Painted Love

Prostitution in French Art of the Impressionist Era

Painted Love

Hollis Clayson

Yale University Press

New Haven & London

Published with assistance from the Louis Stern Memorial Fund.

Designed by Richard Hendel.
Set in Linotype Walbaum type by G&S Typesetters, Austin, Texas.
Printed in Hong Kong
by Everbest Printing Co., Ltd.

Library of Congress Cataloging-in-Publication Data
Clayson, Hollis, 1946–
Painted love: prostitution in French art of the impressionist era / Hollis Clayson.
p. cm.
Includes bibliographical references and index.
ISBN 0–300–04730–4
1. Impressionism (Art)—France.
2. Prostitution in art. 3. Art, French.
4. Art, Modern—19th century—France. I. Title.
N6847.5.I4C58 1991
760'.0449306742'0944361090 34—dc20
90-25889
CIP

The paper in this book meets the guidelines for permanence and durability of the Committee on Production Guidelines for Book Longevity of the Council on Library Resources.

10 9 8 7 6 5 4 3 2 1

FOR JAMES

and to the memory of

JAMES EDWARD CLAYSON, SR.

Contents

List of Illustrations, ix

Acknowledgments, xv

Introduction, xvii

Chapter One — PAINTING THE TRAFFIC IN WOMEN, 1

Chapter Two — IN THE BROTHEL, 27

Chapter Three — TESTING THE LIMITS, 56

The Menace of Fashion, 56

The Invasion of the Boulevard, 93

Chapter Four — SUSPICIOUS PROFESSIONS, 113

Working Women for Sale? 113

Mutual Desire in the New Nightspots, 133

Notes, 155

Bibliography, 189

Index, 197

Illustrations

1. Gustave Courbet, *Les Demoiselles des bords de la Seine (été)*, 1856, oil on canvas, Musée du Petit Palais, Paris. Photo: Ville de Paris, Musée du Petit Palais. © 1991, ARS N.Y./SPADEM. 3
2. Edouard Manet, *Olympia*, 1863, oil on canvas, Musée d'Orsay, Paris. Photo: © Réunion des Musées Nationaux, Paris. 4
3. Anatole Vély, *L'Amour et l'argent*, from *Album Goupil: Salon de 1878*. Photo: Bibliothèque Nationale, Paris. 4
4. Tricoche, "Paris régénéré," *Le Monde Comique*, 1875–76, and *La Vie Amusante*, 1878–79. Photo: Bibliothèque Nationale, Paris. 7
5. "Actualités," *Le Monde Comique*, 1878–79. Photo: Bibliothèque Nationale, Paris. 14
6. Paul Cézanne, *Une Moderne Olympia*, ca. 1869–70, oil on canvas, private collection, Paris. Photo: Harlingue-Viollet, Paris. 17
7. Paul Cézanne, *Une Moderne Olympia*, ca. 1872–73, oil on canvas, Musée d'Orsay, Paris. Photo: © Réunion des Musées Nationaux, Paris. 18
8. Paul Cézanne, *Olympia*, ca. 1877, watercolor, Louis E. Stern Collection, Philadelphia Museum of Art. Photo: Philadelphia Museum of Art. 22
9. Paul Cézanne, *L'Éternel féminin*, 1875–77 or ca. 1877, oil on canvas, J. Paul Getty Museum, Malibu, Calif. Photo: Bulloz, Paris. 24
10. Paul Cézanne, *La Toilette de la courtisane*, ca. 1880, pencil and watercolor on white paper, ca. 1880, Barrett Hamilton Foundation, Little Rock, Ark. Photo: Barrett Hamilton Foundation. 25
11. Edgar Degas, *Notebook 28*, 1877, drawing known as "La Fille Elisa," pp. 26–27, private collection, New York (formerly collection of Ludovic Halévy, Carnet 1). Photo: Author, from *Album de dessins de Degas*, ed. D. Halévy, Paris, 1949. 30
12. Edgar Degas, *Notebook 28*, 1877, drawing known as "La Fille Elisa," p. 31, private collection, New York (formerly collection of Ludovic Halévy, Carnet 1). Photo: Author, from *Album de dessins de Degas*, ed. D. Halévy, Paris, 1949. 30
13. Jean-Louis Forain, *Maison close*, n.d., etching. Photo: Author, from Marcel Guérin, *J. L. Forain, Aquafortiste*, vol. 1, Paris, 1912, p. 21. © 1991, ARS N.Y./ADAGP. 31
14. Edgar Degas, *Le Repos*, ca. 1879–80 or 1876–77, monotype, Musée Picasso, Paris. Photo: © Réunion des Musées Nationaux, Paris. 32
15. Edgar Degas, *Le Client sérieux*, ca. 1879–80 or 1876–77, monotype. National Gallery of Canada, Ottawa. Photo: National Gallery of Canada. 34

16. Jules-Joseph Lefèbvre, *Femme couchée, étude*, from *Album Goupil: Salon de 1878*. Photo: Bibliothèque Nationale, Paris. 36
17. Edgar Degas, *L'Attente*, ca. 1879–80 or 1876–77, pastel over monotype, private collection. Photo: Christie's, New York. 37
18. Edgar Degas, *Le Client*, ca. 1879–80 or 1876–77, monotype, Musée Picasso, Paris. Photo: © Réunion des Musées Nationaux, Paris. 38
19. Edgar Degas, *Au salon*, ca 1879–80 or 1876–77, monotype, Musée Picasso, Paris. Photo: © Réunion des Musées Nationaux, Paris. 40
20. Jean-Louis Forain, *Le Client*, 1878, gouache, private collection, London. Photo: Lefevre Gallery, London, © 1991, ARS N.Y./ADAGP. 41
21. Jules Draner [Jules Renard], "Au salon," *Le Monde Comique*, 1879–80. Photo: Bibliothèque Nationale, Paris. 42
22. Edgar Degas, *La Fête de la patronne*, ca. 1879–80 or 1876–77, pastel over monotype, Musée Picasso, Paris. Photo: © Réunion des Musées Nationaux, Paris. 45
23. Edgar Degas, *Repos sur le lit*, ca. 1879–80 or 1876–77, monotype, Musée Picasso, Paris. Photo: © Réunion des Musées Nationaux, Paris. 47
24. Pablo Picasso, *Le 16 mars 1971*, etching. Photo: Galerie Louise Leiris, Paris. © 1991, ARS N.Y./SPADEM. 49
25. Edgar Degas, *L'Attente*, ca. 1879–80 or 1876–77, monotype, Musée Picasso, Paris. Photo: © Réunion des Musées Nationaux, Paris. 51
26. Edgar Degas, *Dans le salon d'une maison close*, ca. 1879–80 or 1876–77, monotype. Photo: Lefevre Gallery, London. 51
27. Edgar Degas, *Conversation*, ca. 1879–80 or 1876–77, monotype. Photo: Lefevre Gallery, London. 52
28. Edgar Degas, *L'Entremetteuse*, ca. 1879–80 or 1876–77, monotype, Fondation Jacques Doucet, Paris. Photo: Société des Amis de la Bibliothèque d'Art et d'Archéologie, Paris. 53
29. Edgar Degas, *Deux femmes (scène de maison close)*, ca. 1879–80 or 1876–77, monotype, Katherine Bullard Fund, Museum of Fine Arts, Boston. Photo: © 1989, Museum of Fine Arts. 54
30. Jules-Joseph Lefèbvre, *Odalisque*, oil on canvas, 1874, George F. Harding Collection, 1983.381, Art Institute of Chicago. Photo: © 1990, Art Institute of Chicago. 54
31. Jean Quidam [Douglas Jerrold], "Un homme qui suit les femmes," *La Vie Amusante*, 1878–79, and *Le Monde Comique*, 1879–80. Photo: Bibliothèque Nationale, Paris. 57
32. Gaston Coindre, "Le Ridicule," *La Vie Amusante*, 1878–79, and *Le Monde Comique*, 1879–80. Photo: Bibliothèque Nationale, Paris. 59
33. Stop [Louis Pierre Gabriel Bernard Morel-Retz], *Les Prêtresses de l'amour vénal*, 1869, Cabinet des Estampes, Bibliothèque Nationale, Paris. Photo: Bibliothèque Nationale. 61
34. Péry, "Les Cocottes," 1870, Cabinet des Estampes, Bibliothèque Nationale, Paris. Photo: Bibliothèque Nationale. 62

35. Victor Morland, "Ces petites dames," *Le Monde Comique,* 1878–79. Photo: Bibliothèque Nationale, Paris. 62
36. Ernest-Ange Duez, *Splendeur,* 1874, oil on canvas, Musée des Arts Décoratifs, Paris. Photo: Musée des Arts Décoratifs, Sully/Jaulmes. 66
37. Edouard Manet, *Nana,* 1877, oil on canvas, Kunsthalle, Hamburg. Photo: Kunsthalle, Hamburg. 68
38. P. de Haenen, *Paris qui s'en va–Le Cabaret du Père Lunette,* 1889, detail, Cabinet des Estampes, Bibliothèque Nationale, Paris. Photo: Author. 73
39. Pierre-Auguste Renoir, *L'Assommoir,* 1877–78, pen and brown ink with black chalk, Joseph and Helen Regenstein Foundation, restricted gift 1986.420, Art Institute of Chicago. Photo: Art Institute of Chicago. 74
40. Edouard Manet, *Devant la glace,* 1876, oil on canvas, Justin K. Thannhauser Collection, 1978, Solomon R. Guggenheim Museum, New York. Photo: David Heald, © 1991, Solomon R. Guggenheim Foundation. 76
41. Edouard Manet, *La Femme à la jarretière* (originally known as *La Toilette*), 1879, pastel on canvas, Ordrupgaard Collection, Copenhagen. Photo: Ordrupgaard Collection. 77
42. "M. Manet étudiant la belle nature," *Le Charivari,* April 25, 1880. Photo: Bibliothèque Nationale, Paris. 79
43. Henri Gervex, *Rolla,* 1878, oil on canvas, Musée des Beaux-Arts, Bordeaux. Photo: Musée des Beaux-Arts. 80
44. Detail of figure 43. 84
45. Edouard-Théophile Blanchard, *Le Bouffon,* 1878, oil on canvas, Musée d'Orsay, Paris. Photo: © Réunion des Musées Nationaux, Paris. 86
46. "Bréda Street," *La Vie Amusante,* 1878–79, and *Le Monde Comique,* 1880. Photo: Bibliothèque Nationale, Paris. 91
47. Eugène Giraud, *La Salle des pas perdus,* from *Album Goupil: Salon de 1877.* Photo: Bibliothèque Nationale, Paris. 92
48. "Ces dames et l'Exposition," *Petit Journal pour Rire,* 1878. Photo: Bibliothèque Nationale, Paris. 92
49. Victor Morland, "Scènes de la vie parisienne," *La Vie Amusante,* 1878–79, and *Le Monde Comique,* 1879–80. Photo: Bibliothèque Nationale, Paris. 93
50. Map of Paris, 9th arrondissement, from the *Michelin Atlas, Paris par arrondissements,* no. 15, 1st ed. (1989), Pneu Michelin, Services de Tourisme. Photo: Author. 95
51. Alfred Richard Kemplen, "'Monsieur, écoutez donc' . . . L'homme la regarda de côté et s'en alla en sifflant plus fort," illustration for Emile Zola, *L'Assommoir,* 1878, restricted gift of Mrs. Robert S. Hartman, 1987.198, Art Institute of Chicago. Photo: © 1988, Art Institute of Chicago. 97
52. Gillot, "Fantaisies parisiennes," *Le Monde Comique,* 1878–79. Photo: Bibliothèque Nationale, Paris. 98
53. Edward Ancourt, "Sur le boulevard," *Le Monde Comique,* 1875–76. Photo: Bibliothèque Nationale, Paris. 98

54. Jean Emile Buland, *Deux ans à la ville (retour après)*, from *Salon catalogue illustré*, 1881. Photo: Bibliothèque Nationale, Paris. 98
55. Paul Hadol, "L'Araignée du soir," *Le Monde Comique*, 1875–76. Photo: Bibliothèque Nationale, Paris. 98
56. Hippolyte Coté, "Croquis parisien," *Le Monde Comique*, 1879–80. Photo: Bibliothèque Nationale, Paris. 99
57. Edouard Manet, *La Prune*, ca. 1877, oil on canvas, collection of Mr. and Mrs. Paul Mellon, National Gallery of Art, Washington, D.C. Photo: National Gallery of Art. 100
58. Paul David, "Boulevardières," *Le Monde Comique*, 1874–75. Photo: Bibliothèque Nationale, Paris. 101
59. Edward Ancourt, "Au boulevard," *Le Monde Comique*, 1874–75. Photo: Bibliothèque Nationale, Paris. 101
60. Edouard Manet, *Les Bockeuses*, 1878, pastel on canvas, Burrell Collection, Glasgow Museums and Art Galleries. Photo: Glasgow Museums and Art Galleries. 102
61. Pierre-Auguste Renoir, *Au café*, ca. 1877, oil on canvas, Rijksmuseum Kröller-Müller, Otterlo, The Netherlands. Photo: Rijksmuseum Kröller-Müller. 104
62. Henri Gervex, *Groupe à table*, ca. 1880–85 (?), oil on panel, Corcoran Gallery of Art, Washington, D.C. Photo: Corcoran Gallery of Art. 105
63. Giovanni Boldini, *Conversation au café*, ca. 1875–80, oil on panel. Photo: Sotheby's, Inc. © 1991, ARS N.Y./SPADEM. 105
64. Edgar Degas, *Femmes devant un café, le soir*, 1877, pastel over monotype, Musée d'Orsay, Paris. Photo: Réunion des Musées Nationaux, Paris. 106
65. Edgar Degas, *L'Attente*, ca. 1879–80 or 1876–77, monotype, Musée Picasso, Paris. Photo: © Réunion des Musées Nationaux, Paris. 109
66. Detail of figure 64. 110
67. Edgar Degas, *Au café*, ca. 1876–77, monotype, through a prior bequest of Mr. and Mrs. Martin A. Ryerson, 1990.77.1, Art Institute of Chicago. Photo: © 1990, Art Institute of Chicago. 111
68. Jules-Arsène Garnier, *Le Constat d'adultère*, 1885. Photo: Bibliothèque Nationale, Paris. 114
69. "Occupations des fillettes," 1890, Cabinet des Estampes, Bibliothèque Nationale, Paris. Photo: Bibliothèque Nationale. 115
70. Victor Morland, "Coupeau, Lantier, Mes-Bottes et cie.," *Le Monde Comique*, 1879–80. Photo: Bibliothèque Nationale, Paris. 117
71. Pascal-Adolphe-Jean Dagnan-Bouveret, *Repos à côté de la Seine*, 1880, oil on canvas. Photo: © 1990 Sotheby's, Inc. 119
72. *Atelier des modistes*, n.d., wash drawing, Cabinet des Estampes, Bibliothèque Nationale, Paris. Photo: Bibliothèque Nationale. 119
73. "Près du boulevard," *Le Monde Comique*, 1879–80. Photo: Bibliothèque Nationale, Paris. 121
74. Pierre-Auguste Renoir, *Chez la modiste*, ca. 1876–78, oil on canvas, bequest of Annie Swan Coburn, Fogg Art Museum, Harvard University, Cambridge, Mass. Photo: Fogg Art Museum. 123

75. James Tissot, *La Demoiselle de magasin*, 1883–85, oil on canvas, Art Gallery of Ontario, Toronto, gift from the Corporations' Subscription Fund, 1968. Photo: Art Gallery of Ontario 125
76. Edouard Manet, *Chez la modiste*, 1881, oil on canvas, California Palace of the Legion of Honor, San Francisco. Photo: Fine Arts Museums of San Francisco, Mildred Anna Williams Collection. 127
77. Edgar Degas, *Chez la modiste*, 1882–85, oil on canvas, collection of Mr. and Mrs. Paul Mellon, Upperville, Va. Photo: Mr. and Mrs. Paul Mellon. 129
78. Edgar Degas, *L'Atelier de la modiste*, 1882, pastel, acquired through the generosity of an anonymous donor, F79–34, Nelson-Atkins Museum of Art, Kansas City, Mo. Photo: Nelson-Atkins Museum of Art. 130
79. Eva Gonzalès, *La Modiste*, ca. 1877, gouache and pastel on canvas, Lewis Larned Coburn Fund, 1972.362, Art Institute of Chicago. Photo: © 1990, Art Institute of Chicago. 132
80. "Paris pendant l'Exposition," *Le Monde Comique*, 1878–79. Photo: Bibliothèque Nationale, Paris. 134
81. Edouard Manet, *La Serveuse de bocks*, 1878–79, oil on canvas, National Gallery, London. Photo: National Gallery. 135
82. Edouard Manet, *La Serveuse de bocks*, 1878–79, oil on canvas, Musée d'Orsay, Paris. Photo: © Réunion des Musées Nationaux, Paris. 136
83. Edouard Manet, *Le Café-Concert*, 1878, oil on canvas, Walters Art Gallery, Baltimore. Photo: Walters Art Gallery. 137
84. Ferdinand Lunel, *Brasserie le Bas-Rhin et le D'Harcourt*, ca. 1888, Cabinet des Estampes, Bibliothèque Nationale, Paris. Photo: Bibliothèque Nationale. 138
85. Jean Béraud, *Brasserie*, from *Salon catalogue illustré*, 1883. Photo: Bibliothèque Nationale, Paris. © 1991, ARS N.Y./ADAGP. 139
86. Ferdinand Fau, illustration for A. Carel, *Les Brasseries à femmes de Paris*, Paris, 1884. Photo: Bibliothèque Nationale, Paris. 139
87. Ferdinand Fau, illustration for A. Carel, *Les Brasseries à femmes de Paris*, Paris, 1884. Photo: Bibliothèque Nationale, Paris. 139
88. Albert Robida, "Paris nouveau," *Le Monde Comique*, 1884. Photo: Bibliothèque Nationale, Paris. 139
89. Ferdinand Lunel, *La Brasserie Henri IV*, ca. 1880, Cabinet des Estampes, Bibliothèque Nationale, Paris. Photo: Bibliothèque Nationale. 141
90. Edouard Manet, *La Servante de bocks*, india ink and gouache drawing, 1878–80, reproduced in *La Vie Moderne*, May 8, 1880. Photo: Bibliothèque Nationale, Paris. 143
91. Henri Somm [François-Clément Sommier], *La Serveuse de bocks*, ca. 1875–80, pencil, watercolor, and gouache on buff paper, private collection, England. Photo: Private collection. 148
92. Marcellin Desboutin, *Au bal Debray–Fille de brasserie*, frontispiece for John Grand-Carteret, *Raphael et Gambrinus, ou l'art dans la brasserie*, Paris, 1886. Photo: Author. 149
93. Edouard Manet, *Un bar aux Folies-Bergère*, 1882, oil on canvas, Courtauld Institute Galleries, Courtauld Collection, London. Photo: Courtauld Institute Galleries. 151

Acknowledgments

One day about fifteen years ago, I walked into T. J. Clark's office at the University of California at Los Angeles and announced my intent to study the Impressionists' abandonment of urban motifs in the 1880s as a social way of explaining the "crisis" of Impressionism. Clark suggested that I investigate instead the many representations of prostitutes in French art and literature of the 1870s. What seemed then to be merely a fascinating iconography to track – "images of women" – turned out to be a far richer and more important topic than I could have imagined at the time.

I owe my chief debt of gratitude to Tim Clark for both his help and his example. I've been fortunate also to find friendship, support, and high standards combined in Tom Crow, Serge Guilbaut, Nancy Troy, and Marty Ward. The encouragement over the long haul supplied by Carol Duncan, Sandra Hindman, Sarah Maza, Larry Silver, and David Van Zanten has been very important to me. And long before I ever met them, Linda Nochlin's and Griselda Pollock's work helped me a great deal.

Special thanks go to Tom Crow, Nancy Ring, and Julia Sagraves. Tom's comments reignited work on a stalled project. Nancy's nonpareil help with matters both editorial and substantial enabled me to structure and write the book. Julia's careful reading of the text prompted a final key round of rewriting. I also benefited from suggestions made by anonymous readers for Yale University Press.

James Clayson Cogbill just about prevented me from finishing this, but Neil Cogbill was a beacon of confidence and support when the project appeared swamped by teaching and domestic responsibilities. I daily regret that James Clayson did not live to see the completion of this book. He might not have read it, but he would have stopped passersby on the street to brag about it.

My dissertation research in Paris was made possible by an Edward A. Dickson Fellowship in the History of Art from U.C.L.A. In Paris, I profited from the resources and helpfulness of the Bibliothèque Nationale, Archives Nationales, Archives de la Préfecture de Police, and Bibliothèque de la Musée des Arts Décoratifs; and in Strasbourg, from the Bibliothèque Nationale and Institut de l'Histoire de l'Art. Generous private benefactors in Strasbourg and Wichita provided critical financial help that assured the continuation of work on my Ph.D. thesis. I thank the University Research Grants Committee of Northwestern University for a timely award that helped to defray the cost of the photographs used in this book. I thank Patricia Barratt, Janet Cywrus, Neal Meltzer, Theodore Reff, and Richard Thomson for their help in locating reproductions. Finally, I am grateful for the steadfast interest and commitment of Judy Metro, senior editor at Yale University Press, and for the excellent editorial attention given a first book by Karen Gangel, manuscript editor.

Introduction

The germ of this book was my doctoral dissertation, completed in 1984. As plans for that thesis first began to take shape in 1975–76, I felt sure that I was embarking upon an important project. That palpable sense of having urgent work to do was fanned exclusively, however, by fires just igniting inside the academic speciality of art history. Those were the halcyon days of the conceptualization of a materialist history of art for a new generation – "the social history of art." Headquartered at the University of California at Los Angeles in the classes of Tim Clark, Carol Duncan, the late Arnold Rubin, and Karl Werckmeister, the daily discussions with teachers and fellow students were heady, empowering, and very confident. This book grew out of a dissertation first conceived in that warm and optimistic atmosphere, but it has been drawn to a belated conclusion under different conditions of urgency – political as well as professional.

From the vantage point of southern California in the mid-1970s, later nineteenth-century Parisian worries over the morality and safety of prostitution seemed quintessentially Victorian and unfamiliar, if not thoroughly quaint to sexually free and antibiotically and contraceptively protected Americans like my friends and me. Ronald Reagan's presidency and the tragic AIDS epidemic make the story of Parisian fear and contempt toward the moral and venereal contagion of prostitution less foreign. It is instead ominously and painfully familiar. What sexually liberated young person of the 1970s could have predicted or imagined that in the 1980s an oppressive correlation would be drawn between the spread of a sexually transmitted disease, on the one hand, and (supposedly) deviant sexualities and life-styles, on the other? Belief in such a connection has become widespread and has served to heat up the aggressive scrutiny and suspicion of those on the fringes of our own social order – homosexual men, intravenous drug users, aliens, prostitutes, prisoners. In 1990, thanks to the witch-hunts conducted against certain recipients of National Endowment for the Arts fellowships, artists were added to the list of the persecuted. As you read this book, you will be struck by similarities between then and now. Indeed, patterns of suspicion, scapegoating, and social policing have grown up in North America that parallel in many ways the attitudes and institutions that arose from the nineteenth-century Parisian equation of prostitutes with deviant social and sexual practices and the spread of syphilis.[1]

The economy of desire – of exchange – is man's business.
– Luce Irigaray, This Sex Which Is Not One

A main objective of this book is to demonstrate that there was an outbreak of male interest in women prostitutes in French art and culture of the 1870s and earlier 1880s. This particular iconography and its contradictory dialectic of disgust and fascination have not previously been described, let alone analyzed in detail, in the art historical literature. My purpose was to demarcate and call attention to this hitherto unstudied imagery and, at the same time, to problematize it. In other words, I wanted to look closely at a group of pictures that had the subject of female sexuality in common as a means of contributing to empirically precise art history, but I also sought to elucidate issues and problems relevant to women and men in patriarchy. Indeed the operative assumption throughout the book is that art was itself complicit in the regulation of sexualities. It was time to reopen the files, so to speak, on many later nineteenth-century artworks whose apparent familiarity had rendered them stale. Their considerable strangeness had been lost to us or masked by a century or more of admiration and justification. Especially ripe for a fresh look were the complex and problematic works by Paul Cézanne, Edgar Degas, and Edouard Manet that I write about in this book.

In the earliest stages of my work on this project, the principal noun of my investigation may have been prostitution, but the real subjects of my study – in all senses of the word – were the (male) artists, just as they were in their own day in relation to the women they chose to depict in their art. Because I wished to look closely at the actions taken by those artistic subjects upon their frequently elected objects – contemporary Parisian prostitutes, both real and imaginary – I sought to eavesdrop on what was happening between men as they masterminded the circulation of women. The art I am analyzing here records the ideological use of certain women through their transformation into the topoi of a culture, the subject matter of ambitious, mostly male art. Recently, Luce Irigaray, the French feminist, pinpointed the general social and economic pattern in which the production and circulation of the art studied here played a part:

> The society we know, our own culture, is based upon the exchange of women. . . . Why are men not objects of exchange among women? It is because women's bodies – through their use, consumption, and circulation – provide for the condition making social life and culture possible, although they remain an unknown "infrastructure" of the elaboration of that social life and culture. The exploitation of the matter that has been sexualized female is so integral a part of our sociocultural horizon that there is no way to interpret it except within this horizon.[2]

The impact of Irigaray's insight as well as those of other key feminist thinkers, including Simone de Beauvoir, shifted my focus somewhat in the direction of the women (the "subject matter," the "objects"). I tried to see some aspects of this saga of male-modernist art making from the women's side of the canvases. This standpoint seemed increasingly important to me in the 1980s and now as American women struggle to protect their reproductive rights, their rights to their own bodies. So, in the course of writing from an artist-centered, women-as-iconography standpoint, I began to be drawn to the project of imagining and worrying over the absent subjectivities of the depicted women, all the while knowing that there were not "actual" voices and thoughts waiting to be recovered.

At the least, I hope this book persuades its readers that the modernist project of the 1870s and 1880s was a gendered one. Though the seams between the two efforts that coexist here – one empiricist and one feminist – probably still show in what follows, I am not concerned. These ragged edges are the signs that this book has itself been through history; that it was produced over time and under fluctuating intellectual and political conditions which exerted various, uneven pressures on the author and her work.

CHAPTER ONE

Painting the Traffic in Women

The existence of prostitution on a scale so widespread and obvious that it alarmed contemporaries was a distinctive and distinguishing feature of nineteenth-century Parisian culture.[1] And as Parisian streets filled with prostitutes, so did French art and literature. Beginning in the early July Monarchy (1830–48), the prostitute became a regular presence in paintings, poems, prints, and novels and remained so through the end of the century and beyond. It would appear, then, that nineteenth-century French art on the subject of contemporary prostitution mimetically paralleled the rise of a "prostitute problem" in the capital city. This study of a group of such images concurs that the artworks depended upon the events and ideas of their time. That real prostitutes were constant points of reference for artists in the nineteenth century is undeniable. Indeed, in most instances later in the century, artists attempted to depict observable practices. Yet although it is clear that the prostitution problem and the outpouring of images of prostitutes coexisted, the precise correlation between these two phenomena is less certain. Explaining that relationship will be the principal goal of the present work, which focuses upon art made during the 1870s and 1880s.

The generation of artists and writers that matured during the reign of Louis-Philippe was the first to experience the new trademark of modern city life: conspicuous sexual commerce in the streets. For although the prostitute population of Paris was considered large and unruly enough to require systematized police regulation as early as 1800 (the year Napoléon created the office of *préfet de police*), it was during the 1830s that the number of prostitutes working openly in Paris increased dramatically.[2] The steep rise was a consequence of the demographic upheavals of the period: it was among the most striking social by-products of the first stage of growth of the modern industrial city. The women who swelled the ranks were job-seeking migrants from the countryside and unemployed (or underemployed) Parisian laborers. The demand for women in the labor force reached a low point in the middle third of the century, making prostitution a viable, even necessary, choice.[3] The prostitutes' customers were mostly partnerless male workers recently arrived from the provinces, as well as some middle- and upper-class Parisians fleeing from or lacking access to sexual contact with their female social equals.

The consequent impact of prostitution on Parisian life in the 1830s was vivid, and it is therefore not surprising that the first comprehensive, now-classic study of Parisian prostitution, that of A. J. B. Parent-Duchâtelet, was undertaken at this time (the first edition appeared in 1836).[4] The outpouring of representations of prostitutes from many writers and some artists disposed to focus upon modern subjects was in large measure inspired by the newly eroticized contours of city life. Generally speaking, though, artists and writers of the July Monarchy who focused upon prostitutes in their work tended to use them as symbols of the degraded morals or oppressive politics of their time. For example, Alfred de Musset wrote his lugubrious "Rolla" in 1833, Honoré de Balzac's ambitious *Splendeurs et misères des courtesanes* was written between 1839 and 1847, Eugène Sue's *Mystères de Paris* appeared in feuilleton in 1842–43, and Thomas Couture seized upon the prostitute as the perfect symbol of societal decadence in the painting that dominated the Salon of 1847 and was the star turn of his career, *Les Romains de la décadence*. In the same year Alexandre Dumas fils wrote *La Dame aux camélias*.

After a hiatus during the Second Republic (1848–51), the use of the prostitute and the adulteress as principal topoi of modern life in art and literature resumed and continued throughout the Second Empire (1851–70). As in the July Monarchy, the population of clandestine prostitutes (clandestine in the sense of being unregulated by the police) increased during this period. But the Second Empire came to be associated with a particular order of clandestine prostitute: the glittering courtesan, who emulated the fashions and refined postures of the upper echelons of bourgeois and court society. In the 1850s and 1860s representations of the prostitute centered on this figure. This occurred because there were highly visible "real" courtesans to depict, to be sure, but also because the rebuilding of the city by Baron Georges Haussmann and Emperor Napoléon III produced social fears explicitly tied to a discomfort with the blurring of social boundaries in Paris – a state of affairs that artists and moralists alike often found embodied by the courtesan.[5]

Representations of this theme in the July Monarchy and Second Empire shared a tendency toward an overtly symbolic or emblematic use of the subject of the contemporary prostitute. The wealth of examples from the Second Empire includes the following: Dumas fils staged *La Dame aux camélias* in 1852 (Giuseppe Verdi's *La Traviata*, based on Dumas's story, was written in 1853), and the younger Dumas's influential play *Le Demi-Monde* appeared in 1855. Théodore Barrière's *Les Filles de marbre* was staged in 1853, and Emile Augier's *Les Lionnes pauvres* in 1858. The Goncourt brothers' first novel about prostitution, *La Lorette*, appeared in 1853, and their second, *Germinie Lacerteux*, in 1864. The notorious novels of adultery – Gustave Flaubert's *Madame Bovary* and Ernest Feydeau's *Fanny* – appeared in 1857 and 1858, respectively, while Emile Zola's *Thérèse Raquin* was published in 1867.

Charles Baudelaire's "painter of modern life," Constantin Guys, drew contemporary prostitutes throughout the Second Empire, Gustave Courbet's *Young Ladies on the Banks of the Seine (Summer)* (fig. 1) hung in the 1857 Salon, and Edouard Manet's *Olympia* (fig. 2) was the scandal of the 1865 Salon.[6] In spite of the fact that avant-garde artists such as Flaubert, Charles Baudelaire, Gustave Courbet, and Edouard Manet set out to challenge the aesthetic and philosophical bases of many competing academic and popular images, their treatments of the "loose women" of the Second Empire did share a tendency to legibly narrate with their more conventional contemporaries. That is, artists of the mid-century generation tended to stick to the artistic tradition and moralizing logic they had inherited, whereby the life of (or encounters with) a prostitute was eminently narratable. According to this conventional script, "she" conformed to a recognizable type (which prescribed her appearance), acted according to predictable motivations, and met a foreclosed fate.

The argument I present here is that certain artists working in the 1870s and 1880s veered away from this familiar plot and its explicitly moralizing outlook. Indeed, if we sought to gener-

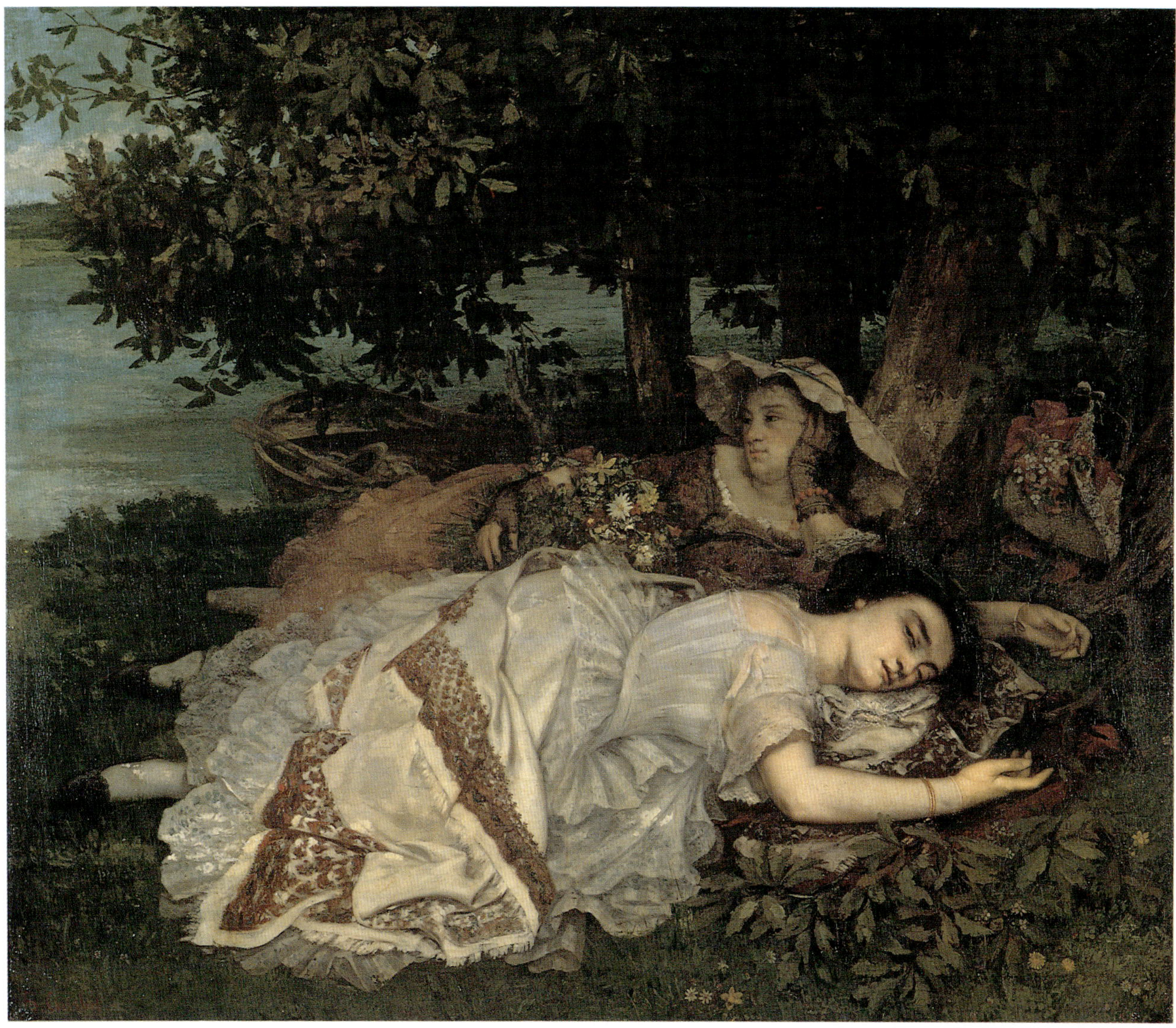

1\. Gustave Courbet, *Young Ladies on the Banks of the Seine (Summer)*, 1856, oil on canvas, Musée du Petit Palais, Paris.

alize about the principal differences between vanguard images of the prostitute from the 1850s and 1860s and avant-garde treatments of the same theme during the 1870s and the early 1880s (the pictures under consideration in the present work), we could point to a comparative absence or avoidance of story line in many of the later pictures. The typical images of prostitutes (Salon and vanguard alike) produced during the July Monarchy and Second Empire provided enough behavioral and social denotations so that an unfolding story could be traced, so that a plausible accompanying text would tend to come to mind for the average viewer. That story telling remained an essential tool of communication for the Salon painter in the 1870s and 1880s is apparent in a work like A. Vély's *Love and Money* from the Salon of 1878 (fig. 3).

In images of contemporary prostitution from the end of the century, there was again a general predisposition to tell a visually legible story. In the late 1880s and 1890s, the illustrated press (*Le Courrier Français*, *Gil Blas*, and *Le Mirliton*, for example) exploded with caricatures and cartoons of prostitutes. But it is Henri de Toulouse-Lautrec's single-minded concentration on brothel prostitutes in his art in the 1890s – resulting in fifty pictures between 1892 and 1894 alone – that has forged an indelible link between fin-de-siècle Parisian art and the theme of

2.
Edouard Manet, *Olympia*, 1863, oil on canvas, Musée d'Orsay, Paris.

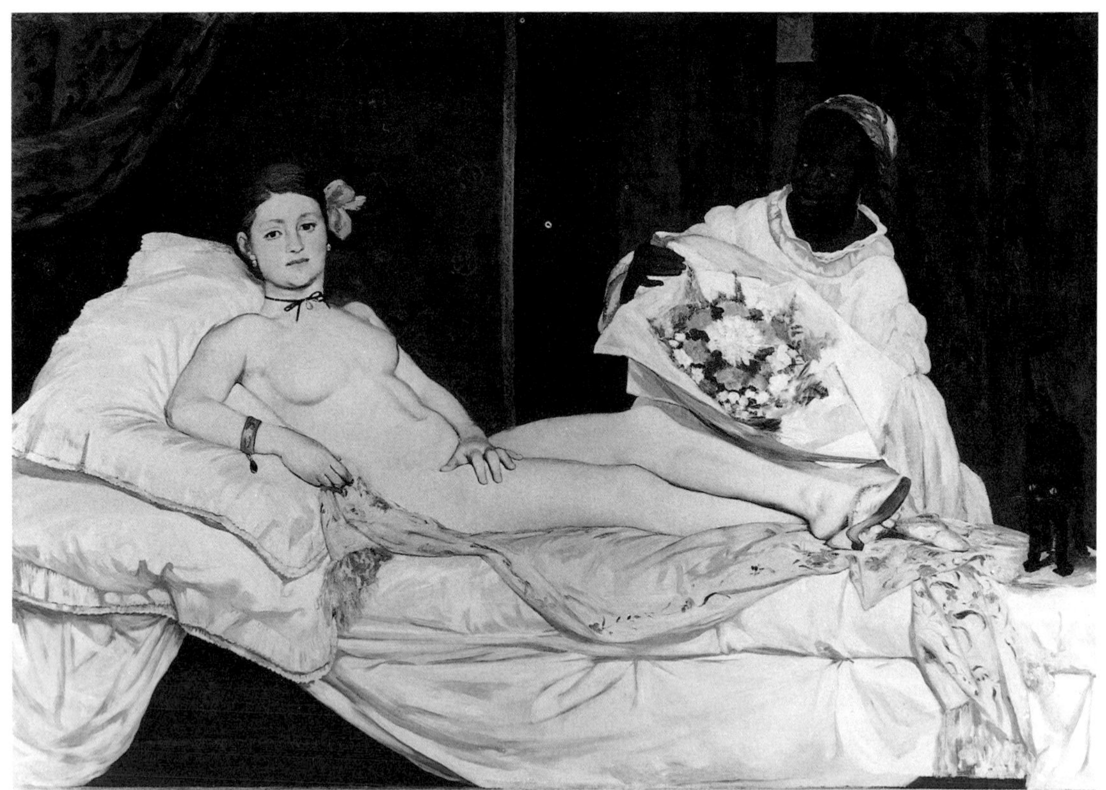

3.
Anatole Vély, *Love and Money*, from *Album Goupil: Salon de 1878.*

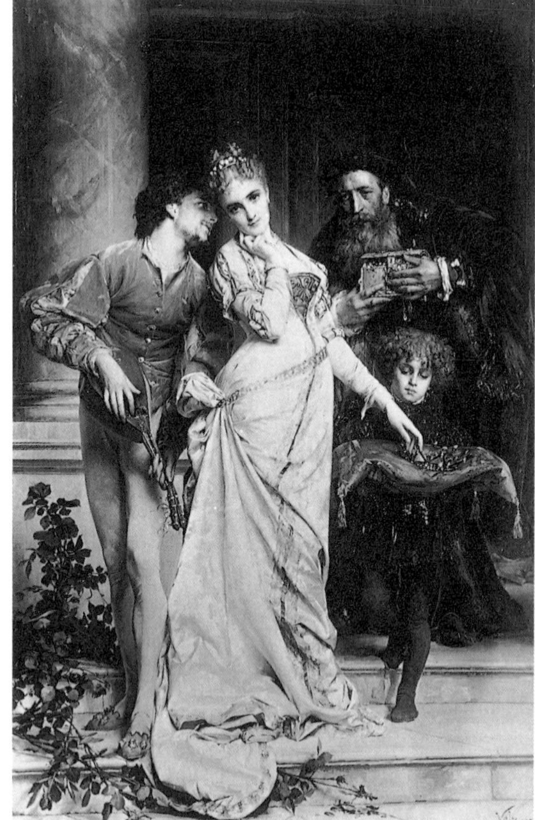

prostitution. A key early example of Paris-based twentieth-century vanguardism was an image of prostitutes: Pablo Picasso's *Demoiselles d'Avignon* of 1906.[7]

But as the prostitute became a mainstay, if not a cliché, of avant-garde focus in the 1890s and early 1900s, the social problem posed by prostitutes in Paris was withering away because of a decline in their number. The disappearance of the problem was principally the result of social and economic changes that followed the first phases of industrialization: an increased demand for female labor, a general lowering of the age of marriage (there were more marriages and fewer consensual unions), a rise in standards of living, and changing family strategies (improved contraception helped limit the number of children).[8] These changes in French private life partially explain why late nineteenth-century and early twentieth-century images of the prostitute are almost invariably interior scenes. No longer conceived as a social or public issue, the theme became associated instead with privatized experience and libertine fantasy.

In this work I recognize the durability and malleability of the theme of prostitution in French art throughout the nineteenth century. Indeed, to paraphrase Griselda Pollock, it is a striking fact that many canonical works held up as the founding monuments of modern art deal with female sexuality, and do so in the form of commercial exchange.[9] My concern is to contribute to an understanding of the extrapictorial reasons for this gendered pattern of representation, but I aim to demonstrate the specificities of a particular episode in the iconography of the prostitute during that century. Lying between well-known earlier and later moments of concentration on the theme of prostitution in the arts, this less-studied case was a no less intense outpouring of artistic enthusiasm for the prostitute.

During the years in question – the 1870s and 1880s – the lions of both the literary and artistic avant-gardes employed the motifs of contemporary prostitution. Although I refer only occasionally to works of literature, my investigation of apposite works of art by members of the Impressionist circle is extensive, virtually exhaustive. The consideration of *pompier* (or conventional) and popular artworks is also extensive but admittedly less systematic. The latter tend to serve a supporting role in the discussions, providing points of comparison with much more thoroughly analyzed vanguard paintings and prints.

Paul Alexis, Edmond de Goncourt, Joris-Karl Huysmans, Guy de Maupassant, and Emile Zola wrote novels or stories on the subject. The earliest books were Huysmans's *Marthe, histoire d'une fille*, which appeared in Brussels in 1876 and in Paris in 1879, and Goncourt's *La Fille Elisa*, published in 1877. Zola's *L'Assommoir* (introducing Nana near its end) appeared in feuilleton form in 1876–77, and *Nana* ran in feuilleton from 1879 to 1880. Paul Alexis's *La Fin de Lucie Pellegrin* appeared in 1880, and Maupassant's best-known stories on the subject, "Boule de suif" and "La Maison Tellier," were published in 1880 and 1881. Paul Cézanne's extraordinary series of *Olympias* – there are three of them – was begun about 1870 and culminated in a watercolor of about 1877. The most controversial public pictures of prostitution made since the mid-1860s appeared on display in Paris between April 1877 and April 1878: Edouard Manet's *Nana* of 1877 (begun in the fall of 1876) and Henri Gervex's *Rolla* of 1878 were both excluded from the Salon and shown at private dealers. Shortly thereafter Edgar Degas began his brothel monotypes. The most unorthodox private images of the brothel undertaken during the entire nineteenth century, they were probably made between 1878 and 1879 (or perhaps slightly earlier, circa 1876–77).[10] Pierre Auguste Renoir's illustrations for Zola's *L'Assommoir* were published in 1878. In 1878–79, Manet made a series of pictures of waitresses in a *bras-*

serie à femmes, the most notorious commercialized form of clandestine prostitution of the period – an interest overtly thematized in his last Salon painting, *A Bar at the Folies-Bergère* (1882). Between about 1882 and 1885, Degas made at least sixteen pictures of milliners, a "traditional" form of covert prostitute of interest to Degas because of both its old-fashioned and its modern characteristics. The enthusiasm of the avant-gardists was shared by pompier contemporaries Ernest-Ange Duez, Jean-Louis Forain, Henri Gervex, James Tissot, and others.

The years with which I am concerned are, of course, the years of Impressionism. Between 1874, the year of the first Impressionist exhibition, and 1886, the year of the eighth and final group show, the Impressionist group forged a high-profile group identity, and its distinctive professional strategy and generally shared style were widely acknowledged. Although the Impressionist attraction to certain subjects of modernity is well known and widely studied,[11] members of the Impressionist circle (like their pompier and caricaturist contemporaries) portrayed aspects of contemporary Parisian prostitution in their art of the late 1870s and early 1880s with greater frequency than has been observed heretofore. One of the principal reasons the presence of this theme in Impressionist works has been overlooked is the gendered nature of art historical practice. The narrative evasiveness of certain pictures in question has also helped to mask the prominence of this theme. Unlike the story-telling clarity that courted outrage in the case of the best-known prostitute picture of the Second Empire, Manet's *Olympia* (see fig. 2), and another troublemaking Salon picture, Courbet's *Young Ladies on the Banks of the Seine (Summer)* (see fig. 1), key images from the later years appear instead to be merely slices of random vision – spectacles of sight, tableaux of disinterested visuality without appeal to the mind – so disorganized that it is difficult to state with any certainty what these painters have to say about their subject matter.

Elucidating the connection between, on the one hand, covert prostitution as subject matter and, on the other, evasiveness as narrational strategy among artists who operated within Impressionist circles during the 1870s and 1880s is among the principal goals of this book. Indeed it has always seemed paradoxical that during the time that naturalist writers specialized in the subject of contemporary prostitution, vanguard visual artists did not appear inclined to deal with the same thematic materials. I shall show that Manet, Degas, and Renoir, for example, were also compelled by the subject during the same years but treated the theme elliptically in their public works, especially when these works are compared to the explicit imagery of their literary contemporaries and of their artistic predecessors and successors. The reserve of many avant-garde depictions of prostitutes certainly departs from the bluntness of contemporaneous pompier and caricatural treatments of the same subject. We shall see, however, that the differences between the various styles of address of the theme of prostitution did not prevent the sundry male-produced artworks from reinforcing certain female stereotypes. In other words, I shall argue that the detachment engendered by avant-garde haphazardness was much more apparent than real, that their self-consciously casual and ambiguous depictions served to reinforce stereotypical notions about the sexual instability, if not patent immorality, of "public women." This was especially pronounced in their images of working-class clandestine prostitutes, discussed in chapter 4.

Representations of the urban prostitute were, of course, shaped by changes in the practice and conceptualization of prostitution in the period. Paris during the early Third Republic was the stage of a heated debate on the status and morality of tolerated prostitution: just after the

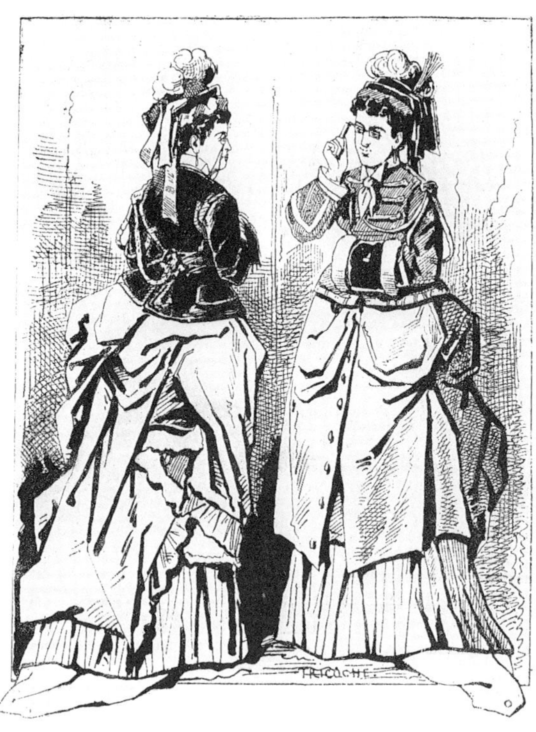

4. Tricoche, "Paris Regenerated," *Le Monde Comique*, 1875–76, and *La Vie Amusante*, 1878–79.

A woman of the world and a cocotte.
– Bah! which one is the cocotte?

suppression of the Commune in 1871, concern erupted about the continuing expansion of covert prostitution and male sexual demand.[12] It appeared certain that the municipal system of regulation, called *réglementation*, was losing its ability to control the profession. Similar concerns had surfaced in the 1830s and 1860s, during which the population of clandestine prostitutes had increased markedly. Around 1880, however, the number of registered prostitutes reached an all-time low (about three thousand in 1883–84), and the collapse of the system appeared imminent. Partially as a consequence of such dispiriting statistics, the "neoregulationist" hysteria of the partisans of the regulatory system in the early Third Republic was noticeably more shrill than the parallel outbursts of the regulationists of the 1830s and 1860s.

Through their "illegal" work in the expanding covert sexual economy, it appeared that prostitutes were responsible for altering the quality of social life. Indeed, it appeared that, thanks to them, social life was turning into economic life. At the same time, women's behavior seemed less governable and female morality seemed less stable than ever before. The question "Is she or isn't she?" became a commonplace obsession of Parisian men and women. The illustration "Paris Regenerated" (fig. 4), whose effectiveness depends upon the comic interchangeability of its figures from different social strata, clearly portrays this conundrum of modern life.

I shall argue that the avant-garde images of the contemporary prostitute made in the unsettled atmosphere of the 1870s and earlier 1880s were responses to the new meanings that were accruing to both the registered and unregistered prostitutes of the day.

The literature of modernity describes the experience of males.[13] Three men, Charles Baudelaire, Georg Simmel, and Walter Benjamin, were pivotal observers of metropolitan life; each saw the prostitute as the most typical figure of urban modernity, because under capitalism, they concurred, the modern social relationship tended increasingly to take the form of a commodity. In their diverse writings, all three pinpointed a lamentable and calculated cooling-off in personal relations as a trademark of modern life.

In the early 1900s, Simmel became the first theoretician of modern culture to posit the existence of a distinctively metropolitan mentality, which he called intellectualist, as opposed to emotional.[14] In Simmel's social theory, the proliferation of this consciousness was tied to the money economy. Largely because of her intrinsic connection with the operations of the money economy, the prostitute emblemizes the gulf between subjective and objective culture that Simmel finds characteristic of modern life. For Simmel, an exchange with a prostitute is both briefer and colder than any other transaction conducted in the society or the economy. "Only transactions for money," Simmel wrote,

> have that character of a purely momentary relationship which leaves no traces, as is the case with prostitution. With the giving of money, one completely withdraws from the relationship; one has settled matters more completely than by giving an object, which, by its contents, its selection, and its use maintains a wisp of the personality of the giver. Only money is an appropriate equivalent to the momentary peaking and the equally momentary satisfaction of the desire served by prostitutes, for money establishes no ties, it is always at hand, and it is always welcomed. . . . Of all human relationships, it is perhaps the most significant case of the mutual reduction of two persons to the status of mere means. This may be the most salient and profound factor underlying the very close historic tie between prostitution and the money economy – the economy of "means."[15]

In Simmel's view, paying for a physical sensation guarantees a double debasement: the experience is both impersonal and of short duration.

For Walter Benjamin, the prostitute's role in the subterranean Parisian economy qualifies her, like no other modern urban figure, for the position of matchless signifier of alienated relations under capitalism. Benjamin adumbrates this conclusion in the course of a demanding commentary on Baudelaire:

> The modern is a main stress in [Baudelaire's] poetry. . . . But it is precisely the modern which always conjures up prehistory. That happens here through the ambiguity which is peculiar to the social relations and events of this epoch. Ambiguity is the figurative appearance of the dialectic at a standstill. This standstill is Utopia, and the dialectical image therefore a dream image. The commodity clearly provides such an image: as fetish. . . . And such an image is provided by the whore, who is seller and commodity in one.[16]

The famous last line of the paragraph projects the doubled symbolic role of the prostitute in the society and economy of the modern city: like no other merchant, like no other good or service for sale, she is all of them at once.

Benjamin's use of "ambiguity" in his discussion of modern social relations parallels Simmel's discussion of the "purely momentary" quality of an exchange for money, the quintessentially modern transaction. Together these ideas constitute a second identity for the nineteenth-century prostitute. She is the living embodiment of the cold cash nexus but is ambiguous, evanescent, and transient as well – a conceptualization at the center of Baudelaire's thinking about the culture of his day. In his widely quoted prescription for modernity, Baudelaire wrote of the need for a dialectical art that could adequately address and record the Janus-faced quality of the new urban experience: "By 'modernity' I mean the ephemeral, the fugitive, the contingent, the half of art whose other half is the eternal and the immutable."[17]

In the characteristically guarded yet actively scrutinizing glance of the prostitute, Baudelaire saw condensed the typical gaze of the modern Parisian. "Her eyes, like those of a wild animal, are fixed on the distant horizon; they have the restlessness of a wild animal . . . but sometimes also the animal's tense vigilance." Simmel has agreed that such prehensile visuality is distinctively modern. It was left to Walter Benjamin to connect Baudelaire's words, quoted above, to Simmel's thoughts: "That the eye of the city dweller is overburdened with protective functions is obvious. Georg Simmel refers to some less obvious tasks with which it is charged. 'The person who is able to see but unable to hear is much more . . . troubled than the person who is able to hear but unable to see. Here is something . . . characteristic of the big city. The interpersonal relationships of people in big cities are characterized by a markedly greater emphasis on the use of the eyes than on that of the ears.'"[18]

We can begin to see that the attraction to prostitution was pervasive in these years – appealing especially to avant-garde painters of modern life but to many men in the larger culture as well – because "she" marked the point of intersection of two widely disseminated ideologies of modernity: the modern was lived and seen at its most acute and true in what was temporary, unstable, and fleeting; and the modern social relation was understood to be more and more frozen in the form of the commodity. In the 1870s and earlier 1880s, prostitution occupied an overdetermined place at the point of intersection of these two ideological structures. Hence, the two seemingly antithetical qualities of modernity central to the avant-garde could be resolved in the figure of the prostitute.

If female bodies are thought of as perennially [sexed], as constant and even embodiments of sexed being, that is a misconception which carries risks.
– *Denise Riley,* "Am I That Name?"

She [the female] appears essentially to the male as a sexual being. For him she is sex – absolute sex, no less.
– *Simone de Beauvoir,* The Second Sex

In the modern period men have relentlessly sexualized women, and markedly so, I wish to insist, in the artistic representations of women that circulated in nineteenth-century Paris. The treatment of – one might prefer to say the scapegoating of – prostitutes deserves therefore to be understood as a subset of the treatment that women received in general. For the prostitute – that quintessentially sexualized and objectified woman – is emblematic of the place of women in the dominant regime of visual representation in the West in the modern period. Teresa de Lauretis puts it forcefully: "Female equals the body, sexuality equals the female body."[19]

One of the reasons prostitutes in particular were at the center of the obsessions and fears of the period was their ostensibly deviant sexuality. The logic of the commodity, as we have begun to see, helped produce the obsession with the prostitute in nineteenth-century Paris, but so did the logic of male desire. Then as now, sexual "deviants" are profoundly worrisome to dominant social groups – especially in times of plague thought to be spread exclusively by the sexually marginal. Those in power tend to divide the population into two opposing and distinct categories: the sexually normal and the sexually deviant, assuming that the variability of human sexuality can be boiled down into these two forms.

Daniel Boorstin's outlook is typical of many mainstream historians: "The daily sexual habits of those who conform to the prevalent mores are seldom recorded and have rarely been chronicled. The history of sexual conduct has tended to become a record of deviants, of contraception and abortion, of polygamy and homosexuality."[20] In addition to a mistaken optimism about our knowledge of the sexual conduct of somatic minorities (prostitutes are usually grouped under the heading of deviants), Boorstin's ideas betray the Manichean habit of thinking about sexuality in terms mentioned above. This standpoint perpetuates a dominant nineteenth-century outlook on the matter and is particularly vexing when it is permitted to structure a historical analysis of prostitution.

Sexual deviance was assumed to be the indelible hallmark of prostitutes of the 1870s and 1880s. "This disgusting sexual life is, after all, the very reason that these women are grouped together and cloistered away."[21] Their deviance had two determinants: high frequency of sexual activity and variability of partner. Although exotic sexual activities may have been imagined (and indiscriminacy of partner choice also played a role), regular sex and diversity of client were the defining procedures. Deviant and illicit were therefore synonymous. Deviance was the opposite of – and a threat to – respectability.

Categorizing female sexuality in this inflexible fashion – into honest or illicit, normal or abnormal – burned a permanent label of deviant into the flesh of the prostitute. Because prostitution was a temporary job for the majority of its nineteenth-century practitioners, defining prostitution as a condition rather than an act – as what one was instead of what one sometimes did – was an error based upon mistaken but widely shared assumptions about prostitutes and their sexuality.

Parisian regulationism, the city-wide, police-administered system designed to survey and control an officially tolerated population of prostitutes, remained in place from 1800 to 1946.[22] Its inscription apparatus called for the enrollment of all women who practiced prostitution and reinforced the habit of thinking that any woman who performed an act of prostitution was a full-time sexual deviant. As a system of thought and action, réglementation did not distinguish between full- and part-time prostitutes. Because the apparatus sought to convert every *insoumise* (a prostitute *outside* police control) into a *soumise* (a prostitute *under* police control), regulationist ideology conflated the two categories. Regulationists recognized that within the registered population, women switched back and forth between the categories of *fille de maison* (resident of a brothel) and *fille en carte* (independent, police-controlled prostitute). But, in their eyes, once an unregistered woman was apprehended for an act of prostitution, she was converted into a permanent soumise. Even if she disappeared from view (that is, never appeared for a sanitary inspection), she was forever "inscribed" on the rolls. In the words of an eminent regulationist doctor: "Inscribing her on the books of regulated prostitution makes her disappear forever from statistics concerning the unregistered."[23]

The abolitionists of the period drew attention to the tyranny and injustice of this pattern of forced identification:

> Despite her protests, she is apprehended and officially registered. From that point on, she will be preoccupied with her sex life (all of her preoccupations will be concentrated on her sexual life); she will be ceaselessly haunted by the desire to escape from the police, while ceaselessly tracked by them. Once submitted to control, it is impossible to even dream of returning to an honest job. Henceforth, her great apprehension will be the abominable visit which will prevent her rising even the smallest bit above the worst vulgarity; her weekly presence in the dispensary tolls the death-knell of her previously pure affection, of her longings for breathable air, of every possible impulse towards good. Prostitute! the police has said, and prostitute she will remain.[24]

Indeed, in the dire opinion of Yves Guyot, the principal abolitionist critic (that is, critic of the regulationist system) of the early Third Republic *police des moeurs*, "Every enrolled woman is at the complete disposition of the *police des moeurs*. In the eyes of the police, every unregistered woman is an *insoumise*."[25]

Regulationist thinking about sexuality and the severe nomenclature that accompanied it may not be altogether unfamiliar, for to this day the tendency is to define sexuality as a state of being rather than a historically specific social practice.[26] Most people consider sexuality to be the principal constituent of the "private sphere." When we address tolerated prostitution in nineteenth-century Paris, we confront an intense struggle between the private and the public spheres, between the individual and the polity, because while licit sexuality was generally assumed to be a private matter, prostitutional sexuality was understood to be the property of the state.

All extraconjugal sexual activity was to be controlled by the municipality, and critical to this state monitoring system was a definition of female sexuality solely in relation to the needs and desires of men. Considering the standpoint of both the framers of regulationist dogma and a portion of the prostitute's clientele, the later nineteenth-century middle- or upper-class Parisian *homo sexualis* had only two heterosexual options: a normal woman (his wife) or a deviant woman (a prostitute or other loose woman).[27] In principle, the categories were mutually exclusive, and the choice posed a crisis of respectability for the married Victorian man and a severe libidinal dilemma for the bachelor. A man was told by society, on one hand, to expend his sexual reserves only within marriage, but, on the other, he learned to expect sexual pleasure only in the bed of the deviant woman.

This system of thought helped to underpin Parisian réglementation. The "régime de la tolérance surveillée" had originally been created to accommodate the sexual needs of a large population of rootless, male sexual *misérables:* solitary working-class men newly arrived in Paris, who had yet to settle into a regular pattern of life in the city.[28] However, the number of solitary, recently uprooted working-class men in Paris declined over the century (which helps to account for the declining strength of the term *dangerous classes* as a bourgeois synonym for *laboring classes* from the time of the Second Empire).[29] As this group was assimilated into the urban mainstream, two things happened: these men gradually espoused a bourgeois model of male sexuality (meaning the adoption of the contradictory code of respectability discussed above), and the main function of réglementation shifted. By the third quarter of the century, the police system had become an institutionalized accommodation of the double-standard requirements of a more socially integrated male population. In part, of course, this ideological shift was brought about by the progressive assimilation of the lower-class male population.

According to the abolitionist point of view, the system became a "veritable insurance company for the man against all risks resulting from his misconduct. It relieves him of the responsibilities incumbent upon him in the most formal manner."[30] Réglementation openly acknowledged that male sexuality was an uncontrollable force that required an outlet. In its essentialist view of sexuality, regulationism conceived sex as an overpowering force in the heterosexual man that shaped not only the personal but social life as well.[31] Though nothing about the system concealed the basic assumption that men were sexually needy, the necessary outlet was to be hidden from view, invisible to all passersby, concealed behind closed doors and heavy drapes. Or if the registered prostitute was to work on the public thoroughfare, she was subject to strict behavioral, geographical, and temporal discipline. The system aimed thereby to control every instance of extraconjugal sexual expression, because prostitution was to be its only form.

Women were positioned at the receiving end of this institutionalized canalizing of male sexual desire. But *desire* is not the right word, at least not within the framework of regulationist ideology. The program instead recognized and sought to accommodate need, because male desire was not recognized as a legitimate demand on the Parisian system of tolerated prostitution. Whereas *need* was understood to be physiological and therefore involuntary if not uncontrollable, *desire* was defined as voluntary impulse and its indulgence seen as a luxury. Evidence of an increase in male desire helped to upset the regulationists of the 1870s. According to the irascible C. J. Lecour, longtime head of the Paris police des moeurs:

> The world of prostitution – establishments and personnel – has changed markedly. The number of police-controlled brothels has decreased: the number will continue its decline. From the standpoint of speculative investment, those houses no longer offer any advantages, and they would disappear if they didn't have their clientele of travellers, soldiers and day-laborers. It would be a mistake to think that in this fact there is cause for public morality to rejoice, for it is more than a simple change of form. Today, one seeks *adventure* at great risk to one's health, and, in many cases, at risk to one's future tranquility. It is a question of the exercise of vanity and the quest for luxury in an unhealthy terrain.[32]

In another context, Lecour aphoristically (and effectively) summarized the problem in this way: "Tolerance for venal and scandalous gallantry has entered our morals."[33] Lecour thereby grants prostitution a horrific power: ordinariness achieved through the complete penetration of the social and moral fabric; an acceptance and toleration of true scandal that trivializes and forces "scandal" into quotation marks.

Parisian réglementation had been put to the test earlier in the century (by sharp increases in clandestine prostitution during the July Monarchy and the Second Empire, and decreases in the number of brothels), but between the Commune and the Boulanger Affair, it appeared that the system was going to be defeated once and for all by the disobedient, deviant women of Paris. Neoregulationist disquiet over the decline of the regulationist program reached fever pitch among interested parties – doctors, police, moralists – who believed that clandestine prostitutes were taking over: "For a certain number of years the chances for prosperity for licensed brothels have definitely dropped. Clandestine prostitution, daily more invasive and audacious, makes quite a contest for the houses and steals away the better part of their clientele."[34] Because clandestine prostitutes were thought to be despoiling the city's public spaces, the citizenry's private morals, and the mandated system of licensed brothels, spokesmen for the police system campaigned to repair the regulationist dragnet.

At least two broad concerns underlay the alarm over the increase of clandestine prostitution: the breakdown of the century-long effort to organize and police sectors of the lower classes, especially women; and the apparent increase in sexuality in the female population as a whole – worries involving *both* lower- and middle-class women. Alain Corbin has rightly observed that the two principal focuses of later nineteenth-century outrage about female sexuality were closely linked; he understands that the fear of the clandestine prostitute and the concern about the sexual recklessness of decent women were two sides of the same coin: "The impression of invasion by the *insoumise* very obviously translated the terror inspired by any thought of sexual liberalization among the bourgeoisie. The line of demarcation between adultery, moral libertinism, debauchery, vice and prostitution was less clear than ever before."[35]

The effort to control working-class women was closely tied to the dichotomous conceptualization of female sexuality already mentioned. The difference drawn between the sexuality of the honest woman and that of the loose woman was, to a degree, a social distinction masquerading as a sexual one: the distinction was equally that between bourgeois and proletarian female sexuality. The female underclass and the sexually deviant were thought (and hoped) to be the same. The regulationist program, established on behalf of respectable French men, required the deviant lower-class woman but needed to maintain that deviance in a marginal space where it could be watched, its trajectories carefully traced.[36] But men of the 1870s and 1880s saw deviance and deviants moving toward the center of their city's life, threatening to upset the social and sexual balance of power.

There is an accusatory tone in neoregulationist discourse. It appears as though the prisoners in the panopticon have gotten loose, that the "weapons" trained on them are without disciplinary effect. But the analogy of a jailbreak is inadequate unless we also imagine the escaped prisoners seducing the guards while the warden looks on, powerless. "In the course of their work, the municipal guards of the service [*des moeurs*] revel in the spectacle of wild misbehavior and saturnalias that police regulations strive in vain to keep within the bounds of decency."[37] Such were the contents and objects of the fear and anger in question, and they point to one of the central contradictions of the philosophy underlying the regulatory apparatus: the sexually deviant woman was needed by the sexually hungry man, but she was frequently characterized as the instigator of increased male demand; indeed these women were believed to have transformed male need into male desire. As a consequence, the women were seen to have increased the demand for illicit sex across the social map, converting men from sexual misérables into sexually ardent victims of disobedient temptresses.

The development that elicited outcries from the regulationists of the 1870s and 1880s was that the women were now openly advertising themselves. Quoting Flévy d'Urville: "Women no longer wait to be admired, they exhibit themselves."[38] (See fig. 5 in which a woman openly seeks to advertise her "freedom.") The following warning, written in 1874 by Léon Rénault, préfet de police, to be sent out to all employees of the *service des moeurs*, echoes d'Urville's opinion. As usual, the prefect claimed to write in the interest of "the honest population":

5.
"Actualities," *Le Monde Comique*, 1878–79.

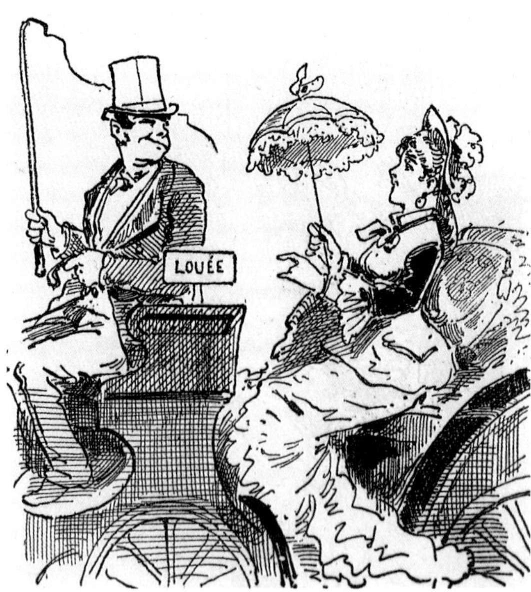

RENTED
Driver, take down that sign; I wish the public to know that I am free, very free in fact.

"Gentlemen, one of the most ordinary solicitation techniques consists in a woman situating herself wearing the showiest outfits and assuming the showiest demeanours among the customers in the front windows of cafés."[39]

Women were blamed for creating an increased male desire for their sexual services by brandishing their own sexual cupidity in the streets. This spectacle was thought eventually and inevitably to infect decent women with a taste for sexual vice – perhaps the biggest concern of all. Male sexuality was to be channelled by the system into an acceptable because marginalized routine pattern, but the new excesses of the deviant woman had decisively upset the equilibrium and respectability of the program.

Honest women were also held liable for the breakdown of public sexual decorum and order in the capital city, values that réglementation was engineered to protect and preserve. Réglementation was to discipline the unruly edges of public conduct; the respectable majority was expected to anchor the social and moral order without intervention by policemen or any other public official.

For the naturalist novelists, there was an in-between category: the adulterous "respectable" woman. Whether writing fiction, diaries, or newspaper articles, they observed – sometimes fretted – that the honest woman could turn into a loose woman at a moment's notice (one need only recall *Madame Bovary* or *Thérèse Raquin*). But their nonliterary writings are also laced with a belief that women were indeed potential adulteresses. The society woman's propensity for infidelity was a favorite theme of the Goncourt brothers' journal: "Adultery is really contagious, just like those crises of hysteria"; and "Those poor society women sometimes end up being treated like the whores that they are."[40] In a *Figaro* column, Zola claimed to find adultery rampant among all bourgeois women: "Among the bourgeoisie, a young girl is kept pure until her marriage; only after the marriage does the effect of her spoiled surroundings and poor education throw her into the arms of a love: it is not prostitution, it is adultery, the difference is only in the words. For, one must really insist, adultery is the plague of the bourgeoisie, just as prostitution is the plague of the people."[41]

But, in the final analysis, it was the clandestine prostitute working the street who played the role of scapegoat in the regulationist drama and as a consequence bore the brunt of repressive efforts, because the lapsed respectable woman was not considered inherently deviant like the prostitute. Any hint of sexual illegality, and the latter was arrested and enrolled. One explanation for the increasing deviance in the culture (exemplified by the growth of extramarital promiscuity) was that vice was contagious. And it was the lower-class clandestine prostitute who was found guilty of spreading sexual licentiousness. Her all-too-visible presence instilled a taste for illicit sexual adventure in her social and moral superiors – or so the story went. The fear of the "contamination" of decent women by venal women was built into neoregulationist thinking.

The protection of proper women was one of the reasons that prostitutes were to be hidden from the eyes of respectable women walking through the city. The decent woman was more likely to have a surprise encounter with an unsupervised prostitute, an insoumise, than with a registered prostitute, whose time and place of appearance in public were limited by established rules. The difference between the practice and the appearance of the soumise and insoumise was certainly exaggerated by regulationist writings, but the insoumise was believed to pose a greater danger to the decent woman: "Clandestine prostitution is much more dangerous than tolerated prostitution; it is a grave danger to morals through its pernicious influence."[42]

What happened to the honest woman if she chanced to observe a prostitute soliciting on the street? The honest woman, when belittled and insulted by the prostitute, was offended by vulgarity; the offense added up to a breach of decorum, as in this account: "The way prostitutes crowd together is a continual source of complaints and recriminations. . . . Honest women can no longer stop at shop windows without the risk of being insulted or being exposed to the propositions of a passerby; they do not want to enter a shop when, in order to do so, they have to elbow their way through a thick group."[43] But it was not only the vulgarity of the boulevard prostitute in the presence of decent women that was the object of concern. No matter how the prostitute acted, her mere presence in a milieu of virtue threatened the moral and social order. Choosing another example of a public, nineteenth-century environmental contaminant – the urinal – the contradictions multiply. *Vespasiennes*, marvels of Haussmann's sanitary engineering, were not offensive to respectable women, even in the most elegant parts of the city. So why couldn't the decorous woman avert her eyes from the abusive prostitute as she would from the man entering or leaving a *pissotière*? After all, the lady was much less likely to witness venal intercourse than she was to view public male urination, a sight also unfit for a proper woman.

Perhaps the regulationist fretted over the possibility that women of his class would only feign disgust at the spectacle of the immoral public behavior of prostitutes but would in fact be tempted to emulate the bestial sexuality of deviant women. In the words of Martine Callu: "Insults, propositions: assaults upon the honor of the physical integrity of honest women capable of reaching the consciousness that she has of herself. It is no longer a question here of the pernicious influence of evil visions upon feminine morality but of the confusion between the honest woman–prostitute that is being fought." The honest woman must therefore never even see the prostitute – "The honest woman must be the antithesis of the prostitute, she must have rejected all sexual desire and pleasure" – because she might envy her apparently powerful sexuality.[44] Prostitution had to be hidden from the dominated honest woman at any price, because, following Callu's argument, it carried a force harmful to the masculine order. The lapsing of the honest woman into the immoral woman – even if such yielding never penetrated her actions and remained merely a shift in consciousness – would erode the patriarchal system of domination.

In this system, because the male depends upon the prostitute for the satisfaction of his libidinal pleasures, he must secure her availability, while controlling and sanitizing her at the same time. The sequestered prostitute was the constant token of the male's political and social power,[45] but also of his sexual neediness and vulnerability – a perpetual reminder that he could become the prisoner of his own sexuality.

What is man that the itinerary of his desire creates such a text?
– Gayatri Spivak, in Displacement *(Krupnik, ed.)*

The vulnerability of certain men to the confusing demands of the modern sexual marketplace is manifest in a series of pictures of brothels painted by Paul Cézanne between 1870 and 1877. Although Cézanne's quirky series seems to be an unusually transparent record of some of the doubts, worries, and fantasies of a bourgeois living through the changes in the sexual economy in the big city, it also introduces one of the trademarks of the avant-garde project as it took shape during this period: the effort to contain and order the anxieties provoked by the modern sexualized woman in general and by the contemporary prostitute in particular.

Between approximately 1870 and 1877, Cézanne painted at least three images of Olympia.[46] He called his Olympias modern and based them, of course, upon Edouard Manet's *Olympia* of 1863. Cézanne's purpose was not documentary, nor did he pretend it to be, but these phantasmic homages to Manet by way of Delacroix address the theater of enticement that existed in the deluxe brothels of Cézanne's day. In so doing, the images confront one of the principal developments in the sexual marketplace of the 1870s but also educate us more generally about the logic (and illogic) of male desire – the force that produced and orchestrated the obsession with prostitution during this period in the first place.

In the first two pictures in the series – both titled *A Modern Olympia*, the former painted circa 1869–70 (fig. 6), the latter in 1872–73 (fig. 7) – the man resembles the artist. This suggests that the pictures had a special personal significance for the painter, because he was not in the habit of including himself in his narrative paintings. The resemblance also suggests that these visions of just-unveiled prostitutes may correspond to the artist's own sexual feelings in ways that are unfamiliar and uncommon in the relatively cool, objective, and normative vanguard painting of the era. Think, for example, of its icily controlled eponym, Manet's *Olympia*, painted in 1863.

Of the idiosyncratic personal quality of some of Cézanne's early paintings, especially his pictures of women, Meyer Schapiro wrote: "In several early works by Cézanne, inspired by Manet, sexual gratification is directly displayed or implied. . . . Cézanne's pictures of the nudes show that he could not convey his feeling for women without anxiety. In his painting of the nude woman, where he does not reproduce an older work, he is most often constrained or violent. There is for him no middle ground of simple enjoyment."[47] Schapiro goes on to argue that for Cézanne the unmanageability of his strong sexual feelings for women led him to displace the theme of eros onto the realm of still life – in particular, onto an idealized and perfectly equilibrated cosmos of apples. The point is that Cézanne could not control the disclosure of his own uneasiness with women and that his strong sexual feelings for women were incommen-

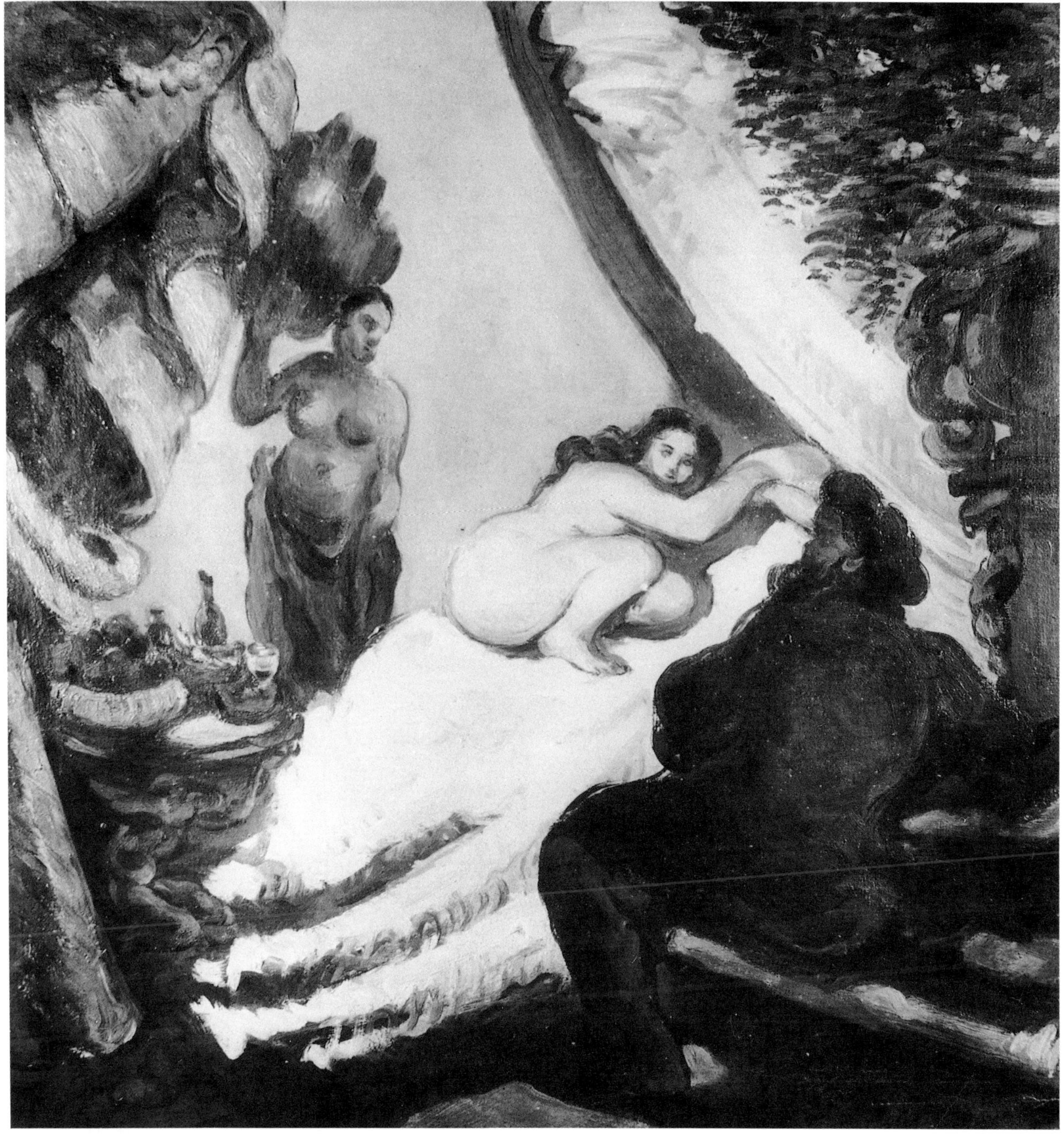

6.
Paul
Cézanne,
A Modern Olympia,
ca. 1869–70,
oil on canvas,
private
collection,
Paris.

surable with the normative painting of the nude. Schapiro concludes sensibly that the marked uneasiness on view in some early paintings is what led him eventually to set aside the theme of sexual fantasy and gratification.

Cézanne exhibited the second Olympia, *A Modern Olympia*, painted in 1872–73 (fig. 7), in the first "Impressionist" exhibition in the spring of 1874. Lionello Venturi has found the painting to be ironic,[48] but in 1874 critics found it to be a deeply disturbed and disturbing painting. The champion of naturalism, Jules Castagnary, for example, found that the picture was spoiled by fantasy and romanticism, both utterly personal in origin and therefore anathema to Castagnary: "From idealization to idealization, they will end up with a degree of romanticism

7.
Paul Cézanne, *A Modern Olympia*, ca. 1872–73, oil on canvas, Musée d'Orsay, Paris.

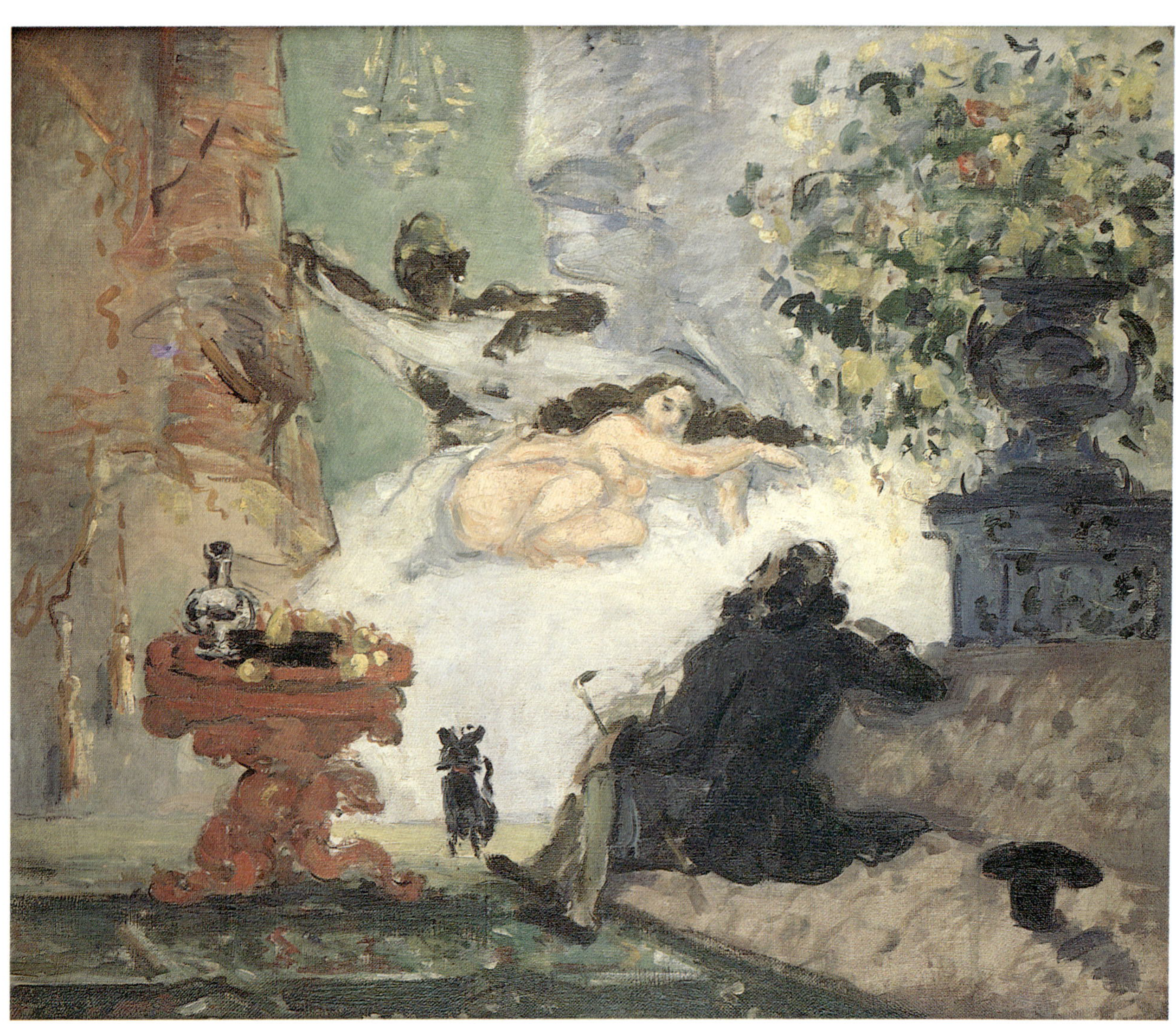

that knows no stopping, where nature is nothing but a pretext for dreams, and where the imagination becomes unable to formulate anything other than personal, subjective fantasies, without trace of general reason, because they are without control and without the possibility of verification in reality."[49] Emile Cardon did not like Cézanne's painting either, because he worried that the public might wrongly take the product of a disturbed artist as a seriously intentioned work: "One wonders if there is in this an immoral mystification of the public, or the result of mental alienation that one can do nothing but deplore."[50] Marc de Montifaud's review was deeply sarcastic but full of interest for this study because she found Cézanne's little picture to be a failed effort at Baudelairean imagery. She consequently situated the image within a world framed by fantasy, literature, and opiates. She wrote:

> Sunday's public decided to laugh at this fantastic figure presented in an opium-filled sky to an opium smoker. This apparition of a little rose-colored, naked flesh that is thrust upon him, in the cloudy empyrean, a kind of demon, who presents herself as an incubus, like a voluptuous vision, this corner of artificial paradise has overwhelmed the bravest, it must be said, and M. Cézanne appears to be nothing other than a kind of fool, painting while agitated with *delirium tremens.* People have refused to see, in this creation inspired by Baudelaire, an impression caused by oriental vapors which had to be rendered under the bizarre sketch of the imagination. The incoherence of it, does it not have the quality, the particular character of laudatory sleep? Why look for an indecent joke, a scandalous motif in *Olympia?* In reality it is only one of the extravagant forms of haschisch borrowed from the swarm of drole visions which should still be hidden away in the hôtel Pimodan.[51]

The fantasies on view in Cézanne's pictures were hardly Cézanne's exclusive property. In the 1870s and 1880s, along with what I have already identified as the *embourgeoisement* of male sexual ideals came a preference for forms of prostitutional practice in which desire – "real feeling" – was convincingly simulated: the "new" male sexuality demanded a new sexual style for the "modern" female deviant.[52] For the up-to-date consumer in the changing sexual marketplace, a Simmelian cold-as-cash, heartless coupling would not do. By the late 1870s, these increasingly widespread demands were channeled toward two sectors of the venal sexual marketplace: the *maison de luxe* (Cézanne's terrain) and various forms of clandestine prostitution (see chapters 3 and 4). The modern man wanted either a dash of recherché aristocratic eroticism (the trademark of the deluxe brothel) or a simulation of bourgeois romance (the specialty of many clandestine prostitutes).

Cézanne's attraction to the fabled allure of the stylized, romantic forms of eroticism offered in the deluxe brothel of the 1870s no doubt motivated the series (see chapter 2). The tension in his pictures bespeaks an altogether modern clash: that between the fantasies of perfect pleasure to be found in such a place and the anxiety that desire will not be fully mutual, that the man will fail to excite the woman. A less-than-ideal erotic experience would threaten to remind the man of his sexual vulnerability. Finding pleasure in the deluxe brothel of this period was apparently a difficult job. The client was to appropriate the woman's desire as well as her body. But the attainment of the Baudelairean delights that awaited the successful customer would have made the risk of failure (of humiliation, of impotence?) worth taking. Cézanne's *Olympia* series addresses these problems.

In the earliest of Cézanne's pictures (fig. 6), the nude woman perches precariously on the draped bed in a surprising position that hints at an unfamiliarity with or dislike for the place: her legs are drawn up beneath her so that she squats while leaning forward and seems to anchor herself on the pillow with her crossed elongated arms. She looks directly at the dark profile of the timorous man who leans back slightly from the spectacle before him. The circumstances of his meeting with her are dramatized by the dark, bare-breasted servant behind the bed who raises a fan, enacting the rhetoric of presentation.

The anatomical features of this young woman provide a key to what this fantastic picture may be about. Her rounded body, pretty face, and long wavy hair exempt her from the stereotype of the lower-class, quotidian prostitute. (Or, to speak in shorthand, her attitude as well as her appearance would be out of place in Edgar Degas's brothel [fig. 18, for example]). The theatrical or operatic quality of the setting and space of the picture conjures up Delacroix more than it does any naturalist picture dating from the Second Empire.

There is a marked difference in scale between the woman and the man that exaggerates the distance between them and implies a gulf between the client and the displayed woman. The oversized baroque vase of flowers at the right edge is in his part of the picture and seems to substantiate the "real" world of the near space inhabited by him and to dematerialize the brightly lit "imaginary" world whose two female inhabitants appear as if projected on a screen before him. The man is the solitary consumer of a confusing spectacle: an attractive young woman is bestowed upon him, but her participation in the transaction seems tentative. She is not made to appear forbidding or dangerous; in fact her precarious pose softens and offsets the drama of her prominence in the space and in the ostensible sexual narrative of the picture. She even appears frail, unpracticed at the role thrust upon her.

This nonrational picture, with its discontinuities of scale and inconsistent, occasionally expressionist handling (the vase, the flowers, and the man's profile), is connected to forms of contemporary Parisian brothel prostitution in real if implicit ways. In it a thoroughly modern anxiety is given form: a classic fantasy of voluptuousness has gone wrong at the eleventh hour. The picture is therefore a melancholy reverie about a missed opportunity in an imaginary world tailor-made for sensual enjoyment. Disappointment, it appears, in the theater of enticement.

The facial features of the pretty young woman are neutral and calm and contribute to the impression that this is a somewhat sad representation of a self-deprecating fantasy. The tentativeness and frailty of Cézanne's Olympia contradict what a man might expect – whether his expectations were shaped by Baudelaire, Delacroix, or reports of deluxe urban brothels – of a beautiful unclothed young woman lying before him, and only him, on an ornamental bed surrounded by the trappings of a specialized, luxurious place of sensual pleasures.

It represents luxuriant sex just out of reach, because the woman – provider of potential sexual gratification – folded up and withdrew the offer. Cézanne suggests that the customer's inadequacy – his own? – destroyed the fantasy. And the veteran of the realm of "luxe, calme et volupté," Olympia, is a temporarily unavailable amateur in Cézanne's picture. It represents a spoiling of the man's prospects for indulging his fantasy, but not, it seems, a total disbelief in the substance of the fantasy that remains otherwise intact: she *is* beautiful and the room would have been the perfect arena for sensual enjoyment. The underpinning of the fantasy is a dream of voluptuous expert sex with no strings attached. But there is despair in the picture about the realization of this desire. Perhaps Cézanne reveals in this brothel image an unconscious realization of the fragility and elusiveness of this illusion in the modern world. Thus the modernity of this Olympia.

The 1872–73 picture (fig. 7) takes up the same theme and reuses the same format, but its irony and humor are new. The ironic and humorous tone of this canvas, vis-à-vis the tentative and sad 1870 painting, is a consequence of changes in both the handling and the story. The uniform choppiness of the paint strokes and the staging of the unveiling on the bed as an ongoing process greatly increase the staccato activity of the picture, especially in the imaginative far space. The fragile curving woman of the 1870 version has been replaced by a rough, slightly grotesque caricature, which modifies the meeting of the man and the woman. The folded-up posture takes on a different significance: this woman rests fully on the left side of her angular and distorted body, which appears to be a natural and stable position rather than an unsure and wavering one. This Olympia is far from conventionally pretty and soft or poised. The client's aspect has also changed. His solidly anchored sitting position and the addition of hat and cane give him an air of composure and savoir-faire as he looks in and up at the pink Olympia edged in blue shadows, an Olympia who lies and crouches before him, only for him. The painting presents a lively and available grotesque regarded without apparent emotion by the seated man.

The mutual lack of conviction in the meeting between the two in the 1870 version has been replaced by an altogether more confident and urbane exchange: the sophisticated gentleman is unmoved by the extraordinary spectacle before his eyes. The man – the artist? – is shown to be under full emotional control but appears slightly foolish. Certain accessories in the room add to the burlesque quality of the scene: the jaunty, vibrating deep red table and the impudent terrier. Here is an interior equipped and furnished exclusively for the pleasure and indulgence of the senses, but when the covering is swept off the woman, something incongruous is revealed.

This image seems witty and even slightly absurd compared to the 1869–70 version, but the absurdity of the situation carries an altered message, a subtly changed view of the prospects for and even the desirability of sexual gratification in luxurious circumstances. The fantasy of voluptuousness is here unmistakably diluted – undone – by the recognition of the implausibility of finding gratifying and uncommercialized sensual pleasure in the deluxe sexual marketplace. Yet Cézanne has somewhat distanced the client (himself) from the experience of disappointment with this turn of events by granting him (himself) greater control over the situation and, by extension, over the venal woman.

Cézanne's third *Olympia*, the watercolor version done around 1877 (fig. 8), presents a view of prostitute, servant, and client substantially different from the two discussed above. Although painted in a more generalized style, the setting of the work seems less fantastic: most of the operatic equipment is gone, replaced by a common armchair, framed mirror, modestly dressed domestic, and man *en habit noir.* The servant and client contemplate the featureless, reclining blond nude from above. They seem to watch her, stare at her, as if she were a person apart, as though they were mourners or concerned visitors attending someone suffering from a serious if uncommon illness. Olympia is stiffly arranged, rigid like a naked corpse, with arms pressed into frozen contradictory imitations of sensuality (behind the head) and modesty (the chaste hand at the groin).

The bearing of her two spectators hints at a bewilderment; they seem to manifest focused concern but at the same time remain somewhat detached and immobile, all the while fundamentally in control of the situation. The two onlookers are differentiated from each other: the

8.
Paul
Cézanne,
Olympia,
ca. 1877,
watercolor,
Philadelphia
Museum
of Art.

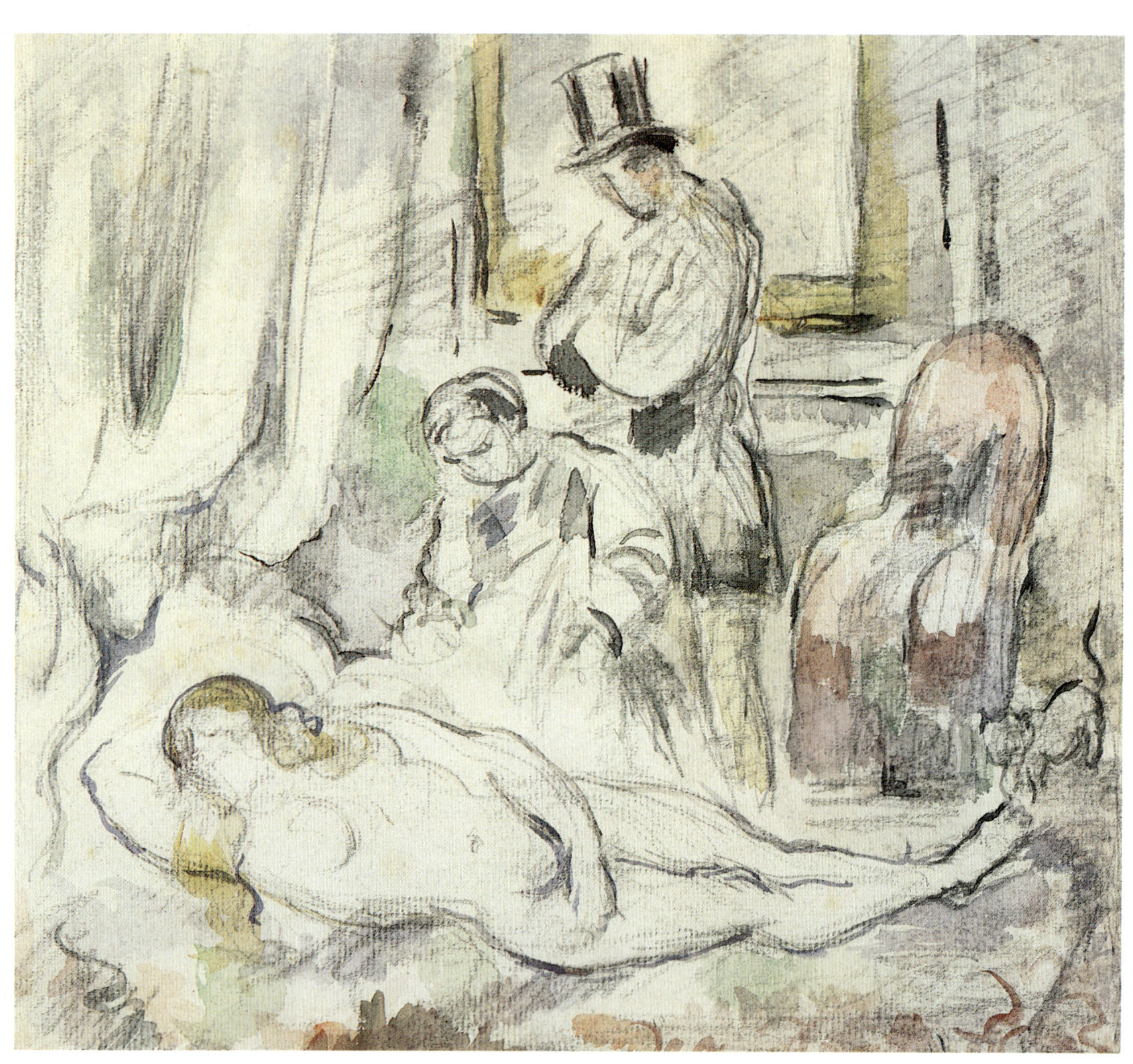

woman sits or kneels and leans slightly forward; the man stands behind her with his arms folded, more removed than she from the blond nude, whom he looks at nonetheless. The intensity of their scrutiny of Olympia is suggested by the dark strokes that denote their eye cavities. These faint indications of facial features are all the more significant because the nude's face is empty. Olympia's separation and tense immobility are enhanced by the cat, whose arched back and flaring eyes in Manet's original had stood for sensuality gone rampant, which now saunters in casually from the right edge of the painting.[53] The forms of this watercolor – its heavy, dark, vibrating contour lines, strongly rectilinear structure, and blocky transparent patches of colored wash (reds, yellows, greens, and blues) – freeze the picture's imagery of a conundrum.

Perhaps the puzzlement of Olympia's small but privileged entourage – the collaborator in the provision of paid pleasures and the potential consumer of her sexual services – is, at one level, provoked by her immobility, by her simply not acting according to the sexual agenda. But, perhaps, the puzzlement exists on, and is caused by, another level of bewilderment: the confusion in finding that there is no mystery, no eroticism in this nakedness. Another reading of the third *Olympia* is equally in order. The reclining figure of the prostitute (her body marks out the flat base of the picture's triangular order) is held down by the two stares, although she has no eyes of her own. This conventional Salon-type nude appears fixed, pinned down, rigorously controlled – in every way unlike the 1870 *Olympia.*

The sequence of Olympia images shows that there was a marked change, one might even say a development, in Cézanne's portrayal of this subject over a seven-year period, what we might today call a deconstruction of the fantasy of perfect voluptuousness in the lair of the beautiful, erotically able prostitute. The change in the series shows an increasing awareness of the impossibility of finding pleasure in the sexual marketplace, while the direction of the images is also toward an ever-greater containment of female force and male anxiety.

The direction taken by Cézanne's thoughts and feelings on this subject is vividly exemplified by his *The Eternal Feminine* (fig. 9), done at the same time as the watercolor version of Olympia (circa 1877).[54] In this picture, a nude, faceless woman is enthroned beneath a canopy while a gathering of men from diverse professions (painter, bishop, musicians among them) surround and pay tribute to her. This outpouring of veneration is hardly portrayed as a serious ritual but rather as a caricature of the homage paid blindly to sexualized womankind – her faceless nudity and vagina-shaped awning the signs of her sexualization. Cézanne seems to have found the theme of the luxury prostitute (the woman of *The Eternal Feminine* fits that definition as well) appropriate to his increasing pessimism (or even cynicism) about finding "real" eroticism in its old fantastic forms in the modern world and his increasing effort to gain control over his means of representation and over the themes he chose to paint.

A watercolor done about 1880, entitled (apparently by Cézanne himself) *The Courtesan's Toilette* (fig. 10), duplicates the scenario of the 1877 *Olympia,* but with small and telling alterations. The changes constitute an image that closes off the pictorial and ideological cycle Cézanne initiated with the *Modern Olympia* of 1869–70.

A maidservant and a man appear bewildered by the reclining courtesan, but the modern dress and furnishings of the 1877 *Olympia* are replaced by an archaic, romantic-biblical setting complete with tub. Most important, in this case Cézanne appended a text which, though crossed out, has been deciphered to read:

9. Paul Cézanne, *The Eternal Feminine*, 1875–77 or ca. 1877, oil on canvas, J. Paul Getty Museum, Malibu, Calif.

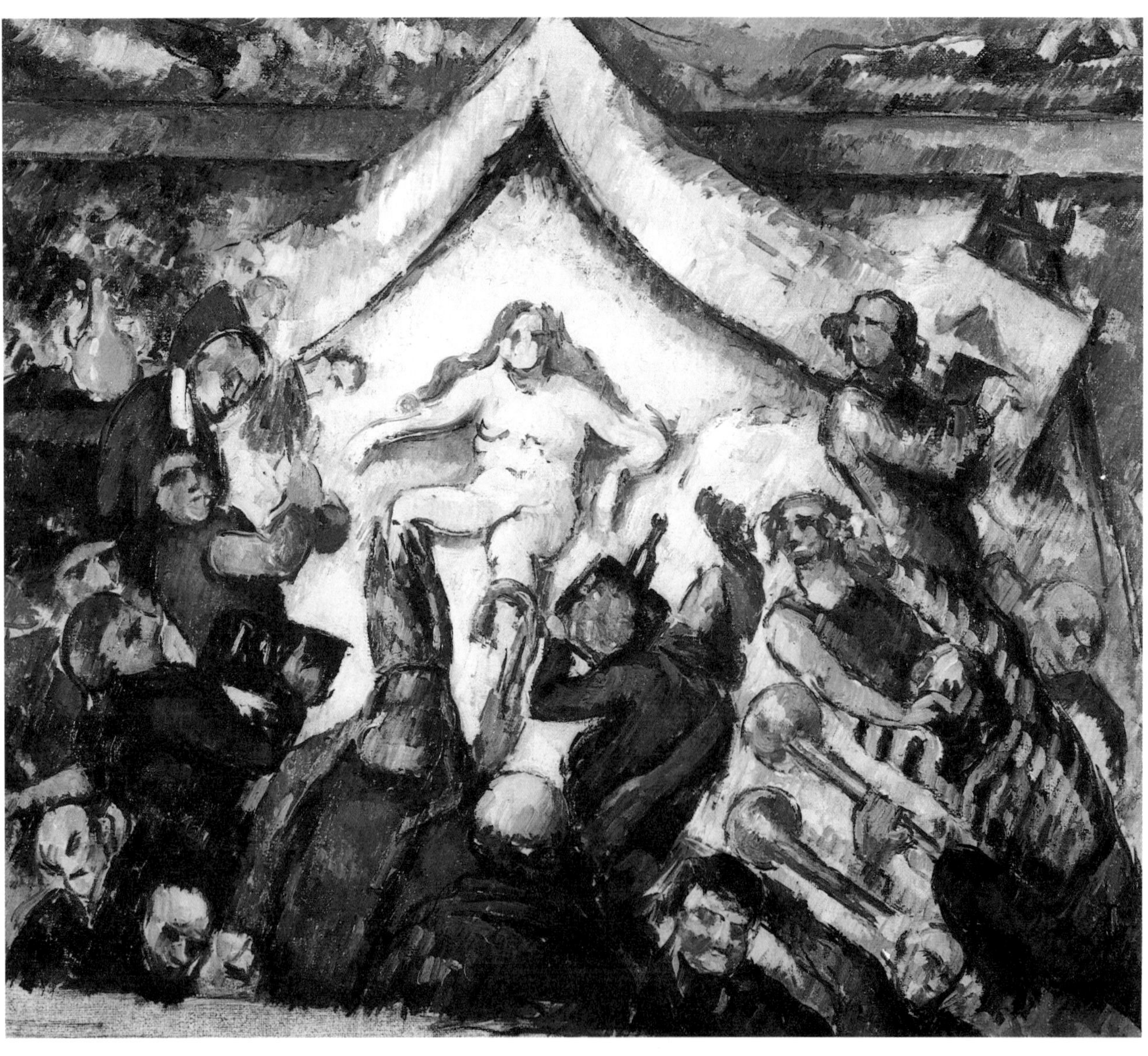

10. Paul Cézanne, *The Courtesan's Toilette*, ca. 1880, pencil and watercolor on white paper, Barrett Hamilton Foundation, Little Rock, Ark.

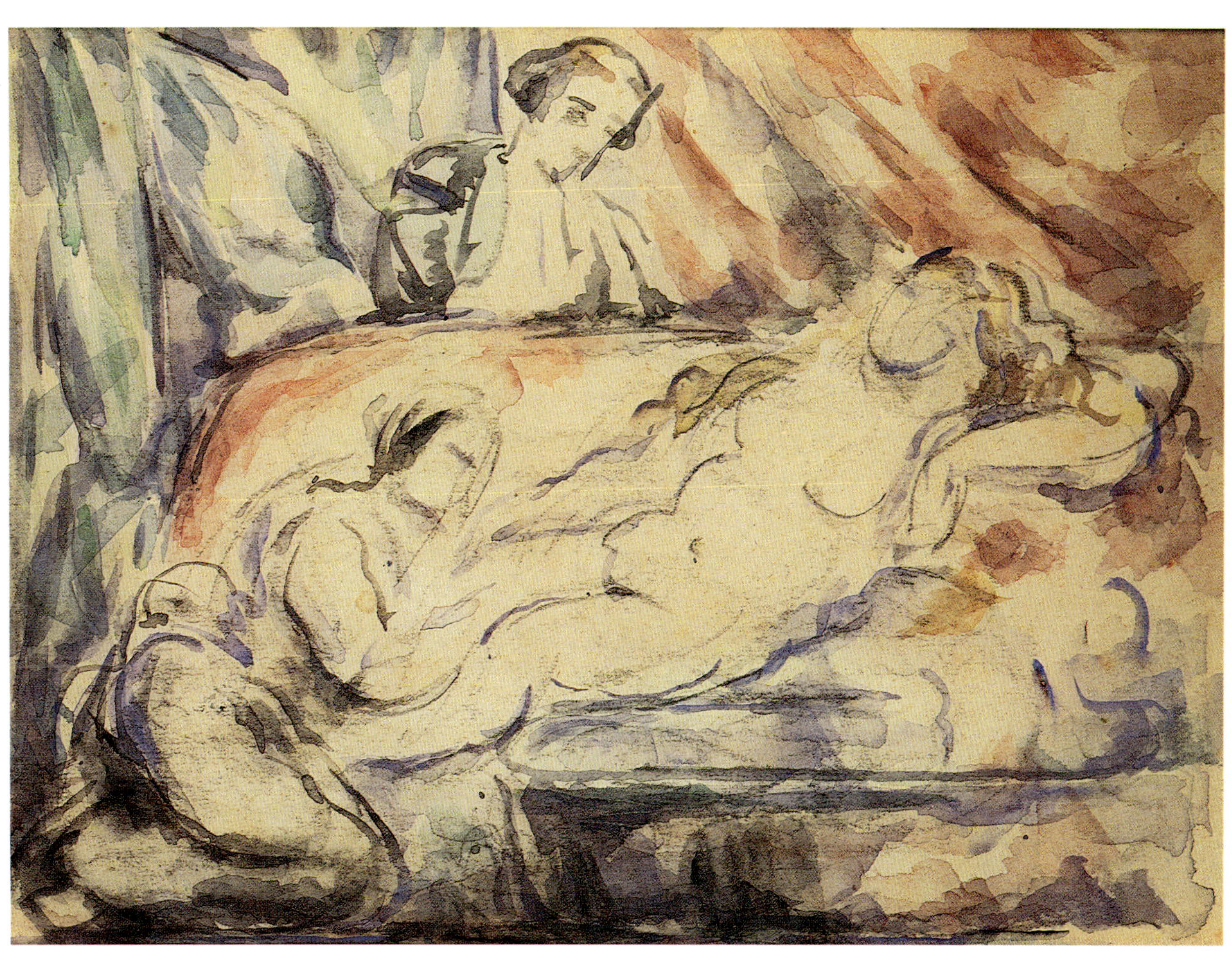

When she rises from the bath, the [zealous ?] servant
pours on perfumes for her refreshment.
And, with breasts palpitating and head thrown back,
free from care she takes in the intrusive glances.[55]

With this ensemble of picture and poem, Cézanne has restored a vexing theme to the safer world of literature, vouchsafed its generality and timelessness, and protected himself from appearing to have enlisted his own libidinal feelings in its construction. With the last line of his rather pathetic poem, Cézanne struggled to demodernize the subject matter of desire in the fantasy brothel. Instead of the trademark "burning glances" of the professional, deluxe prostitute, his literary courtesan appears nonplussed by the prospect of an admirer's importunate advances. But the strain to return to the fantasy bordello of a Delacroix is borne out by the patent mismatch between the text and the picture: the onlooker is stiff and inactive, the courtesan almost equally so.

This examination of a small group of images by Cézanne introduces in microcosm a central theme of this book: the ways in which the painters of the Parisian avant-garde devised the means to attain an appearance of truthful representation of and detachment from the charged subject of contemporary prostitution, while simultaneously perfecting a strategy of ideological containment of the erotic force of the women portrayed. I shall be tracking what becomes a trademark of vanguard art of the 1870s and 1880s: the devising of pictorial styles that appear to avoid (and evade) the explicit "expression" of sexual feelings, while at the same time achieving a measure of control over "their" elusively described women.

This analysis will permit us to conclude that on the matter of sexual ideology – that is, when we focus upon artists' depictions of women – the painters of the Impressionist group had much more in common with their pompier and popular contemporaries than they perhaps would have been willing to admit. In any case, the similarities we shall uncover between apparently dissimilar artistic enterprises certainly outnumber those typically enumerated in the art historical literature.[56]

CHAPTER TWO

In the Brothel

In the late 1870s, Edgar Degas made more than fifty small monotype prints of brothel interiors.[1] In doing them, the artist sought to fulfill two ambitions: to create formally experimental and innovative prints and to record a provocative contemporary practice. Modernist interpretive theory has reconciled the apparent contradiction between the two objectives. Indeed, modernists have argued that the two projects not only did not conflict but actually strengthened and reinforced each other. As a consequence, modernist art historians have tended to regard the simultaneous appearance of (documentary) accuracy and pictorial modernity as a hallmark of the best later nineteenth-century art. Certainly the most influential postwar modernist explanation of the operations of later nineteenth-century painting is Clement Greenberg's. In 1949 he reasoned that the "paradox in the evolution of French painting from Courbet to Cézanne is how it was brought to the verge of abstraction in and by its very effort to transcribe visual experience with ever greater fidelity. Such fidelity was supposed, by the Impressionists, to create the values of pictorial art itself. The truth of nature and the truth, or success, of art were held not only to accord with, but to enhance one another."[2]

A first encounter with Degas's monotypes tends to affirm Greenberg's point of view. Because the prints visualize prostitution in an idiosyncratically fragmented, messy, and daring shorthand, the series looks casual and dispassionate and, as a consequence, seems to present a "true" (because of being straightforward) account of its subject. According to this way of seeing them, the monotypes appear both unencumbered by tradition and unburdened by doctrine.

The strong appeal of Greenberg's account resides in the openness of its dialectical argument. The scholar of Degas's prints can have it both ways; modernist orthodoxy gives the formalist her radical aesthetics but without depriving the social scholar of her investment in the unvarnished realism and objectivity of the series. Not surprisingly, until recently the best studies of Degas's demanding prints were based upon such Greenbergian assumptions.[3] My account differs from its modernist predecessors by calling attention to the ideological qualities of the monotypes – to their various "untruths" – and, in so doing, arguing that in Degas's prints (as in much avant-garde art on the subject of prostitution), truth, modernity, and modernism were incompatible.

My analysis of the monotypes opens with a historical overview of the actual practice of brothel prostitution in Paris at the time. The capsule history segues to a discussion of Degas's related sketchbook drawings. I then proceed to a reading of Degas's prints, which unfolds in three distinct stages, each of which is increasingly detail-oriented.

In the first section, I discuss Degas's negation of the dominant conventions for rendering unclad female bodies and make the case that these bodily unorthodoxies were politically and aesthetically critical. This first stage of my discussion targets for disagreement the modernist accounts outlined above, while it aligns with the principal conclusions reached by Charles Bernheimer, a literary historian, in his account of the monotypes published in 1987. Bernheimer reasons that the prints are "critical" because the "images sever the metaphorical bond between artist and viewer and the signs of his creative triumph over the prostitute's erotic threat"[4] and that they insist thereby upon the commodification of gender relations.

The second part of my discussion will amplify and revise the first part by pointing out instances of Degas's reliance upon the predictability and prejudice of physiognomic codes and stereotypes, especially in the handling of various figures' heads. This portion of my argument points out the heterogeneity and internal contradictions of the codings used for bodies in the prints.

The third and final part of the analysis reconnects Degas's handling of the bodies of Parisian sex workers to the conventions (both aesthetic and sexual-political) that the prints appear to overturn but, in the end, do not. This final portion of the argument, like the first, focuses upon the means used to represent women's bodies, but with a concentration upon Degas's eroticization of prostitutes' buttocks.

The practice of brothel prostitution was inalterably changed by the rebuilding of Paris initiated during the rule of Napoléon III (1852–70). The number of filles de maison remained roughly the same during the last half of the century, but the number of tolerated and licensed houses decreased steadily. From 300 in 1840, the number declined to about 190 in 1860, to 128 in 1878, and to only 70 in 1886.[5] Because the business expanded at the extreme ends of the social spectrum of brothel prostitution, the types of houses that remained in operation changed a great deal. Located for the most part between the exterior boulevards and the fortifications, houses of the most squalid variety, catering to the least elite customers, carried on and prospered. The second-rate houses almost disappeared, while the number of maisons de luxe (often called *grandes tolérances*) increased, mostly in proximity to the newly prosperous *grands boulevards*, the commercial center of Paris, and particularly in the streets adjoining the Madeleine, the Bourse, and the Opera.[6] During 1878, the year of an Exposition Universelle in Paris, establishments in the deluxe category doubled their earnings.[7]

Vital to the prosperity of the maison de luxe was its provision of recherché, aristocratic forms of sexual services and fabulous interior decoration.[8] In every way, the operators of the top houses endeavored to outdo the no-nonsense brothels of modest *tenue*, or standing. Whereas, for example, a display of stylized, professional sexual enthusiasm was apparently rare in the neighborhood tolérance, it was de rigueur in the deluxe house. The experts usually considered the average brothel worker uninterested in (or even incapable of) showing any emotion on the job. Gustave Macé, an old hand of the service des moeurs, described "normative" brothel prostitutes like this in 1888: "These mercenaries of official prostitution, despite the absence of physical desire, are in constant contact with men, and having only the joy of others to live on, they subject themselves to an absolutely mechanical job."[9] Likewise, the style and dress of the "average" brothel prostitute were apparently quite plain compared to those of the deluxe whore: "Contrary to similar establishments that are more chic where the women are dressed only in a peignoir or chemise, the pensioners in the cheapest houses are more dressed."[10]

Popular houses had distinctive architectural features as well, in the form of a ground-floor tavern (called an *estaminet*), while the best houses had a salon.[11] The contrasting layouts of the establishments reflected their different relationships with the outside world: the estaminet opened to the street, whereas the grande tolérance was completely closed off and shuttered.[12]

As we shall see, a broad gulf separates Degas's brothel monotypes from his contemporaneous drawings of downstairs life in the *maison populaire* (figs. 11 and 12). The differences demonstrate that the artist was conversant with the architectural and social contrasts between upper and lower categories of brothel. The sketchbook drawings are closely related to passages of Edmond de Goncourt's 1877 novel, *La Fille Elisa*, and were probably done at the time of its publication.[13] In the sketchbook drawings of young *pensionnaires* (residents of the brothel) interacting with their potential customers in the estaminet, socializing appears intimate, friendly, and gender-balanced, not much like commercial sexual relations at all. There is a social interchange – talking, drinking, playing cards – and the sexes are not segregated into buyers and sellers. Unlike the fragmented monotype compositions that we shall examine closely, a completely narrative unit appears on the page of each of these drawings, which helps to knit together and equalize the men and women shown relaxing congenially. The milieu of these pictures is the estaminet of a popular house near a military school or *caserne*. All of the men in the drawings wear their military uniforms but, perhaps out of respect for the women, have removed their hats. And the room is shown to have been decorated to please the clientele, complete with a picture of a Napoleonic soldier and his cannon on the wall. The rather primly dressed prostitutes wear what was customary in such circumstances (chemiselike garments that left the arms bare), altogether modest costumes by comparison with the outfits of the monotype sex workers.

These unassuming sketchbook drawings correspond to the scene set in a brothel near the Ecole Militaire in Goncourt's novel.[14] Goncourt's energetic indecorousness is a far cry from the low-key, demure camaraderie represented in Degas's drawings. Some of Goncourt's pensionnaires yell and bat their eyes, while others take awkward poses against the wall, attempting to stave off a longing to nap. The final line of the scene – atmospheric rather than descriptive – emphasizes the rudeness of the goings-on: "Noisier and wilder, the orgy continued, despite the somnolence of the women."[15]

Whether or not there is an exact narrative match between the drawings and this scene in the novel is not the important question. Within the conventions of representation available to the two artists, each has produced an imagery of mutualized fellowship, of extroverted, emotionally credible interaction. Goncourt uses the language of noise and ongoing action, while Degas invests his scenes with warmth and equality by momentarily capturing the actions and

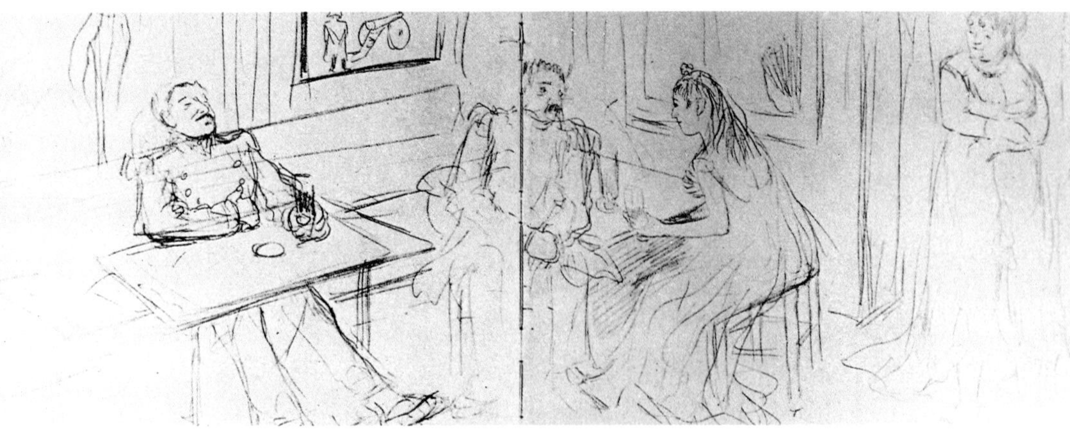

11. Edgar Degas, *Notebook 28*, 1877, drawing known as "La Fille Elisa," private collection, New York.

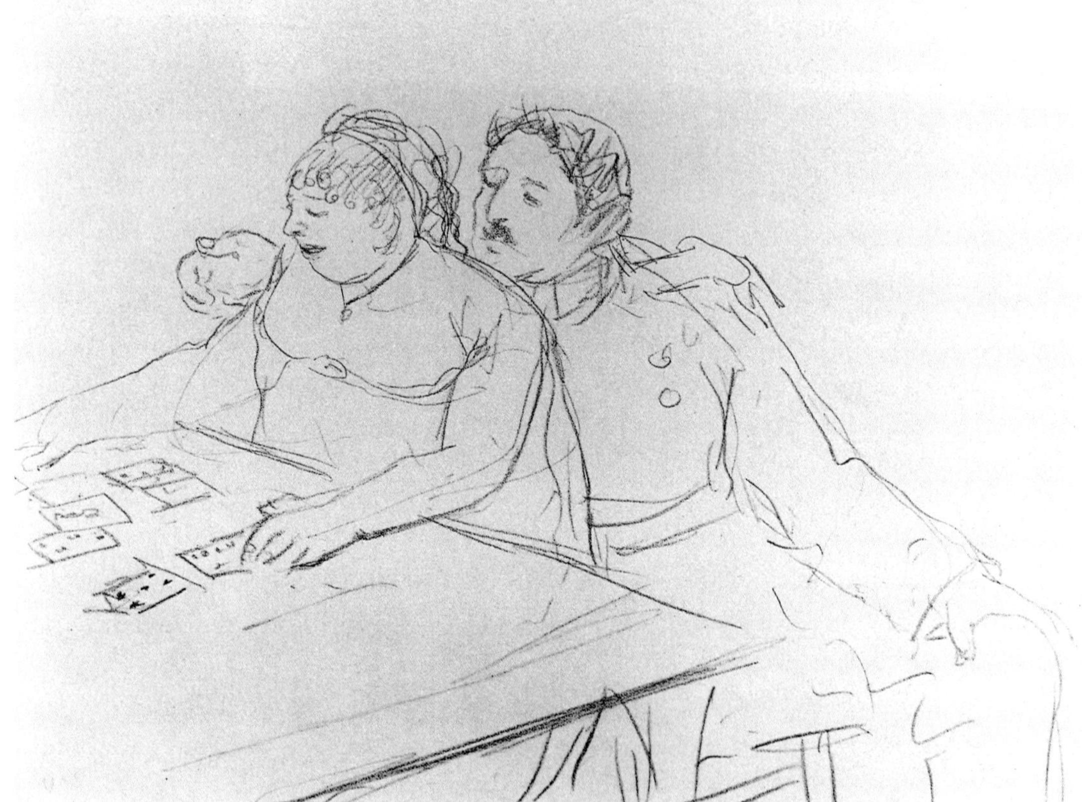

12. Edgar Degas, *Notebook 28*, 1877, drawing known as "La Fille Elisa," private collection, New York.

demeanor of his figures and by completing their stories within the edges of his notebook pages. Degas is right in step with Jean-Louis Forain on this matter. Forain's undated etching of a *maison close* (fig. 13), intended as a book illustration,[16] is quite close in composition and spirit to Degas's drawings, in spite of Forain's characteristic spectacularizing of the full bosoms of prostitutes.

In Degas's monotypes, compositional structure and the temperature of human relations are otherwise. Furnishing and clothing are also different, but it is the absence of comfort or warmth in the monotypes that sets them apart from the drawings.

13.
Jean-Louis
Forain,
Brothel, n.d.,
etching.

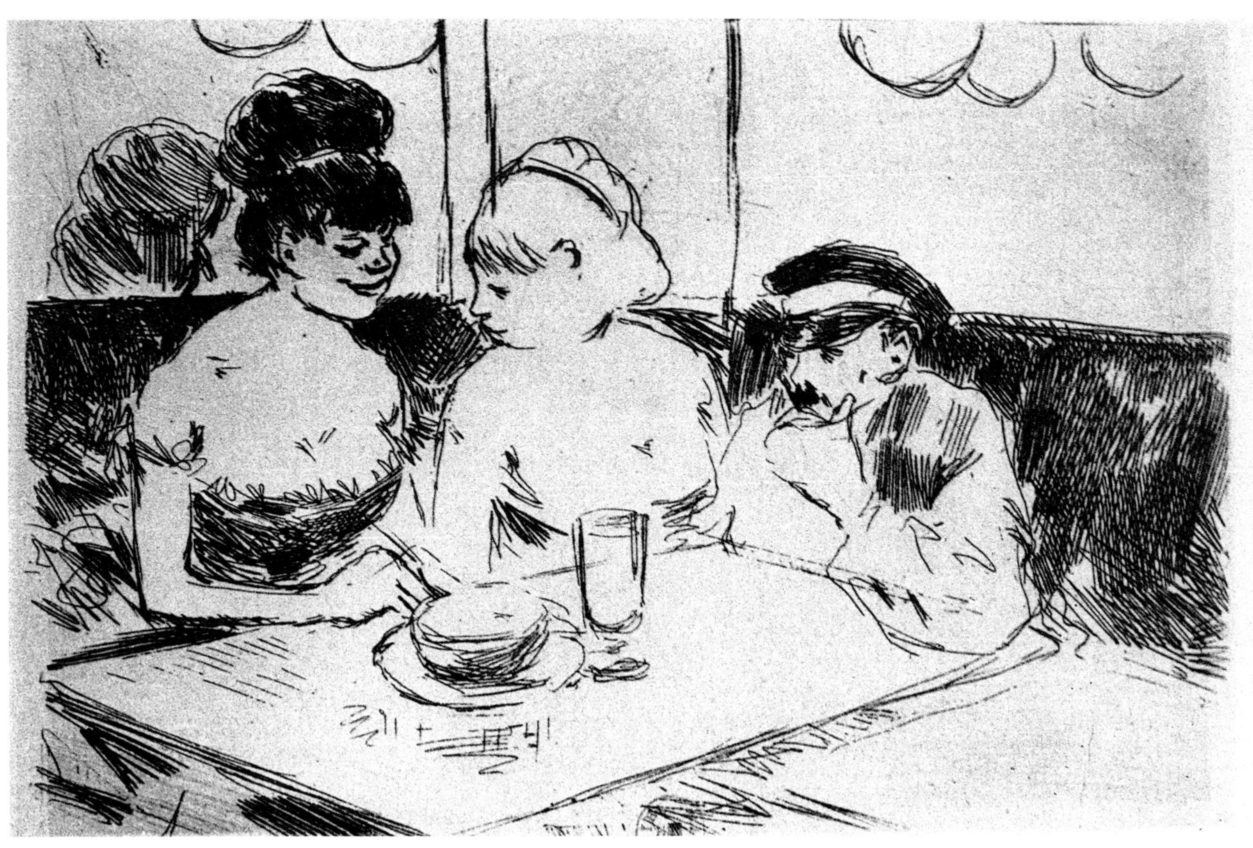

14.
Edgar Degas, *Repose*, ca. 1879–80 or 1876–77, monotype, Musée Picasso, Paris.

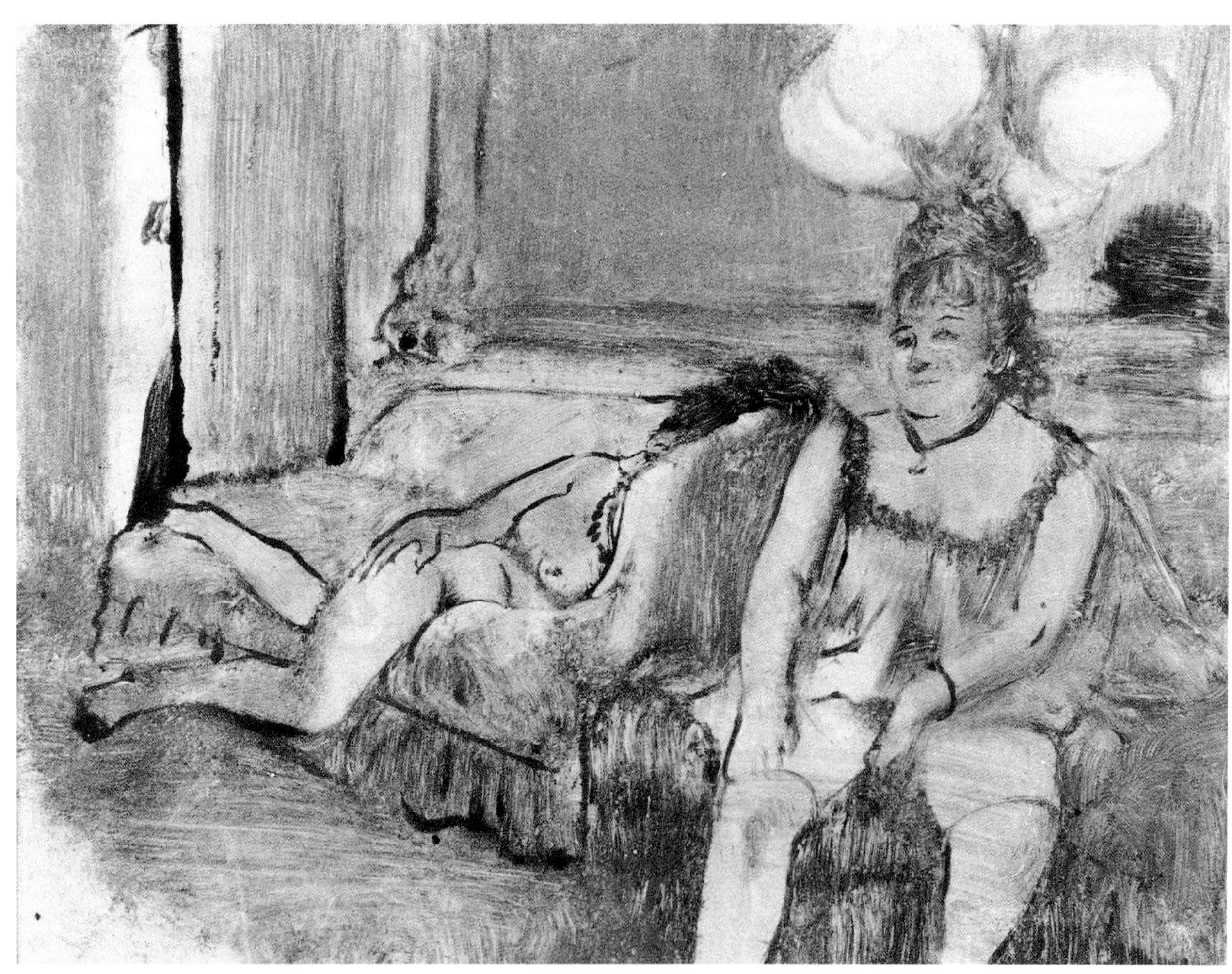

In *Repose* (fig. 14), the loose and irregular application of the printer's ink to the metal plate – Degas used a brush, rag, and sometimes his fingers – is seen in the paper print in the unevenness of the dark lines and the blurriness and varied densities of the tonal areas. As we have noted, this look has been read in the twentieth century as the sign of a relatively nonchalant and rapid manufacture. The relative "sincerity" of a drawing, with which a monotype has much in common, is often determined on the basis of the presumed freedom and speed of its execution. So also with Degas's prints. The composition of *Repose*, with its cutoffs and fragmentations, characteristic of most of the monotypes, has contributed to this impression. The man entering the room at the left has to be deduced from minimal bits: a hat brim, part of a face, a hand, and a pant leg. The legs of the seated woman are sliced through at the shins. And the oblique angle of view runs counter to the rules of conventional viewer-oriented pictures.

The man at the door sets the immobility of the two women in a specific temporal framework: he arrives, but they are not yet aware of him, because they do not shift position as they would be expected to. They maintain what appear to be relaxed, unselfconscious, gravity-bound positions: the twisted, reclining naked woman hugs the sofa edge with a draped leg, and the other sits with her legs apart and a hand resting between her thighs at the groin.[17] The women appear, then, to attend to their own reveries or, more likely, to be simply blank, not actively involved with each other or with the arriving man and not animated individually by an interior state. Consequently, the print is devoid of subjective prediction: it does not carry hope for the emotional coalescence of its three figures. The whole format insists that nothing of consequence is going on, or, perhaps better said, it does not construct a proper narrative out of its parts: these are just the sheer material facts of an average brothel, laid out broadly and greasily, observed from a nonparticipatory, offstage oblique angle. It is a virtuoso semblance of nonchalance.

The likelihood of a connection between Degas's monotypes and novels about prostitutes must be addressed. Among the likely reasons that Degas upheld the disparaging view of the erotic atmosphere of the brothel, which is evident in the monotypes, and identified the pensionnaire as the alienated and commodified modern woman par excellence were the impetus and example provided by his literary predecessors and contemporaries (from Eugène Sue and Honoré de Balzac to Emile Zola, Joris-Karl Huysmans, and Edmond de Goncourt). From the time of Sue, following the analysis of Peter Brooks, writers discovered in "her" the preeminently narratable life and condition. Paraphrasing Brooks, because the prostitute is preeminently someone with a novelistic destiny (whose plot is by definition a deviance) and because "she" gives access to an eminently storied subworld, she was taken to be the "last refuge of the narratable."[18] What better theme, then, to provide content for an art form that all but forecloses upon narration? What more effective way automatically to sustain "a plot" while the forms themselves conspire to muffle and confound the telling of a story? In sum, what better way to be (to *appear* to be!) a realist and a modernist at once? Even in the face of my relentlessly social discussion of Degas's monotypes, we can see that a reading of the prints as reports upon the "modernity" of prostitution cannot be undertaken apart from an active discussion of their formal language.

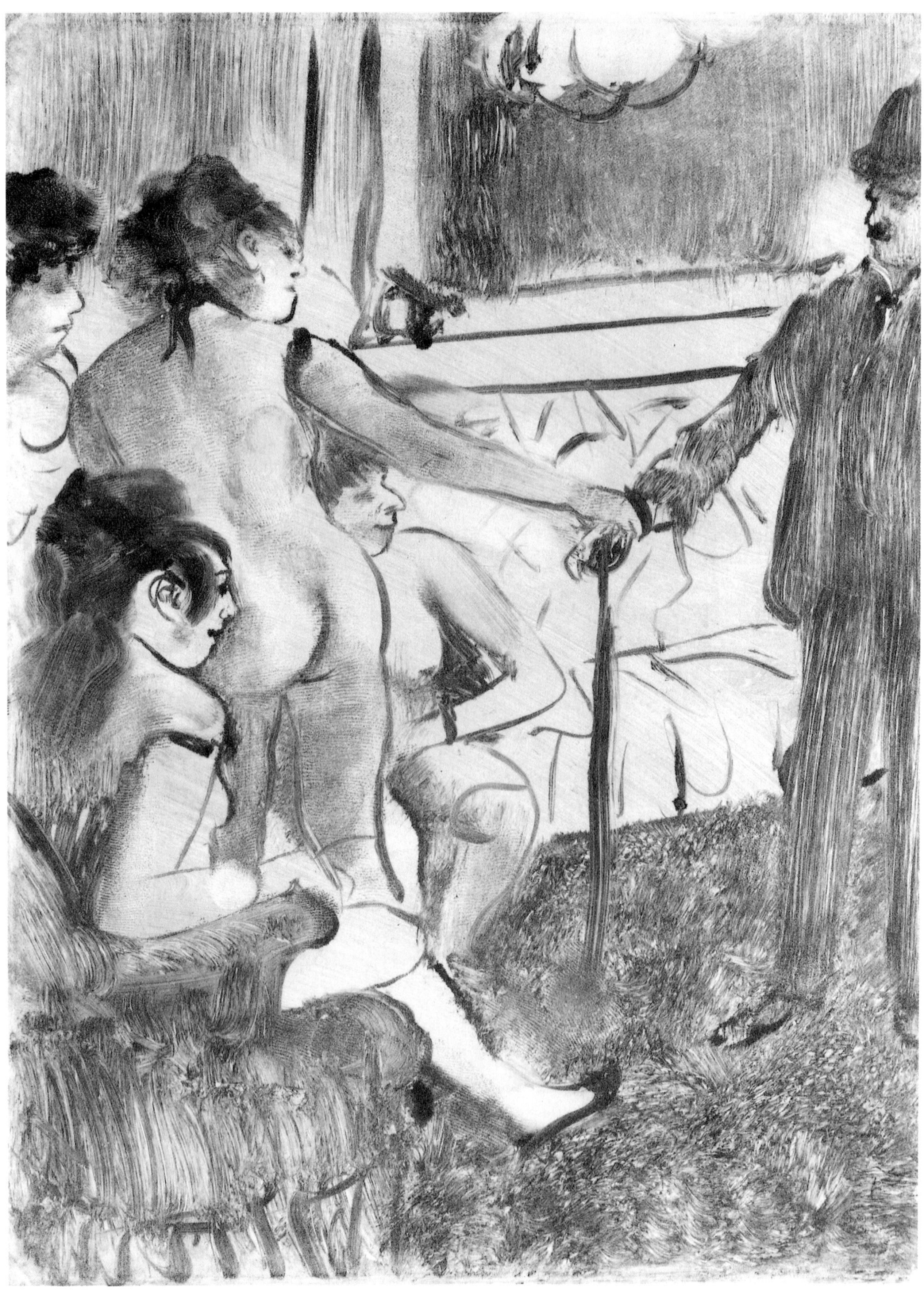

In *The Serious Customer* (fig. 15), four prostitutes face a timid client. The composition is structured to suggest that only a random slice of the activity has been committed to the plate, because the parts are incomplete at all four edges. The body of the naked woman (who stands with her back to us) is made up entirely of Degas's fingerprints. She reaches out her hand to the reticent man, whose form is all streaky brush or rag marks, encouraging him or mocking his timidity, or both. It is a group effort next to which the man appears especially small. His unmodeled, suited body appears flat and insubstantial next to the sculptural roundness of the women's ample bodies. He is also psychologically small: they appear at ease operating in their communal seminakedness while he appears shy even though protected by his street clothes from head to foot.

On balance (look again at figs. 14 and 15 and see fig. 18, for example) the monotypes propose that their Parisian brothel was a brutalized and brutalizing ghetto of women, an enclave of urban coldness for men par excellence. In asserting this outlook, Degas was in fact out of step with the majority of Frenchmen at the time. He was viewing the subject of the brothel anachronistically, against the grain of the most up-to-date and widespread opinion. Because he insisted that the prostitute was a material commodity, he (like certain abolitionist critics of regulated prostitution)[19] was ignoring the discursive forms of the most modern prostitutions of the day: the simulated and increasingly popular warmth of clandestine prostitution (the subject of chapters 3 and 4) and the suave eroticism of the deluxe brothel. For the most part, then, the series constitutes a backward-looking construction of the essential prostitute, which allowed Degas to carry out his visualization of a dehumanized ghetto of prostitution but in a radical pictorial form that provided his gloss on the subject with the appearance of the forthright and the new nevertheless.

The function of Degas's fantasy of brutalized, infantilized women and slightly humiliated men has both personal and social dimensions, even though the images were never meant for male strangers, let alone women.[20] One dimension of the motivation for the series that bridges the gap between the public and the private was, undoubtedly, aesthetic: to use the modernist language of incompleteness and half-legibility (which, Greenberg reminds us, was in part generated by the effort to accurately transcribe the seen). But in spite of and because of the well-known commitment to particular conceptions of modernity and its telltale forms (venal sex, for one) on the part of Degas and his circle, in order for Degas to maintain a view of prostitution that insisted upon one plausibly modern, material definition of it – its brutishness and commodification, its being another enclave of modern urban coldness – he had to ignore the ideological forms of the fashionable and new prostitutions of his time.

Throughout the monotypes the rooms are decorated with stuffed sofas and chairs, chandeliers and sconces with round glass globes, and mirrors in carved frames. The women wear little or transparent or no clothing at all. In view of the consistent "facts" of the settings of Degas's prints, his real-world point of reference may have been one of the fashionable forms: the deluxe brothel. After all, only at the pinnacle of the sex business could naked prostitutes be counted on to appear in carefully ornamented rooms and to assume enticing, rehearsed poses. The rituals of overture acted out by the nude women in the living rooms of the house were very carefully orchestrated. A later nineteenth-century witness emphasized the coexistence of silence and stylized erotic blandishments during a typical meeting between a client and the women in a salon: "The serious client makes his entrance. None of the women would address a

15. Edgar Degas, *The Serious Customer*, ca. 1879–80 or 1876–77, monotype, National Gallery of Canada, Ottawa.

16.
Jules-Joseph Lefèbvre, *Reclining Woman, Study*, from *Album Goupil: Salon de 1878.*

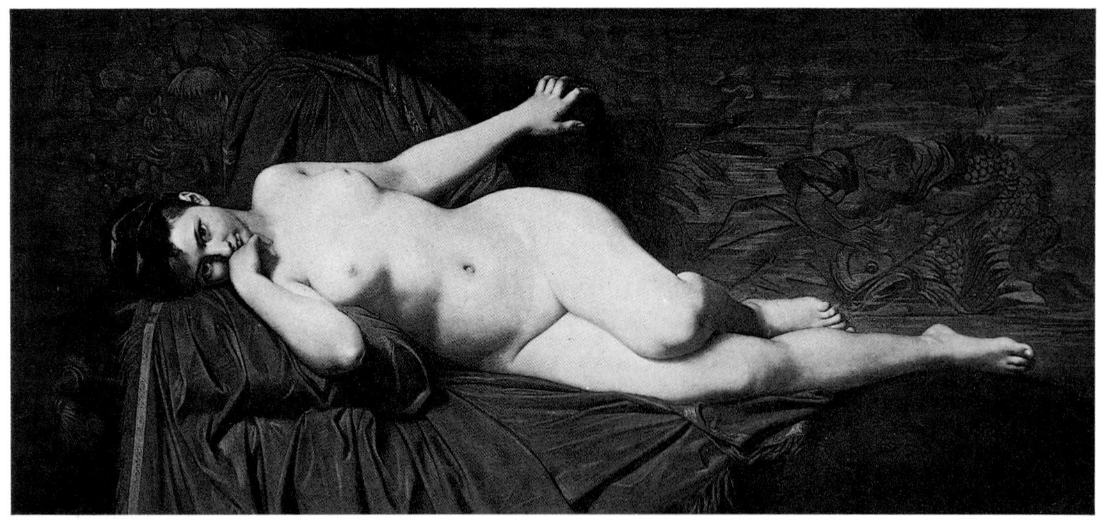

particular verbal invitation to him; but they all dispatch burning glances his way, strike exciting poses, smile and even wiggle their tongues, to make it clearly understood that they can put one thousand voluptuous refinements at the client's disposition."[21]

The best houses, though plain on the outside, were extravagantly decorated on the inside. "The twinkling of ornamented mirrors, a profusion of gilt, the glitter of lights" – these were the desired effects. The decoration of one such house, opened in 1875, cost 1,500,000 francs.[22] The general nakedness of the wards of Degas's brothel (as well as certain elements of decor in the series) urge us to keep the erotic trademarks of the grande tolérance in mind as we continue to chart the unique course that the prints steer between documentation and fantasy, unorthodoxy and stereotype.

The main vehicle of Degas's critique is the body. And the construction of the female bodies in the prints breaks with the canons of decorous nudity institutionalized by Salon oil paintings. The painting by Jules Joseph Lefèbvre entitled *Reclining Woman, Study* (fig. 16) is typical of the nude of the late 1870s. (It belonged to Alexandre Dumas and hung in the Art Exhibition of the Exposition Universelle of 1878.) Using T. J. Clark's definition, the nude, as practiced in the Salon, was a "picture for men to look at, in which Woman is constructed as an object of somebody else's desire."[23] The genre made Woman appear simultaneously chaste and sexually open. The decorous yet sexy exhibition of the body was meant to stimulate the drives of the male viewing subject while also confirming his superiority, to excite and to calm him at the same time. In Lefèbvre's painting, we find the typical, anatomically perfect reclining body whose address of the viewer is both flirtatious and demure.

17.
Edgar Degas, *Waiting for the Client*, ca. 1879–80 or 1876–77, pastel over monotype, private collection.

Degas's break with the conventions of nudity involves an alternative anatomy to be sure – swollen, thick bodies with drooping breasts instead of smooth, fluid, hairless ones with erect, hemispherical, or conical breasts. But it is also a matter of an alternative construction of what the body on display conveys and connotes. Degas's development of an alternative canon of female physicality in the brothel monotypes refused in large measure the erotic codings of the Salon nude. We shall trace that refusal in several of the monotypes.

In *Waiting for the Client* (fig. 17), three prostitutes respond to a customer in the living room of the house in diverse ways – he is just discernible as the narrow dark slice at the left border. The closest young woman in the bright orange stockings leans forward angularly, apparently

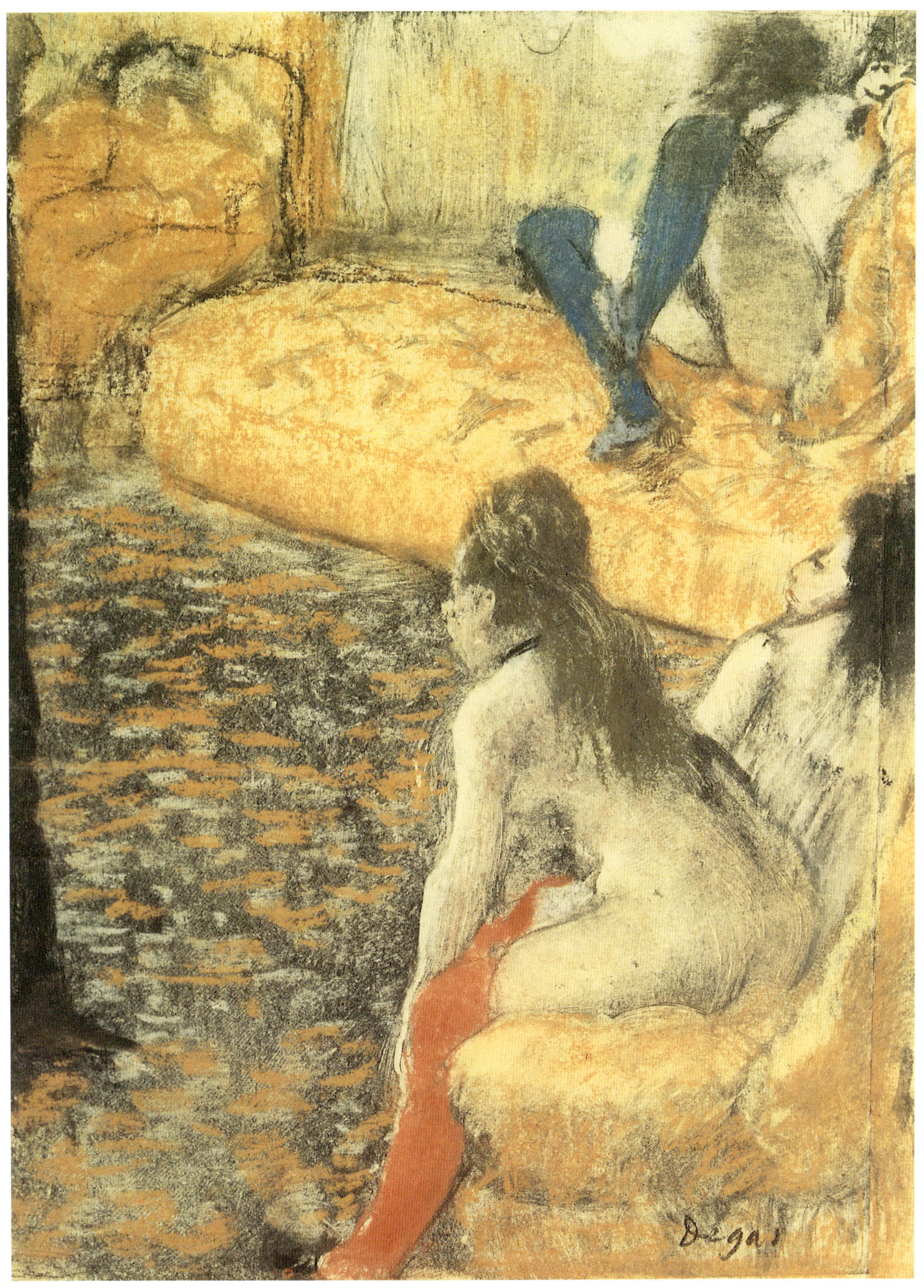
Degas

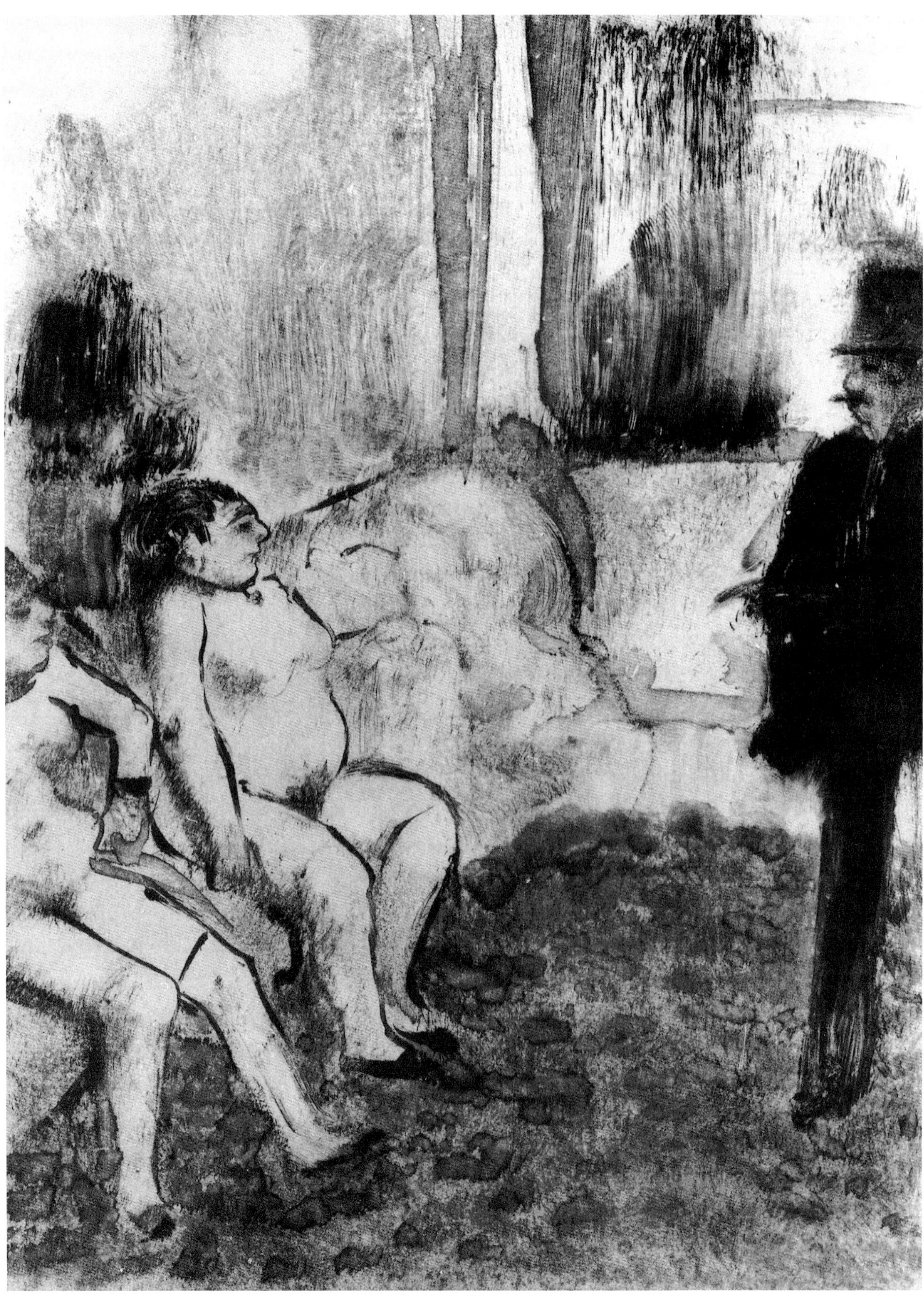

responding with her entire body to the man's proximity; her profile may suggest words spoken in his direction. Her immediate colleague is somewhat cooler in her response to business at hand: also on the near couch but with her lower body concealed, she leans against the furniture with shoulders hunched while looking toward the client with eyes slightly veiled. On the far side of the room, the woman in royal blue stockings leans back into the sofa cushions, her feet on the edge; she spreads her thighs in view of the man and wears a smile, a spare but clear upturned line. Her attitude is a far cry from the facetious propriety devised for the coy woman in Lefèbvre's painting (fig. 16).

18. Edgar Degas, *The Customer*, ca. 1879–80 or 1876–77, monotype, Musée Picasso, Paris.

The composition of *Waiting for the Client* is certainly intricately structured. Degas has varied the scene by flanking the relatively restrained and partially hidden central woman with two women who are physically forthright in their address of the customer. Neither decorous nor inhibited – one assumes a boyish sitting position at the front, the other brandishes genitalia at the back – the women get on with the preliminaries, encouraging the man to make a choice between the two of them without waiting passively to be noticed, without too much professionalized enticement, and without the appurtenances of a falsely heart-felt seduction.

In *The Customer* (fig. 18), another moment of selection is played out. The customer is again fragmentary but moved on stage. He wears a hat and he smokes, underscoring his already considerable physical distance from and social disregard for the pair of naked prostitutes. The thickset woman at the center, shoulders stiff and arms pulled into her side, looks done up like a package of flesh, ready to be taken. As usual, Degas varies the scene by contrasting the positions and actions of adjacent figures. The near woman rests a bent arm jauntily on her upper thigh and flexes her legs; the tilt of her head and the set of her mouth appear conversational, yet there is not a trace of coquetry. The two women carry out this stage of their unrelentingly physical work without recourse to elegant maneuvers or to any of the bodily conventions of romantic intimacy.

In the Salon (fig. 19), the last print we shall examine in some detail, is an exceptionally complex composition that brings together nine prostitutes with the mistress of the house and a customer in top hat. The madame and the man – the two representatives of the world of at least semirespectability – close off the two horizontal rows of filles like parentheses at either side of the page. Their uprightness – both physical (they are vertical) and moral (they are dressed) – emphasizes the difference between them and the sprawling filles. Among the prostitutes, the diversity of sitting and reclining positions has been maximized, but it is a variation within the limits imposed by the series' established code for the specialized language of the prostitute's body. Contrary to the client and the madame, the women are in various states of undress and assume varied positions of abandon (from enthusiasm to inattention to collapse) – the physical evidence of their existence outside the society whose rules they trespass or do not know.

In spite of the transgressiveness of the way their bodies are figured, the women of the monotypes do not appear rude in their disregard of the etiquette of intimacy – both prostitutional and bourgeois, venal and romantic – or particularly bad-mannered in their occasional self-absorption. The point is that their childlike, *bête*, good-natured otherness does not conflict with the obligations and circumstances of their work as Degas has defined it in the monotypes. Their particular, tenacious physicality seems intended to embed them in a world of the sheerly material, where the subjective self has been suspended, cancelled, or long since overridden. Degas's prostitutes lead an existence in which the self and the body have become the same and the women's sexuality has been lost to the world of exchange.

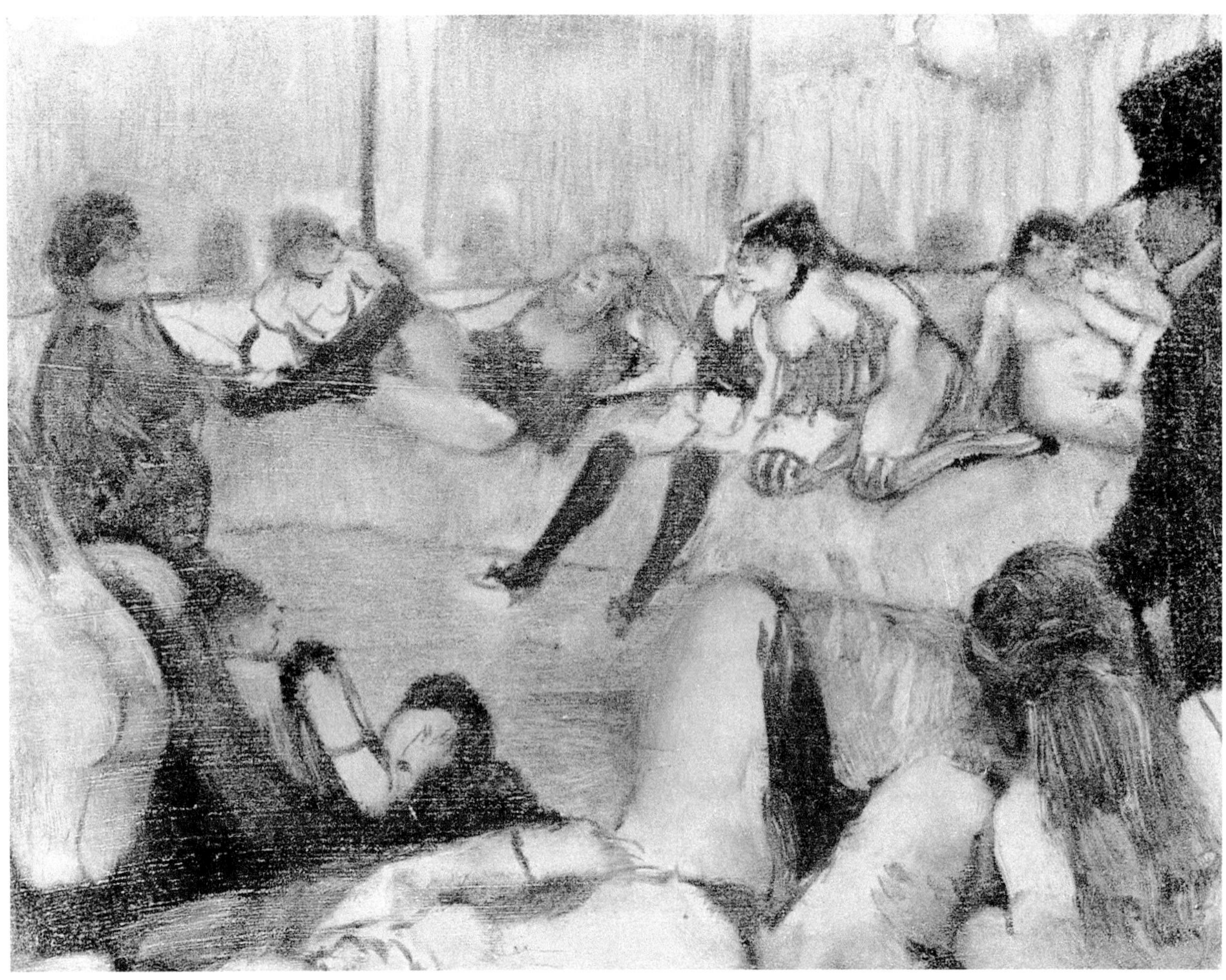

19.
Edgar Degas, *In the Salon,* ca. 1879–80 or 1876–77, monotype, Musée Picasso, Paris.

In order to fix the prostitutes in a condition of material being for others (as opposed to the aestheticized, disingenuous variant of woman as object embodied by the Salon nude), Degas portrayed a relatively old-fashioned, even primitive form of sexual commerce – primitive compared to the two more modern forms we have already mentioned. What is given in the prints is convincing, even appears to be "the truth" about relations in a brothel, because Degas has constructed a deceptively guileless visual language in which to declare the unwavering appropriateness, the absolute suitability of these women – their bodies, their actions – for their circumstances. For Degas to portray the brothel convincingly, he reverted, though not completely, to an increasingly outmoded type of brothel commerce. Describing the whore as material commodity, to undercut the general outlines of narcissistic male fictions about prostitution, seems to have required this.

Thus *The Customer* (fig. 20), Jean-Louis Forain's version of brothel operations of 1878, which is more closely aligned with the preferences of the late 1870s for stylized seductions, differs considerably from Degas's graphic works. Relying upon the outline of the economy of brothel prostitution developed to this point in the chapter, we may say that Forain's watercolor operates on the basis of an ideology of prostitution, which is, on the one hand, more old-fashioned and conventional, while, on the other, more modern than that underpinning Degas's monotypes.

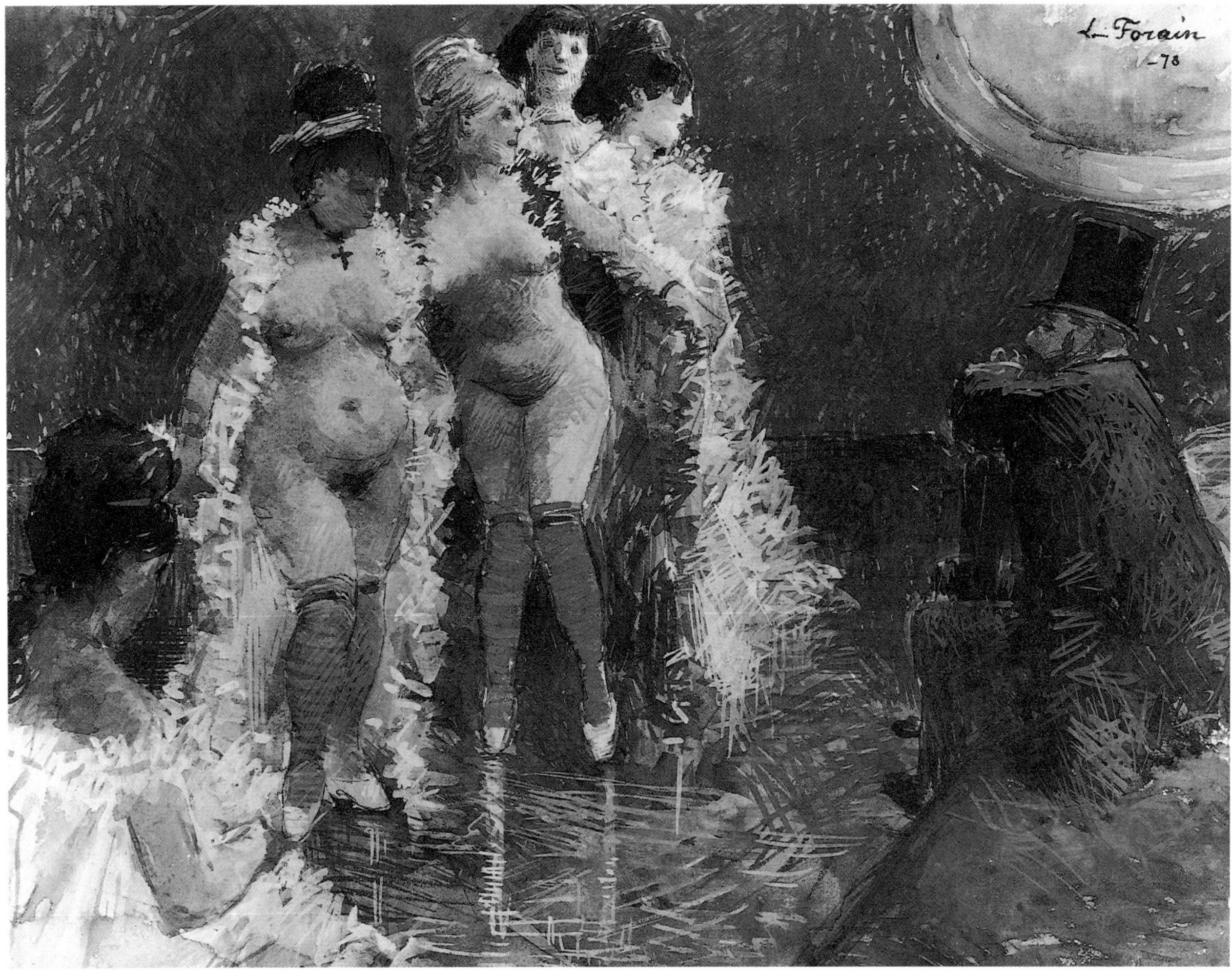

20. Jean-Louis Forain, *The Customer*, 1878, gouache, private collection, London.

In Forain's picture, the prostitutes stand and perform while the client sits and observes. The generous display of flesh is posed for the inspection and pleasure of the potential buyer, the confident customer, whose savoir-faire is inscribed in his sitting position: planted on a banquette with his chin calmly resting on the handle of his umbrella, he resembles the suave customer in Cézanne's second *Modern Olympia* (fig. 7). Here the women have sprung into enthusiastic action for the customer and use the conventions of seductive flirtatiousness and coquettishness, of the aestheticized and eroticized display of the body. Unlike Degas's women, these fleshy prostitutes have firm, round breasts, not to mention bodies that curve and taper at the waist. The picture seems to rely upon an oddly current mixture of attitudes. On the one hand, there is old part-cliché, part-fantasy of the beautiful, sensual, enthusiastic, endlessly obliging prostitute: a Salon nude finally agreeing to go home with the libidinous male spectator (just like the man whose brain and hands are activated by Salon nudes, as shown in fig. 21, "At the Salon"). On the other hand, the most up-to-date forms of male sexual preference are recognized: a professional seduction is blended with the friendly and persuasive imitation of real sexual feelings. This admixture would be comforting to the libidinous man because sexuality is on sale, but its commodification is effectively masked. It is appropriate that the customer in Forain's brothel salon appears morally and socially cool and superior, and a bit detached from the whole thing, as though Cézanne's fantasies had been brought under control.

21.
Jules Draner [Jules Renard], "At the Salon," *Le Monde Comique*, 1879–80.

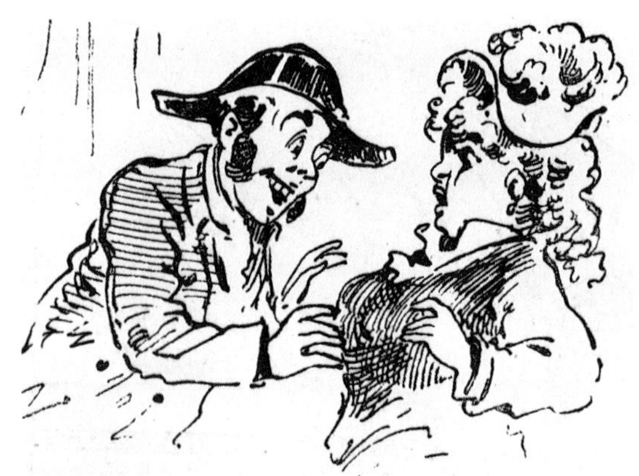

Excuse me, madam, but all this nudity stirs up my brain.

A very self-satisfied J.-K. Huysmans admired Forain's picture for the reasons we have outlined:

> What is prodigious in this work, is the strength of reality it emits; these whores are brothel whores and none other, and if their postures, their irritating odor, their spicy flesh, under the gaslight that lights up this watercolor heightened with gouache, with a precise truth which is really strange, are, unquestionably for the first time, so firmly, accurately rendered, their character, their bestial or puerile humanity is no less accurately recorded. All the philosophy of love for sale is in this scene in which, after having entered voluntarily, pushed by a stupid desire, the man reflects and, become cold, ends by remaining unmoved by their offers.[24]

For Huysmans, the essence of prostitution was a woman's ability to stage the sale of her body to a stranger with persuasive and uninhibited ardor even in the face of a cool and unenthusiastic customer.

With his monotypes, Degas parts company with Huysmans and Forain. For Degas, it is the exteriority, cancellation, or extinction of self that is the essence of the seller's position in prostitution. According to Huysmans and Forain, the knowing and repeated subversion or denial of self enacted over and over again in the ritual of seduction that somehow remains friendly is the essence of the matter. Huysmans is the complete cynic: it is the knowing and professionalized transformation of one's sexuality into a commodity that earmarks the true brothel prostitute. He sadistically gourmandizes over the women's enlightened because masochistic awareness of her irredeemably debased sexuality.[25] He is delighted to assert the traditional prerogatives of male spectatorship. The prostitute is thus conceptualized as an immoral but tantalizing woman, a conscious human, though of a slightly different because lesser species, who practices a debased and self-debasing skill. For Degas, the brute, material prostitute exemplifies unconscious human otherness, the loss of a person to the world of sexual exchange.

Degas was not alone in his search for a particular and definitive syntax for the brothel prostitute's body. The regulationists were eager to discover a distinctive set of physical characteristics for the women who populated the official ghetto of prostitution. The uncovery of such a normative anatomy would have been – need it be said – very much in the interest of those who favored réglementation. Such a list of features would have helped to justify the stringent control of prostitutes and their separation from the rest of society. Parent-Duchâtelet attempted a classification in the 1830s but found physical diversity when he had gone looking for uniformity.[26] The only shared physical characteristics he identified were hardly intrinsic to the breed: plumpness and harsh voices.

Nor could later apologists for réglementation admit to having found any distinctive physical characteristics that distinguished filles decisively from other women. The failure to classify prostitutes by aspects of their physical appearance spoiled any prospects for a theory of causation based on physiological determinism. This in turn underscored one of the biggest threats posed by prostitutes: they looked like average women.

The vain attempt to discover shared physical traits, however, did not prevent the development of psychological stereotypes by the regulationists. "The flaws particular to prostitutes,"[27] to use Parent-Duchâtelet's phrase, frame a mentality in opposition to bourgeois norms of decency. Among the traits that the regulationists thought typified the prostitute were immaturity, instability, disorderliness in behavior and appearance, financial prodigality, voracious excess in food, alcohol, and conversation, and a susceptibility to lesbianism – part of a general propensity for sensual excess.

Coexisting with their negative characteristics were the "good qualities of prostitutes,"[28] which included a well-developed sentimentality (apparent in religiosity, fondness for children and one another, and nostalgia for their childhoods and birthplaces); modesty in the presence of other women and men who were not potential sexual partners; and charity and kindness toward the less fortunate. In brief, a set of characteristics that revealed the utter disorderliness and "otherness" of these women and thus established the pressing need to hide them away. But, at the same time, the listing also revealed their thoroughly stereotypical femaleness, their "ordinariness," since sentimentality, modesty, and charitableness were the admirable attributes of decent women. Gustave Macé, for example, recognized the ordinary and diverse looks of registered prostitutes while he simultaneously relied upon stereotypes of temperament:

> What strange prostitutes these brothel girls are. Pretty, ugly, stupid, spiritual, all of them have their moments of folly and of despair; they can go instantly from laughs to tears, from threats to caresses. If you overhear their confidences, they name fate as the cause of their first abandonment, and in order better to inspire the pity of the clients, they renew that eternal and ancient story of young girls who were seduced. Not one of them was born for this line of work and it is only out of need that they exercise this repugnant work. Their moral corruption is rarely complete, for in their own rooms, bare, dilapidated, are found objects of piety, dried flowers, souvenirs of their birthplaces and honestly written books. . . . Most of these girls are excessively superstitious.[29]

As we have seen, the regulationist failure to discover a venal female body type did not prevent Degas from digging into the project of inventing a prostitutional body and demeanor with gusto (and consistency). His coding for the prostitutes' appearance is the visual equivalent of the regulationists' discovery of a prostitutional character or psychology. But Degas did not rely upon a received image of bodily otherness; he created one of his own. (As we shall see, however, in devising many of the heads in the series, he was less inventive and stuck quite closely to a fixed corpus of "low types.")

Because Degas's brothel workers look and act the same regardless of who is around, one could argue that Degas's prostitutes have an essence. This reading is reinforced by the comportment of the women in the prints that contain neither actual nor implied customers. *The Madam's Name Day* (fig. 22), for example, presents such a single-sex occasion.[30] The prostitutes celebrate the name day of the madam, their overseer, and share a time of *gaieté bête*, or childish fun, bringing her flowers, patting her on the back and head, kissing her, all in the manner of partying children, but wearing the signs of their permanently debased condition: their immodesty about their nakedness and the ungainliness of their anatomies "covered" only by body ornaments specific to the slattern (neck ribbons or necklaces and brightly colored stockings). The uninhibitedness of the minimally inflected nakedness is familiar from other prints, but in this context there is enjoyment on the faces, and there is no customer-oriented obscenity of the body, nor a need for it. All the more reason to argue that the ideology of the brothel prostitute engendered by the prints proposes not that these inmates are unkind or rude or even misbehaved but that they are different from all other women. They do not resemble respectable women, and they are more rudimentarily "primitive" than other kinds of prostitutes (such as the clandestine varieties discussed in chapters 3 and 4).

The Madam's Name Day may bring to mind the rustically simple and childlike prostitutes of Guy de Maupassant's short stories. This particular print, the proud possession of Pablo Picasso, has often been (mis)identified as a Degas-planned illustration for "La Maison Tellier," because Ambroise Vollard used it for that express purpose in 1934. And of all the women in Degas's monotypes, these filles are most like the good-hearted and fun-loving prostitutes of Maupassant's fiction.

Maupassant's literary moves were almost always countercultural and ironic, and especially so when telling stories about *filles inscrites* (registered prostitutes). In those tales Maupassant regularly ironized regulationist cant. While his literary contemporaries' narratives of the prostitute (for example, Huysmans's *Marthe* and the Goncourts' *Elisa*)[31] appear to revere the "scientific" findings of the sociologists and medical men and use them to produce fact-laden stories about unstable, hedonistic, and immoral women, Maupassant demotes the pseudoscientific to the *idée reçue*, the received idea or cliché, as part of his larger project of satirizing conventional moral hierarchies. In Maupassant's stories, the prostitute and her standard characteristics (she is fat, sentimental, religious, nostalgic, and emotionally volatile) function as the levers with which to prize loose the bourgeois agenda of morality from its hypocritical underpinnings.

Maupassant's plots are clever reversals of the natural order. In his best-known stories on this subject, "Boule de suif" of 1879–80 and "La Maison Tellier" of 1880–81, he made the prostitutes the only moral citizens of France circa 1870. The key instances are the patriotic actions of the story's heroine, the prostitute named Boule de Suif (ball of wax), which are greeted by the cold-blooded cruelty of "respectable" society; and the religiosity and kindness of the wardens of Madame Tellier's brothel on the occasion of her niece's First Communion in a small village. According to Maupassant's script, when the prostitute is virtuous, the contemporary world is truly turned upside-down. But even Maupassant's supposedly unmoralizing view really belongs to a standard kind of literary irony.

Maupassant's sarcastic disruption of period clichés about the bordello prostitute disentangled the two strands of received wisdom about "her": that the fille was vicious and venal, on

22. Edgar Degas, *The Madam's Name Day*, ca. 1879–80 or 1876–77, pastel over monotype, Musée Picasso, Paris.

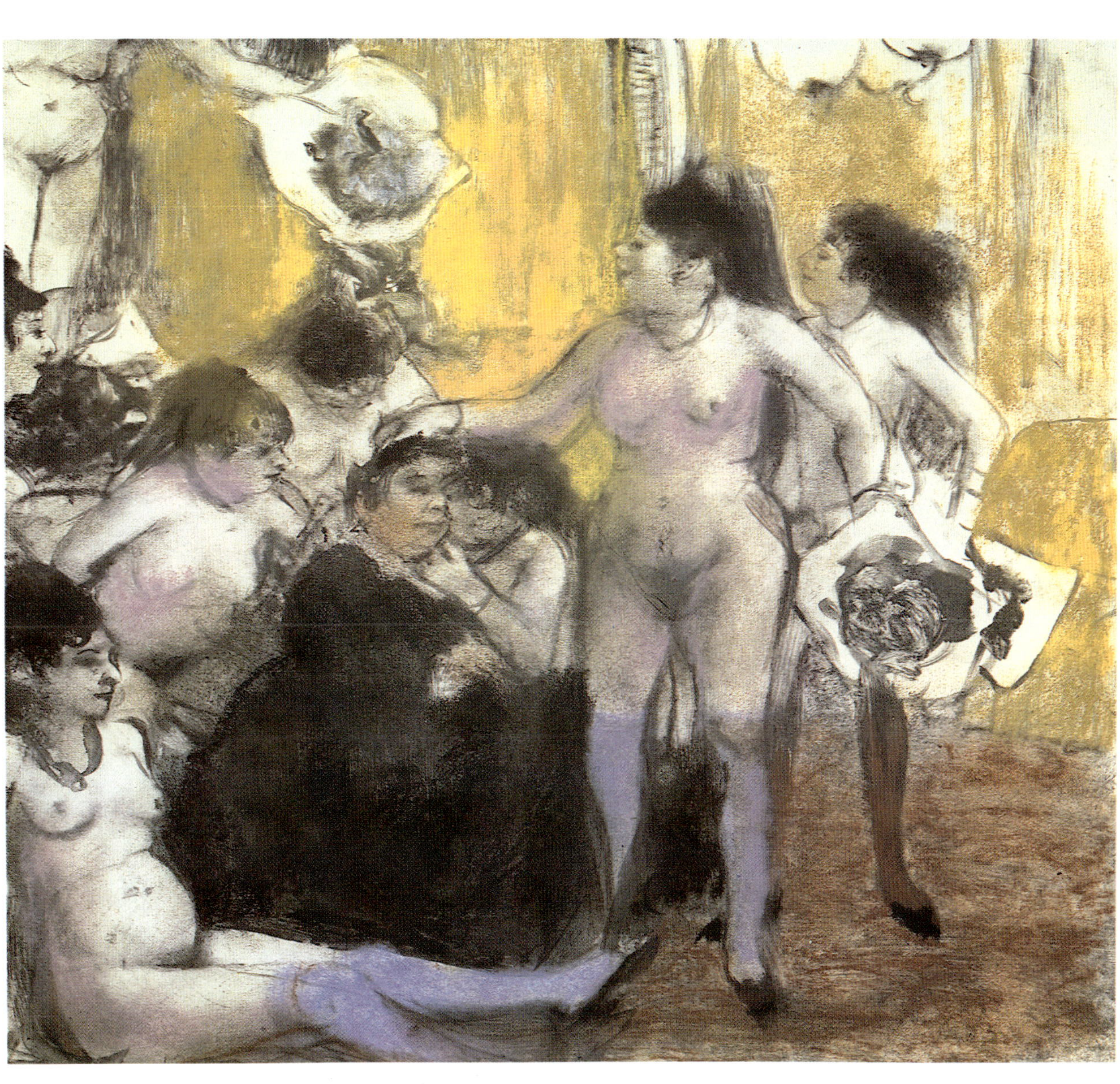

the one hand, and childlike and simple, on the other. By substituting virtue for venality in the character of the prostitute, Maupassant satirizes the coexistence of viciousness and childishness in the regulationist stereotype of the prostitute, but his work does not resolve the opposition between the two halves of the regulationist bromide. Degas's brothel monotypes *do* effect (or certainly strain to effect) a novel synthesis, because they enact a visual resolution of the conflict between the venal and the childlike. But as we have seen, the monotypes do so at the cost of any simple realism and by avoiding almost altogether the narration of actual prostitutional business – that is, depicting the kinds of exchange that involve body contact.[32]

In Degas's representations of women alone on a bed upstairs in the working rooms of the house, the atmosphere and body language of the downstairs salon(s) are rehearsed, but with a slight inflection that accords with the phase of the job to be performed in these small spaces. The same format is used in most of these prints (*On the Bed*, fig. 23, is quite typical). A woman sits back on the bed with her legs apart; one knee is bent more than the other so that the pubic area is exposed, but the skin and exterior genital organs are concealed by the distended, black, totally opaque triangle of hair.[33] This repeated body position encapsulates the distinctive and compromised mode of seduction and excitation that Degas has invented as a suitable trope for the essence of the brothel prostitute. In this position there is the clumsy and uncontested collapse of the body combined with the raw obscenity of spreading one's legs to the buyer. It is the identity and simultaneity of the two operations to the point of their conflation that is the distinctive representational operation. Such a conflation in Degas's images serves to reconcile the two sides of the regulationist prostitutional dichotomy in the field of the visual.

As in much of the neoregulationist discourse, the world of the monotypes is shown to be populated by a species that is singularly well adapted for life within its confines: subjective selves transformed into objective commercialized matter, a view with which neoregulationists could have heartily agreed. But there are decisive differences between the terms and focus of Degas's images and the campaign of the regulationists. First, although both emphasize the brothel prostitute – one of Degas's pictorial specialties and the centerpiece of réglementation – the regulationists spent most of their energy on the problems posed by the clandestine prostitute. They worried about the dangers posed by her skillful commerce in erotic adventure, an apparently attractive alternative to both anesthetizing conjugality and perfunctory brothel sex.

Degas's prints also seem to engender some persistent attitudes toward the customers of his brothel (even though the prints are less than clear on this issue). You may recall that there was no place in neoregulationist discourse for an expression of concern about the well-being of the client of the maison de tolérance, because when the system was running smoothly, he was assumed not to be running any health risk. Neither was there room in this discourse for comment on the relative satisfaction or happiness of the consumer with his purchase, because the absence of disease was the only qualitative concern of the brothel police, and any loose talk about pleasure would have contradicted the founding definition of prostitution as a *mal inévitable* (inevitable evil). Degas, however, does make an attempt to represent the experience of some brothel clients, or at least of certain anticipatory rituals.

In monotypes that include a client in the public rooms of the house (such as *The Serious Customer*, fig. 15, and *The Customer*, fig. 18), the customer is not made to appear emotionally stimulated or pleased by the prospect of choosing one of the women before him. Quite the contrary. Charles Bernheimer's phrase is apt: "Degas associates hesitancy and ambivalence rather than voyeuristic power with the threshold position."[34] This appearance of physical (and, by im-

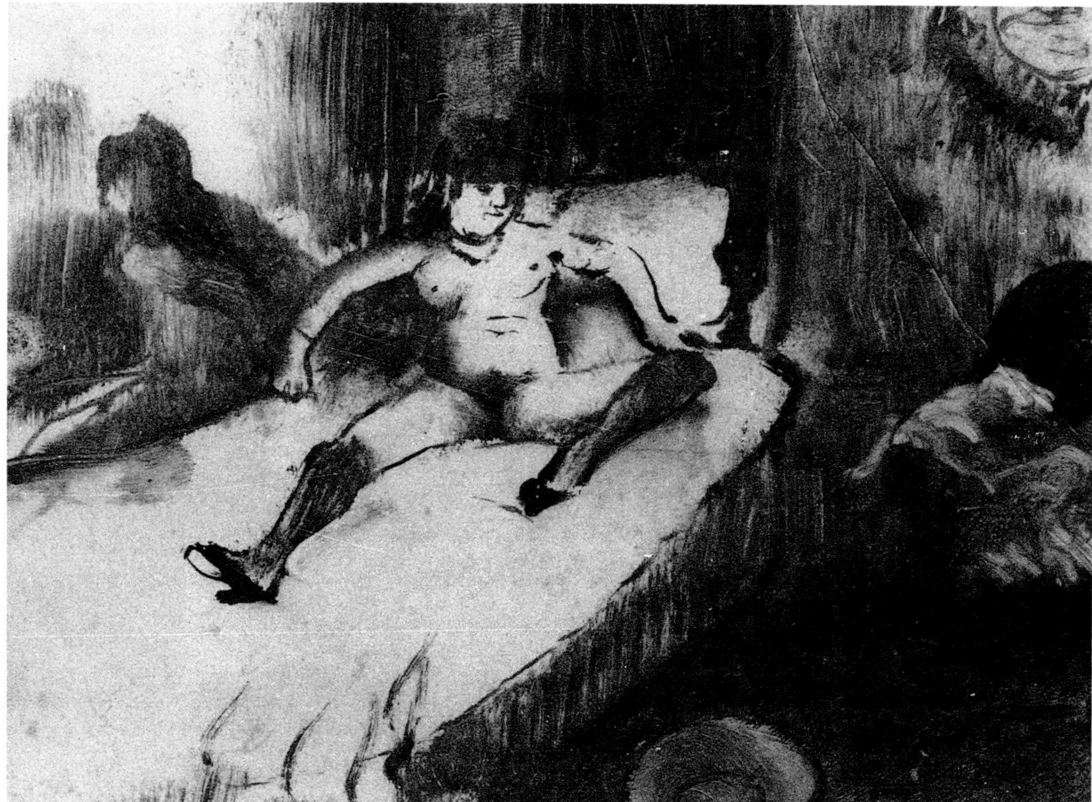

23. Edgar Degas, *On the Bed*, ca. 1879–80 or 1876–77, monotype, Musée Picasso, Paris.

plication, emotional) alienation of the buyer from the goods for sale is the opposite of the climate of selection in Forain's *The Customer* (fig. 20) in which the social and psychological superiority of the client remains intact. It differs as well from the easy sociability of interaction that Degas incorporated into his *Fille Elisa* drawings (figs. 11 and 12).

In the monotypes, Degas pictures the diminutive and reticent customers of the brothel as buyers in a sexual market where the goods lack the cachet of refinement, where the codes in operation seem to conflict with their own, or with what they anticipated finding there. It appears, in other words, that Degas imagines that the customer of the middle- to high-class brothel – a member of his class? – would be somewhat humiliated and perhaps socially and psychologically compromised by the experience.

Yet the social signs given to Degas's brothel customers are elliptical in the end. The man in *The Serious Customer* (fig. 15), for example, wears a soft rather than a top hat, suggesting a lower-middle-class rather than an upper-middle-class clientele. This was perhaps another means of distancing himself from the men of the prints, of discouraging any reading of the series as self-representation, and perhaps another ideological way of suggesting the otherness of the place and its people.

Degas further suggested the foreignness and distinctiveness of these cloistered women by providing them in many cases with conventionalized simian faces. Over twenty years ago, Eugenia Janis called attention to what she called "vulgar facial characteristics"[35] in the prints, while John Richardson observed that Degas regularly frizzed the women's hair into bangs "over criminally low foreheads."[36]

The solitary figure in *On the Bed* (fig. 23) has such a face. So do the inveigling women in *The Serious Customer* (fig. 15) and the thickset, seated figure in *The Customer* (fig. 18). These faces are clearly stereotyped, and, as Janis's and Richardson's language strongly implies, their use records Degas's concurrence with some socially benighted attitudes in circulation at the time about the recognizability of members of the underclasses. I use the term *stereotype* here to describe physiognomic convention, because stereotypes are "evaluative concepts held by groups about other groups, most frequently and effectively by dominant groups about marginal groups" and because sociologists often distinguish stereotypes (which are deviant) from social types (which are normative).[37]

Douglas Druick has published the most detailed study of Degas's use of the scapegoating procedures of physiognomic stereotype. He has not looked at the brothel monotypes with this issue in mind, but he has certainly proven that Degas used physiognomic facial codes "assigned" to members of the criminal lower classes in several of his exhibits in the 1881 Impressionist exhibition: namely, in the lost pastel *Criminal Physiognomies*, as well as in *The Little Dancer* sculpture, which features the face of an adolescent girl.[38]

Linda Nochlin has examined several works by Degas in search of traces of anti-Semitism. Her investigation showed that Degas's increasingly anti-Jewish attitudes were not detectable in his work in any overt way, but that "before the period of the Dreyfus Affair, Degas, like many other Frenchmen and women, and even like his erstwhile Impressionist comrade, Pissarro, was anti-Jewish only in terms of a certain *representation* of the Jew or of particular 'Jewish traits.'" Nochlin was also able to conclude that the "signifiers that indicated 'Jewishness' in the late nineteenth century were . . . firmly locked into a system of negative connotations."[39] Nochlin's observation appears borne out by Anthea Callen's argument that the handling of certain male clients' heads in Degas's brothel monotypes betray the explicit use of anti-Semitic stereotype.[40] Callen argues that Degas made an effort to provide several of the overwhelmed and humiliated clients with obviously caricatured and specifically Jewish faces. The man in *Conversation* (fig. 27) is among those Callen has discussed in this way.

The important point about the appearance of stereotyped faces in the brothel monotypes is that they suggest Degas thought of these women not only as sexual deviants but as threatening *social* deviants – like other typed components of the Parisian criminal underclass.[41] This caricatural practice inflects otherwise *un*conventional bodies with a very strong accent of the conventional.

That Degas used facial types in this particular context is perhaps not completely unexpected, for, as T. E. Perkins has argued, women give rise to very powerful stereotypes because their socialization is problematic. She suggests that a group undergoing shifts in structural position – as was the population of Parisian prostitutes in the late 1870s – will throw up new stereotypes, and that if its challenge is threatening, these will be pejorative. But – bear this in mind as we continue to interrogate the social purpose of the prints – stereotypes are inevitably subject to internal contradictions and therefore are perpetually precarious.[42]

Biographical readings of Degas's prints have been essayed, in which the artist's sexuality – latent or lived – has been correlated (I use a merely inferential verb here on purpose) with his idiosyncratic brothel prints. Most recent accounts of this vexed issue follow Vincent van Gogh and Pablo Picasso in attributing the unorthodoxy and scurrilousness of the

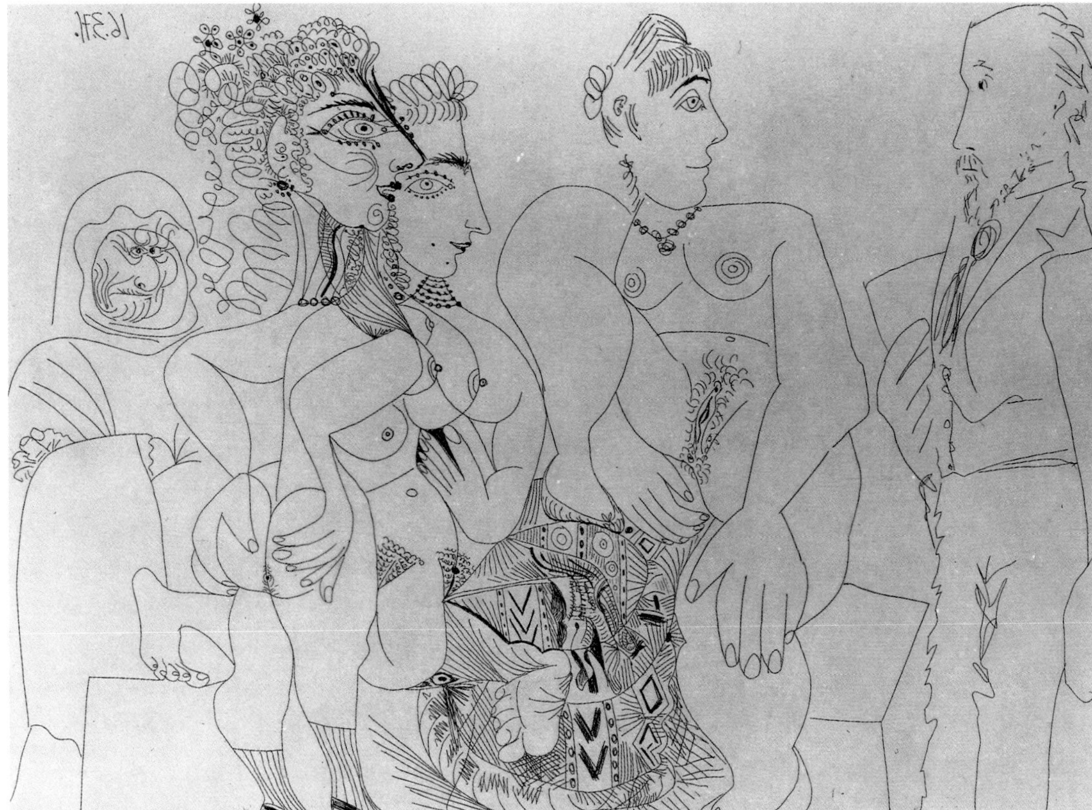

24. Pablo Picasso, *March 16, 1971*, etching.

pictures to sexual abstemiousness, if not to dysfunction, on Degas's part.[43] In the summer of 1888, while in Arles, Vincent wrote the following to Emile Bernard: "Degas lives like a small lawyer and does not like women, for he knows that if he loved them and fucked them often, he, intellectually diseased, would become insipid as a painter. Degas's painting is virile and impersonal for the very reason that he has resigned himself to be nothing personally but a small lawyer with a horror of going on a spree. He looks on while the human animals, stronger than himself, get excited and fuck, and he paints them well, exactly because he doesn't have the pretention to get excited himself."[44]

Picasso acquired his first brothel prints by Degas in 1958, eventually owning eleven of them (all now in the Musée Picasso), but it was not until the spring of 1971 – between March and May of his ninetieth year – that he began making etchings (about forty of them) based upon his Degas monotypes.[45] The project was inspired to some degree by Eugenia Janis's 1968 monotype catalog and also by his reexamining the prints in his collection with Brassai and (on another occasion) with William Rubin early in 1971. At this point Picasso asked, "What do you think Degas was doing in those places?"[46] Picasso's answer to this question is in the prints he made in 1971.

In the etchings, Picasso often includes Degas as an outsider (as in the case of the work reproduced here in fig. 24). He is represented as an awkward wallflower who stands at the margin of the sheet looking on, watching, but never participating. In an exchange with Pierre Daix concerning the etchings, Picasso is reported to have said: "Degas would have kicked me in the pants if he'd seen himself like this."[47] According to the old Picasso, Degas is not just an outsider, but a hapless one at that. He is the only man in the house but is unequivocally separated from the cavorting tangles of exaggerated women.

The intertextuality of the two brothel series is historical as well as structural, but the bodies (if not the faces) of Picasso's prostitutes are completely different from those in Degas's prints, and Picasso's Degas-as-customer should not be confused with the position of the clients represented in Degas's prints. Indeed Picasso's exhibitionistic women exemplify in extreme yet condensed form a convention for the figuration of sexualized women that Degas undoubtedly set out to avoid, in spite of the fact that his practice was linked to its ideologies and reflexes by a bond as strong as any chain. Pictorial evidence of the continuities is presented below.

Picasso's etchings fantasize the male artist's proverbial control over the threat of female sexuality. His whores' desire is exhibited only for the flattery of male narcissism.[48] As John Richardson has put it: "There was nothing senile or passive about Picasso's voyeurism; on the contrary, there was something almost sadistic about it."[49] The defenseless, dead Degas is scapegoated in the old Picasso's alarming misogynist fantasies.

In his own prints, Degas's undermining move was the poisoning of the voyeur's standard domineering grasp of the sexualized woman by forcing the recognition that the viewer or client's psychic advantage was actually (only) economic. Whereas Picasso's etchings figure the ultimate misogynistic cultural perception (sexual woman as a prostitute), Degas in some measure reverses the terms so that one gets the prostitute demoted (elevated?) to a package of devenustated flesh for sale.

Yet certain prints – this is slippery terrain – record traces of Degas's erotic attraction to the discreet charms of the sexual deviant. If we look at certain passages of Degas's handling of the naked prostitutes' bodies, we encounter tattletale examples of descriptive specificity and illusionistic veracity that send readable little messages about the artist's pleasure in the sight of the hypersexual body of the brothel prostitute. The only bodily feature given fully tonal, sculptural treatment in the monotypes is the convex, symmetrical prostitutional buttocks.

Sander Gilman discusses the nineteenth-century preoccupation with Hottentot steatopygia (protruding buttocks) as an anatomical symbol of atavistic female sexuality.[50] The female buttocks came eventually to function as *the* semantic sign of primitive sexual appetite and activity, and not only for black women. Havelock Ellis (the early modern scholar of the psychology of sex) argued that only people "in a low state of culture" would perceive the "naked sexual organs as objects of attraction." He managed nevertheless to naturalize an erotic interest in the large posterior of black women by naming the buttocks at the top of his list of secondary sexual characteristics properly admired by "cultured people." Gilman explains: "The nineteenth-century fascination with the buttocks as a displacement for the genitalia is thus reworked by Ellis into a higher regard for the beautiful."[51] Nineteenth-century conceptualizations of deviant or primitive female sexuality were tied to the image of the buttocks.

This anatomy-centered ideology retrieves Parent-Duchâtelet's unsuccessful attempt to map a physical anthropology of the prostitute by discovering – even in the teeth of its absence – a moral semiology of the flesh. It apparently worked like this: although it was known that prostitutes resembled decent women (a fact much fretted over), European women with prominent buttocks were nevertheless believed likely to be sexually transgressive individuals. Nineteenth-century Parisians were always on the lookout for a reliable physiognomic code.[52]

In view of the currency of these ideas, it is not surprising that an artist of Degas's physiog-

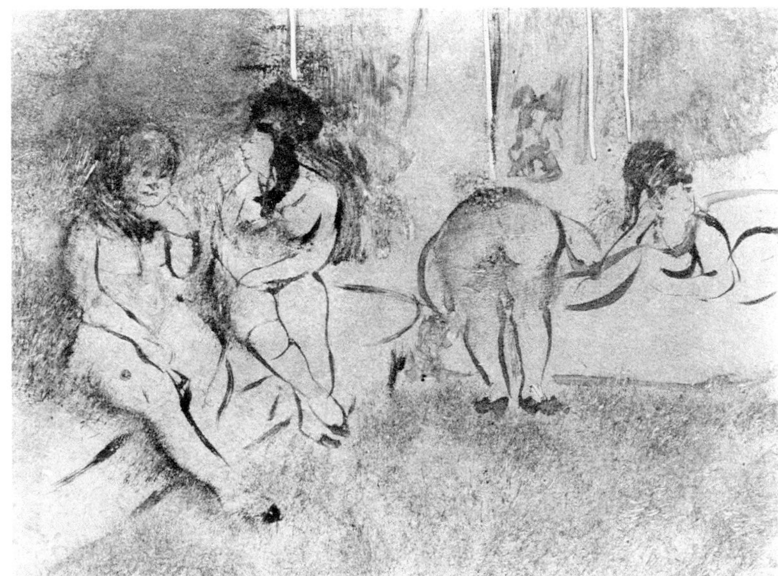

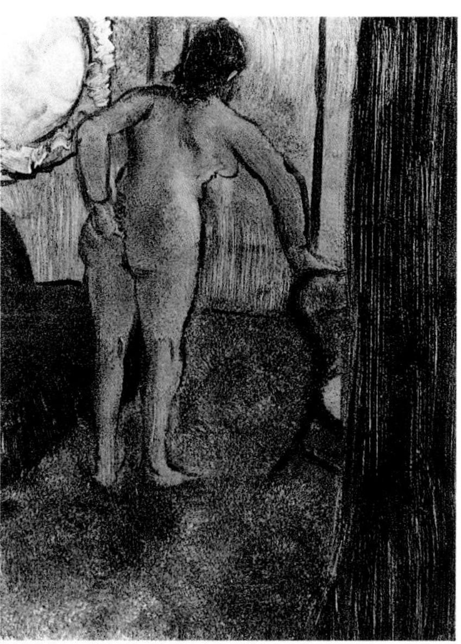

nomic interests and sophistication, in his one attempt to devise an imagery of brothel workers, would use prominent derrieres as part of the women's already corpulent bodies. But Degas used the fleshy buttocks of the prostitute in two distinctively different ways.

In one of the prints entitled *Waiting* (fig. 25), which depicts the women passing the time in a downstairs salon, the second girl from the right is shown acting the part of the quintessentially bête prostitute by upending her derriere without giving a second thought to etiquette. In *In a Brothel Salon* (fig. 26), the solitary fille attending to an itch functions in a similar way. Both of these particular prints showcase Degas's tendency to suspend the standard hierarchy of the appeal of particular body parts seen from certain viewing angles and to fix the prostitute's primordial inelegance by these bodily means. In short, in monotypes such as these, Degas distances himself from the voyeuristic male protocols of the Salon nude.

25. (l.) Edgar Degas, *Waiting*, ca. 1879–80 or 1876–77, monotype, Musée Picasso, Paris.

But the alternative way that Degas showed and used the backside of the prostitute's lower body is exemplified by the enticing display of the posterior in *The Serious Customer* (see fig. 11), which appears daring but darkly erotic at the same time. The sculptural, erotic, and tactile appeal of the buttocks is also on view in *Conversation* (fig. 27) and *The Procuress* (fig. 28), both of which feature carefully rounded, strategically placed posteriors. And it is not at all surprising that the darker partner in the lesbian monotype called *Two Women (Scene in a Brothel)* (fig. 29) consists almost entirely of buttocks and is without a head. (Note too that a rather conventional white nude is used here for the passive partner, similar in shape and position to Lefèbvre's *Reclining Woman* [fig. 16].)

26. (r.) Edgar Degas, *In a Brothel Salon*, ca. 1879–80 or 1876–77, monotype.

I wish to suggest that the latter way of representing the brothel prostitute's derriere, the way that inscribed its erotic appeal, on the one hand exceeds the limits of any purely physiognomic project, and on the other hand connects Degas's approach to that of contemporary painters of the Salon nude (not to mention the old Picasso).

See, in this connection, another prototypical Salon nude, again by Jules-Joseph Lefèbvre: his *Odalisque* of 1874 (fig. 30). In it, the painstakingly modeled, sculptural curves of the woman's lower body seen from the back constitute the most heavily eroticized zone in the pic-

27.
Edgar Degas, *Conversation*, ca. 1879–80 or 1876–77, monotype.

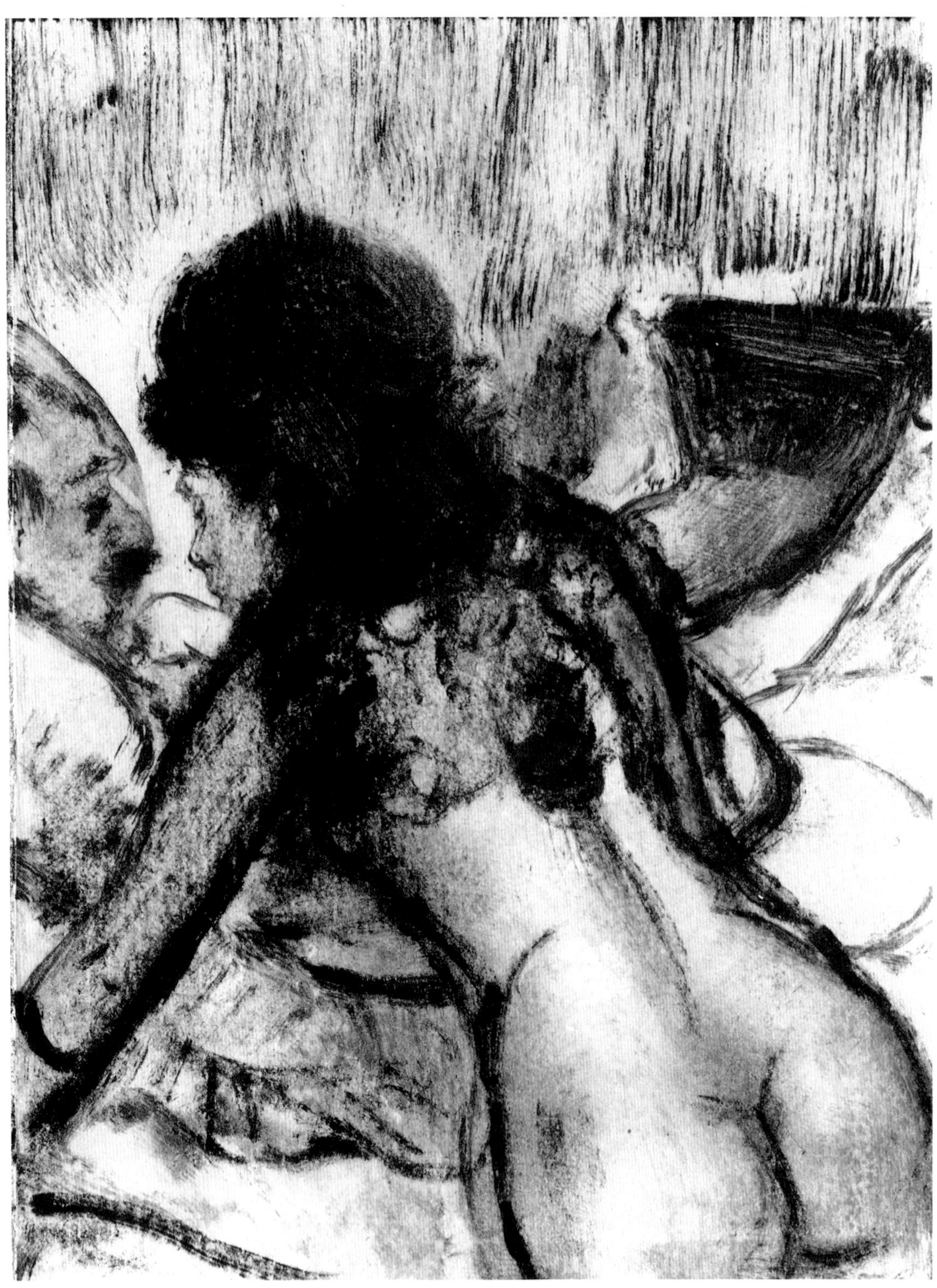

28.
Edgar Degas, *The Procuress*, ca. 1879–80 or 1876–77, monotype, Fondation Jacques Doucet, Paris.

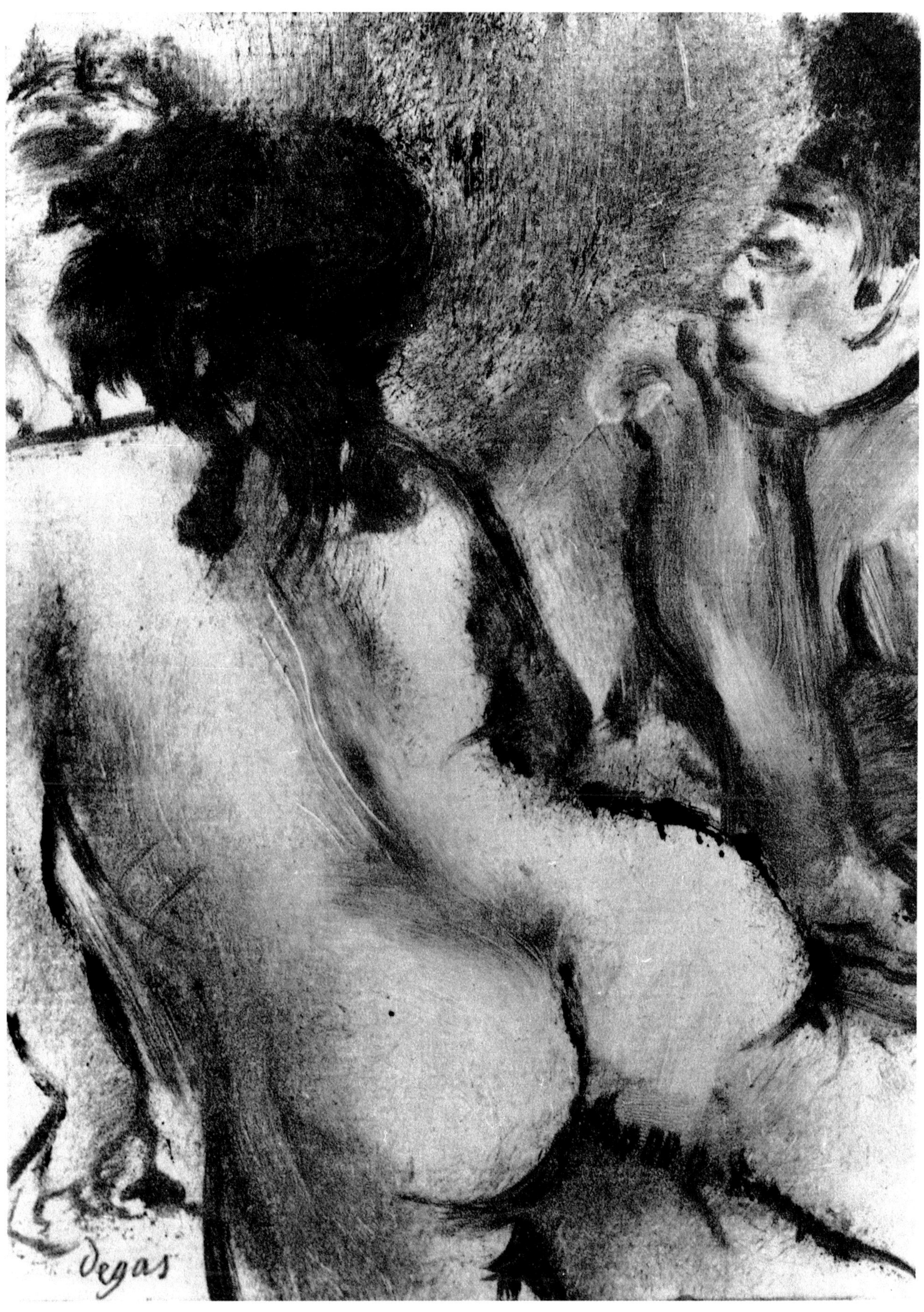
Degas

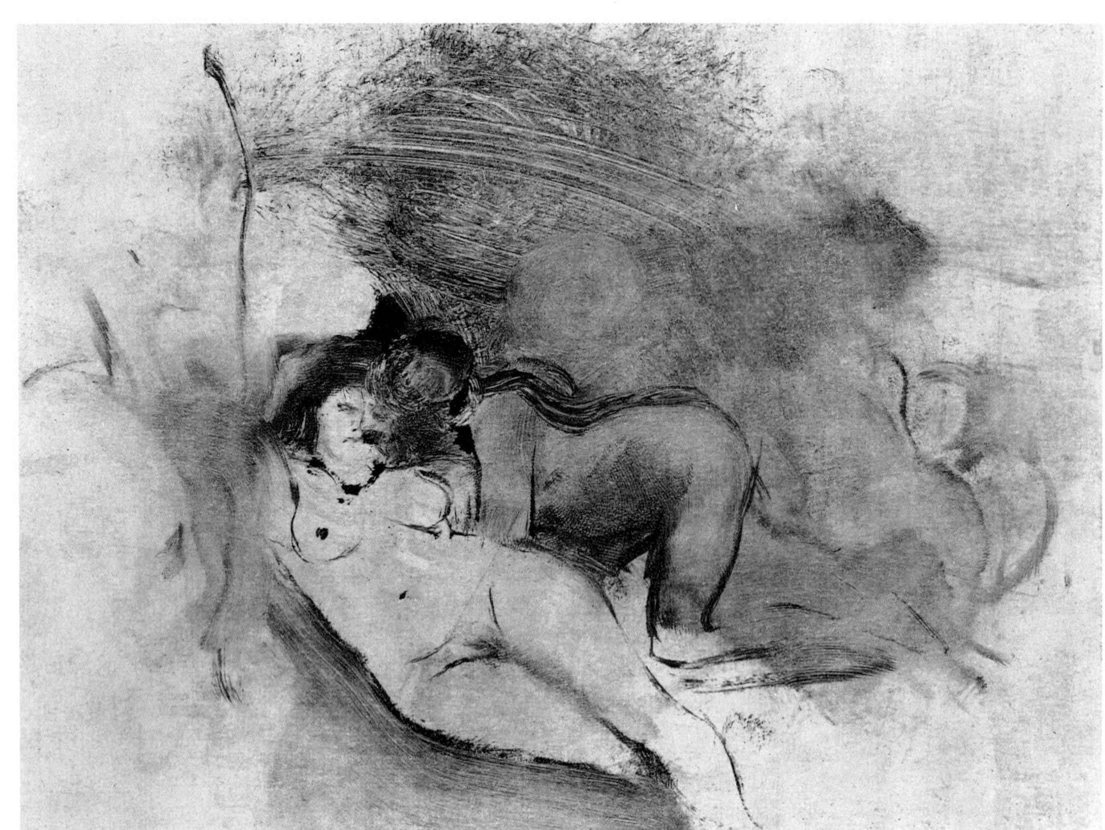

29.
Edgar Degas, *Two Women (Scene in a Brothel)*, ca. 1879–80 or 1876–77, monotype, Katherine Bullard Fund, Museum of Fine Arts, Boston.

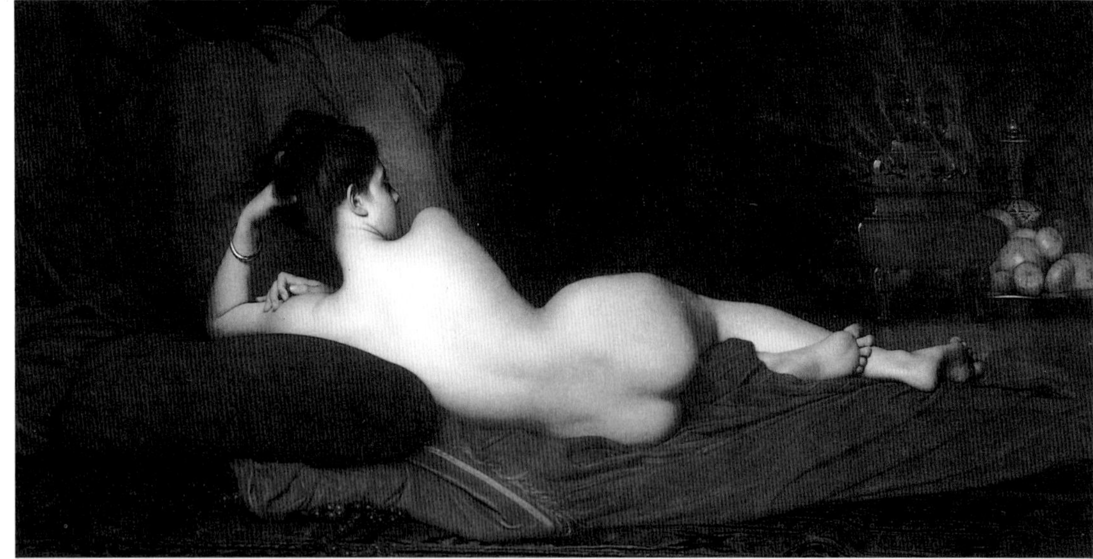

30.
Jules-Joseph Lefèbvre, *Odalisque*, 1874, oil on canvas, George F. Harding Collection, 1983.381, Art Institute of Chicago.

ture (especially insofar as the curves of the buttocks serve here as a gateway to the woman's genital area, suggestively encased by red velvet).

The eroticized handlings of this part of the female body that appear in the brothel monotypes betray Degas's vulnerability to the erotic appeal of the fleshy buttocks by endowing this part of the body with a persuasive volumetric tactility that the flattened out and blurred bodies of the series do not otherwise possess. In them we witness a record of desire and attraction.

In the monotypes overall, so many female features and parts are blurred, occluded, flattened, disfigured, elided, and congealed into ink that the relative three-dimensionality and clarity of these particular body parts stand out and invite comment. This observation converts the series into an even more complex, heterogeneous, and contradictory attribution of traits to brothel prostitutes than we had apprehended heretofore. On the one hand, the women are vulgar and unsophisticated: their bodies are flawed and improper, their heads those of lower-class reprobates. But on the other hand, a certain erotic appeal in the uninhibited use of their fleshy bodies is strongly implied, especially, as we have seen, by the clearly modeled and demarcated telltale posteriors of figures 15, 27, and 28, for example.

The conventions of male spectatorship are not fully abrogated by Degas's prints after all. While Degas demystifies most of the reigning fantasies of the prostitute, at the same time he displays an erotic fascination with the bodies from which he otherwise alienates the represented client, "the spectator," and himself. In the hindquarters of the prostitute, Degas upholds the textuality of her body,[53] restoring to otherwise de-eroticized figures the old (apparently indispensable and unavoidable) spice of the erotic appeal of the sexual deviant and social miscreant.

CHAPTER THREE

Testing the Limits

The Menace of Fashion

The time-honored signifier of social difference is clothing. In Thorstein Veblen's words, "Our apparel is always in evidence and affords an indication of our pecuniary standing to all observers at first glance."[1] But by the second half of the nineteenth century, clothing had become more uniform, and, as a consequence, people (especially men in their monochrome costumes) began to look increasingly alike. The difficulty of reading clothing accurately did not, however, prevent exercises in costume detection from becoming obsessions (this *was* also the age of Sherlock Holmes). As clothing became a less accurate (or at least less easily read) guide to social standing, people began to worry over it more and to take its role as an index of character more seriously.[2]

The personal quality that the male inquisitor might have wanted to ascertain most from a female's appearance was sexual morality: What was the woman's moral character? Was she a *femme honnête* or perhaps a *fille?* This decoding was particularly tricky in the case of a woman being observed, because female appearance was apparently especially hard to judge and confusion could result in considerable distress and embarrassment. (Look again at fig. 4, "Paris Regenerated," for example.)

Jean Quidam's "A Man Who Follows Women" of 1879 (fig. 31) recounts the story of a man who struggles, unsuccessfully, to determine accurately the sexual propriety of a strange woman encountered on the street. The city police knew that misjudging the integrity of respectable women was a problem, but rather than try to establish a system for labeling prostitutes, they complicated matters considerably by insisting that all women resemble one another. The police regulations governing the appearance of the card-carrying indecent woman, the *fille isolée* or *fille en carte*, forbade her to wear any distinctive clothing or accessories. Nothing on her exterior was to offend public morality by calling attention to her indecent interior. The elusory goal of the mandate was the uniform appearance of all women.[3] No less an authority than Parent-Duchâtelet reckoned, however, that even if all women's clothing were identical, men in need of a prostitute would always be able to recognize one (in spite of the contrary evidence of confusion on such matters in a journalistic picture like Quidam's).

The other side of the widespread perplexity over female appearance was that, as a consequence of the belief that moral meanings were immanent in mien, women attempted to control the image they were transmitting.[4] For some, this resulted in a fear or virtual suspension of

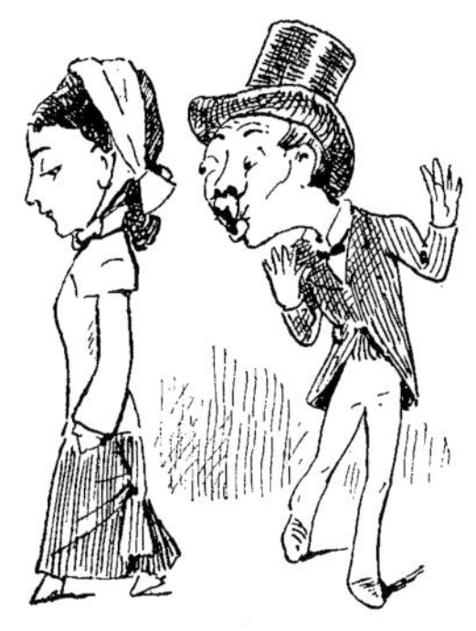

– Oh! good grief! but she looks nice! Ah! here's the woman that I've always dreamed of. Let's see! five and four is nine, and ten and ten, – ten francs. I have ten francs.

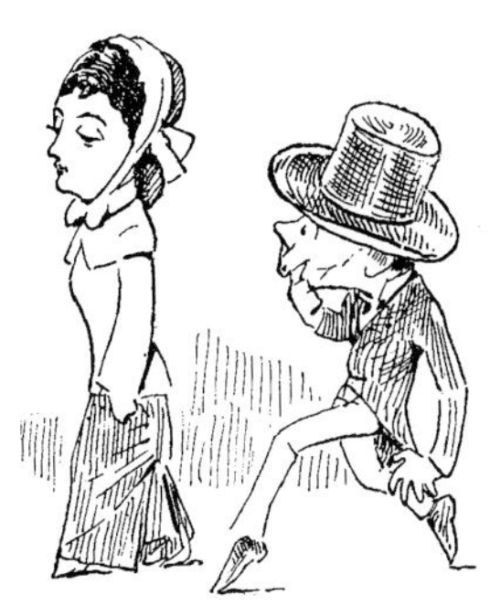

– The dickens! she has the air of being an honest woman! That's charming, but annoying; I don't know what to offer her. But don't act like you're following her.

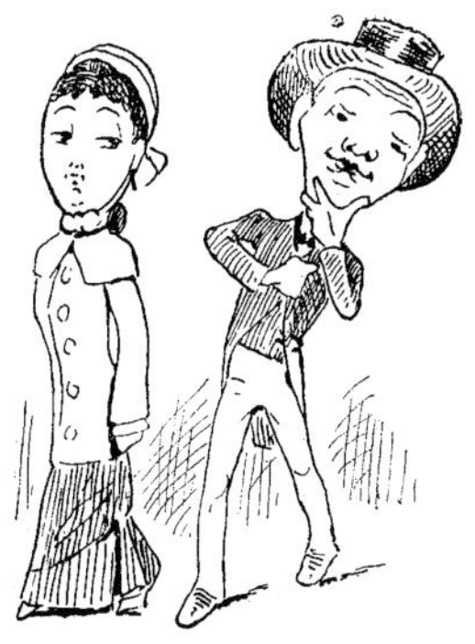

– Good grief! she's turning around! I'll act like I'm checking my watch. But I look rather stupid all the same! I want to get out of here.

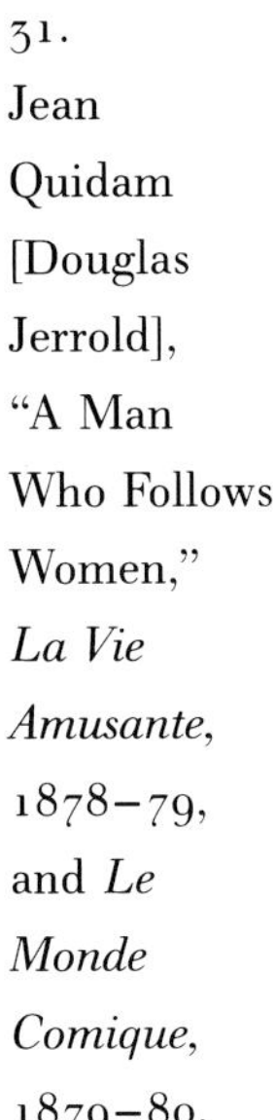

31. Jean Quidam [Douglas Jerrold], "A Man Who Follows Women," *La Vie Amusante*, 1878–79, and *Le Monde Comique*, 1879–80.

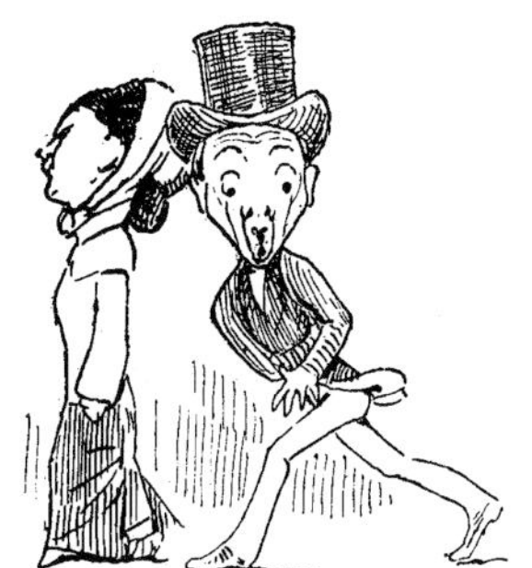

– But no. Let's see, let's be enterprising. Hm! Ms . . . Really, I don't dare. I must seem so stupid! And should I say Madam or Miss?

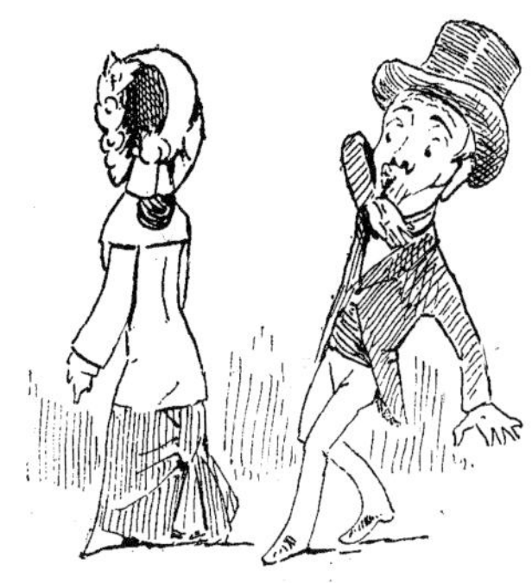

– Sir, I beg you not to follow me, or . . .
– But, Ma . . . Mademoiselle, I'm not following you at all; believe me, if I had even noticed you, I would have headed in the opposite direction.

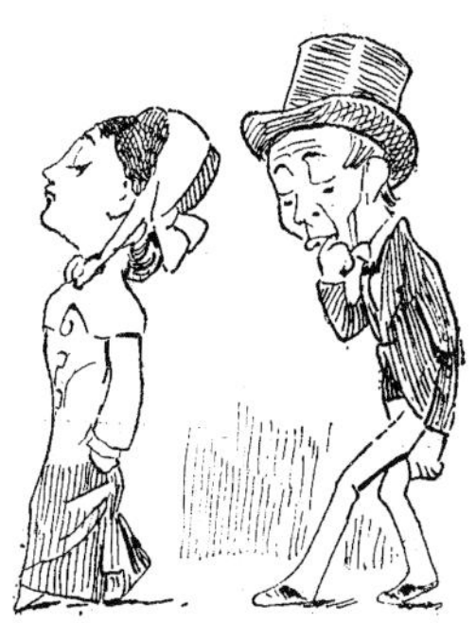

– My God! Did she snub me! I' don't really have the courage to speak to her. It's very nice to say: 'Be brave!' But the woman has to put herself into it after all.

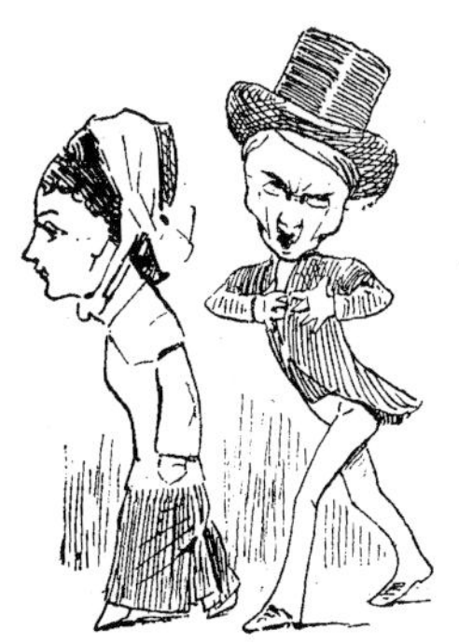

– No, let's see, I'm going simply to say to her: "Ah! Madam, listen to the voice of a heart . . . – the voice of a heart . . ." No, let's be original and plain! No, after all!

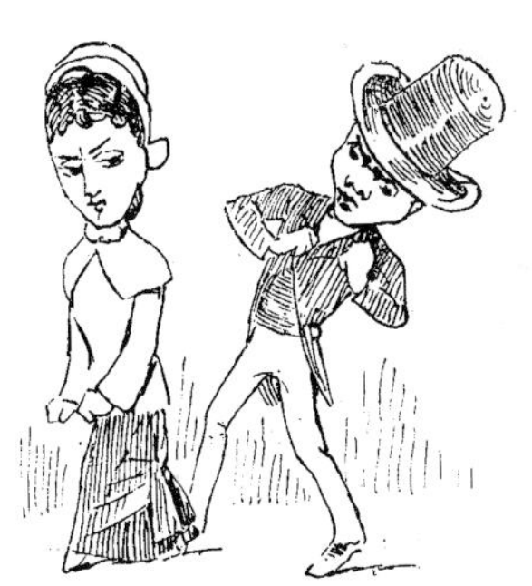

– It is best to be polite, I think. In stories, they are polite, I think. Let's see! let's take our courage in two hands. "Madam, listen to the voice . . ." – Yes, that's working. Oh! good grief! she's turning around! Lord! is this annoying!

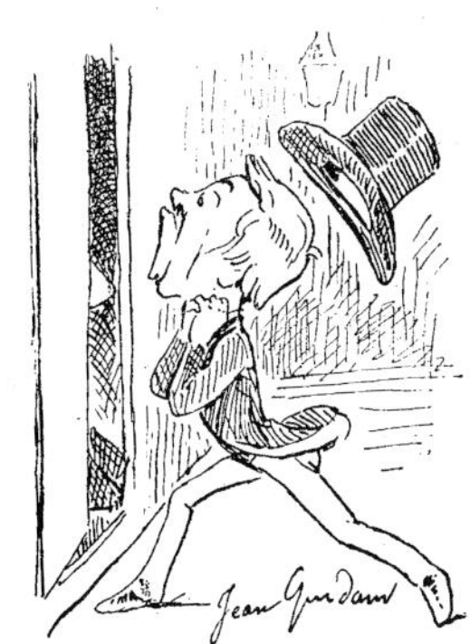

– Ah! I don't care, let's go! "Madame, lis . . ." In the name of a dog! she's gone inside. I really don't have any luck! I always happen upon honest women.

expressiveness, the proverbial Victorian self-discipline. Richard Sennett has written about the increasing self-consciousness of respectable women: "There arose out of this dilemma a need to pay great attention to details of appearance and to hold oneself in, for fear of being read wrongly or maliciously; indeed, who knew, perhaps if one gave off miniature signals of being loose, one really was. . . . One's only defense against such a culture was in fact to cover up, and from this came the stony feminine fear of being seen in public."[5]

It is not mere coincidence that the age of anxiety about prostitution and the morality of appearance was also the first golden age of the mass-produced garment and the Parisian department store.[6] Thanks to the "democratized" availability of previously undreamed-of quantities of diverse but standardized goods, large stores caught on and shopping was forever altered.[7] Throughout the 1870s and 1880s, women became increasingly active in the interlocking realms of consumption and fashion.[8] Respectable women apparently felt at ease shopping inside of stores but found the negotiation of sidewalks and streets – inevitably involving encounters with strangers – unpleasant and likely to pose moral risks and inconveniences.

Shopping and following fashion were in large measure compensatory activities. Because women had less social and political power than men, they sought avenues of expression that at least felt and appeared powerful. Hence the durability of Georg Simmel's (deceptively patronizing) explanation of this phenomenon: "Fashion [is] the valve through which woman's craving for some measure of conspicuousness and individual prominence finds vent, when its satisfaction is denied her in other fields. . . . In a certain sense fashion gives woman a compensation for her lack of position in a class based on a calling or profession."[9] Sheila Rowbotham clarifies the larger political matrix of women's increasing interest in fashion and self-adornment: "A dominant group is secure when it can convince the oppressed that they enjoy their actual powerlessness and give them instead a fantasy of power."[10] Being on top of fashion provided just such an image of power.

But the power conferred by this expertise was not purely imaginary. First of all, self-adornment could be a form of economic empowerment, because women were the principal consumers in the new shops and stores lining the boulevards. Even though the economic role of the nonworking woman was restricted largely to shopping, an activity that does not generate exchange value, the financial impact of female consumption was enormous.

At the same time, the increasing activity of women in the fashion sphere signaled yet another upsurge of female power: a new obsessiveness with (and parallel ability to modulate and control) their own sexual attractiveness made women seem more powerful and less vulnerable, at least according to male commentators. Self-adornment and sexual allure were closely connected in the latter half of the nineteenth century because dress had come to distinguish gender in more exaggerated ways. By the early Third Republic, fashion was no longer conceived as an entity separable from a woman's beauty; it was no longer a "priceless frame for female beauty."[11] Woman and her costume *together* created womanliness. No one believed this more passionately than Baudelaire: "What poet would dare, in the painting of pleasure occasioned by the appearance of a beauty, to separate a woman from her costume? Where is the man who, in the street, at the theater, in the woods, has not enjoyed in the most disinterested manner, a toilette knowledgeably put together, and retained an image of it inseparable from the beautiful woman to whom it belonged, making thus out of the two, the woman and the dress, an indivisible totality?[12] Simone de Beauvoir's gloss on this pattern of belief reminds us of the enduring way that men have tended to judge the erotic eligibility of women: "In woman dressed and

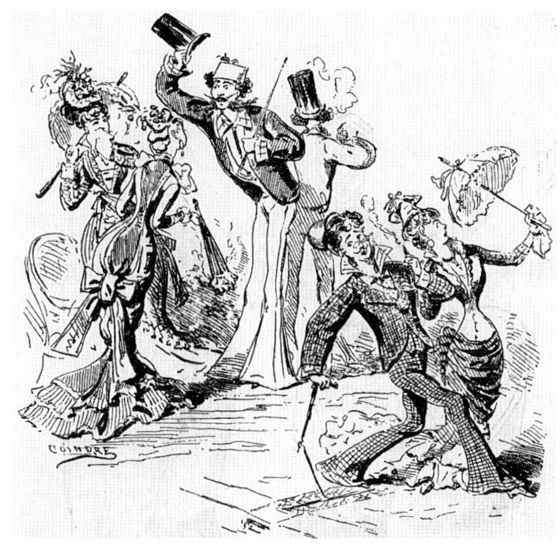

32. Gaston Coindre, "Ridicule," *La Vie Amusante*, 1878–79, and *Le Monde Comique*, 1879–80.

If you want to succeed in society and especially among the demimonde, you have to inspect carefully the minute details of the toilette. To greet one of these young ladies and leave the leather insides of your hat resting on your forehead is the ultimate embarrassment.

adorned, nature is present but under restraint, by human will remolded nearer to the man's desire. A woman is rendered more desirable to the extent that nature is more highly developed in her and more rigorously confined: it is the 'sophisticated' woman who has always been the ideal erotic object."[13]

Power was certainly at stake insofar as self-enhancement could substantially alter a woman's sexual attractiveness.[14] Women appeared to be remaking themselves in the sphere of consumption and, as a consequence, seemed more powerful and less governable by men. But men found this form of power problematic in many instances. Coindre's cartoon "Ridicule," of 1879–80 (fig. 32), for example, warns men against appearing foolish by committing a fashion faux pas before the powerful women of the demimonde.

To be in fashion, then, was to exercise an exclusively female form of power that had considerable force. By breaking the boundaries of their assigned roles through the activity of self-adornment, women were crossing over into the established codings of prostitution. It is not surprising, therefore, that women who customarily followed the dictates of period fashion in clothes found themselves regularly denounced as fatuous or indecent, as the examples discussed below will demonstrate.

Cementing the connection among the issues of clothing style, morality, and female power in the later nineteenth-century discourse on fashion was another important innovation in the production and social meaning of clothing: the birth of haute couture – high fashion in the modern sense – which originated in the designs of Charles Frederick Worth during the Second Empire. For the first time, fashionable women's wear was seen as the creation of a single designer. Although Worth owed a portion of his success to having the Empress Eugénie as a regular client, the majority of his customers were not aristocrats. They were instead demimondaines and *grandes cocottes* (courtesans), women whose success depended entirely upon their looks, whose fussiness about the details of fashionable dress was a trademark.[15]

That the unique, elaborately planned, fashionable appearance of a demimondaine or courtesan was vital to her success points to a fundamental difference between the common prostitute and the high-class one, best explained by Beauvoir: "The essential difference is that the first carries on trade in her pure generality – as woman – with the result that competition keeps her at the level of a miserable existence; whereas the second endeavors to gain recognition for herself – as an individual – and if she succeeds, she can entertain high aspirations. Beauty and charm or sex appeal are necessary here, but are not enough: the woman must be publicly *distinguished* somehow, as a person."[16]

Because of the early correlation between high fashion and sexual immorality, the morality of always being in fashion was thought to depend upon the already-established good character of the wearer. A decent woman for whom shopping was an obsession rather than a simple devoir was in danger of falling from the path of respectability and manageability, whereas the deviant woman who dressed to the nines was ipso facto immoral and could also inflict societal damage by infecting the lady with an uncontrollable taste for extravagant clothes.

The High Priestesses of Venal Love by Stop (fig. 33), which figures the stereotypical connection between extravagantly well-dressed women of the Second Empire and immorality, casts enthusiasm for fashion in a central, starring role. Worshipping at the shrine of love and money, of Cupid and coins, has produced results for these attractive young women of the late Second Empire. This pattern of veneration has enabled a life of sartorial luxury. This calculus of venality reckoned that the way for the morally reckless woman to obtain the money to be in fashion was by selling love.

"The Tarts" by Péry (fig. 34) pushes the link between fashionable women and sexual immorality to its outer limit by showing well-dressed prostitutes using their fashionable clothing to hook customers: they sell themselves to afford the elaborate clothes, which in turn guarantee a brisk turnover in "affaires." And the calculating fashion mavens of Victor Morland's "These Little Women" of the late 1870s (fig. 35) prefer a lingerie salesman from a department store to a viscount.

As a cartoon like "The Tarts" (fig. 34) vividly shows, the female stereotype that linked fashion to Cupid tended to advance the assumption that a woman would take off her clothes in order to have nice clothes. An excessive attachment to the cause of clothing – a slavery to fashion – could bring about de facto prostitution. The classic formulation of this bromide (favored by those who would not admit that prostitution had pressing economic causes) had been devised in the 1830s: a principal cause of prostitution was the "desire to have fun or to acquire beautiful clothes, especially in Paris."[17] The idea remained current for decades: "The reasons are simply three quarters of the cardinal sins: coquetry, laziness, gourmandise – and the rest."[18] Emile Zola's characterization of the young Nana's impassioned longing for material comfort is a paradigmatic example of this formulation. Her desire for luxurious things exceeds the normal yearning for material well-being that Zola would vouchsafe any member of Nana's class, because the author has Nana experience a desire for luxury as heat running up her thighs. In *L'Assommoir*, he wrote:

> Then, trotting in the mud, splashed by the coaches, blinded by the resplendence of shop windows, she had longings that twisted in her stomach, like clothes, longing to be well set, to eat in restaurants, to go out to events, to have her own room with her own furniture. She stopped completely pale with desire, she felt rising all along the length of her thighs a heat from the pavement of Paris, a ferocious appetite to bite into those pleasures that turned her upside down, there in the midst of the throng on the sidewalk.[19]

The reversible relationship between handsome clothing and dubious sexual morality (immorality enabled fashionability, and the desire to be fashionable caused venality) lay at the

33.
Stop [Louis Pierre Gabriel Bernard Morel-Retz], *The High Priestesses of Venal Love*, 1869, Cabinet des Estampes, Bibliothèque Nationale, Paris.

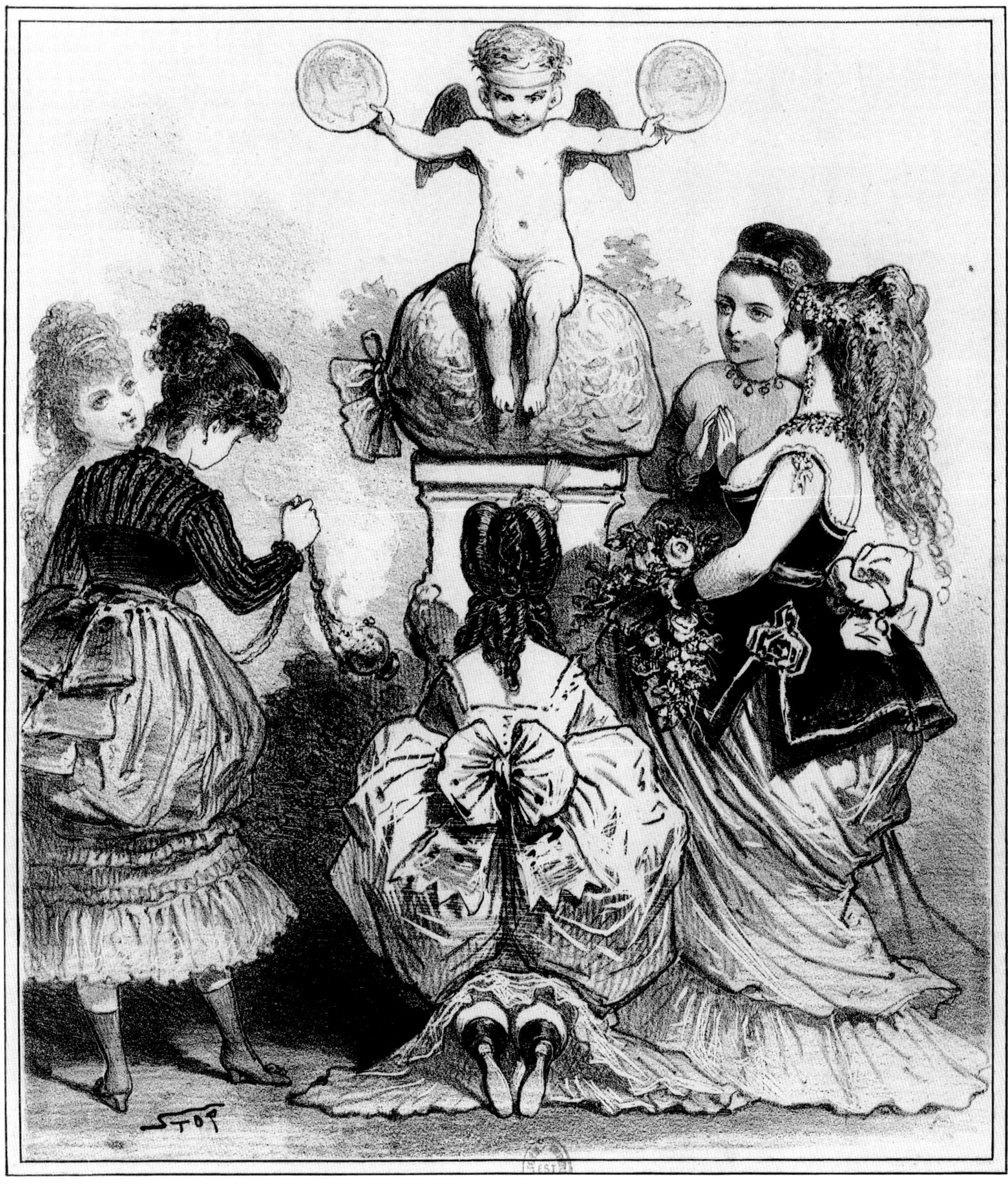

heart of the history and myth of the later nineteenth-century courtesan, because once having secured a means of support, her life was consecrated to the display of her fashionable possessions and ostentatious idleness. The characteristically luxurious way of life of the successful *grande horizontale* was thought to dazzle honest women to a menacing degree. Using the weapon of lavish, highly styled clothing, the courtesan could undermine the stability of the social order by driving moral women to imitation.

34. (l.) Péry, "The Tarts," 1870, Cabinet des Estampes, Bibliothèque Nationale, Paris.

35. (r.) Victor Morland, "These Little Women," *Le Monde Comique*, 1878–79.

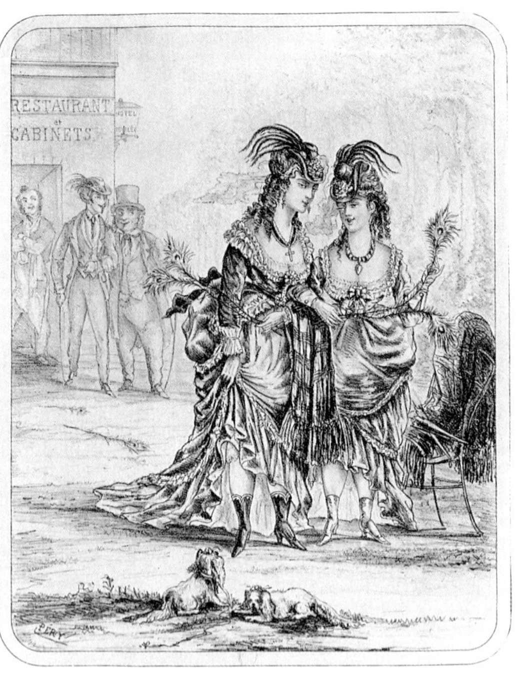

– *What do you think of the latest fashion, Fany?*
– *Oh! my dear, I find it excellent. "Affairs" are going much better now.*

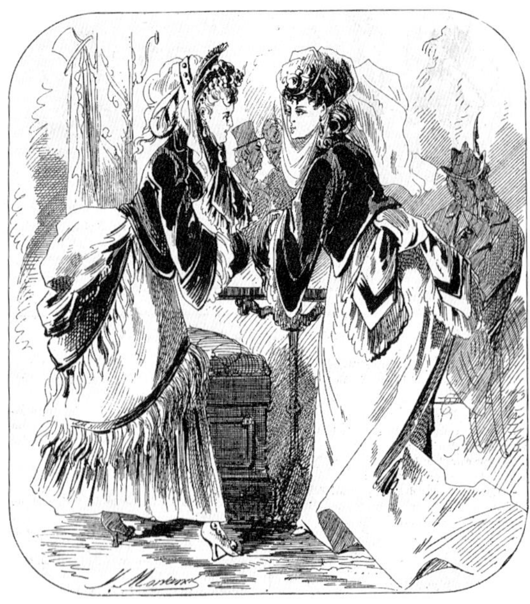

– *He has a very respectable air, the young man with you . . . Is he the son of a good family . . . a viscount?*
– *Much better than that! he's a lingerie clerk from* Plaisir-des-Dames*!*
– *Ah!*
– *Yes . . . and think about it – he has on him his week's savings.*
– *Off you go, you lucky dog! . . .*

> Thanks to society journals which discuss clothes, relationships, lovers, parties and the fitting up of prostitutes, to plays in the theater and to novels, many of which have supported, with an incontestable talent, the rehabilitation of the courtesan, there has been a pronounced evolution in morality; the unhealthy curiosity which pushed honest women towards courtesans at the beginning of this evolution (but which did not prevent them from keeping their distance) has gradually been succeeded by another sentiment. Jealous of the prostitutes who are highhandedly carrying off their husbands, brothers or fiancés, they have set about imitating them, copying them. The salons are transformed; the *cocodette* has made her appearance, to the applause of the blasé young people and the soft old men who find in her the offhandedness, the language, even the odor of the fashionable *cocotte.*[20]

Surely Alexandre Dumas fils had this very issue in mind in 1890 when he wrote: "*La Dame aux Camélias* . . . could not be written today. . . . Courtesans and society women share designers . . . Not only do they wear the same clothing, but they use the same language."[21]

It was the view of a naturalist insider that respectable people condemned the high-class prostitute only out of deep-seated envy and desire:

> Oh, matrons, if you had the youth of these prostitutes, and if you, young ladies, had the same elegance; if you, upright bourgeois, could obtain their favors without completely ruining yourself, and if you, colorless young people, dared to have the courage of your convictions, no one would cry out against prostitutes![22]

The three foregoing later nineteenth-century observations remind us of the inherent complexity of the courtesan's relationship with other women, which Beauvoir explained:

> She [the courtesan] needs them [other women] as critical judges and spectators, as confidants and accomplices, in order to create that counter-universe which all women oppressed by man require. But feminine rivalry here reaches its culminating point. The prostitute who trades in her generality as woman has her competitors; but if there is enough work to go around, even in their disputes they are conscious of their solidarity. The hetaira who seeks individual fame is *a priori* hostile to any other woman who, like herself, covets a privileged position.[23]

But just as the courtesan's ostentatiousness irked respectable women, it pleased many respectable men. Her lavish expenditures for luxury goods displayed her commercial success and that of the man (or men) financing her. A married woman of means mirrored the wealth and status of her husband, but a courtesan, shunning decorum, could exhibit the wealth of her keeper in an even more forthright way: her opulence could effectively signify a lover's amassed wealth without his having to exhibit it directly, and in ways that were simply not available to the man's wife.[24]

The competition between moral and immoral women of means, then, was fought on the battleground of high fashion. Indeed, the luxury of the courtesan's way of life paraded through Paris placed the honest, well-to-do woman in a predicament. Imitation of the hyperfashionability of the courtesan's costume, detail for detail, was out of the question because deviations from the norms of high fashion indecorously emphasized the sexual function of the toilette.[25] But imitation was taboo for other more fundamental reasons as well. The courtesan's lover – that sexual and financial slave of the woman who wore showy and overblown styles – would never want or permit his wife (or daughter or sister) to dress in the same way, in spite of the pleasure he took in the courtesan and her seductive style. This prohibition was a question not only of decorum but of economics as well: the man – as financier of two women, two households – was not prepared to pay for two displays of sumptuous living. The spendthrift mistress satisfied her underwriter's vanity, but a wife's parallel extravagance might have ruined him.[26] Because there was no divorce in France until the passage of the *loi Naquet* in 1884,[27] a disgruntled married woman, who might have sought to dissolve her marriage under other legal circumstances, was especially sensitive about the social prohibitions upon her sartorial competition with a mistress.

An ordinary woman's lively interest in shopping and clothing provoked worries of another sort. It was believed that women were vulnerable to a form of psychological distress known as the delirium of consumption, an exclusively female affliction. In manuscript notes to his 1883 novel about department stores, *Au bonheur des dames*, Zola wrote that "women are thus dazzled by the accumulation of merchandise. That is what has made the success of the *grands magasins*."[28] A commentator for *Le Figaro*, who called himself Ignotus, identified a particular form of nervous agitation produced by department store displays: "The creation of these grand bazaars has given birth to new passions in the moral order as in the pathological . . . There's no doubt about it, it is a new style of neurosis!"[29]

Because the majority of customers at the principal department stores were middle class (the trade was cash and carry; there was no credit), the female shopper was frequently denounced as neglectful of her proper domestic duties, leaving the morality of her forays into the public sphere open to speculation. Zola certainly thought along these lines: "The department store tends to replace the church. It marches to the religion of the cash desk, of beauty, of coquetry, and fashion. [Women] go there to pass the hours as they used to go to church: an occupation, a place of enthusiasm where they struggle between their passion for clothes and the thrift of their husbands."[30]

Ignotus discovered indelicacies in the appearance of some shoppers, and, as a consequence, he correlated a zeal for shopping with the onset of sexual stimulation: "The women I see are wearing today's clothes. Corsets make their hips stick out. Dresses without gathers at the waist mold their bodies like wet fabric. The tips of their breasts appear under the fabric, as under the marble of certain Florentine statues. From time to time, a woman searches in her pocket for a miniscule purse. It's surprising that someone who spends so much has such a tiny purse!"[31] Not every shopper was improper but a marked enthusiasm for shopping – synonymous with vanity – on the part of an otherwise respectable woman suggested a dubious character and an exaggerated and unhealthy concern for her own personal appearance, which in turn suggested her attempt at sexual attractiveness. In short, nice women did not succumb to the allure of the sales counter: "The woman of a relatively elevated breed – which sane maternal or conjugal passions preserved from this particular neurosis – only goes to the grand bazaars in order to spend very modestly for the household."[32]

Betraying an excessive passion for shopping was a risky move, but appearing overdressed was a good deal more so, because to be judged vulgarly turned out was deadly in polite society. In extreme cases, an extravagantly dressed woman, especially if the extravagance was slightly incorrect, could be taken for a courtesan – especially if she and her husband were not known to be wealthy enough to cover the cost of her clothes. The moral signification of personal appearance was clearly an obsession of the age, even in the most unimpeachably modest circumstances. The force of this obsession was in some sense justified, given the potent messages sent by clothing during this period. As Georg Simmel suggests below, the power of the language of clothes was so great that its vitality could be appropriated by the clever, subversive have-not; the display of extravagant fashion could work as a form of resistance on the part of the social underdog:

> The fact that the demi-monde is so frequently a pioneer in matters of fashion is due to its peculiarly uprooted form of life. The pariah existence to which society condemns the demi-monde produces an open or latent hatred against everything that has the sanction of law, of every permanent institution, a hatred that finds its relatively most innocent and aesthetic expression in the striving for ever new forms of appearance. In this continual striving for new, previously unheard-of fashions, in the regardlessness with which the one that is most diametrically opposed to the existing one is passionately adopted, there lurks an aesthetic expression of the desire for destruction, which seems to be an element peculiar to all that lead this pariah-like existence, so long as they are not completely enslaved within.[33]

We now turn to an extended consideration of three Salon-bound paintings of the mid-1870s, each of which explicitly thematized the convergence of female sexual immorality and fashionability of dress. The relative straightforwardness and legibility of these pictures sets them apart from the typically "evasive" vanguard picture discussed in chapter 1. To encounter this kind of highly detailed forthrightness in pictures by Ernest-Ange Duez and Henri Gervex, so-called pompiers, may not be surprising, but it is less familiar in the work of Manet, whose *Nana* is probably the only celebration of a high-class prostitute in the avant-garde record.

Worries about the sexual morality of female sartorial display were condensed and contained in two paintings that appeared in the Salon of 1874, Duez's *Splendor* and *Misery*. These pictures, designed as a pair, won a third-class medal.[34] *Splendor* (fig. 36) is the only half of the diptych that survives, although descriptions of the critics provide some idea of the appearance of its companion, *Misery*.

In the broadest sense the subject of Duez's works is the juxtaposition of two types of promenading prostitutes. The contrast between the two was not only one of social rank – a *fille galante* in *Splendor* and a *chiffonnière* (ragpicker) in *Misery* – but also one of age.[35] The age difference (and perhaps a portrait likeness between the two?) made it possible, perfectly logical in fact, to read the images sequentially[36] rather than as representations of two coexisting forms of contemporary prostitution. The social dissimilarities between the two prostitutes automatically provided a moral for the works, and the substantial age differential amplified the cautionary message. Because of these legible points of contrast between the two prostitutes and the long visual tradition of "before and after" images,[37] none of the critics saw the paintings as two facets of a heterogeneous and dynamic contemporary situation, as two coexisting and competing forms of prostitution in the capital in the 1870s. Only Zola implied such a reading, but perhaps the implication is only a consequence of the brevity of his remarks: the title is sufficient to make the antithesis understood, he wrote.[38]

In characterizing the woman in *Splendor*, critics remarked on the combination of youth, insolence, and swagger. Duez did indeed give her an insolent, youthful beauty marked and diluted by the professional artificiality of an excessive elegance. The colors of her face are the sure consequence of heavy makeup: pursed red lips, darkened eyebrows and eyes, cheeks covered with powder. The skin is slightly pink and flushed beneath the powder, and the puffiness of her cheeks and the pouches over her eyes are probably caused by a lack of sleep (and the possible abuse of alcohol or tobacco). The look of degraded youthfulness is also carried by the visibly reddened ear against which her earring sparkles. The brassy yellow of her dyed hair sweeps across her forehead.

Duez dresses her in *the* correct fashion of the day (a swept-back skirt topped by a jacket),[39] but her suit is an especially lavish example of the current style of street dress. It is made of rich, heavy materials: the gray fabric is ornamented with gold brocade stripes on the bodice and at the skirt borders, and an abundance of brown fur trims every edge of the garment. She holds her left glove in her right, gloved hand (the gloves are bright ochre) to permit a secure hold on the small white dog.[40] She is surrounded by darkness, and the various metallic objects (earring, rings, dog leash) sparkle in what appears to be the artificial gaslight of evening. She stops or slows down her perambulation to fix a calculated glance upon the passerby.

Duez's pair of canvases represents two extremes of prostitution according to stereotype and convention. He painted the cliché of the well-turned-out young courtesan of the boulevards in her prime up against the old vagrant-outcast from the edges of the city, a failure from the margins of society, and implied that one way of life would succeed the other. Various accounts of prostitution on the Parisian boulevards during the 1870s describe the strong competition that a

36.
Ernest-Ange Duez, *Splendor*, 1874, oil on canvas, Musée des Arts Décoratifs, Paris.

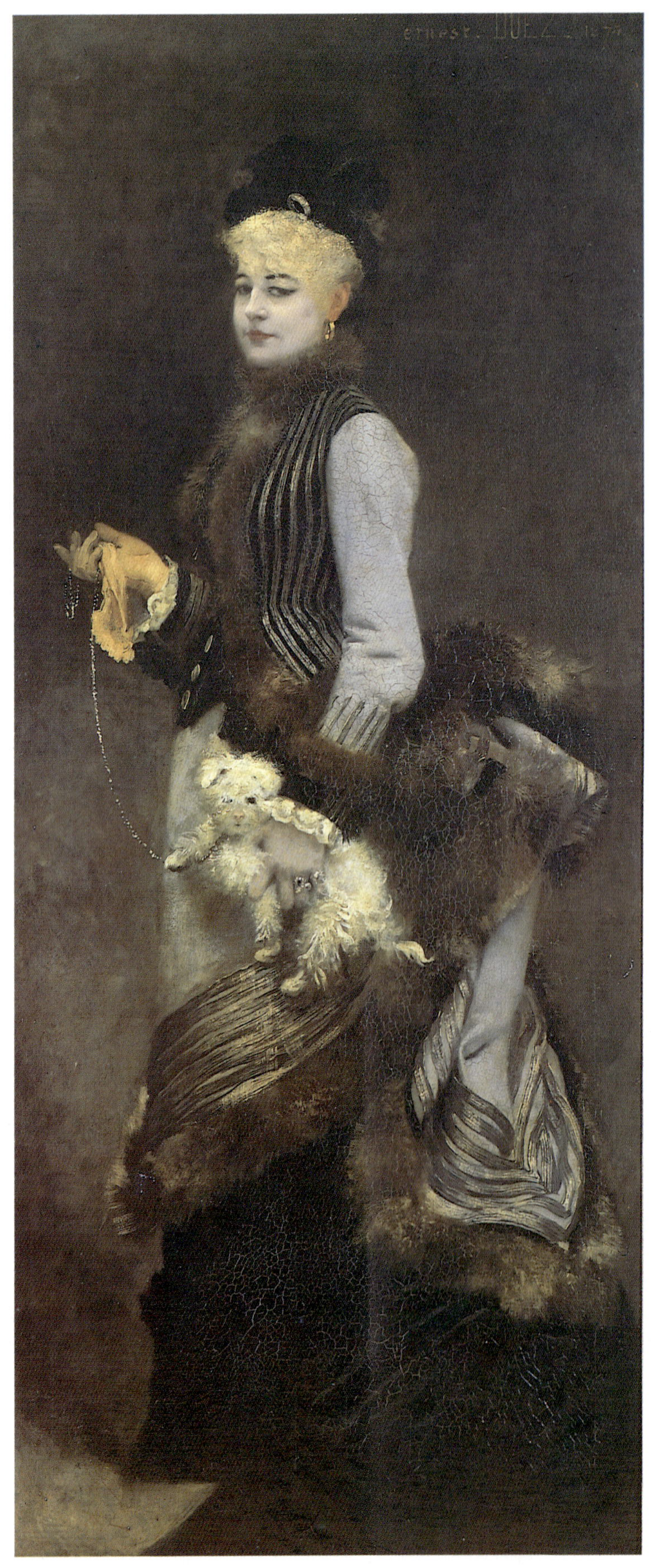

young prostitute like the one in *Splendor* encountered from other prostitutes, especially at night – filles who were desperate, aggressive, hatless, working the sidewalks and passages in darkness and gaslight.[41] But Duez was not a documentary artist and did not conceive his diptych in terms of coexisting, competing kinds of prostitutes. He painted instead two halves of a sequential dichotomy. His only modernizing touch was the correlation between professional venality and the hyperfashionability of 1874.

Duez's before-and-after canvases were read like pages from their probable eponym, Balzac's *Splendeurs et misères des courtisanes* of the 1830s. The moral caveat that critics found in the pictures was linked to their reading of the connotations of the prostitutes' clothing and deportment. They showed concern that the well-turned-out young courtesan could infect decent young women with an enthusiasm for extravagant clothes, without regard for the consequences.

The critic L. Janmot took Duez's intent to moralize for granted when he wrote this discouraged observation for *Le Contemporain:* "It is fine for him to bring out through his talent the strictness and the poignancy of these two contrasts. Will the sight of the hideous ragpicker stop those tempted to start like she did by making them feel afraid of ending up like that? I doubt it."[42] Janmot thus rehearses the view encapsulated by *The High Priestesses of Venal Love* (fig. 33). In his view the possibility of ending up as a wrinkled ragpicker was unlikely to deflect the path of the committed and venal slave to fashion.

Paul Mantz's review in *Le Temps* was also confident that the young woman of *Splendor* was flanked by the image of her certain future in *Misery:*

> It is a very moral diptych or, at least, strongly imbued with literature. . . . [On one side] superb and young, with dyed yellow hair, powdered and velvetized cheek, insolent, radiant, there she goes, clicking the asphalt of the boulevard with the little heel of her victorious boot. . . . There, right alongside, the same woman seen thirty years later, shrivelled, sordid, in tatters, letting all her rips betray misery and vice, and holding in her hand like an ironic symbol of past follies an old pair of pink satin slippers.[43]

His (and the artist's) reliance upon the moral denotations of fashion parallels and reinforces the concerns we have been mapping. Two of Mantz's images are especially vivid: a belief in clothing as *the* sign of the prostitute's immoral monetary success, captured by the phrase "sa bottine victorieuse," and his mention of Duez's apparent inclusion of an old pair of pink satin evening slippers in *Misery* as a reminder of the old woman's former costume prerogatives.

Although the prostitute of *Splendor* was unmistakably a hyperfashionable woman of the day, Duez's prizewinning diptych of 1874 used a traditional, moralizing iconography of prostitution, which originated in prints and novels of the 1830s. And any threat that a courtesan like Duez's might have posed to the social and moral order of 1870s Paris was contained by the cautionary flanking depiction of her subsequent defeat and ruination in *Misery.* If *Splendor* exemplifies the safe picture of the hyperfashionable courtesan of the 1870s, Manet's *Nana* of 1877 was the threatening way to represent the untamed challenge of the expensively clad fille galante.

Manet's *Nana* (fig. 37) was begun in October or November 1876, presented unsuccessfully to the Salon jury in the spring of 1877, and displayed for several

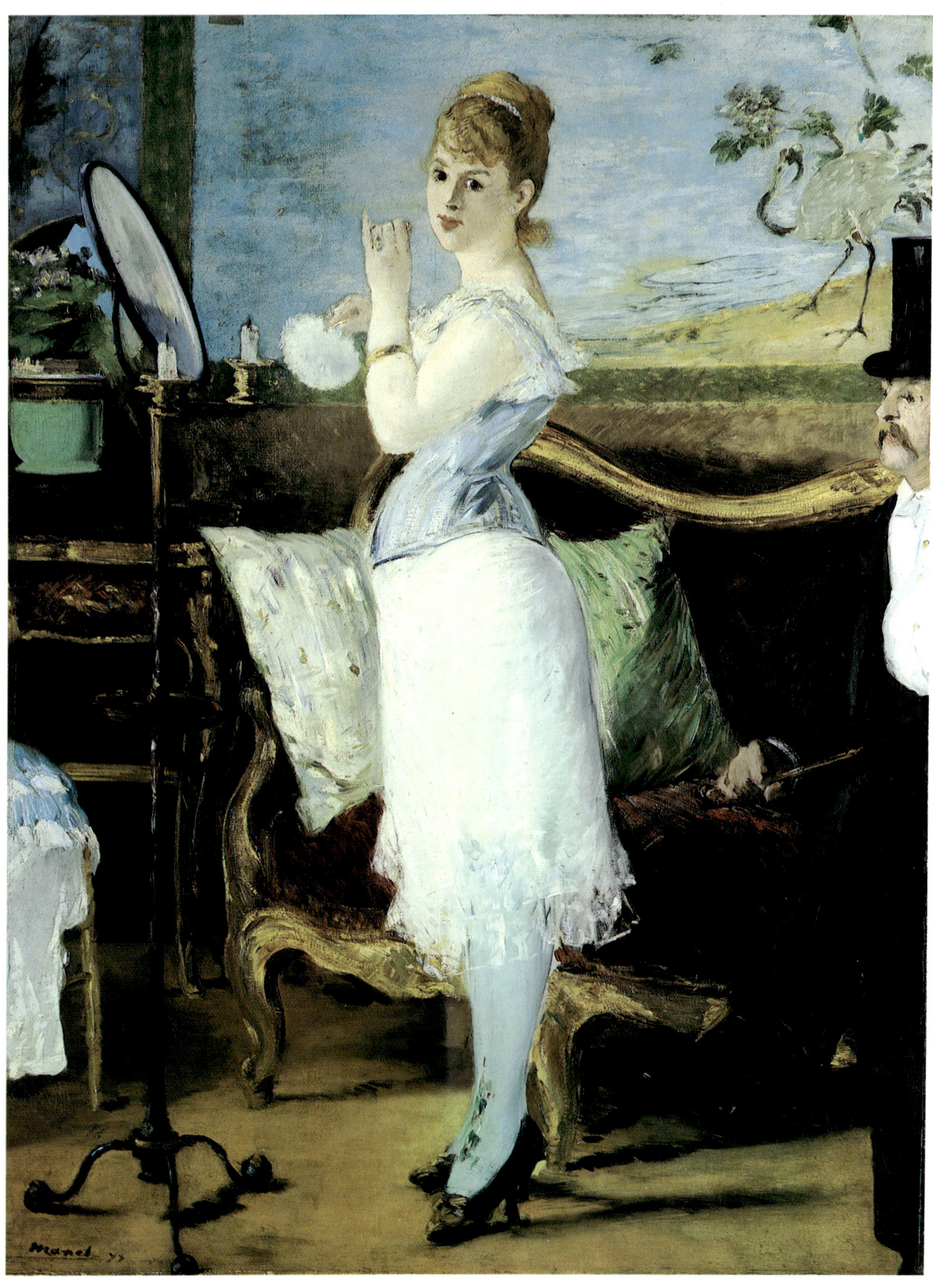

37.
Edouard Manet, *Nana*, 1877, oil on canvas, Kunsthalle, Hamburg.

weeks in May 1877 at Giroux, a merchant of bibelots on the boulevard des Capucines. The painting was probably named after Emile Zola's fictional heroine of *L'Assommoir* and *Nana*, but whatever the precise relationship to Zola's Nana, Manet's was conceived in overtly Baudelairean terms. She is a figure whose allure depends upon – is in fact identified with – her costume. Baudelaire's thoughts were bread and butter to a woman like Nana: "She must paint herself up to be adored."[44]

In the painting, Nana gets ready to go out, while a gentleman in top hat waits off to one side, seated on a burgundy velvet settee. Only half of the seated man is in the picture, but this is not a painting assembled with the goals of the "instantaneous glimpse picture" in mind.[45] Not an evasive or elliptical picture, it is a deliberate synthesis of the look and period reputation of the courtesan, distilled in a unitary image in which the man plays a secondary, though still decisive, role. This is in many ways an odd picture for Manet to have painted. Among his works on the theme of the contemporary prostitute, *Nana* is unique, both aesthetically and ideologically. Rehearsing the observation made at the outset of this chapter, the picture is probably the only straightforward glorification of a prostitute in the avant-garde record. Indeed, it appears that the theme of the hyperfashionable, immoral woman was never treated with reserve and evasiveness by visual artists of the 1870s and 1880s.

Manet's art is filled with frontal female faces,[46] but Nana's face is quite different from the others. Both its position and expression are distinctive. Although her body is in profile, her head turns between forty-five and ninety degrees from the plane of the body, and the face tilts slightly back from a strict vertical axis. Her head turning away from the plane of the body calls our attention to the discontinuity between what she is looking at now and what she has been doing. She addresses an outside spectator, aware that she is being admired. The diagonal placement of her head gives it a certain insouciance, but the facial features combine conventional flirtatiousness with a somewhat patronizing and practiced flippancy. The slightly raised left eyebrow gives the face a note of alertness and sternness that stiffens its otherwise coquettish expression. Nana's attractive features encourage attention, but all the while she professionally appraises the potential visitor. And at the same time, her body carries out the task of self-adornment, uninterrupted. This complex relationship between body and countenance is a critical part of Manet's definition of Nana and her kind.

Nana applies her makeup with the aid of a mirror, but unlike most women she is able to work on the project with both hands. Considering the customary limits of manual dexterity and hand-eye coordination, as well as plain efficiency, this two-handed technique is extraordinary. This pose is coupled with the theatrical exaggeration of her hands: the right hand holds a powder puff limply while the left hand, holding her lip rouge, includes a consciously chic extension of the little finger. These are not practical hand positions, and maintaining them while she looks away accentuates their – and her – artificiality. Nana is defined quite precisely as someone who applies makeup in her underwear not only while someone watches (the observer is the anonymous viewer of the painting, not her gentleman, for he is looking at her posterior), but *in order to be watched.*[47] This is not just an image of narcissistic adornment practiced by a venal woman but, rather, the *process* of adornment on display.

The body – soft, curved, and plump – also fixes Nana's shamelessness.[48] (A look of well-fed voluptuousness could at the time be as suggestive as expensive clothing.) The only exposed skin, her left arm, is made to appear as fleshy as possible: the bracelet pushes into her forearm, and her upper arm is splayed against her side. Manet has emphasized the breadth and softness of the flesh of the upper arm by rhyming it with the white powder puff to the left of her forearm. Her swaybacked posture is partially explained by the force of her corset but also suggests an immodest ease and relaxation at this display, in addition to enhancing the robustness of her physique. That she is presented as managing a somewhat relaxed posture while wearing high-heeled shoes further suggests how practiced she is at the art of adornment and display. It goes without saying that such shoes are not de rigueur for this stage of the toilette. The roundness and fullness of Nana's body are emphasized and reiterated in the appointments surrounding her. The gilt frame of the couch suavely echoes the curve of her stomach, and the pillows on either side of her haunches emphasize the breadth of this area. The bird decorating the wall is the key evidence: it is a crane, *une grue*, a slang term for prostitute.[49] In effect, Manet depicts Nana's body as equivalent to these various forms of decoration and display.

As discussed above, one of the reasons that a gentleman would frequent such a woman was to consume extravagantly by proxy. The dress code of the period constrained a man from adorning himself. Manet plays upon the contrast between the simplicity and formality of his clothes and the complexity and informality of hers. Like the men in the salon of Degas's brothel, however, he keeps his hat on in Nana's boudoir, which is an abrogation of good manners and a sure sign of his casual disrespect for her.

In addition to his wearing a hat, the man's indifferent manner may signal the routine nature of their relations – as though he were accustomed to waiting. In Robert Herbert's apt phrase, "She has a saucy independence and seems capable of controlling the man who supports her," or, in the more extreme formulation of Gotthard Jedlicka, "The young woman Nana is so to speak a modern allegory of being-for-sale. The man is an allegory of the duped buyer."[50] By suggesting that the buyer has been duped, Jedlicka wants to call our attention to a disequilibrium in their otherwise fully commodified relationship, one in which equality *should be* achieved through the leveling effect of the exchange of money (Jedlicka is echoing Simmel's outlook on the matter).[51] Because Jedlicka presumes that the man is subject and the woman is object, he seems both struck and displeased by an image of a forceful, purchased woman who is not fully controlled by her buyer.[52] Manet shows Nana involved in a to-and-fro of display and enticement with the viewer, a transaction in which the man on the settee has no part. The painting proposes that money does not buy the domestication of Nana's sexual force. And this disequilibrium was, of course, the outcome of the courtesan's simultaneous independence and dependence: "No man is absolutely their master. But their need of man is most urgent. The courtesan loses her means of support entirely if he ceases to feel desire for her."[53]

The question remains: Why was the painting rejected from the Salon of 1877? What is it about this particular image that placed it outside the bounds of propriety at this particular moment? Werner Hofmann argues that the inclusion of the man in the painting was the reason for the rejection, believing that the inclusion of a "customer" was ipso facto unacceptable, whereas Robert Herbert has argued instead that by using the Zolaesque title *Nana*, "Manet was deliberately courting a scandal."[54] Indeed, acknowledging and looking into the intertextuality of the works by Manet and Zola appears crucial to understanding the rejection of the painting by the Salon.

Manet's explicit debt to Zola must be sorted out first, starting with the facts of chronology. Zola's *L'Assommoir*, which introduced the character of Nana, was published in feuilleton from April 13 to June 17, 1876, in *Le Bien Public* and from July 9, 1876, to January 7, 1877, in *La République des Lettres*. Chapter 11, which featured Nana, appeared in November 1876. On

July 26, 1878, Zola wrote, "I have the plan of Nana." On October 16, 1879, the first installment of that novel appeared in *Voltaire;* on January 7, 1880, Zola wrote the last line.[55] (In 1878, between *L'Assommoir* and *Nana,* Zola published a volume in the Rougon-Macquart series, titled *Une page d'amour.*) Because Nana had appeared in the serialized *L'Assommoir* in the fall of 1876, Manet's painting (begun in October or November 1876) probably owes its title to Zola's creation.[56] It is then frequently argued that Zola could have been in turn inspired by Manet's canvas in the development of his novel.[57]

The scheme of Zola's *Nana* has been well studied. An attractive, poor, and uneducated *jeune femme du peuple* (lower-class young girl), both sensual to an unusual degree and tainted by her early environment and her genetic legacy of alcoholism, ripens into a monster-courtesan. Beneath the author's claim to objective historical reconstruction and commitment to uncompromising naturalism lay a legible ideological scheme: the construction of a *courtisane du peuple* (popular courtesan)[58] who would take vengeance on the classes oppressing her own and be undone by her own "appetite for luxury and easy pleasures."[59] The consensus of art historians in this matter is that Zola's *Nana* and Manet's *Nana* are not alike. For example, Beatrice Farwell has written, "Manet's *Nana* as a human statement has little in common with Zola's which is more symbolic and sermonizing than pleasurable";[60] and Françoise Cachin finds that unlike Zola's character, Manet's "Parisian cocotte has nothing truly fatal about her" and is "without bitter or tragic connotation."[61] My discussion of the two Nanas distinguishes between them in other ways.

The ideological differences between the two Nanas are clear and stark in chapter 5 of Zola's novel, which provides the closest subject parallel to Manet's picture. It includes the scene in which Nana, the actress, performs her toilette in the company of the Comte Muffat, the prince, and the Marquis de Chouard. This episode is a particularly forceful example of Zola's recurrent association of deviant female sexuality, male sexual desire, and extreme male discomfort, analyzed by Chantal Bertrand-Jennings: "The bestial character of the sexualized woman is also made tangible by the mixture of dirtiness, suffocating closeness, stifling heat and nausea which marks all the locations of feminine intimacy in *Nana.*"[62] Even before the comte arrives at Nana's loge, his uneasiness predicts his pursuit of a sexualized destination: he is "stricken with a malaise, a repugnance mixed with fear" and inconvenienced by "suffocation by the thick, overheated air dragging along with it a strong odor." But he is deeply – inexorably – attracted to the secrets of the theater: "hurrying his step, almost running, carried away by the frisson of this fiery opening onto a world he didn't know." Once inside the loge, the discomfort accelerates, and he experiences a "feeling of vertigo" and "afraid of swooning in this odor, increased tenfold under the low ceiling, he sits down."[63]

Throughout the scene, Nana is minimally clothed ("tranquilly, while carrying out her toilette, she walks by in her pantaloons in the midst of the men"), at ease and consistently congenial, sharing champagne and chatting with her guests. She executed her toilette with concentration and diligence but did not forget that she had company: "Wanting to show her responsiveness to a compliment paid to her by the old man, she acted by swinging her hips." Muffat's reaction, which unfolds in distinct stages, is the narrative and ideological justification for the toilette scene. Initially shocked and confused by the novelty and extremity of what he has witnessed, he resolves to resist because Nana is evil; and the evil is clear to him because it differs from the intimacies of his marriage: "He who had never seen the Countess Muffat put on her garters was witnessing the intimate details of a woman's toilette . . . in the midst of this odor so strong and so sweet. . . . But he promised himself to be strong. He knew how to defend himself."[64] Intense confusion follows his departure from the loge, experienced as strange physical sensations, mostly unfamiliar smells. Finally, at the end of the chapter, he realizes that he is conquered. This is Zola's characterization of his capitulation to Nana:

> So, Muffat, his head on fire, wanted to go home on foot. All internal combat had ceased. A flood-tide of the new life was drowning forty years' worth of ideas and beliefs. While he was walking along the boulevards, the rumbling of the last carriages deafened him with the name of Nana, the gaslamps made Nana's nudities, her supple arms, her white shoulders dance before his eyes; and he felt as though she possessed him, he would have renounced everything, sold everything to have her for one hour, this very evening. It was his youth that was awakening finally, a greedy adolescent puberty, suddenly burning in his Catholic coldness and in the dignity of his maturity.[65]

In giving in to the *idea* of giving in to Nana, Muffat has given in to himself, to his repressed sexual desire, but – as Zola troubles to specify – he has also yielded on fronts other than personal: economic, religious, and social standards are all threatened by desire for this woman, are all to be transgressed. This chapter is a showcase for Nana's simultaneously good-natured and vulgar use of her body – the corporeal signature of the sexual deviant. Clothing and makeup here serve only to define Nana's sensuality, a quality that is converted into a potentially destructive force, but only *when she is desired* by a prosperous and repressed man.

Zola's treatment of the courtesan's toilette in the dressing room is quite unlike that in Manet's *Nana.* In Zola, uniting a partially dressed working-class woman with a formally dressed aristocratic gentleman heightens his sexual edginess and vulnerability to passion, which are barely contained by the mandatory facade of respectability, while intensifying Nana's unworldliness and unhampered sensuality. She had no need to plot or scheme to undermine his control, his grip on his principles. Zola seeks to maximize the difference between the woman and the man through the transformation of Nana into an evil force, one that will damage or even destroy the whole social and economic order by unsettling its topmost stratum, personified here by the comte. Nana is an effective personification of corruption in the novel, because, owing to Zola's choice of unorthodox origins for her, she is a double menace, by virtue of her class *and* her sex. (Nana's ruination at the end of the story helps to defuse the threat posed by woman and by the people.) Small wonder that some of Zola's critics drew his face on cabaret walls (as in fig. 38, at the Cabaret du Père Lunette, which shows him staring at a naked idealized woman in Dr. Frankenstein fashion), because his novel reduces a specific fictional character to an essence – to the principle of sex as corruption.

Though many of the discrepancies between Manet's and Zola's *Nana*s are rooted in differences between their respective media, there are also different objectives in play. Compared to the attentiveness and discomfort of Comte Muffat in Nana's dressing room, for example, the composure and lack of interest of Manet's gentleman make the painted Nana's toilette much more public than its analogue in Zola's scene, because it is directed toward an outside spectator. In Zola the rituals of costume and makeup stimulate Nana's visitors. Manet appears instead to emphasize the routine quality of their bargain or, at least, the restraint shown by the man under the circumstances. The meeting in Manet's picture is something of a nonencounter because it is shown as an unexceptional moment of established intimacy and familiarity.

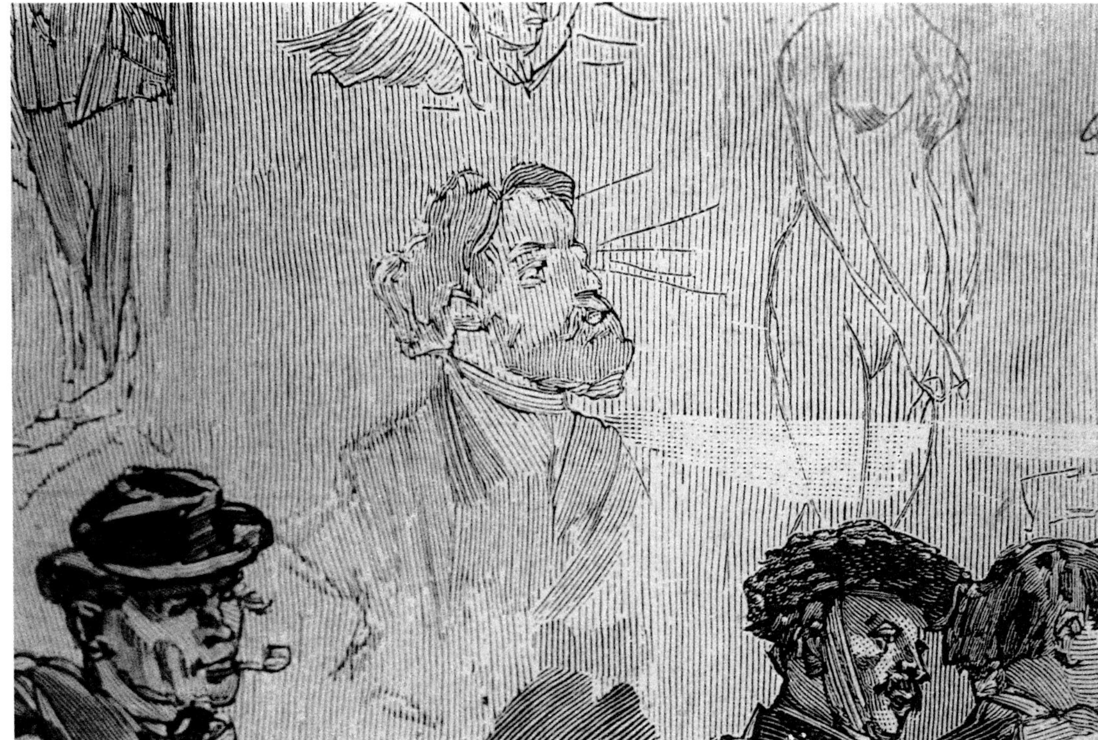

38.
P. de Haenen, *Disappearing Paris – The Cabaret of "Papa Eyeglasses,"* 1889, detail, Cabinet des Estampes, Bibliothèque Nationale, Paris.

The vanity of both figures is emphasized by Manet, whereas vanity is not a central theme in Zola's text. Manet's version of the observed toilette works almost as a critique of the substance of Zola's, but it is undertaken at Nana's expense; for, while the man's vanity is passive, hers is active. His mere complacency makes him vain, but her vanity comprises the elaborate makeup procedure, the luxurious undergarments, and her eye contact with the viewer. But vanity, as we have learned, is *the* powerful weapon of the courtesan. In de-emphasizing the man's agitation in this context, Manet's image might agree with the following nineteenth-century definition of *courtisane*, which establishes the Veblenesque link between buyer and courtesan: "The rakes take on the payment of courtesans, not for the pleasure that they find with them, but out of a sentiment of ridiculous vanity."[66]

An obvious difference between the two is that resplendence of costume is not part of Nana's minimal and theatrical toilette in Zola's loge scene, whereas the sumptuousness and physical effects of undergarments are indispensable to the meaning of all three of Manet's *Nanas*. For Zola, flesh, rather than what covers it, is the instrument of domination. Zola almost always succumbs to this allegorized use of the exposed body, and it is only when the scene shifts away from Nana the beginner, in a sexualized private space, to Nana at the zenith of her powers, in a public arena, that Zola's clothing imagery falls more closely in line with Manet's.

Pierre-Auguste Renoir, however, in his handling of a similar subject, relies less on the link between the courtesan and her costume. He, too, became involved in devising an imagery of Nana in the late 1870s, providing illustrations for a deluxe illustrated edition of *L'Assommoir* published in 1878.[67] In the drawing that served as the basis for one of his four illustrations for the book (fig. 39), he depicts a scene in which the young Nana invades the sidewalk in the company of five girlfriends. "All six, arm in arm, taking up the whole width of the street, were going along dressed in light colors with ribbons tied around their bare heads."[68] Evidently Re-

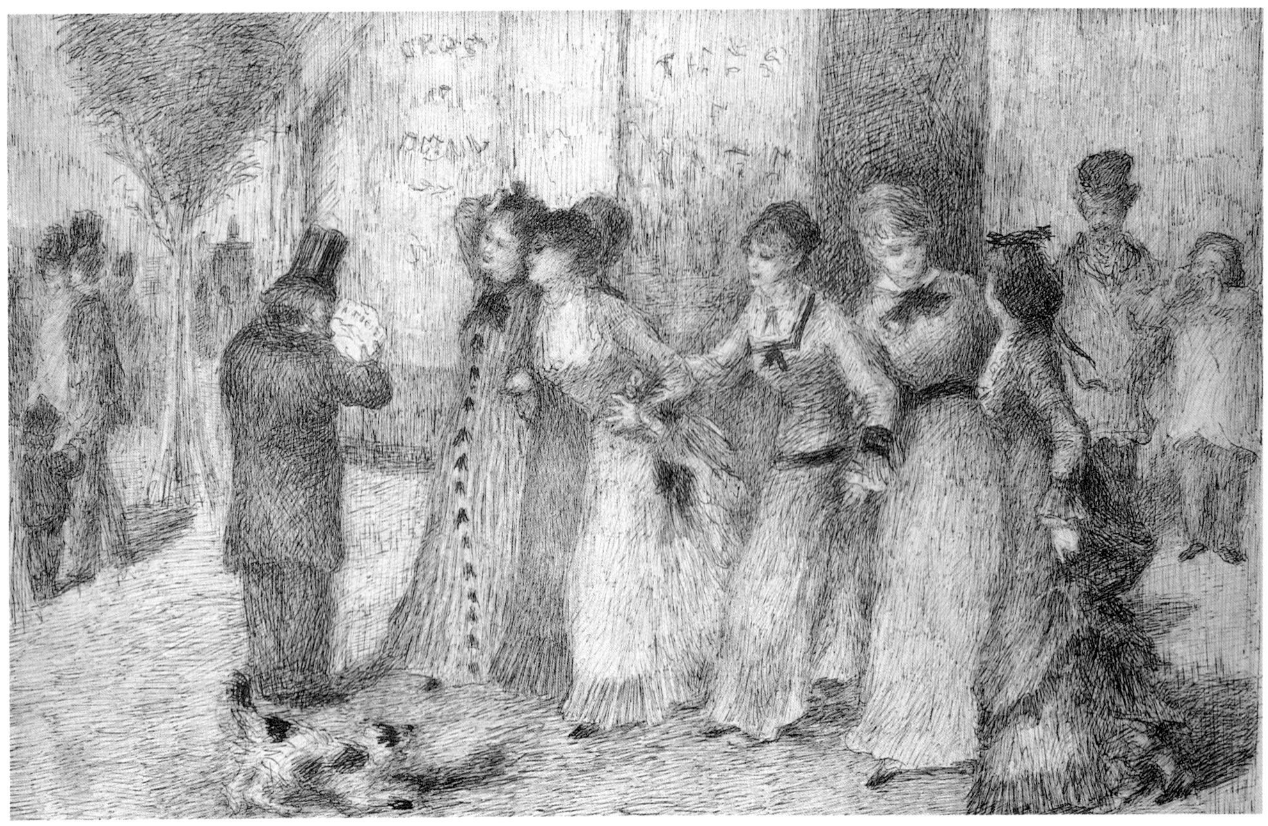

39. Pierre-Auguste Renoir, *L'Assommoir*, 1877–78, pen and brown ink with black chalk, Joseph and Helen Regenstein Foundation, restricted gift 1986.420, Art Institute of Chicago.

noir was drawn to a passage in which Nana dresses in an attractive, slightly transgressive (that is, hatless) outfit as a way of being noticed by men. The workers at right watch the chain of young women, but the newspaper reader in top hat at left appears unmoved by the nearby expanse of energetic, audacious, and girlish pulchritude.

In chapter 11 of Zola's *Nana*, her distinctive costume for the Grand Prix at Longchamp becomes the unmistakable sign of her worldly success. It is the weapon that attracts and reconquers men and makes honest women envious, even admiring. Nana's attire at the race track is not only extravagant and new but in its details departs from the high fashion of the 1860s. Zola projects the enticing modes of the late 1870s onto the Second Empire: "The little bodice and the tunic of blue silk clinging to the body, caught up in back in an enormous puff, sketched out her thighs in an impudent way in those days of ballooning skirts." She dominates the occasion by her controlled presentation, with each detail of costume in careful focus. Not wishing for a moment to enhance Nana's advantage, the respectable women refused to bet on the horse named Nana: "It would certainly not do to work toward the success of a dirty slut who was outdoing all of them with her four white horses, her servants, her air of being able to swallow up the whole world."[69]

Throughout the chapter, Zola endows Nana's toilette with social and sexual power. Even though at the start of the event Nana lacked the conventional indicator of prominence (entry to the weighing-in enclosure, granted only to ladies), she was able nonetheless to consolidate her dominance of the event – "there was finally only one crowd, only one hubbub, and it surrounded her landau." She could in the end confidently denounce the other women using quality of dress as a metaphor for power: "Insofar as the entry to the weighing-in area was absolutely forbidden to 'filles,' Nana was making sharp remarks about the respectable women whom she found dowdy with silly faces."[70] The courtesan took her revenge on the honest world through fashion.

Manet and Zola (and Renoir, too) use showy clothing to identify the courtesan, and both Manet and Zola employ it to fix Nana's social and economic hegemony. Unlike Zola's imagery, however, Manet's picture collapses the distinction between public and private displays of fashion. Furthermore, Manet's is firmly planted in the world of the late 1870s. Manet has dressed his Nana in the undergarments of the day – her blue corset was quite up-to-date[71] – and has therefore revised the Second Empire model upon which he undoubtedly relied. But Zola displays sentiment that is thoroughly representative of the late 1870s insofar as his *Nana* unquestionably registers neoregulationist panic about the dangers of working-class female sexuality.[72] Manet's painting also offers a strong image of female sexual force, but one that, à la Baudelaire, secures Nana's power in what is visually immanent – her adornment – rather than in a narration of her interactions with men.[73]

Repeating the question posed earlier: What was it about Manet's *Nana* that placed it outside the bounds of Salon propriety in 1877? We can now see that the painting brought several already inflammatory motifs into combustible contact: that Zola's courtesan wore a luxurious and indecorous toilette in the company of a blasé upper-class lover apparently exceeded the limits of tolerance at the time. This reading is supported by the discussion of the critical reaction to *Nana* and her surrogates that follows.

After the display at Giroux in 1877, *Nana* was never again exhibited during Manet's lifetime (its next showing was not until 1895), so the multiple references to *Nana* in reviews of Manet's 1880 one-person exhibition at *La Vie Moderne* gallery appear puzzling at first. It turns out, however, that *Nana* had two de facto surrogates on display in the 1880 show and had thereby a vicarious second outing in the art world of Paris. The stand-ins for *Nana* were the oil *Before the Mirror*, done in 1876–77 (fig. 40), and a pastel done in 1879, known as *The Toilette* or *The Garter* (fig. 41).[74] These two pictures are not connected to *Nana* in any conventional, programmatic sense – they are not parts of a series – but because the two pieces shown in 1880 were also understood to be connected to or referred to explicitly as *Nana*,[75] I have chosen to reunite the three works in this analysis of critical reactions to *Nana*.

In spite of the commotion evidently caused by *Nana* when it appeared in Giroux's grand boulevard shop window, few reviews of the painting appeared in the press in 1877.[76] In the sparse criticism, commentators seized upon Nana's costume – what one critic called her "très grand négligé"[77] – as the key to the picture and to what Manet was saying about the courtesan. *Le Tintamarre* ran a four-stanza poem, "Nana," dedicated to Edouard Manet and signed "Un impressionniste." Generally banal and moralizing, it does claim that this is Zola's Nana and contains this rather interesting second stanza:

> More than nude, in her chemise, the fille shows off
> Her feminine charms and the flesh that tempts. There she is.
> She has donned her satin corset and is getting dressed
> Calmly, near a man, who has come there to see her.[78]

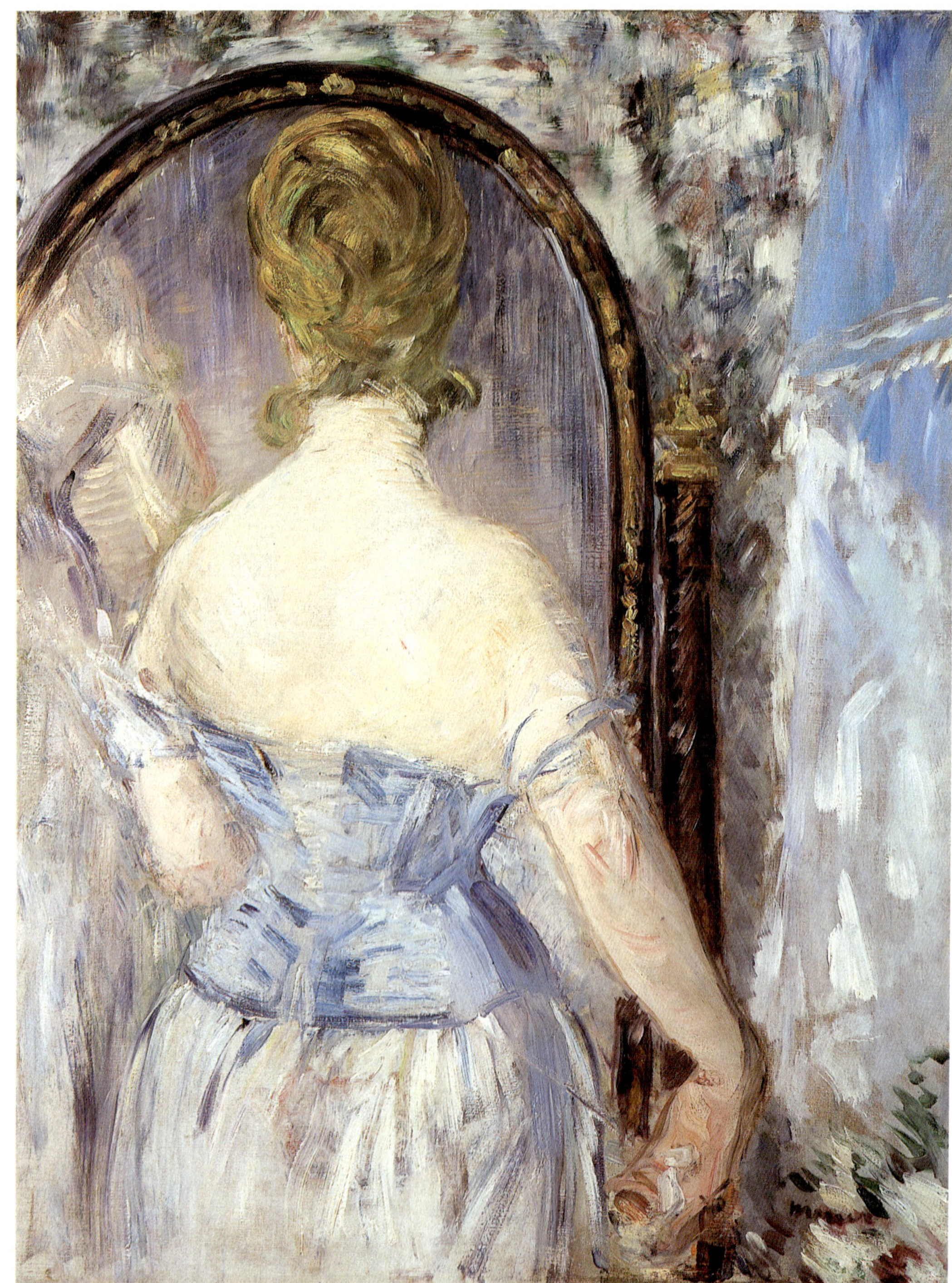

40.
Edouard Manet, *Before the Mirror,* 1876, oil on canvas, Justin K. Thannhauser Collection, Solomon R. Guggenheim Museum, New York.

The phrase "plus que nue" is an important one. Why is a woman who reveals no more flesh than she would in evening dress called "more than nude"? It is Nana's audacious yet calm appearance in the secret cloak of expensive and beautiful lingerie before a spectator that is immodest and that automatically denotes her impurity. Never mind that Manet has fastidiously arranged Nana's arms so that the upper part of her breasts is not shown; wearing a chemise and corset is a brazen "display of her charms" nevertheless. (Indeed, wearing expensive lingerie in front of an observer and possessing feminine charms are synonymous in the mind of this critic.) Because of this shamelessness, the "impressionniste" writes, "she is sordid one hundred times over, this whore."[79]

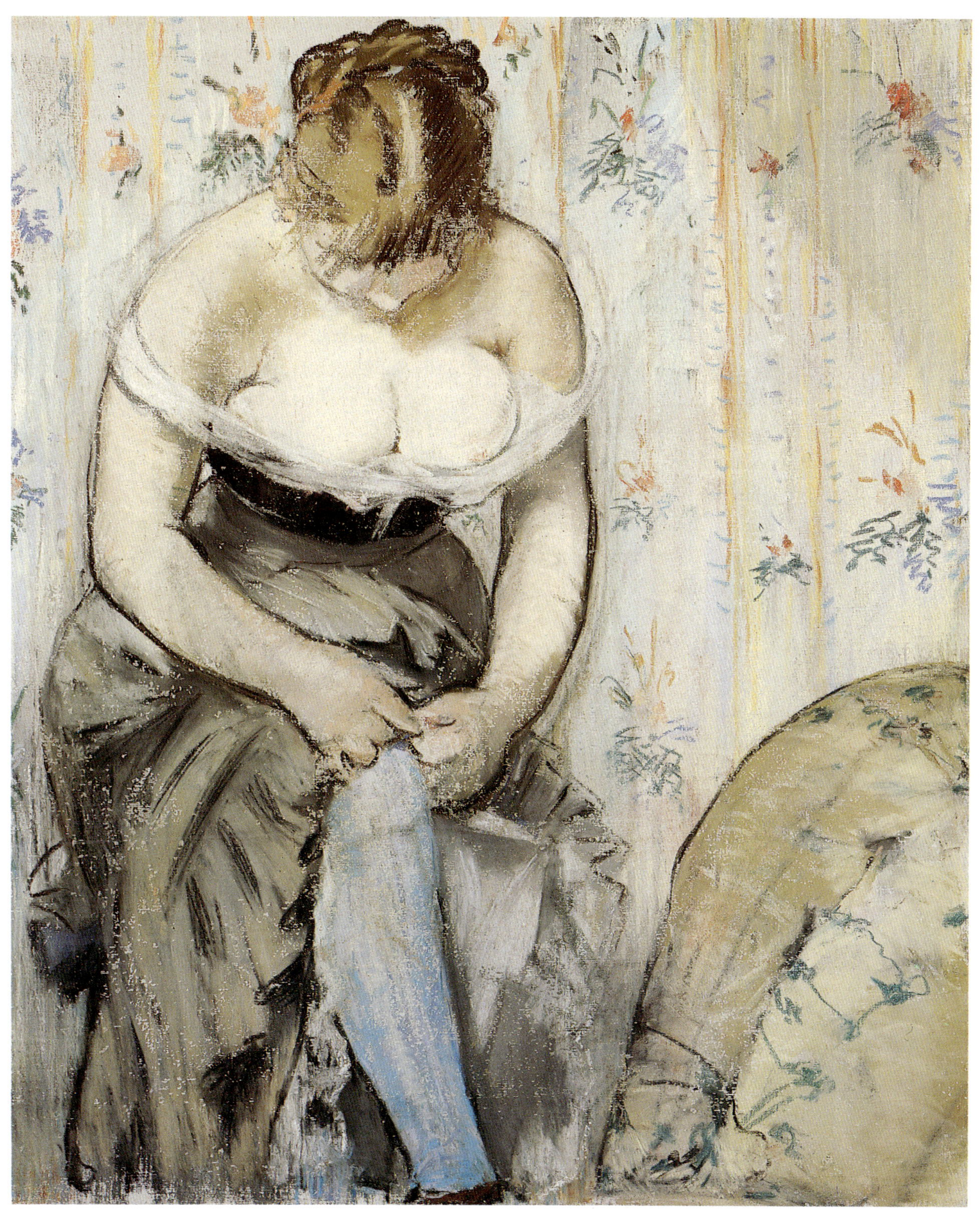

41.
Edouard Manet,
The Garter (originally known as *The Toilette*), 1878, pastel on canvas,
Ordrupgaard Collection, Copenhagen.

J.-K. Huysmans's long review, which appeared in a Belgian journal, also focused upon the importance of Nana's unselfconscious appearance in luxurious undergarments. In Huysmans's judgment Manet accomplishes a goal unattained heretofore: he painted "la fille."[80] Moreover, one of the ways to capture this type was by rendering with considerable expertise the "luxury of glimpsed underclothing."[81] Huysmans's analysis culminates in this aphoristic observation: "The aristocracy of vice is recognizable today by its lingerie." But rather than merely congratulating Manet on his mastery of the most luxurious and decadent forms of women's underwear, Huysmans acknowledges the artist's use of them as both a sign of success and an instrument of domination. Apropos of the former, he writes in part, "Silk is the trademark of courtesans who rent out at a high price," and regarding the latter: "Nana has thus arrived, in the painter's tableau, at the summit envied by her equals, and, intelligent and corrupted as she is, she has understood that the elegance of stockings and slippers . . . is, to be sure, one of the most precious adjuvants that *filles de joie* have invented for overthrowing men."[82] Given our familiarity with Huysmans's viewpoints, we are prepared for his way of interpreting the predatory Nana's sexual dominion: we are likewise unsurprised by his lack of interest in Nana's economic dependence upon the man.

Before the Mirror (fig. 40), shown in the 1880 exhibition and probably painted at the same time as *Nana*,[83] repeats many of the same ingredients. It shows the back of a blond woman in a sky-blue corset and white chemise before a looking glass. It is not a rehearsal of *Nana* because the three crucial items – gentleman, application of makeup, and confrontation with the viewer – are missing. Nevertheless, when it was shown in 1880, two commentators, both of whom were familiar with Manet and his work, assumed that this was Nana. Paul Alexis called it the audacious *Nana before the Mirror*,[84] and, to conclude an article on *La Vie Moderne* show, Gustave Goetschy wrote (wanting to assure his readers that Manet captures bodily likenesses): "Everyone belongs to his race, his time and his milieu; society women are really society women, *filles* are real *filles*, rascals are real rascals, and Nana is really Nana!"[85] The painting was not called *Nana* in the catalog, so it was certainly the familiar blue and white undergarments in the context of vanity that prompted this identification. But the pastel called *The Toilette* or *The Garter* (fig. 41) appears to have been the most noticed and provoking item in Manet's 1880 show.[86]

Paul Sébillot, quoted in *L'Artiste*, saw Nana in the pastel: "We must not forget one work which attracts the public the most through the risqué quality of its subject: it is a woman *en déshabillé* who is attaching her garters, and whose position leaning forward reveals what the poets call 'the opulent treasures of the bodice.' This is pure naturalism, something like a page of *Nana*."[87] Even though he means Zola's *Nana*, which was still running in feuilleton during Manet's exhibition, the reference to any Nana will do as an indication of the potent association between an indecorous modern toilette and the courtesan.

In an angry commentary on the pastel, Bertall was not reminded of Nana but connected the aggressive address of a frontal body shaped by an extreme corset – the support for what David Kunzle has called the "new sartorial aesthetic of the [18]70s"[88] – with filth and sordidness in this otherwise unaggressive image. "What is that horrible woman coming here to do, turned as she is shamelessly towards the public, pulling up her blue sock above which are arranged sordid linen surmounted by a corset barely holding back a ghastly chest, whose tortured and repugnant folds overflow in the direction of the spectator? Why?"[89]

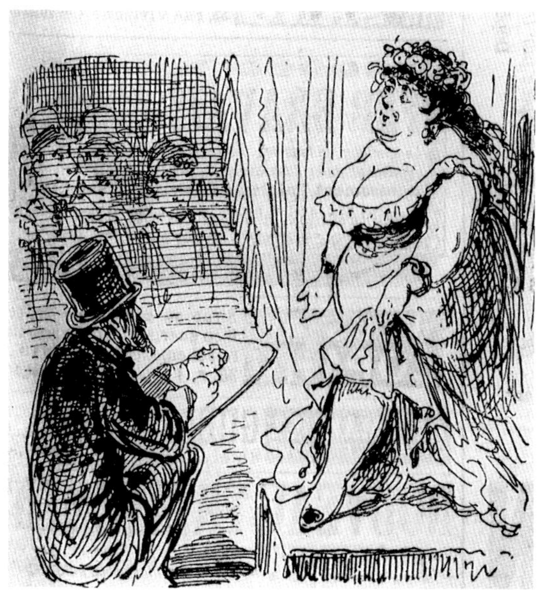

42.
"M. Manet Studying Beautiful Nature," *Le Charivari*, April 25, 1880.

The anonymous review of the show published by *Le Temps* praised the exhibition, especially the pastels, but found one of them unspeakable: "In this seductive genre there are choice morcels. I am not speaking of the *Toilette* of this coarse *fille* leaning over and pulling up a stocking of white silk."[90] Again, then, an abrupt dismissal of an otherwise modest picture whose only departure from the standard iconography of woman at her toilette is the expansive and compressed bosom. A caricature of the work was published in *Le Charivari* at the time of *La Vie Moderne* exhibition (fig. 42). The cartoon, entitled "M. Manet Studying Beautiful Nature," connects the extremity of exposed breasts to vulgarity and ugliness as did the remarks of Bertall and Sébillot, by mocking any connection between this toilette and decorous feminine beauty.[91]

Unsurprisingly, *The Toilette* was the only work in Manet's private show that Huysmans found worth mentioning in his account of the 1880 art season. The consistency of his enthusiasms is apparent. He is delighted to find another prostitute: "One, *la Toilette*, representing a woman with a low neckline, the top of her chignon and the tip of her nose are gaining ground on her departing chest, while she attachs a garter to a blue stocking, fills one's nose with the prostitute who is dear to us. To envelope his people with the scent of fashion to which they belong, such has been one of M. Manet's most constant preoccupations."[92] Huysmans put his expert finger on the issue: Manet's use of a vulgar "fashion vignette" enabled commentators of all stripes to discover a prostitute without the aid of a suggestive picture title, because they all knew that a respectable woman would not have been shown that way.

Another instance of a painting that displays female sexuality as something of a threat, and that locates this threat specifically in the realm of modern fashion, is Henri Gervex's *Rolla* (fig. 43). Sent to the Salon of 1878, this painting was abruptly removed by a Beaux-Arts administrator more than a month before the opening of the exhibition because of its *inconvénance*, or impropriety, in spite of the fact that the twenty-six-year-old Gervex had been exempt from jury deliberations since winning a prize in 1874.[93] Like Manet's *Nana*, *Rolla*,

43.
Henri
Gervex,
Rolla,
1878, oil
on canvas,
Musée des
Beaux-Arts,
Bordeaux.

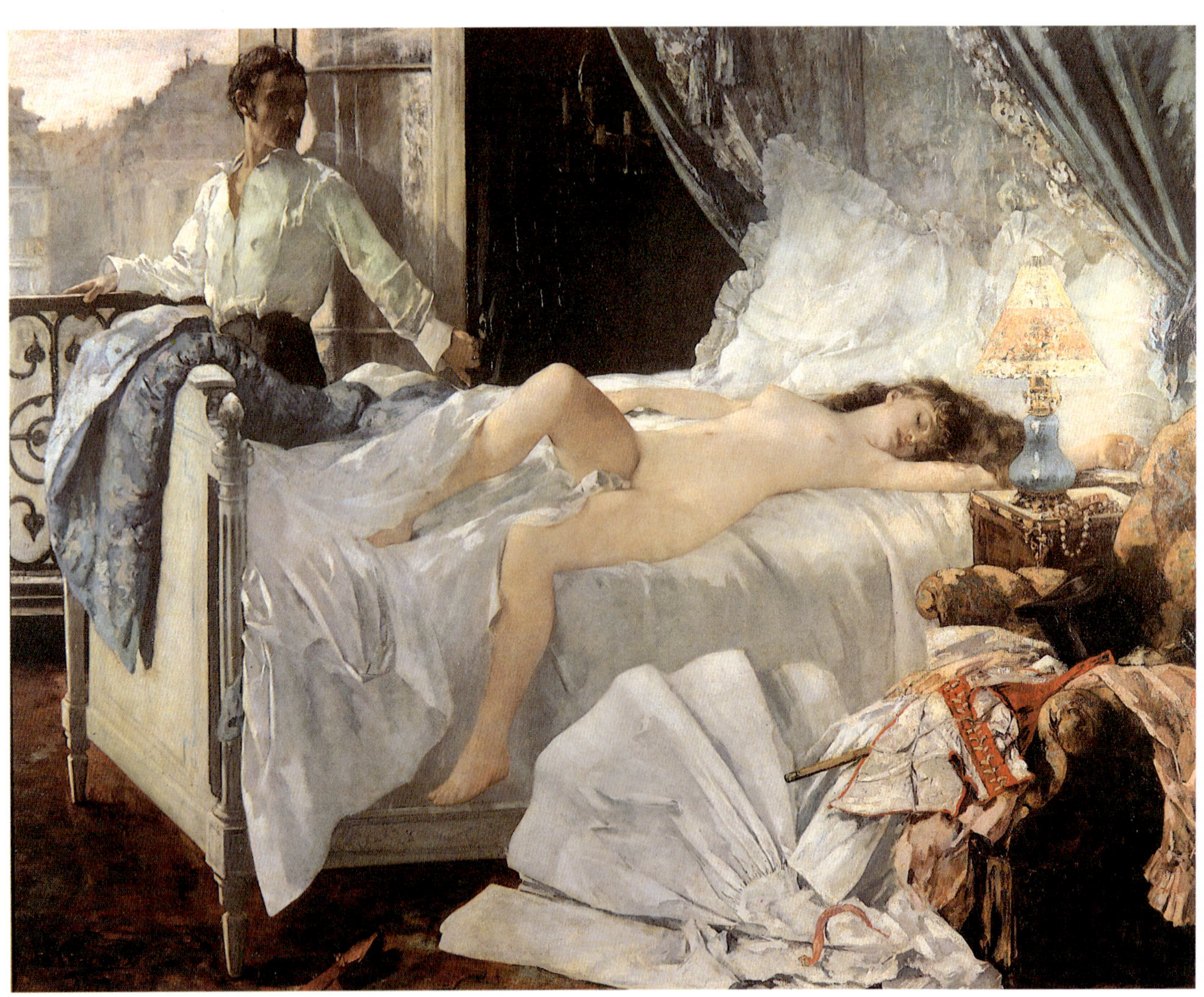

too, was exhibited in a commercial space. It was on view at M. M. Bague, a private dealer located at 41, rue de la Chaussée d'Antin (just northeast of the Opera), from April 20 to July 20. The three-month-long exhibition was well attended, and the society and art press had plenty to say in 1878 about Gervex's painting, in contrast to their relative silence about Manet's *Nana* the preceding year.

Gervex's painting had a lurid and well-known literary source: it was based on Alfred de Musset's poem "Rolla," published in 1833 and 1840.[94] The poem, a paradigm of July Monarchy romanticism, chronicles the disgrace that befalls Jacques Rolla, a son of the bourgeoisie, in the big city. The narrative of his decline – he squandered his fortune and committed suicide – is interleaved with lamentations over the moral and spiritual decadence of contemporary life. The nineteen-year-old Rolla becomes the "most debauched man" in Paris, "where vice is the cheapest, the oldest and the most fertile in the world."[95]

The poem tells a second story as well, that of Marie (or Maria or Marion), a pure young girl who becomes a degraded urban prostitute. Her story amplifies the poet's theme – a world in moral disarray – and provides the instrument of, and a sympathetic companion for, Rolla's climactic self-destruction. Musset is clear about his young prostitute's status: she was forced into a *prostitution de la misère* by economic circumstances ("what had debased her was, alas, poverty / And not love of gold"), and he frequently distinguishes her situation from that of the venal women of the courtesan rank ("Your loves are golden, lively and poetic; . . . you are not for sale at all"). He is also insistent about the tawdry circumstances in which the young woman had to practice her miserable profession ("the shameful curtains of that foul retreat," "in a hovel," "the walls of this gloomy and ramshackle room").[96]

The segments of the poem from which Gervex drew his story – and which were published in press reviews of the painting – are these:

> With a melancholy eye Rolla gazed on
> The beautiful Marion asleep in her wide bed;
> In spite of himself, an unnameable and diabolical horror
> Made him tremble to the bone.
> Marion had cost dearly. – To pay for his night
> He had spent his last coins.
> His friends knew it. And he, on arriving,
> Had taken their hand and given his word that
> In the morning no one would see him alive.
>
> . . . .
>
> When Rolla saw the sun appear on the roofs,
> He went and leaned out the window.
>
> . . . .
>
> Rolla turned to look at Marie.
> She felt exhausted, and had fallen asleep.
> And thus both fled the cruelties of fate,
> The child in sleep, and the man in death![97]

It was a moment of inaction, then, that Gervex chose to paint – that of weary repose for her and melancholic contemplation for Rolla, following the night of paid sex and just prior to his suicide.[98]

If we compare the room and its furnishings in Gervex's painting to the squalid interior described in Musset's poem, the discrepancies are apparent. Whether a hotel room or private bedroom, the space is well appointed with a Louis XVI bed and night table and a wall-mounted brass candelabrum with convex mirror. The pink and blue pastel scheme of the bed and its furnishings, the small glowing bedside gas lamp, and the discarded clothing contrast markedly with the brown, green, and yellow of the armchair and the rose-colored rug. The red of the corset and the discarded shoe are added spots of discordant color. The conflicting color systems – pale and cool, dark and warm – give an improvised if not sloppy look to the condition of the room in spite of the elegance of the prominent bed.

In Musset's poem, Rolla sees the sun rise over the rooftops while "the heavy carts were beginning to roll" and "a forlorn band of wandering singers murmured an ancient romance in the square."[99] Musset's phrases are images of Paris in the 1830s, and they do not tally with the city seen through the window in Gervex's painting. In it the morning light flows into the room from Haussmannized Paris. The stylized floral motifs of the iron balustrade and the mansarded buildings on the facing street are characteristic of those that had recently been built in the northwest part of the city. A critic for *L'Evénement* proposed that the setting of the painting might have been the boulevard des Italiens,[100] the most chic section of the newly prosperous and fashionable grands boulevards of the Right Bank, a *beau quartier* of Paris in the 1870s.

In his careful editing of Musset's story – his inclusion of the current, his exclusion of the old-fashioned – Gervex obviously updated it,[101] but in so doing he also changed its significance for Parisians of the late 1870s, perhaps unwittingly. Like its source, Gervex's *Rolla* tells a story about a debauched bourgeois and a prostitute. But the careful building of a recognizably modern Parisian context, inhabited by modern people and props, resulted in a picture that situated the overtly sexual content of its narrative as a contemporary issue. The explicit eroticism of the details of Gervex's picture comes into focus upon close inspection of the painting.

The repose of the nude young woman in the painting is languid, but studiously controlled and decorous in every detail. There is nothing to be discovered in the treatment of her skin, anatomy, or pose that differentiates her from the canonical nude of the period. Gervex's nude is little changed, in fact, from that classic of the genre, painted by one of his teachers in 1863, Alexandre Cabanel's *The Birth of Venus*.

The smooth surfaces of her pale flesh accord with Musset's description of the girl's skin:

> Is it on snow, or on a statue
> That this golden lamp, hanging in the shadow,
> Casts the blue shimmer of the swaying curtain?
> No, the snow is more pale, the marble less white.
> It is a child, sleeping.[102]

But Gervex's Marion is a young woman, not a child. She lies sleeping on her back with her arms in customized odalisque position: the turn of her head toward the viewer and the extension of her left arm back alongside her head set a viewer-oriented seductiveness even though her eyes are closed in sleep. The left leg falling over the edge of the bed is Gervex's only concession to nakedness, to the operations of a real body. It is the one element of the body that suggests unposed fatigue, although the leg is made weightless through its bent knee and floating foot. The right knee, primly raised and tilted, corrects any impression that this body departs from the Salon norm – especially since the bed sheets are gathered up strategically between her legs to the groin at the center of the canvas, a traditional compositional strategy that simultaneously announces and conceals the woman's genital area. The bed is rumpled, but the sheets and pillowcases are well made and impeccably clean, and the bedstead and curtains are in perfect repair. Disarray, yes, but nothing dirty.

Gervex attempted to give the face some specific features. It is not an abstracted mask: the nose and mouth are thick, the eyes, brows, and mouth bear appropriate traces of makeup, and the parted lips resemble a breathing mouth in slumber. Her long thick chestnut hair, with its gathering of curls about the forehead, also betrays the artist's concern to individualize and modernize the usual, unstyled, loosely flowing hair of the Salon nude.

The mustachioed Jacques Rolla is anchored to the far side of the room: he stands upright at the open window, with his right arm resting on the wrought iron balustrade and left hand grasping the frame of the open casement window. His wrinkled shirt is open at the neck and cuffs. (Perhaps we are to think that he engaged in the hurried coupling of the prior evening with his shirt on, but surely not with his trousers on. In either case, Gervex has given him a shirt to strike his pose. A naked male torso would, after all, have been out of the question in the context of Salon propriety.) He looks thoughtfully but without specific focus across the room, past the woman lying before him.[103] His detumescent condition is narrated by bed clothes: the serpentine mass of blue comforter with pointed tip hanging over the end of the bed overlaps Rolla's pelvic area, suggesting a colossal, flaccid phallus emanating from his trousers.

In the jumbled pile of clothing in the right foreground (fig. 44), we can distinguish an inside-out red corset lined in white, two garments – one white, one pink – beneath the corset, a rose garter, and a stiffened white petticoat on the floor. Again, still life works as sexual metaphor in the painting: an upside-down top hat lies atop the prostitute's underwear, and the sharp tip of a cane pokes out between the white garment and the corset. The scale and angle of the exposed cane even give the chair on which it rests a bodily presence, to the degree that the clothing enacts a surrogate intercourse in the foreground of the postcoital human scene. Marion's body is thus hemmed in by the phallus – limp at her right, erect at her left – and her body inclines toward the stiffened male sex in the chair, as do her stiffened petticoats from the floor. Furthermore, the layering of the pieces of clothing provides a startling sartorial chronology for their lovemaking: she was apparently out of her corset before he put down his hat.

Of the many critics assessing the *Rolla* scandal in the Parisian press in 1878, only two thought that technical incompetence or stylistic unorthodoxy was responsible for the decision to remove the painting from the Salon.[104] But even judgments ostensibly confined to matters of form also touched on the issue of morality.

Jacques Liber, writing for the short-lived *Paris-Plaisir*, was an avid supporter of the picture; he believed that the artist had been censored for his stylistic independence and originality, for trying "to get off the beaten track and get away from academic convention."[105] If Liber meant to refer to specific portions of the painting, it is hard to know which they might be – perhaps the arguably Manet-esque handling of the clothing in the lower right corner, the roughness and thickness of which differ somewhat from the otherwise thin glazes and smooth surfaces of the

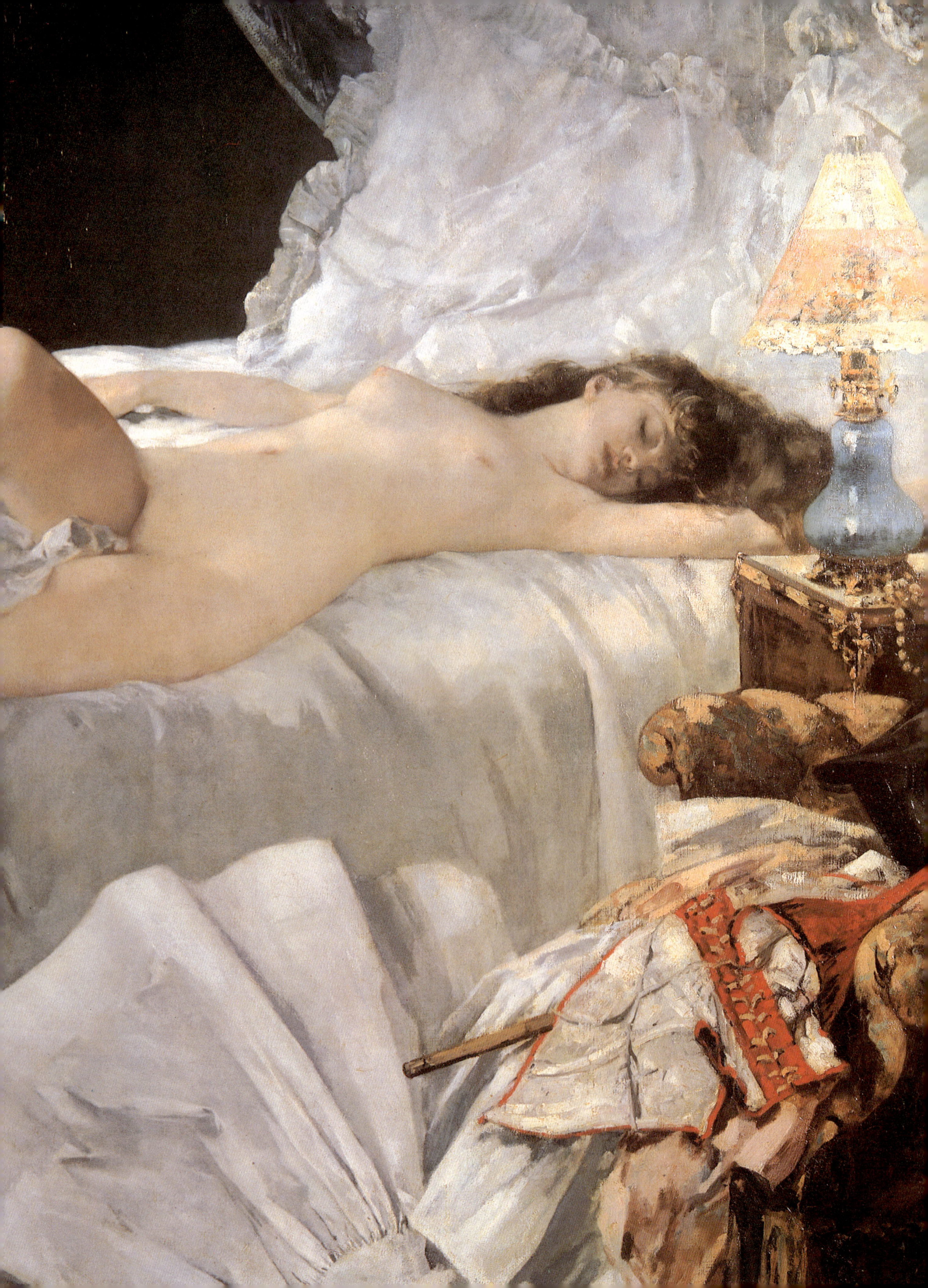

work. In spite of Liber's passionate defense of Gervex's painting style, one senses in his review that the critic was foregrounding an aesthetic defense even though he actually believed the key issue to be the moral hypocrisy of the Salon administration.[106]

At the other end of the spectrum of reaction to the technical qualities of the painting was the opinion of Alexandre Weill, addressed to the publisher of *L'Evénement.* The only critic who found the painting justifiably banished for its technical incompetence, he also wrote the most vituperative denunciation of it:

> Have you seen the painting of Rolla? Its ugliness is complete. [Jacques] Rolla has the look of a military officer's orderly preparing to give a liniment to an anemic creature with breasts narrowed down to the size of lemons, with spindly legs hacked up by a white sheet – more like a shroud than a sheet – and with a stifled and decayed holiness. There is nothing immoral in this painting, except perhaps the desire to pass the artist off as a victim of the administration. The administration did well to refuse it or not to admit it. The artist will do better another time.[107]

It is a clichéd invective that, in the lingua franca of negative criticism of figure painting, makes fun of the narrative and the laughable social types that result from an artist's lack of ability. He preemptively closed off debate on the morality of the picture's iconography by intentionally misreading the easily identified figures: the Parisian dandy is demoted to a batman, and the correctly voluptuous nude is found bleached, angular, and sour. Such a denunciation implies that the content of the picture was as crude as its form.

The balance of commentators defended Gervex's artistic competence, even excellence, and claimed that the nude was normal. Whether or not a specific critic found a "normal nude" synonymous with a "moral nude" depended explicitly, of course, on the critic's view of the health and morality of the contemporary genre of the nude[108] and implicitly on the critic's ideas about contemporary Parisian prostitution.

Exponents of the painting, angry about its removal from the Salon, found its exclusion absurd, because the permitted eroticism of the Salon seemed to promise a congenial environment for *Rolla,* as well as hypocritical, because the morality of most nudes of the late 1870s was dubious at best. Others agreed, and Balsamo, a writer for *Le Petit Parisien,* put it exceptionally well: "We find that the administration has proven . . . its exaggerated susceptibility to a ferocious form of false modesty. The young woman is nude, certainly. But if you are going to amuse yourself by proscribing academic studies from the Salon, every year there are nudities, each one more nude than the next."[109]

In a lengthy article in *Le Soleil,* Emile Cardon, a vigorous defender of *Rolla* against those responsible for its removal, focused on one "ordinary" 1878 Salon picture, *The Buffoon,* by Edouard-Théophile Blanchard (fig. 45), in order to reveal the cause of Gervex's offense. He sensibly found no difference between them on the scores of morality and decency; the contrast was one of furnishing: "To my mind, the serious difference between the two paintings is that the buffoon is dressed in a superb red velvet costume like those worn by the jesters of Francis I, while M. Gervex's Rolla is in shirtsleeves, and wears trousers bought chez Renard or Dussautoy."[110] Cardon is certainly *not* proposing that the contemporary clothing in *Rolla* was intolerable – there had been modern-life images in the Salon for decades – but rather that its use within the already provocative situation of the picture was the unacceptable move. Other critics probed the specifics of this unacceptability.

44.
Detail of
fig. 43.

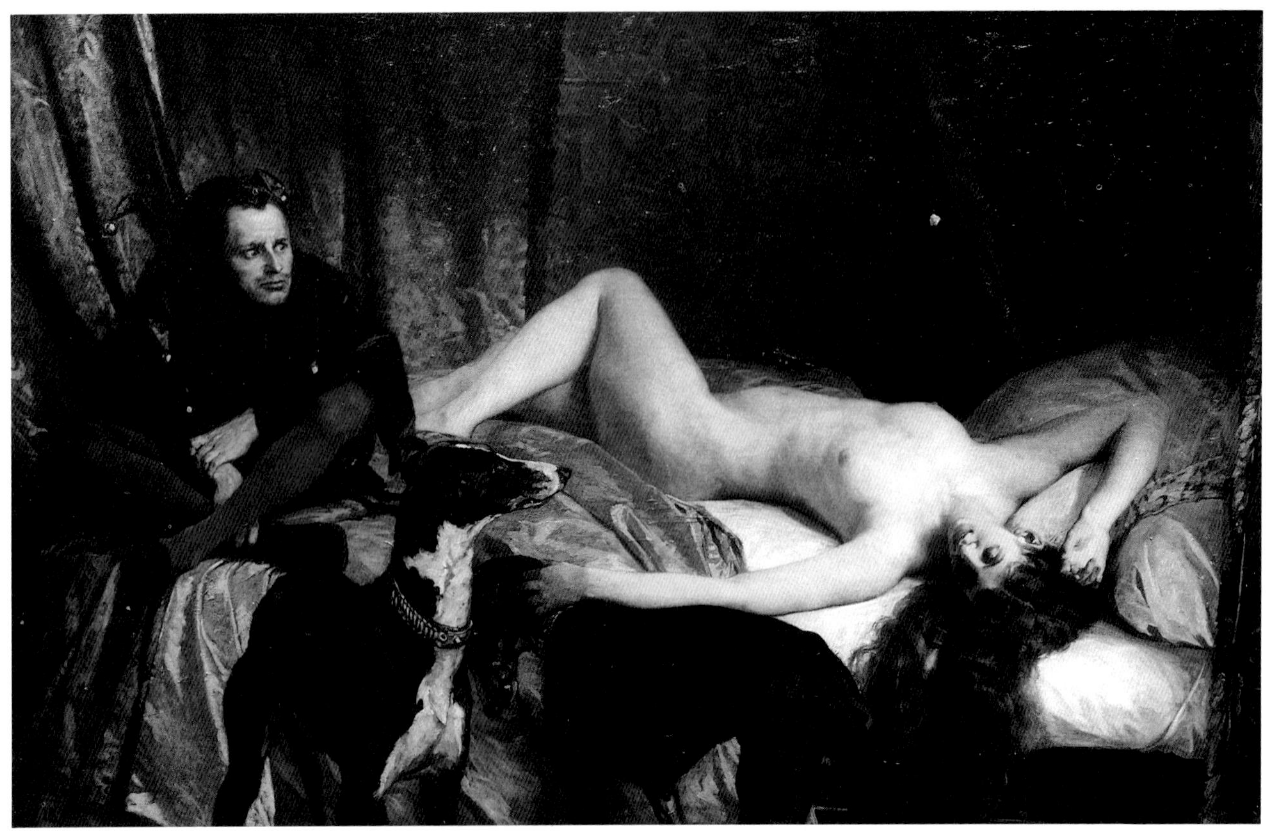

45.
Edouard-Théophile Blanchard, *The Buffoon*, 1878, oil on canvas, Musée d'Orsay, Paris.

The anonymous review published in *Le Temps*, for example, bears out what Cardon suspected. Even though the female figure was found consistent with other Salon nudes, the critic judged the painting immoral, because "here, the accessories have spoiled everthing. The nude is beautiful enough in itself to do without the spiciness that makes it suddenly indecent; near the bed a stack of petticoats is piled, coiffed ironically by a black top hat; the cane is not far away. Here is the anecdote that leaves a dirty stain, the goad to filthy laughter. That unfortunate hat, a garter mislaid amidst the skirts: here are the trappings of vaudeville in the middle of a serious drama."[111]

Roger Ballu, writing in *La Gazette des Beaux-Arts*, also objected to the ways in which the trivial and coarse baggage of a contemporary sexual episode jarred an otherwise standard Salon melodrama. The work was immoral in spite of its fine visual qualities, because it showed the "morning after an orgy of love."

> I would like to be able to admire without reservation this body of such delicate tone, of such fresh color in the midst of the whiteness of bed clothes: but, alas! the whiteness is that of an undone and ruffled bed, with falling sheets: all the hideous equipment of debauchery. The details are painted with a frank touch and a truth of color of incontestable merit, but do you know what these details are? A rose satin garter, a starched petticoat, fallen in the disorder on the floor; a man's hat, brutal and insolent, that sprawls on top of the dress precipitously thrown and rolled up in this armchair! Oh! to be young, to have the honor of being an artist, to sense one's own talent and make such a work! To make use of sacred art to excite wanton and lustful instincts, that is a profanation, and I say this from the bottom of my heart.[112]

In an energetic and intelligent defense of the painting in *Le Bien Public*, Paul Sébillot regarded the objects of Ballu's condemnation in a different light. His telling inventory of the canvas deserves to be quoted in full:

> On a bed that one barely sees beneath white, embroidered sheets and rich pillow cases, Marion sleeps completely nude, with one leg hanging outside the bed, the other bent in half; the petticoats, dresses and all the accessories of the modern toilette cover the upholstered armchair in their picturesque disorder; the necklace and jewels that play a role in the poem rest upon the richly ornamented night table which is almost concealed by the surrounding disorder, and amidst the whiteness and pale objects, a top hat makes its black mark.[113]

For Sébillot, it was not a question of the morality of the ensemble; modernity was the issue. The work is "conceived in a modern sentiment" and – in the painting's favor – "absolutely in keeping with the poem that provided its theme." "But," he continues, "modernity applied to certain subjects has not yet triumphed over academic prejudice: it is modernity that forced the painting's exclusion from the Salon." Like all the other experts, he found the figure of Marion delicate, calm, and chaste, but he called it a "modern nude," nevertheless, because of what accompanies it: "I know very well that there is a black hat in a corner: it appears that this black hat is the truly guilty party, it is the hat that makes a painting improper that would not have been without it. . . . One is accustomed to the nudity of the heros and heroines of antiquity: the modern nude shocks, but not our modesty, it shocks the prejudices of an academic educational system, and a painting becomes a danger to morals according to the nobility of its accessories."[114]

"Le Sphinx," columnist for *L'Evénement*, reached a similar if more lively conclusion about the removal:

> M. Gervex, although quite young, is hors concours; as a consequence, it was not for the jury to accept or refuse him. It is therefore only administrative modesty that was scandalized. Yes, the same administration that admits the brothels of M. Gérôme with so much enthusiasm, does not allow Rolla to live right in Paris, does not countenance his buying his clothes from a first-rate source, does not allow his shirt, wrinkled by the orgy, to come from a shop in vogue. No! no! Oh! our censors are riding herd on morality . . . or rather on moralities since they have two. . . . Put the young Marion on a velvet divan and give Rolla a turban to wear . . . [and] you will be admired by these men; your work will be hung in the exhibition, and without fear a young woman will take her mother to see your "entry." But a young girl upon a modern Parisian bed (although of the purest Louis XVI style), with a man in shirt sleeves, and, upon an armchair, a black top hat of the latest style, an umbrella (*bone Deus!*), a corset (horrors!), and on the carpet, a skirt! . . . Hurry up, young man, get all of this away from us![115]

Almost all of the critics were preoccupied by Marion's underwear, topped by the black hat and intersected by the cane (one called it an umbrella). Pertinent to our investigation of this pattern of absorption and to our understanding of Gervex's inclusion of the controversial still life is a story published in the 1920s about Edgar Degas, who assumed the role of sympathetic, paternal vanguardist by offering advice to the eager, up-and-coming pompier in 1878.[116]

Gervex recalled, more than forty years later, that the discarded clothing was Degas's idea. Ambroise Vollard reported that Degas had offered Gervex specific advice during a visit to the younger artist's studio to see the unfinished *Rolla:* "You have to make them understand that 'your' woman is not a model. Where's the dress she's taken off? Then put a corset on the floor!"[117] In an interview conducted by Félix Fénéon in 1920, Gervex recalled doing exactly what he was told: "It was at his instigation that I put this petticoat so stiffly starched, this corset, all this lingerie in the foreground."[118] Degas was apparently satisfied that his suggestion accounted for the painting's removal. His reaction to the event, according to Vollard, encouraged Gervex to see the cowardly inability of the Salon to exhibit an unavoidably contemporary, sexualized woman: "You see . . . they understood that she's a woman who takes her clothes off."[119]

We shall never know with certainty whether Gervex was disappointed or pleased by the events of the spring of 1878. Without registering his feelings about the rejection, he reported to Fénéon in 1920 that he knew it was the "modernity" of the discarded clothing that inculpated his otherwise inoffensive painting: "This nude would certainly have passed muster, illuminated as it is by the conflict of lamp light and the first rays of sun at dawn, but these feminine remains gave, it appears, a spice of modernity to the work that was too irritating."[120]

Gervex's memoirs, published in 1924, grant no credit to Degas for the offending motif and indicate that the action taken by the Salon administration came as a genuine surprise to the young artist. In these recollections, his official reminiscences about *Rolla,* he highlighted two aspects of the painting that he said he "counted upon" to guarantee its success: the technically demanding lighting (combining daylight and gaslight within the same canvas) and the still life – "several details that seemed audacious at the time, such as the crush of feminine lingerie near the bed, the way it is piled next to the nude flesh of the woman."[121] But he reported that all the "camarades" who visited his studio to see the picture prior to the Salon predicted only the greatest success for it. The comrades included Manet, Degas, Alfred Stevens, and Princess Mathilde Bonaparte – all of whom Gervex trusted, and none of whom found the picture immoral.

But hearsay evidence recorded years after the event and the self-serving memoirs of the seventy-two-year-old painter are not very reliable sources of information concerning Gervex's actual work on *Rolla* in 1878. After all, by the 1920s Gervex had become a rich member of the French Institute and was nearing the end of an exemplary career as a successful artist; he had been richly rewarded by the state and generously patronized by prosperous and loyal private clients. But a return to the painting itself can tell us something about his inclusion of the still life, for, even though the "dépouille féminine" was probably Degas's idea, it was the young Gervex who worked out the foreground jumble in detail (see fig. 44).

The choreography of the cane, hat, and corset in the chair shows that Gervex immersed, even lost himself, in the licentiousness of his subject, allowing small but apparently irresistible indecencies to intrude upon the field he had chosen in 1878, the terrain of the Salon nude.[122] Indeed the lack of restraint that Gervex showed in placing the cane in the still life points to the vulnerability of the genre of the nude, to the ways in which the nude was almost always a strained synthesis of opposing forces, perpetually in danger of slipping out of equilibrium as a consequence of even the smallest push in the direction of deviance. Gervex's handling of the discarded clothing shows that he had ideas about the sexuality of the prostitute – notions in wide circulation at the time – that worked against maintaining the chaste equipoise required of the acceptable Salon nude.

The high heel, the skirt, the impracticable bonnet, the corset, *and the general disregard of the wearer's comfort which is an obvious feature of all civilized women's apparel, are so many items of evidence to the effect that in the modern civilized scheme of life the woman is still, in theory, the economic dependent of the man – that, perhaps in a highly idealized sense, she is still the man's chattel.*
– *Thorstein Veblen,* A Theory of the Leisure Class

Aside from Degas and Gervex in their private discussions of work in progress on *Rolla,* only one writer mentioned the corset in the painting in 1878, and he, Le Sphinx, abruptly recanted, or was forced by his publisher to disavow, his initial enthusiasm only three days later. This omission from all other inventories of the foreground still life is somewhat surprising to a present-day viewer, because the corset is such a prominent and colorful *repoussoir.* It is hard to miss it and the adjoining starched *jupon* on one's way to the nude, because they establish such a deliberate obstacle to the nude's accessibility and put such an unavoidably modern and deviant twist upon her voluptuousness. Perhaps mentioning a corset by name would have exceeded the limits of normal art critical decency. But why could a petticoat and garter be named, and not a corset? The question, then, is why a corset – why this corset painted in this way – provoked discomfort and controversy at the time.

That Parisians of the 1870s were riveted to the significance of outer clothing is abundantly clear, but, as already suggested by our investigation of *Nana,* they were also interested in and knowledgeable about women's underwear. David Kunzle and Anne Hollander have shown that underwear – corsets and lingerie – even became an artistic cult in their own right,[123] but, then as now, a man's interest in ladies' lingerie was commingled with sexual feelings in ways that a woman's concern with female undergarments would probably not be.

Among the upper echelons of both sexes, the fascination with corsets was, first of all, a simple matter of fashion, based upon the foundation requirements of the dress styles of the decade, particularly from the mid-1870s on. That is, the shape of fashionable women's outer garments changed in such a way that everything depended on, and drew attention to, the sophisticated engineering that went on underneath. Beginning about 1874, for the first time in Parisian memory the natural contour of the female hip was defined, and thereby featured, by extending the fitted bodice downward over the hips. As worn by the most fashionable women, this extended bodice, called appropriately a *cuirasse bodice,* was very tight and formfitting. The fashion required the curve-molding and shaping work of a formidable and elaborate foundation garment, a special corset called a *corset-cuirasse.*[124]

By the end of the 1870s, beginning in 1877–78 and continuing until the reintroduction of the bustle around 1882–83, the lines of the bodice were extended to the knees, and eventually to the floor, describing a pencil or tubular silhouette. Extremely tight, almost preventing the wearer from walking, these dresses obviated the need for jupons and redoubled the need for a strong corset. This form-fitting dress style brought unprecedented attention to the body of the well-dressed woman, as well as creating interest in the corset, the substructure that made the styles not only popular but possible. These dresses, which molded the figure in front and around the hips, required complex undergarments, making it unthinkable to get along with a homemade article, as was commonplace in the 1860s. The widespread popularity of corsets gave the ready-to-wear underclothing industry a boost and caused a growing number of illustrations of these garments to appear in magazines of the 1870s.

But Gervex's Marion took her corset off. Irrespective of a corset's style and manufacture, removing one's stays had long been, iconographically, a symbol of female dishonor, of taking leave of social decencies. A woman shown next to her abandoned corset had abandoned morality. That her corset is represented inside out inflects that condition of surrender. It enforces the disarray of the situation and suggests the haste with which clothing was removed and discarded. It denotes the sexual impetuosity of the woman and hence her hypersexuality or deviance.

Gervex painstakingly showed the pattern of laces. This is another detail that implies the haste of their lovemaking, because the still-laced corset shows that Marion evidently got out of it the quick way, by releasing the clasps up the front (or perhaps Rolla did the job?) rather than going to the trouble of unlacing. It also shows, perhaps needless to say, that Jacques Rolla was not involved in the old erotic ritual of helping his lover unlace her corset, although the showy red exterior and plain white interior of Marion's corset are meant to be seen and appreciated on rather than off.

If we assume that Marion undid the undergarment herself, then the corset, in combination with the tranquil nude, suggests that her venting of sensual energy was voluntary and rather enthusiastic as well. The male viewer always welcomed the illusion of sexual enthusiasm or at least cooperation in a nude. The ideal nude did not have to convey (and could not have conveyed) the painting's complete erotic message. It was shifted to the surrounding emblems, that defensive armor so ostentatiously and carelessly laid aside. The body is automatically eroticized and rendered deviant by the abandoned corset. Another aspect of the shock in associating that body with that garment was that her perfect form (*pace* Alexandre Weill) does not appear to require molding. It was vital, however, to the impact of the painting that Marion's body be as it is: an agitated, alert, imperfect body might have suggested rape or at least a lack of cooperation, in which case the picture would have functioned altogether differently. Thus, the calm of the body vouchsafes the indelible impression of Marion's willingness, of her professional, prostitutional subordination to male desire, which she appears to have enjoyed. Paradoxically, Gervex's adherence to the conventions of the nude, at least with regard to the body, was a cause of the painting's removal. It in fact called attention to the contradictions usually masked by the nude.

The design and color of Marion's corset informed the astute observer at the same time that, unlike Nana, she was no "aristocrat of vice." Marion's corset is plainer and shorter than that worn in the 1880 cartoon "Bréda Street" (fig. 46), and its simplicity is a far cry from the stylishness and luxury of Nana's sky-blue satin corset-cuirasse. Marion's lacks lace decoration, is not made of comparably delicate and expensive fabric, and, judging from the limpness of it, is certainly not the cuirasse type then in fashion, lacking as it does the proper busk. (It was the busk that created the hard restraining surface that forced the breasts in and up to create a so-called pouter pigeon uplift and an exaggerated concavity at the waist.)[125]

Marion's corset appears to be a cheap ready-made one, bought in a *grand magasin,* and as such it exemplifies the general availability of relatively standardized, machine-made costume at the time. Brightly colored corsets were trendy items. Recent arrivals on the fashion market, they became common only in the late 1870s.

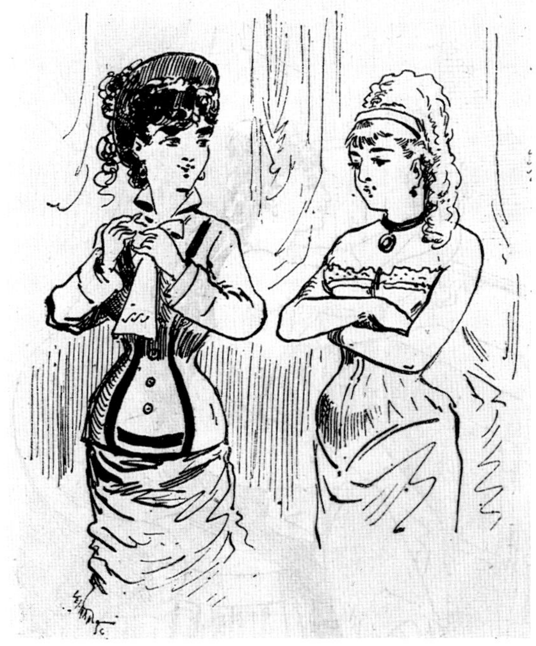

46. "Bréda Street," *La Vie Amusante*, 1878–79, and *Le Monde Comique*, 1880.

– *It looks like the little viscount left me because his noble parents didn't want him to have a mistress.*
– *You just need to get him to marry you. That would take care of everything.*

The elaborate corset series drawn by Henri de Montaut for *La Vie Parisienne* between 1874 and 1882 documents that fashionable, respectable women wore and were preoccupied by corsets.[126] Among young lower-class women, however, tight corsets were, to the male observer, a vivid sign of sexual willingness and therefore intemperance. A description of a group of underage prostitutes (between the ages of twelve and eighteen), soliciting customers just off the grands boulevards, tells us that they were "bothered by high-heeled boots that they were not accustomed to, hampered by corsets they had recently begun wearing."[127] So Marion's adoption of just such a foundation garment declared her departure from adolescent sexual innocence and announced that she cultivated and drew attention to her illicit sexuality.

Standing in front of Gervex's picture of a discarded, red corset men must have experienced a disorienting ambivalence that they would have been hard-pressed to put into words. In the spirit of Veblen's argument, the corset would have confirmed the viewer's power over women, because a corset concealed and transformed the female body into a pleasant, artifical shape and showed the woman's eagerness to bend her flesh in ways dictated by a male-dominated culture. But, as our analysis has already suggested, the removal of this token of obedience denoted the woman's flagrant rejection of the dominion of men, their fashion system, and their "morality." Without removing the armor of chastity, however, a woman could not respond to a man's sexual entreaties, nor, perhaps, to his fantasies of sexual mastery. And, as we have stressed elsewhere, those male fantasies underpinned the genre of the nude.[128]

From our familiarity with Marion's underclothing, we know quite a bit about her street clothing. Because her corset is not of the cuirasse type, it is doubtful that she could have been wearing one of the constricting and revealing tied-back dresses of tubular silhouette of the late 1870s. The full, starched petticoat that jars into view alongside the bed – in Gervex's words, "this petticoat so stiffly starched" – assures us that Marion was wearing a dress with a full skirt.[129] This interests us because, according to a variety of representations of women in street clothes, a woman in a tightly fitted dress could be respectable or an aristocrat of vice (that deter-

47. (l.) Eugène Giraud, *The Hall of Missteps*, from *Album Goupil: Salon de 1877*.

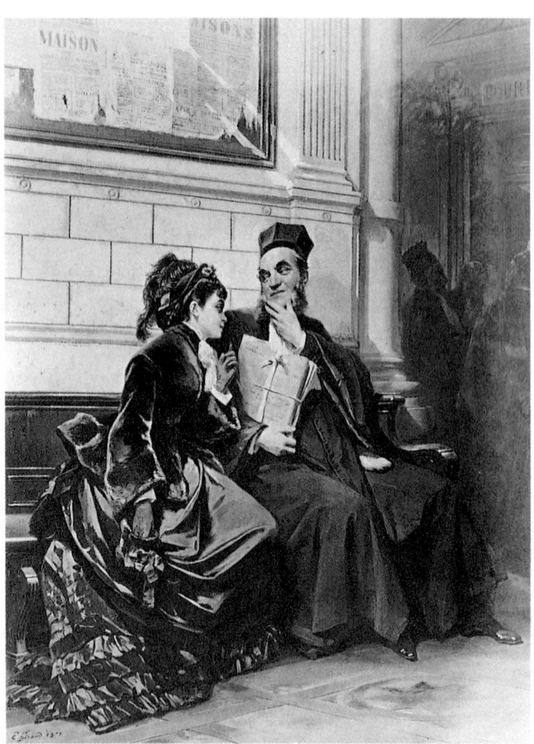

48. (r.) "These Women and the Exposition," *Petit Journal pour Rire*, 1878.

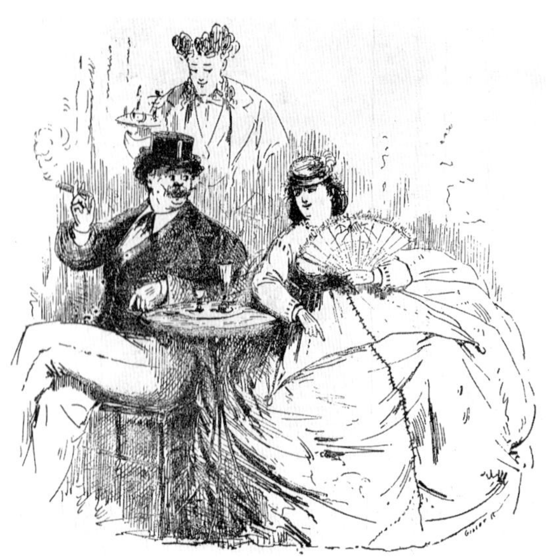

– That's all you're paying?
– That's all you're exposing?

mination depended on factors other than the cut of her costume), but the lower-class, public prostitute – registered or not – is regularly shown wearing full skirts, presumably old-fashioned or cast-off dresses.

In *The Hall of Missteps* of 1877, by Eugène Giraud (fig. 47) – one of the rare paintings of a modern prostitute to appear in the Salon about the time of *Rolla* – the fille leaning over intimately toward the official of the court is wearing a full skirt. The café prostitute shown in a *Petit Journal pour Rire* cartoon of 1878 (fig. 48) makes a pun on the "exposing" going on at the 1878 Exposition Universelle. She is shown in the fullest of skirts. Another example of this style of dress is in the "Scenes of Parisian Life" of 1879 (fig. 49), run by both *Le Monde Comique* and *La Vie Amusante*, in which the woman demands a wallet from her admirers.

The courtesan or demimondaine of 1878, unlike the lower-class prostitute, is invariably shown wearing the straight profile. All of the fashionably dressed demimondaines wear this style in the "Ridicule" (fig. 32). Manet's *Nana* wears no starched petticoat, and other well-turned-out women involved with men from classes considerably above their own (fig. 46, for example) are also shown wearing the pencil silhouette.

Marion's undergarments and our deductions about her street clothes refine our understanding of her status and way of operating as a prostitute in 1878. Unsurprisingly, given what we have learned of their sexual charge, corsets were worn by prostitutes at work in the living rooms of some brothels, but the combination of corset and petticoat was unheard of. We become more and more sure that Marion's dress allowed her to be read as a lower-class prostitute who worked independently of a maison de tolérance, out on the street, especially because there were no popular licensed brothels on the grands boulevards, where the painting is set.[150]

Policemen could not control the spread of sexualized street vice – they were particularly ineffective in the grands boulevards district – so young men like Jacques Rolla remained un-

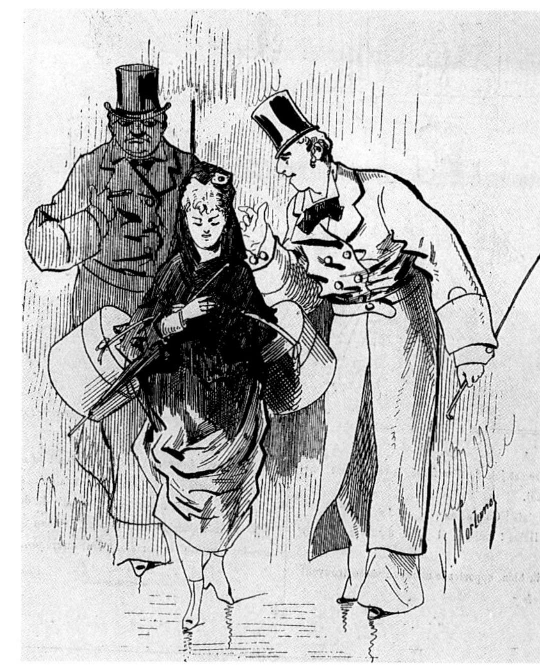

49. Victor Morland, "Scenes of Parisian Life," *La Vie Amusante*, 1878–79, and *Le Monde Comique*, 1879–80.

– *Miss! . . . miss! – listen to a heart that only seeks to cherish you!*
– *And a wallet!*
– *The devil! . . . there are costs.*

protected from the temptations and dangers of the swarm of sexually illicit women. It seems inevitable that this issue would have surfaced in the *Rolla* criticism because of the ways in which the picture represented a young *bourgeois célibataire* who had been with a prostitute apparently from *les classes populaires.* We have already seen that the painting's props emphasized the vivid physicality of Rolla's contamination; the top hat and cane enacted and symbolized the sexual capitulation of Rolla to the power of female deviance and the social capitulation of an upper-class man to a lower-class woman. Rolla drowned in the rising tide of sexual vice. The woman was the culprit, and Rolla her victim.

The Invasion of the Boulevard

No where are the Nymphs of the pavé to be seen in greater force than on the Boulevards. As soon as the lamps are lit, they come pouring through the passages and the adjacent rues, an uninterrupted stream, until past midnight. The passages Jouffroy, Opéra and Panoramas, on wet nights swarm with these women. At the cafés on the boulevards, particularly on the Blvd. Montmartre, the muster, always, is considerable. Only glance at one of these creatures, and you will be entrapped in a moment unless you have the moral courage to resist.

– *Anonymous,* Paris after Dark: Night Guide for Gentlemen

For it's no longer the night, the evening, from the lighting of the gas lamps until eleven o'clock *when the* hétaïres *operate. It is all day. It's not in the remote neighborhoods that they search out their booty, it's in the most lively center of Paris.*

Between noon and midnight, pass by the left sidewalk of the rue du faubourg Montmartre – you see that I'm precise – you will encounter twenty, thirty, forty girls, aged between fifteen and eighteen – there are some who are twelve! – hatless, décolletées, *provoking, shameless, brushing up against you with an elbow or a shoulder, barring your way while telling you things in the loudest voice that would make a rifleman blush. Where do they come from? It is easy to tell from their demeanour; they walk dragging their feet, bothered by high-heeled shoes that they are not accustomed to, encumbered by corsets that they haven't worn for long. It's the riffraff from the* bals de barrière *who, enticed by impunity, have descended upon Paris.*

– *Georges Grison,* Paris horrible et Paris original

Various commentators – including moralists, journalists, social observers, policemen, and writers of specialized guides to sex in Paris – reported that bands of predatory lower-class women regularly invaded the grands boulevards, which were the pride of fashionable Right Bank Paris. Statements about this occurrence (the majority written between the late 1860s and 1889) vary in tone and purpose but tend to fall into two general categories. One variety, like the first passage quoted above, lightheartedly celebrates a nocturnal movement of energetic and attractive young women who, when the gaslamps are lit, arrive on the boulevards to establish their beachheads in the neighboring cafés.[131] The other kind, exemplified by the second text, judgmentally describes a contamination of the neighborhood by a squalid street *racolage*, or solicitation, that lasts all day, practiced by grim, aggressive, and vulgar young girls.[132] But certain "facts" appear in reports of both kinds: particular sections of the boulevards brimmed with opportunities for sexual commerce (especially but not only in the evening), the girls came from "elsewhere," and the boulevard Montmartre (between rue Drouot and rue du Faubourg Montmartre) was the most thoroughly contaminated section of the grands boulevards. (See the map of the *quartier*, fig. 50.)

No doubt accounts of women aggressively putting themselves on sexual display in "the city of open living" are partly fantastic and partly documentary.[133] On the one hand, they describe the increasingly open forms of sexual commerce that characterized the urban erotic economy in the years following the Commune; on the other hand, they are also symptomatic of the chimerical neoregulationist disquiet about the takeover of the city by clandestine prostitutes.

Not surprisingly, the always-courtly travel guides of the period avoid any mention of street prostitution in their descriptions of the grands boulevards precincts. Karl Baedeker's 1874 description of this series of avenues is exemplary: "It constitutes a series of streets, of which the seven-part component, on the right bank of the Seine, today surpasses all the streets of the universe, as much by the richness of its architecture as by the luxury of its stores and the splendid decoration of its cafés."[134] According to Baedeker, the only differences that the tourist might

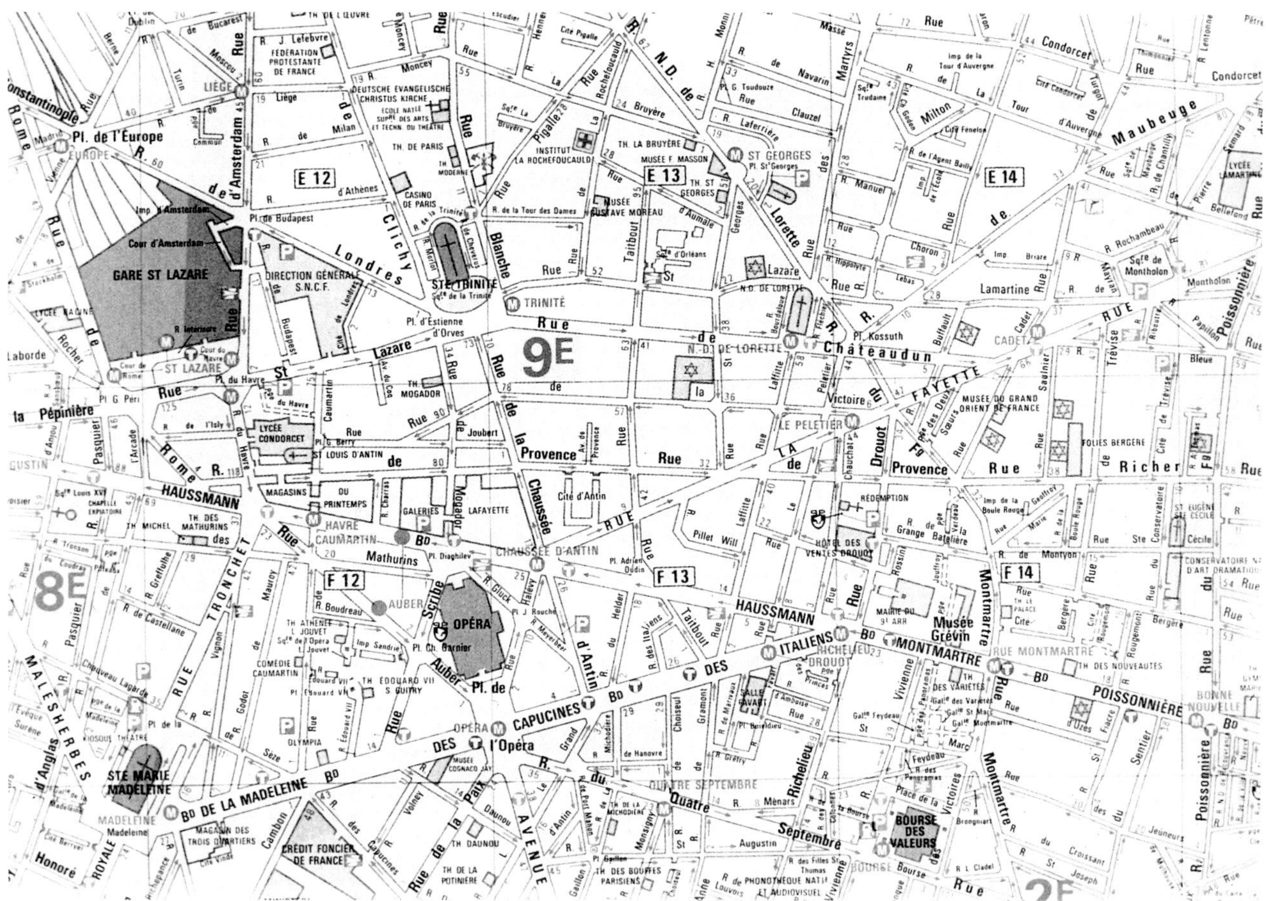

50. Map of Paris, 9th arrondissement, from *Michelin Atlas, Paris par arrondissements*, no. 15, 1st ed., 1989.

experience between day and night on these streets were those of relative comfort, ease of circulation, and visual opportunity:

> The most convenient time for this promenade is the morning, between 9 AM and noon, when the crowd is not yet too dense. Later, between 2 and 6 PM, and in the evening between 8 and 11 PM, there is such a crowd, especially between the Madeleine and the boulevard de Sebastopol, that it is no longer possible to examine at one's leisure the buildings, the stores, etc. Nevertheless you repeat this promenade in the evening, when hundreds of thousands of gaslamps transform night into day, and you can also see the interior of all the beautiful stores, thanks to the brilliant lighting system most have adopted.[135]

Baedeker's geographically precise recommendations give the city a discursive form that follows the canons of many such tourist aids. It is strictly pavement, architecture, *éclairage* (lighting), stores, and cafés. (It is as though the Paris that really mattered would survive a neutron bomb explosion.) The contemporaneous social texture of the city is not part of the account beyond a passing mention of the *foule* (crowd). This tactful and respectable text summons up a lively spectacle but, in keeping with the tastes and sensitivities of Baedeker's probable readers, constructs a city whose features do not seem to exist in a historical or social context.[136]

Certain Impressionists saw this glamourous quarter of the city through a Baedeker-like mythologizing lens. Claude Monet's well-known *Boulevard des Capucines* of 1873–74 (now in the Nelson-Atkins Museum, Kansas City), for example, depicts an especially chic section of the grands boulevards in terms that parallel guidebook discourse, by turning urban social incident into a homogenized, blurred field of pure vision. Monet's painting uses a high, nonparticipatory point of view from which all foliage, architecture, and traffic blend together in the same wintry atmospheric haze. Like Baedeker's text, the picture presents the terrain as merely an engaging spectacle.[137]

Although Claude Monet kept his distance from the foule down on the streets and sidewalks, many artists of the period, like the commentators encountered at the opening of this chapter, represented the subject of the "invasion" of the boulevard by morally dubious women. The verbal imagery of this invasion and occupation, whether admiring or disparaging, dealt with the unending attempts of these sex workers to attract the interest of men, usually while walking the streets. The visual imagery of invasion also had its orthodoxies: the installation of the marauding women in cafés dominated the interest of virtually all artists working on the theme, as will be apparent from the examples that follow. The prevailing image of boulevard prostitutes was that of women occupying tables at cafés (either sitting or standing nearby) while drinking and sometimes smoking.

The only exception to this general rule was in the specialized world of book illustration. Alfred Richard Kemplen helped illustrate a deluxe version of Zola's *L'Assommoir*, published in 1878.[138] Kemplen's portrayal of Gervaise's desperate (and unsuccessful) attempt to earn money as a street-walking prostitute (fig. 51) is the only picture of ambulatory racolage made during this period. The ineffectiveness of Gervaise's attempt to "hook" the passerby is underscored by the text that accompanied the illustration.[139]

The caricaturists who sold their work to the urbane illustrated papers tirelessly drew pictures of the solitary invader who settled in a café to attract men. No other motive is ever attributed to her presence there. In "Parisian Fantasies" of 1878–79 (fig. 52), for example, the waiter cooperates by helping the calculating woman settle in a favorable spot for solicitation. Interested men are already lining up in the background. In "On the Boulevard" of 1875–76 (fig. 53), Edward Ancourt's joke about the parasitic café woman turns upon the parallel between the opening of the hunting season and her inability to hold off her quotidian hunt for men. The unladylike confidence and angle of her sitting position – her devil-may-care air as she leans back in the chair – reinforces what the caption, the cocktail on the table, and the cigarette in her mouth have already fixed: this woman is not respectable.

During this period smoking was regarded as a daring habit for women, a sign of their worldliness and fast living. *The Return after Two Years in the City* (fig. 54), J. E. Buland's country-versus-city *Salon* picture of 1881, clearly conveys this message. Smoking cigarettes showed that the country girl had taken on questionable city ways, much to the perplexity of her rustic family. Such behavior was no guarantee that a woman was for sale, but the habit did suggest an inclination toward transgressive behavior. Nor, apparently, did respectable women take strong drink in public, especially during the 1870s, when civic consternation about drunkenness was at its peak in France. Indeed it was only during the decade that followed the Commune that public abuse of alcohol was seen as a code phrase for working-class irrationality and as a violation of law.[140] Public drunkenness was associated principally with excesses of male behavior, but, according to Susanna Barrows, "females who did imbibe strong beverages courted social ruin and most often sank into those two spheres of the underworld: crime and prostitution."[141]

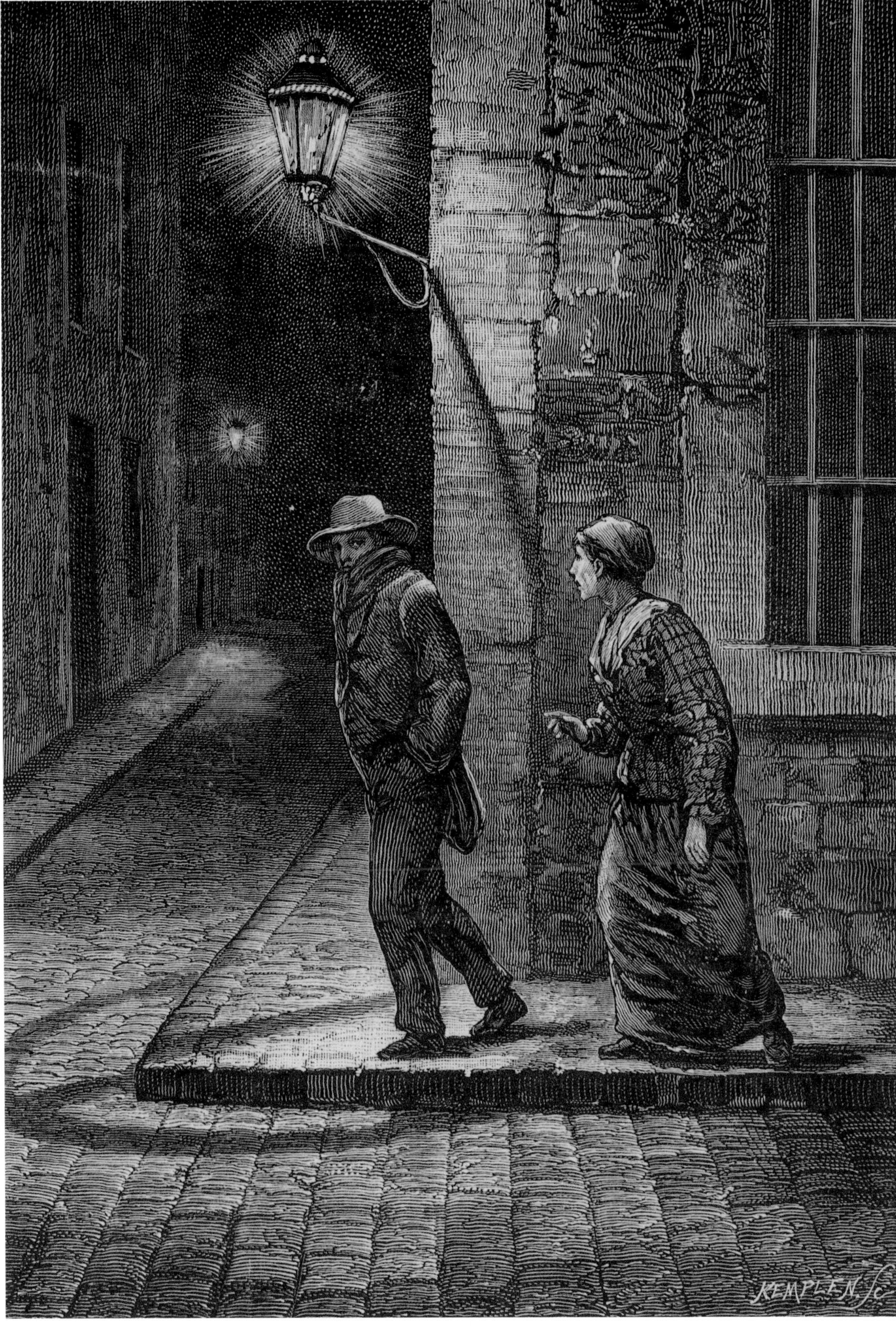

51. Alfred Richard Kemplen, "'Sir, please listen' . . . The man gave her a side glance and went on, whistling even louder," illustration for Emile Zola, *L'Assommoir*, 1878, restricted gift of Mrs. Robert S. Hartman, 1987.198, Art Institute of Chicago.

52. (l.) Gillot, “Parisian Fantasies,” *Le Monde Comique*, 1878–79.

53. (r.) Edward Ancourt, “On the Boulevard,” *Le Monde Comique*, 1875–76.

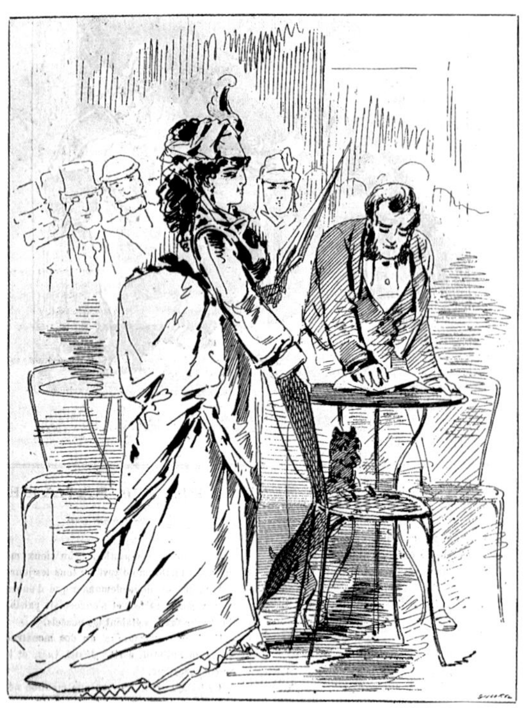

– Here, glue yourself right there. It's a good spot.

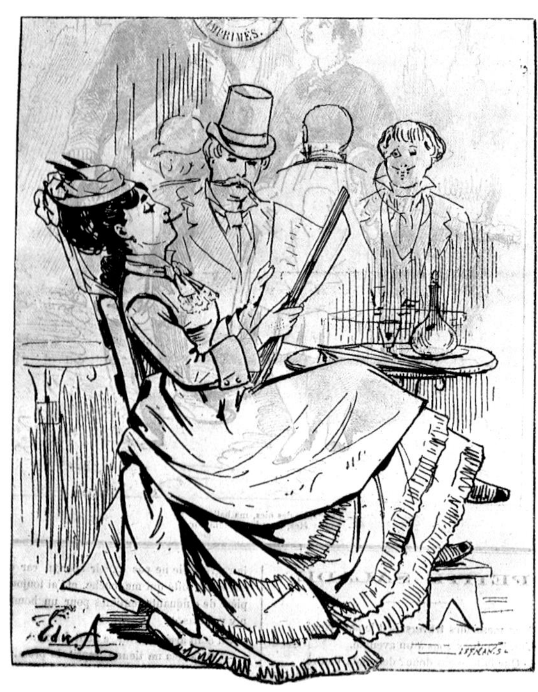

– “Hunting season opens the 29th . . .” Goodness! if I had to wait until then . . .

54. (l.) Jean Emile Buland, *Return after Two Years in the City*, from *Salon catalogue illustré*, 1881.

55. (r.) Paul Hadol, “Evening Spider,” *Le Monde Comique*, 1875–76.

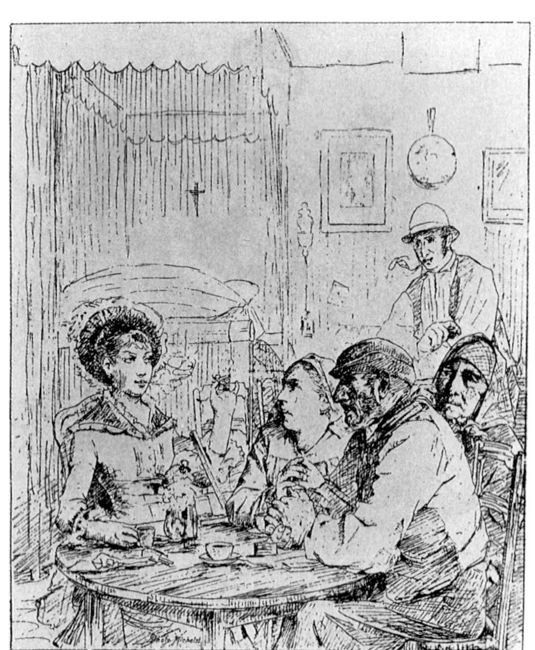

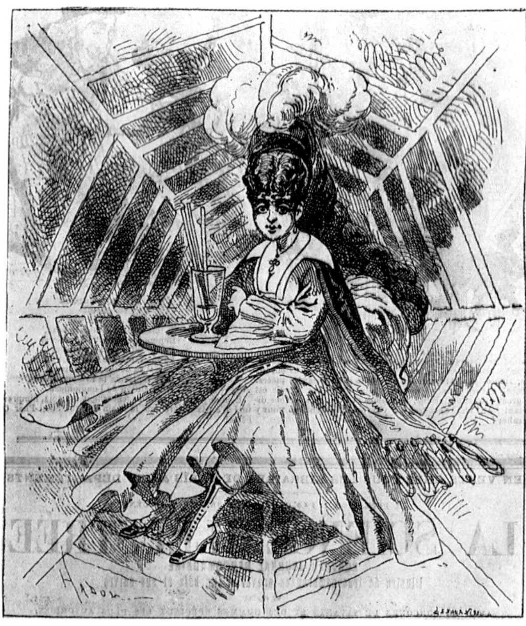

– Five o'clock! The absinthe hour. Penelope has spread out her web.

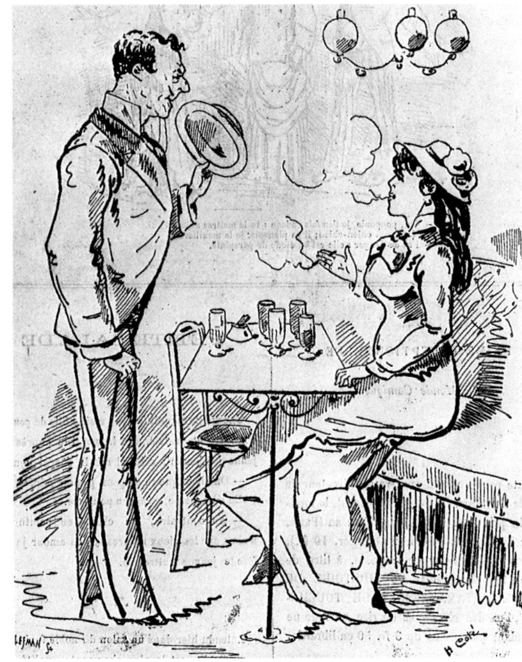

56.
Hippolyte Coté, "Paris Sketch," *Le Monde Comique,* 1879–80.

– *Late again, baron. I was drinking while I waited.*
– *What an effort it was to escape, my dear! My wife, my mother-in-law wanted me to accompany them.*
– *What blood-suckers those women are!! Finally, I have you, my big one. What are you offering me?*

Many journalistic pictures of café women (an expression of moral disapprobation during the period) consuming alcohol suggested that their moral and social status was quite low. Hadol's ingenious "Evening Spider" of 1875–76 (fig. 55) overtly links a solitary, web-dwelling aperitif drinker to sexual ensnarement. A slight variation on the same theme appears in H. Coté's "Paris Sketch" of 1879–80 (fig. 56). The unaccompanied woman has worked her way through five drinks while waiting for her detained "baron." The joke in the last line of dialogue centers on her gusto for strong drink. This picture also works off the common assumption that a boulevard café was *the* appropriate rendezvous spot for illicit lovers from different social orbits.

For the image makers of the avant-garde – in whose pictures indeterminacy was becoming something of a trademark – a woman seated on her own in a café was not necessarily identifiable as an "urban slut."[142] Manet's *The Plum* of 1877–78 (fig. 57) is such a case of descriptive imprecision. The conventional traits of "the café woman" are disarmed by Manet. While she is solitary and seemingly down-and-out, she is not working on any seduction; nor is she eating her brandy-soaked plum. Moreover, she has not even lit her cigarette. The image is vintage Manet. It includes all the ingredients of the usual social coding for "the indecent café woman," but here the codes are muffled and brought to a stalemate, though certainly not refused. The painting does not escape agreement with the dominant ideology of the immoral, solitary woman in a café, but neither does it actively contribute to the reinforcement and dissemination of these ideas.

Manet's picture is semantically open-ended by comparison to Hadol's café spider (fig. 55) *and* relative to Degas's presentation of a solitary café visitor in his pastel-enhanced monotype *Woman in a Café* of 1877 (private collection, New York). The fresh-faced young woman in pink of Manet's *The Plum* appears positively chaste compared to the very painted figure in Degas's

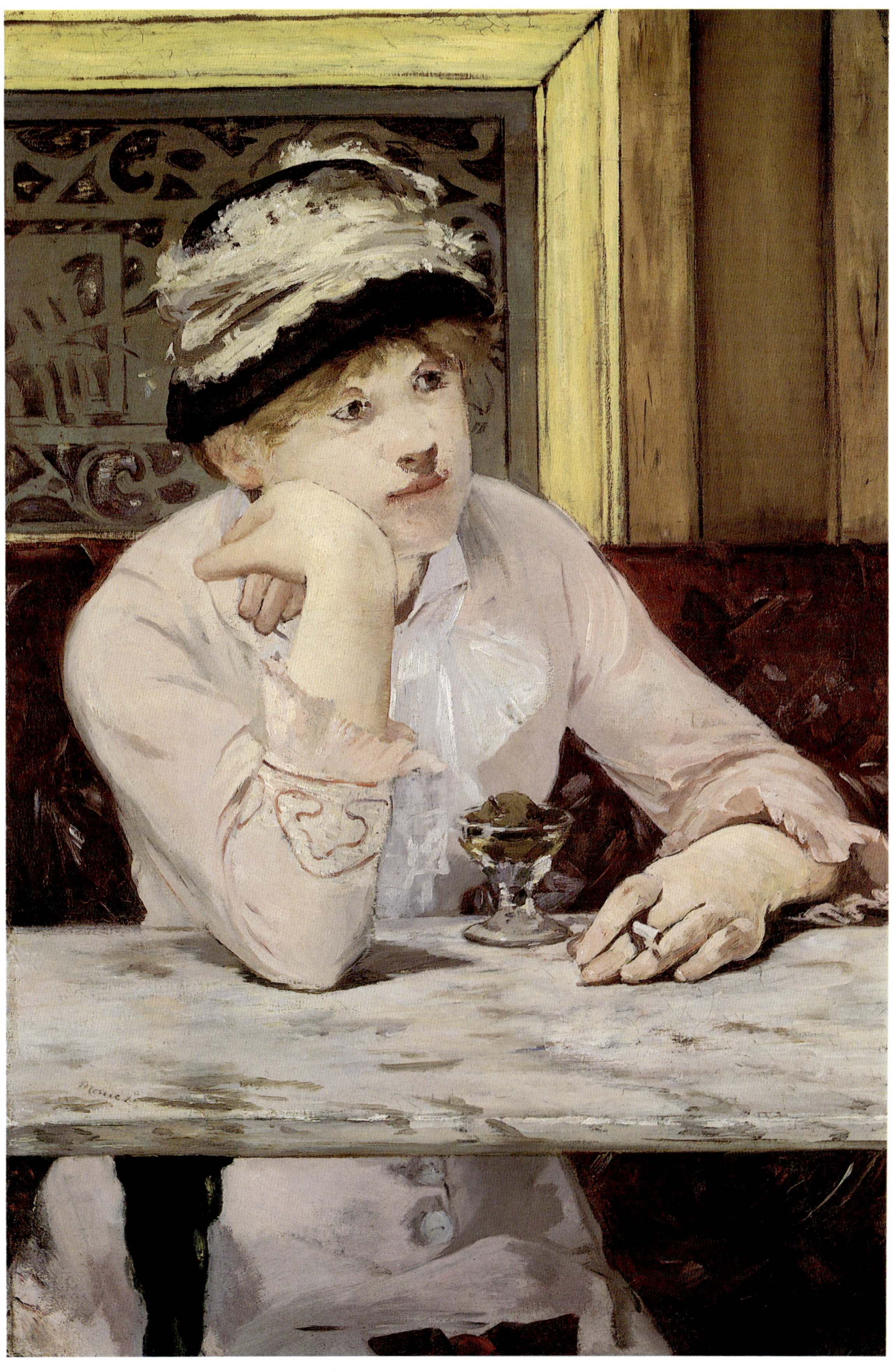

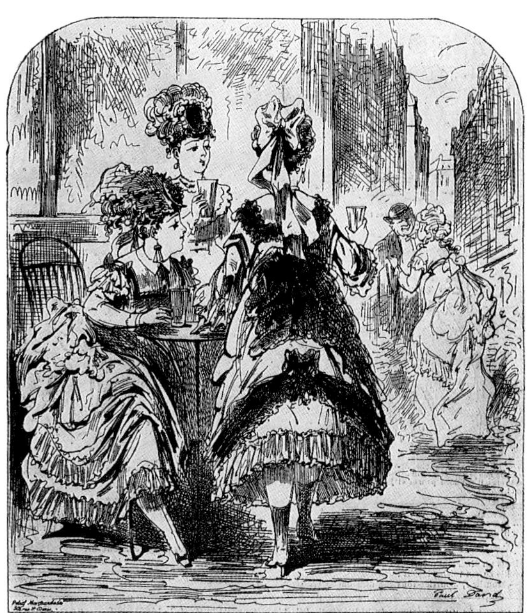

– *Pauline would have a beer with us. Call her.*
– *Can't you leave her alone! She's tending to her "affairs."*

58. (l.) Paul David, "Boulevard Women," *Le Monde Comique,* 1874–75.

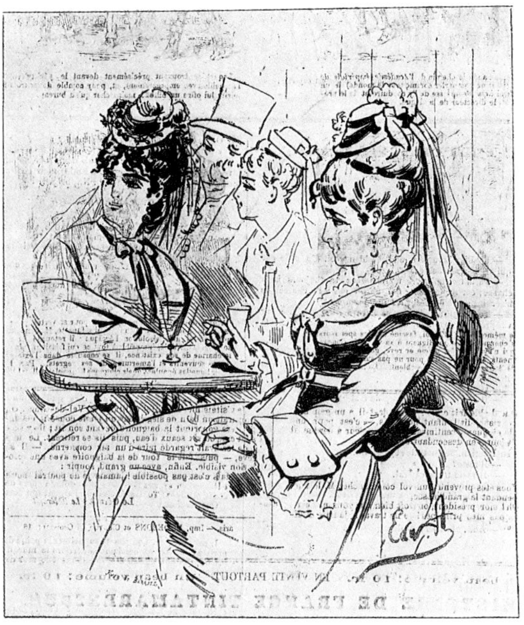

– *Men! . . . They say that we run after them!*
– *Not so often!!!*

59. (r.) Edward Ancourt, "On the Boulevard," *Le Monde Comique,* 1874–75.

small picture (only 5 1/8″ × 6 3/4″).[145] Although Degas's woman has no spider web, the heavily made-up and gaudily dressed figure playing solitaire and having an aperitif is surely meant to be identified as a slattern who is on the lookout for a man (or is using the café as the rendezvous point for an illicit assignation). Unlike Manet's young woman who appears introverted and lost in thought to the point of ignoring her surroundings, Degas's figure is definitely oriented outward. Only a tart would play cards wearing gloves, let alone such flashy black ones.

The stigma of impropriety that adhered to almost any café woman on her own was erased in pictures that show more than one woman sharing a table. By and large, the rule seems to have been (at least in the realm of representation) that the predatory lamp was lit only when the marauding woman was alone. When friends were together, they were understood to be socializing and relaxing. In "Boulevard Women" (fig. 58), for example, a trio of friends in the foreground is having a beer as a respite from "work." The woman in the distance ("Pauline") had planned to join them but had another "affaire" to attend to. In Ancourt's "On the Boulevard" (fig. 59), the two young women relax and confer about the conventional wisdom concerning their tendency to run after men. Although the women in Manet's *Women Drinking Beer* of 1878 (fig. 60) are not necessarily prostitutes, the pastel fully shares the format and assumptions discussed above. The women shown here are completely inner-directed and absorbed by their refreshment and relaxation. (The distinction was not hard and fast, but beer seems to have been the beverage of choice for times of morally neutral relaxation and sociability, whereas strong spirits were more likely to accompany café-based racolage.)

The masculinist idea that unchaperoned bourgeois women in a café could be morally indecent or were at least inviting sexualized attention – that it was daring if not wrong for such women to be out in public without men – underlay an influential topos of female modern life during this period. Certain middle-brow painters of respectable women sharing a visit and re-

57. Edouard Manet, *The Plum,* ca. 1877, oil on canvas, National Gallery of Art, Washington, D.C.

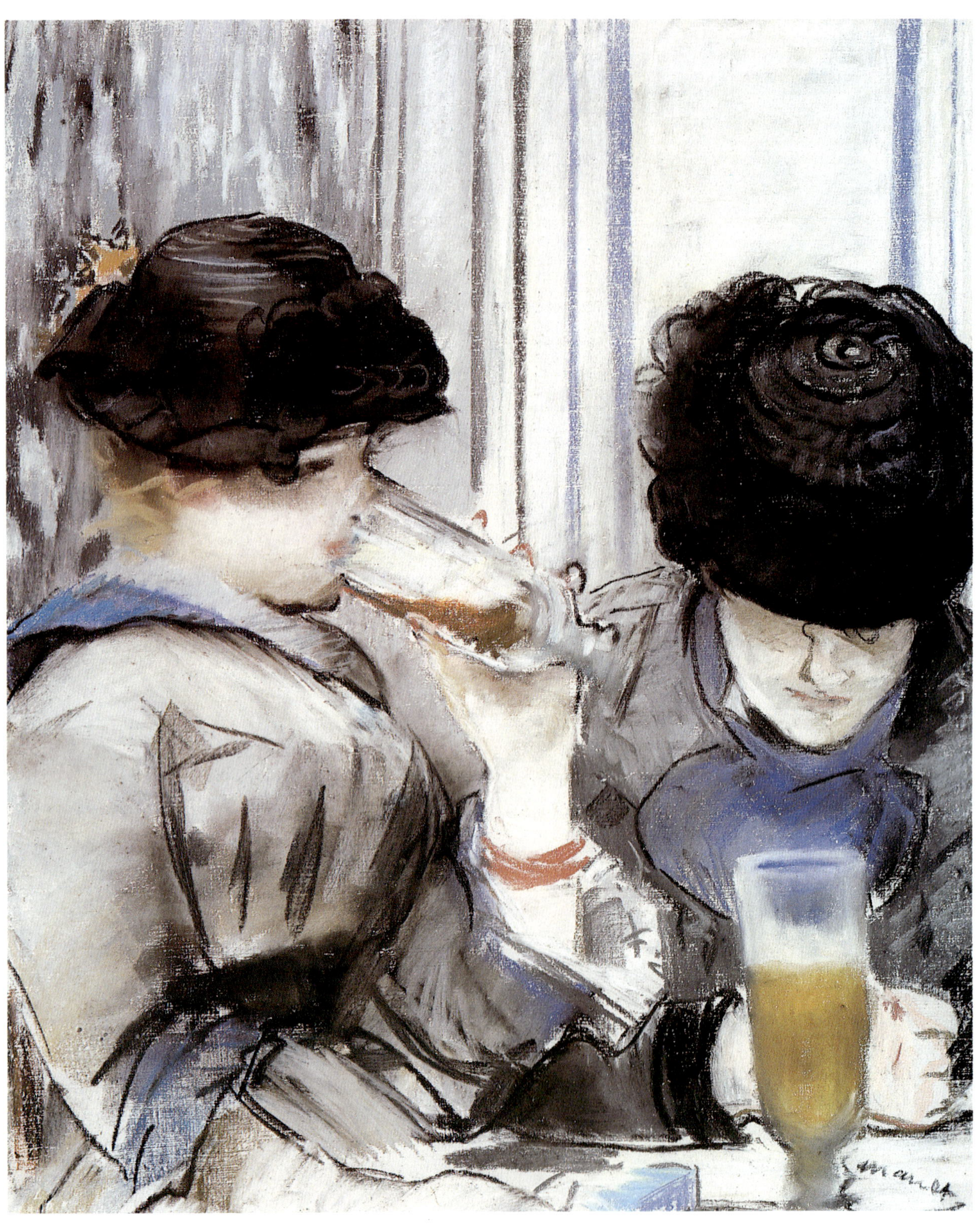

60.
Édouard Manet,
Women Drinking Beer, 1878, pastel on canvas,
Burrell Collection, Glasgow Museums and Art Galleries.

freshment in a café often included a male admirer in such a scene. It appears that conceptualizing almost any woman in a café as a sexual object was an essential part of many records of this modern subject.

In Renoir's *At the Café* of circa 1877 (fig. 61), for example, two thoroughly respectable women rivet their attention upon a man who has paused at their table to chat.[144] We know they are respectable because of their appearance, but Renoir could not resist showing this twinned female pulchritude acknowledged by a second man who is eavesdropping: the fellow in the top hat at the left (considered to be a likeness of Georges Rivière, a supporter of the Impressionists) leers appreciatively in the direction of the women. In a café picture attributed to Gervex, *Group at Table* of about 1880–85 (fig. 62), two seated women chat and read side-by-side, but there is a man close by to add the apparently indispensable note of male attraction to the "charms" of women seated in a café. Giovanni Boldini's *Café Conversation* of circa 1875–80 (fig. 63) puts a slightly different twist on an example of the same genre of modern-life painting. The two well-dressed women in his painting are alone on a café terrace, but their attention is not centered on their refreshment or on each other. They are busy meddling, looking at something or someone beyond the right margin of the picture. The demeanor of the woman at right suggests, for example, that the explorations of her eyes are flirtatious.

The iconographies of these café subjects fall, therefore, into three general categories (which convey in turn interconnected beliefs about women in cafés): (1) a woman alone was *likely* to be a prostitute and was *likely* to be soliciting; (2) prostitutes together were relaxing, not working, and would be left alone by men; and (3) unchaperoned, respectable women would be ogled by men and might flirt back.

Degas's *Women on the Terrace of a Café in the Evening*, a pastel over monotype of 1877 (fig. 64), appears at first to be an example of the second category: an image of prostitutes taking their ease, having a drink, resting their feet, getting caught up with one another (especially since a man is shown hurrying past them in the distance). Upon close inspection, however, it is instead a picture that crosses the boundary between genres and blurs certain of the usual distinctions drawn between ways of picturing prostitutes at work and prostitutes at rest.

Degas borrowed the picture from its owner, Gustave Caillebotte, to exhibit it in the third Impressionist exhibition in 1877. It bore its present title, but its setting has long been identified as a café on the notorious boulevard Montmartre.[145] Reviewers of Degas's twenty-two-piece exhibit in the 1877 show found that the picture was especially truthful.

Georges Rivière, friend and partisan of the independent group, recorded his view of Degas in his journal, *L'Impressionniste*. Unlike many twentieth-century critics, Rivière, like Edmond Duranty (a close friend of the artist and author of the 1876 *La Nouvelle Peinture*), believed that Degas was as concerned with narration in his work as he was with aesthetic issues. "M. Degas," he wrote, "how best to speak about this essentially Parisian artist, whose every work contains as much literary and philosophical talent as it does expertise in drawing and the science of coloration? . . . Here are some women at the door of a café in the evening. There is one who clicks her fingernail against her teeth, saying: 'not even that,' which is a poem in itself. Another rests a large gloved hand on the table. In the distance, the boulevard with its gradually thinning swarm. Again it is an extraordinary page of history."[146] It is not surprising that Rivière found an anecdote in *Women on the Terrace of a Café*, because he believed that a legible story was a characteristic part of Degas's art. As Carol Armstrong has shown, Duranty tended to look for a real-

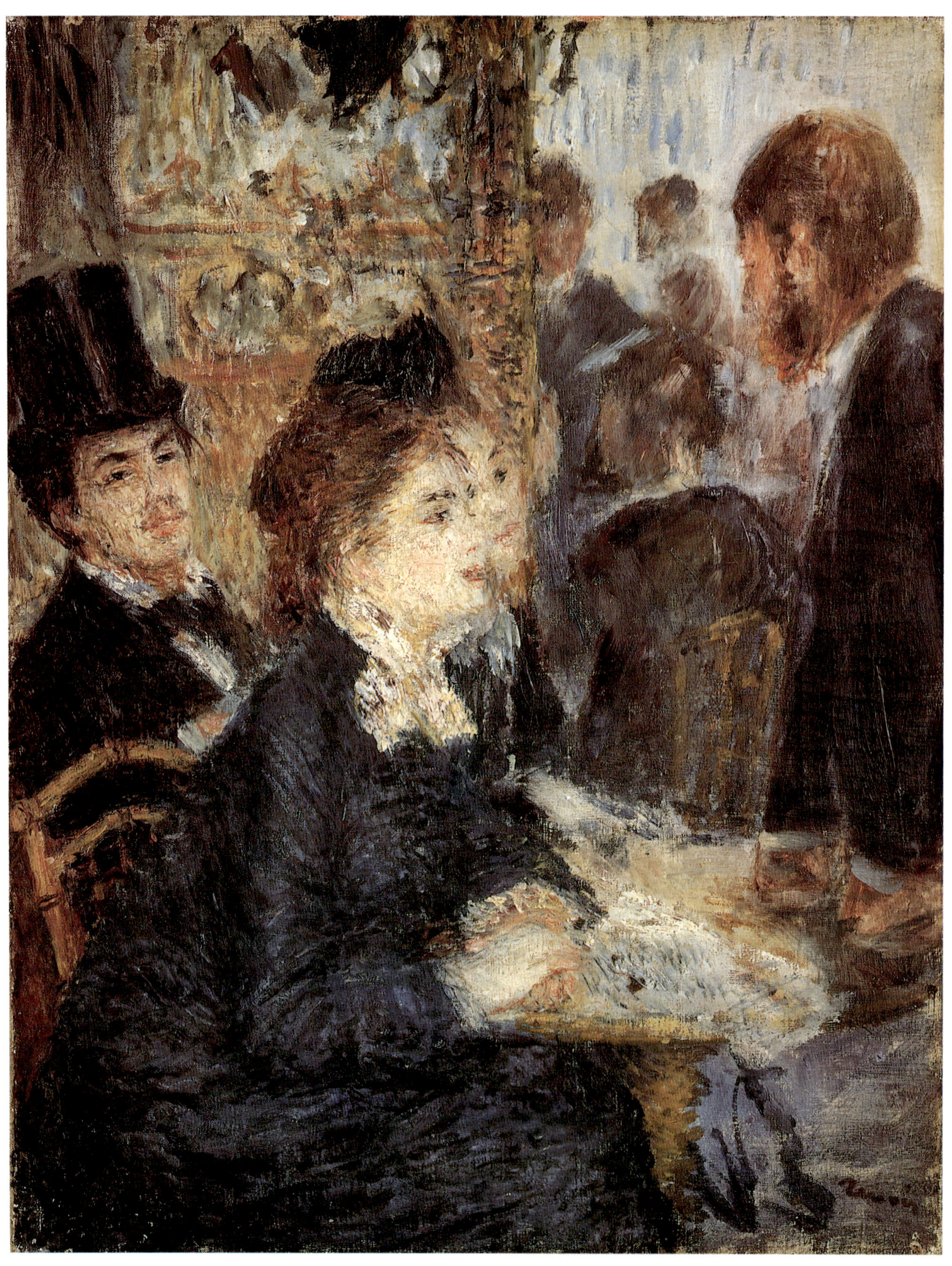

61.
Pierre-Auguste Renoir,
At the Café, ca. 1877, oil on canvas,
Rijksmuseum Kröller-Müller, Otterlo, Netherlands.

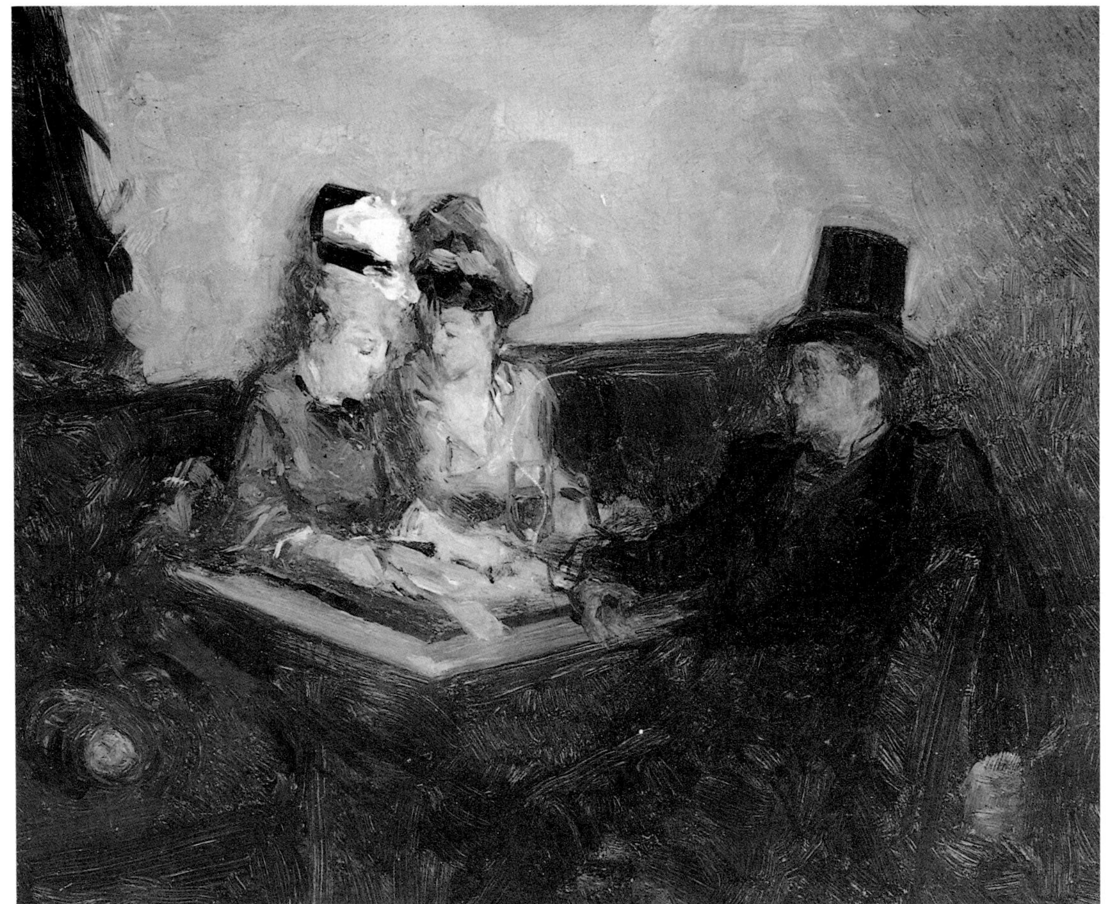

62.
Henri Gervex, *Group at Table*, ca. 1880–85 (?), oil on panel, Corcoran Gallery of Art, Washington, D.C.

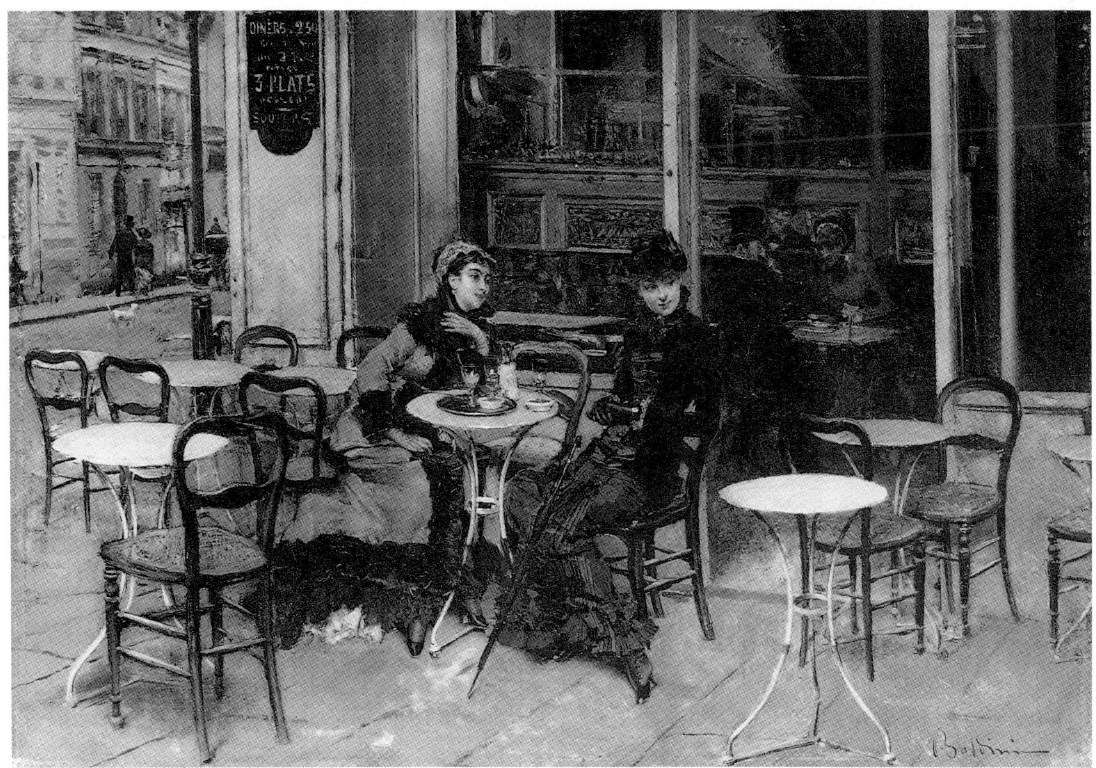

63.
Giovanni Boldini, *Café Conversation*, ca. 1875–1880, oil on panel.

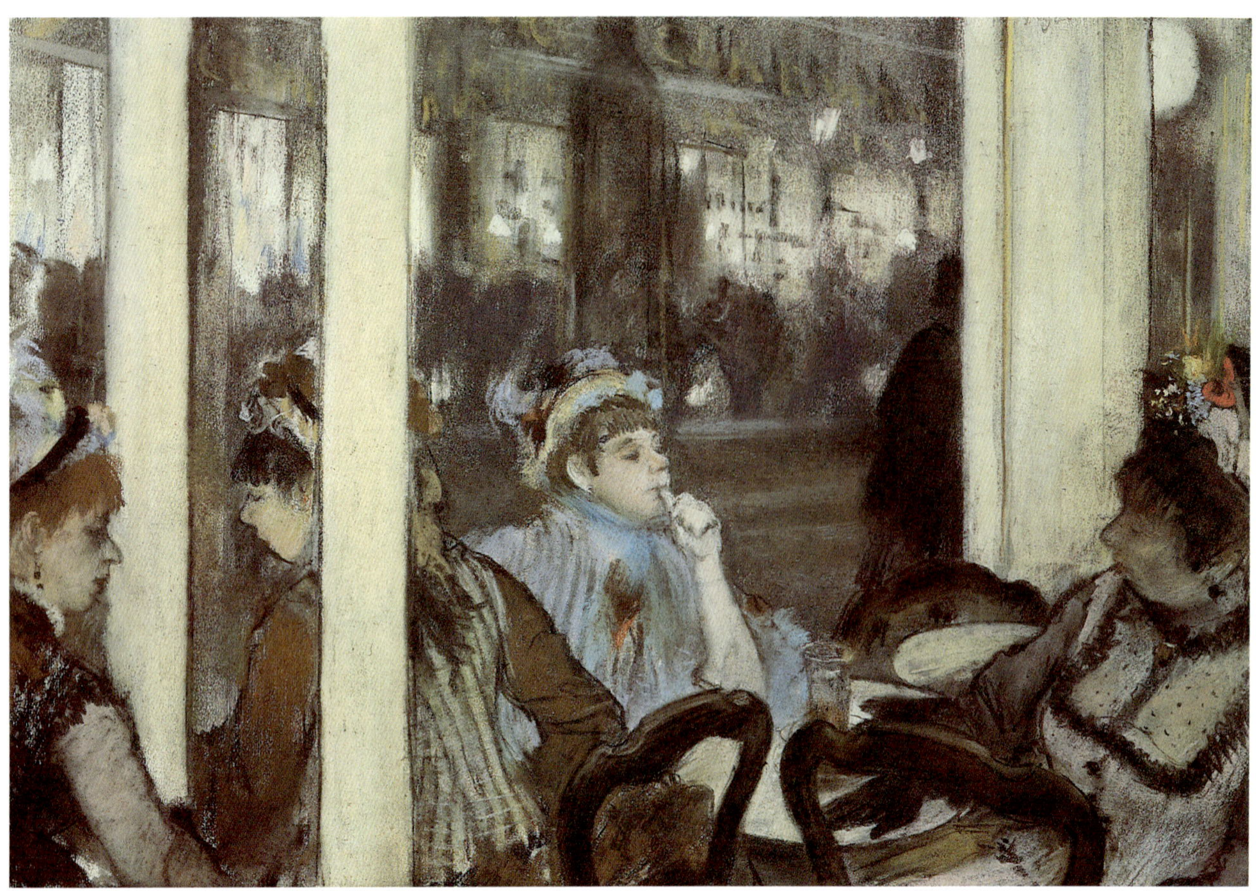

64. Edgar Degas, *Women on the Terrace of a Café in the Evening,* 1877, pastel over monotype, Musée d'Orsay, Paris.

ist textuality in Degas's art. Both Duranty and Rivière wanted to find a straightforward social physiognomics of class and profession in Degas's pictures that was not there, so they had to make do, as we shall see, with the "language of bodily impropriety and gestural inuendo" in Degas's work, to borrow Armstrong's excellent phrase.[147] But Rivière's concoction of a story is not entirely inappropriate to what is in the picture, even if it does rest heavily on that one provocative thumb-in-mouth maneuver, a matter to which we shall return.

In a generally sympathetic review of the third Impressionist show published in *Le Petit Parisien,* Alexandre Pothey emphasized the truthfulness of Degas's observation of his motif as he wrote: "Monsieur Degas seems to have issued a challenge to the philistines, that is to say to the classics. *Women on the Terrace of a Café in the Evening* are of a terrifying realism. These painted, blighted creatures, sweating vice, who recount to one another the doings and gestures of the day, you have seen them right enough, you know them, and you will come across them again in a little while on the boulevard."[148] The critic Bernadille wrote this in *Le Français:* "Monsieur Degas lacks neither fantasy nor wit nor observation in his watercolors [sic]. He has gathered at the tables of a bistro, or in the cafés-concerts and the corps de ballet, types of a cynical and quasi-bestial truthfulness, bearing all the vices of civilization written in large letters on their triple layers of makeup. But his wit has a heavy hand and a crude expression."[149] The writer Jacques published these comments in *L'Homme Libre:* "The studies in the boulevard cafés are no less finished and no less curious, though cruel – passably so. I would be permitted to criticize a certain accentuation of detail. But the whole constitutes an incomparable page in the book of contemporary anecdote."[150]

We postwar modernists are accustomed to being counseled away from detecting an anecdote in Degas's pictures, but the consensus reached in these sample reactions of 1877 is that Degas's pastel tells a story about immoral women who, while they relax, trade stories about their work, complete with vernacular gestures. The critics also find that the picture was an expert and accurate record of prostitutional appearance (paint and makeup) and character (vice and quasibestiality). A careful inventory of Degas's image will help us to see why the critics were confident in identifying the women as vulgar prostitutes trading stories at a café, in spite of Degas's general avoidance of traditional anecdote and narrative convention.[151]

The setting of the work is initially difficult to decipher: the viewer is looking out onto a gaslit evening boulevard from the interior of a café. Seen from the threshold of the terrace, the view of the blurred buildings, street traffic, and opposite sidewalk is overlapped and interrupted by the four women, their tables and chairs, and the three plain beige pillars supporting the roof.

The two women at right are seated and appear quite firmly planted at a small round table, although only one drink is before them. The central figure, the woman in blue, assumes the position that fascinated Rivière, while the woman at the extreme right edge of the sheet turns away from the table, rests her full forearm upon it, and looks down somewhat querulously. The other figures, the two at the left, are gathered around another of the small tables. Of these two, the woman with black hair and brown sleeves – who is sliced and splayed by a pillar – is in an animated posture: between sitting and standing, she is slightly bent over, elbows flexed. Her facial profile suggests that she is speaking. Her partner appears to listen dully.

Through this arrangement, Degas emphasizes the impermanence and irregularity of their presence on the terrace. As usual in Degas's work, the appearance of casual variety is the result of diligent compositional work. The heads of the four women are all on the same level, allowing us to understand that they are all seated, though our comprehension of the position of the two figures at left depends on the clarity of the positions of the two at right. Within this frieze of seated women, which fills up the lower half of the sheet, diversity has been maximized. The positions of the four heads create an alternating rhythm, a series of reversals: facing right, left, right, left. The women at either edge of this series face into the center, closing it off as with parentheses. Because the heads alternate in direction, there is the appearance of randomness in the moment observed and of disconnection between the women at the moment.

The variation of pose, and resulting lack of cohesion, suggest that this is not a normal, settled café gathering. The four women do not form a group but, rather, compose a fidgety ad hoc assembly, as if each has taken a temporary seat for the sake of convenience. This seems the point of the solitary drink on the table and the animation of the woman in brown.

Their positions, each different from the next, further connote the women's lack of decorum and their indifference to the world surrounding them. Their disconnection from their immediate milieu is underscored by the furtive disappearance of the man in the dark suit, a faceless diagonal form in the middle distance. He appears to move steadily off to the right, away from the women in order to disappear quickly behind the broad column.

As one surveys the women from left to right, the figure at far left presents a sullen, downturned, heavily made-up face in profile. The briskly moving figure appears to chat animatedly before finding a calm and composed sitting position. The central figure leans languorously and rudely into her vernacular gesture. The woman at far right does not sit up to the table: she appears to have rapidly taken her position without having bothered to rearrange herself according to conventional standards of etiquette. Her ample bosom, squeezed by a corset and covered by transparent material, is the most prominent sculptural form in the drawing. Even this ripe anatomical feature is absorbed into the formal scheme of the lower half of the sheet by rhyming the shape of the black tuile trim with the chair back. Degas also used different colors, patterns, and materials for each of the costumes. The women wear the obligatory hats (required by the regulationists), which in this case are gaudily ornamented.[152]

Degas establishes the appearance of an animated conversation kept up in spite of the women's coming and going. Critics easily identified the occupation of these women, even though Degas's image of boulevard prostitutes obviously differs from other images of the subject. One difference is that these figures appear to relax, to bustle off to work, and to be at work – all at the same time. By mixing these pursuits and by joining together the genres used to depict them, Degas suggests that, for the prostitute, work and leisure are not mutually exclusive, especially not on the terrace of a boulevard café, locus of work *and* play for a street prostitute. Blurring the borders between established formats allows Degas to propose that the commodified woman remains just that, at work and at play. Stopping work does not alter her prostitutional status. Prostitution is not what she *does* but, according to the terms of this picture, what she *is*.

This outlook toward contemporary lower-class prostitutes is reminiscent of that found in Degas's brothel monotypes, discussed in chapter 2. Another link between this pastel and the brothel prints (and another characteristic of the 1877 café picture that differentiates it from the others we have examined) is the use of a thumb-in-mouth gesture by one of the conversing prostitutes.

Degas uses the same action in *Waiting* (fig. 65), one of the brothel monotypes owned by Picasso. To this second version of the print, Degas added bits of clothing (stockings), altered body details (darkened and enlarged pubic areas), and included additional gestures.[153] The woman second from the right employs the decisive action of the 1877 pastel-enhanced monotype. In view of Degas's use of the same hand movement in these two particular contexts, Rivière's reading of the motion – a girl's complaint about a niggardly payment from a client or regret that she did not have enough customers that evening – does not exhaust its possible meanings.

In *Waiting*, four varieties of simultaneously relaxed and enticing bodies (a portmanteau configuration often found in the brothel monotypes, as we discussed in chapter 2) are lined up. As usual, it is hard to separate the "natural or inner-directed" from the "staged or outer-directed" in this syntax of the body. What concerns us here is that in the framework of brothel display and inveiglement, the woman may be shown mimicking (and thereby promising?) fellatio. Although Degas did not set out to refer to this act directly in the pastel he exhibited in 1877, he certainly relied on the thumb-in-mouth gesture (fig. 66) to enforce the scurrilousness of the street prostitute and to collapse further the distinction between work and play for the prostitute's mouth. In the artist's otherwise very similar monotype, *Café Scene* of 1876–77 (fig. 67), the absence of just such a gesture (and the presence of the prim, bespectacled standing woman) allows the seated women to appear comparatively less coarse than their analogues in the 1877 pastel. The gesture in *Women on the Terrace* says: only a vulgar woman would place a

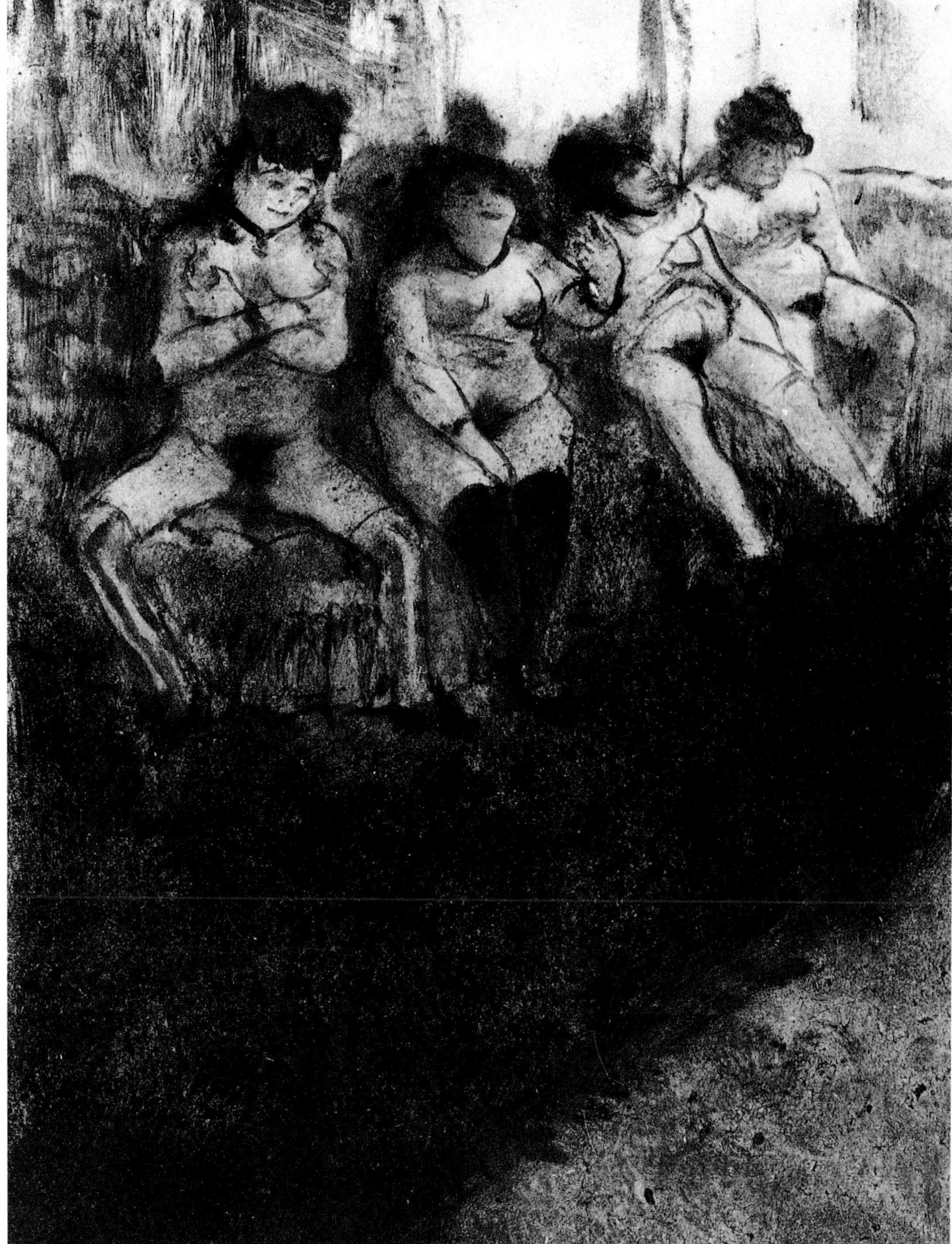

65.
Edgar
Degas,
Waiting,
ca. 1879–80
or 1876–77,
monotype,
Musée
Picasso,
Paris.

thumb in her mouth in such a way.[154] This in turn reminds us of the extraordinary degree to which Degas's trademark – the isolation and precision of the typical professional gesture – is a multilayered allusive device rather than a univocal, anecdotal means of representation and reportage.

Thus, although Degas's picture is reserved, elliptical, and noncommital compared to the average, anecdotal boulevard cartoon (like fig. 52, for example), his use of gesture forcefully

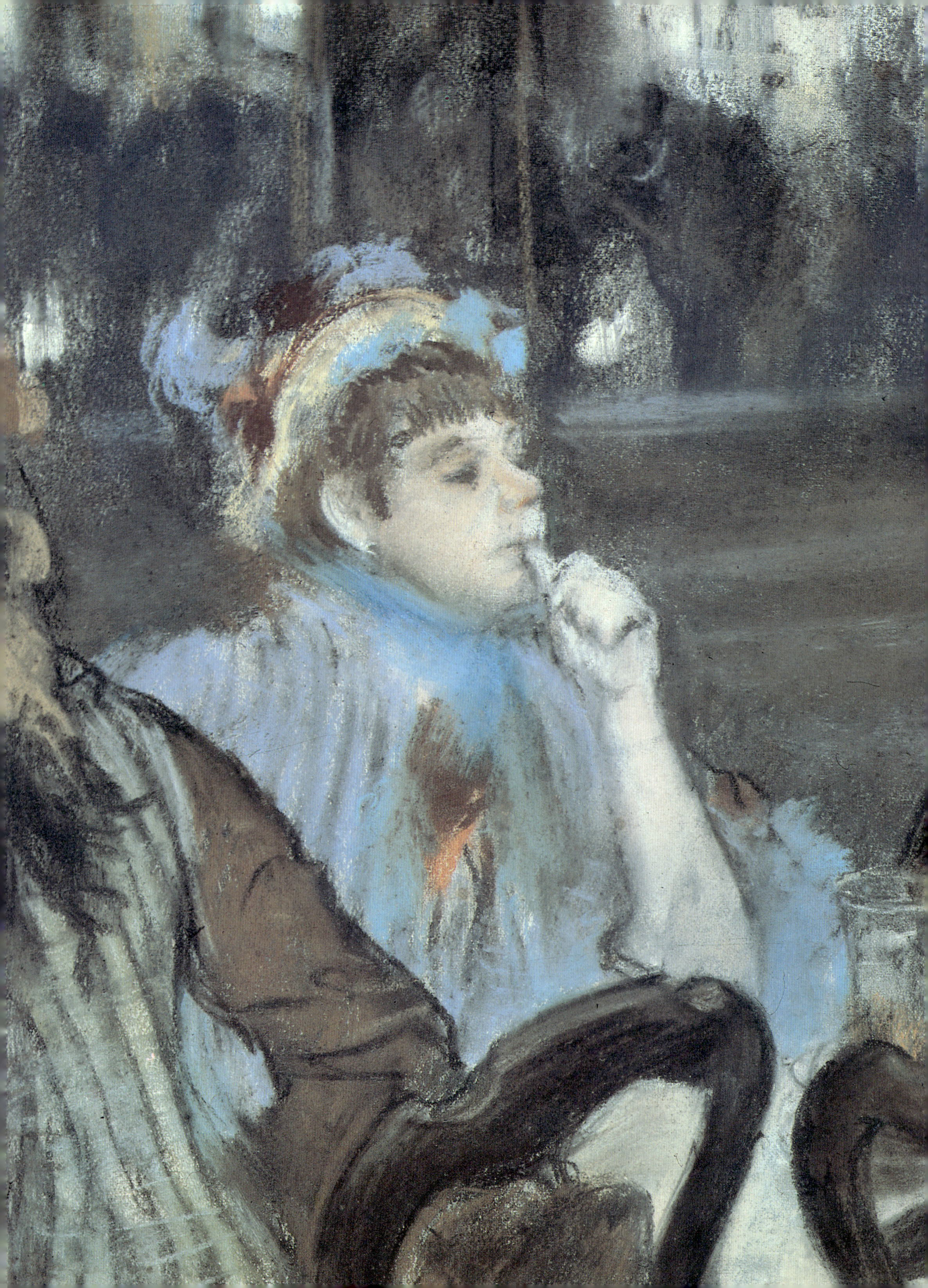

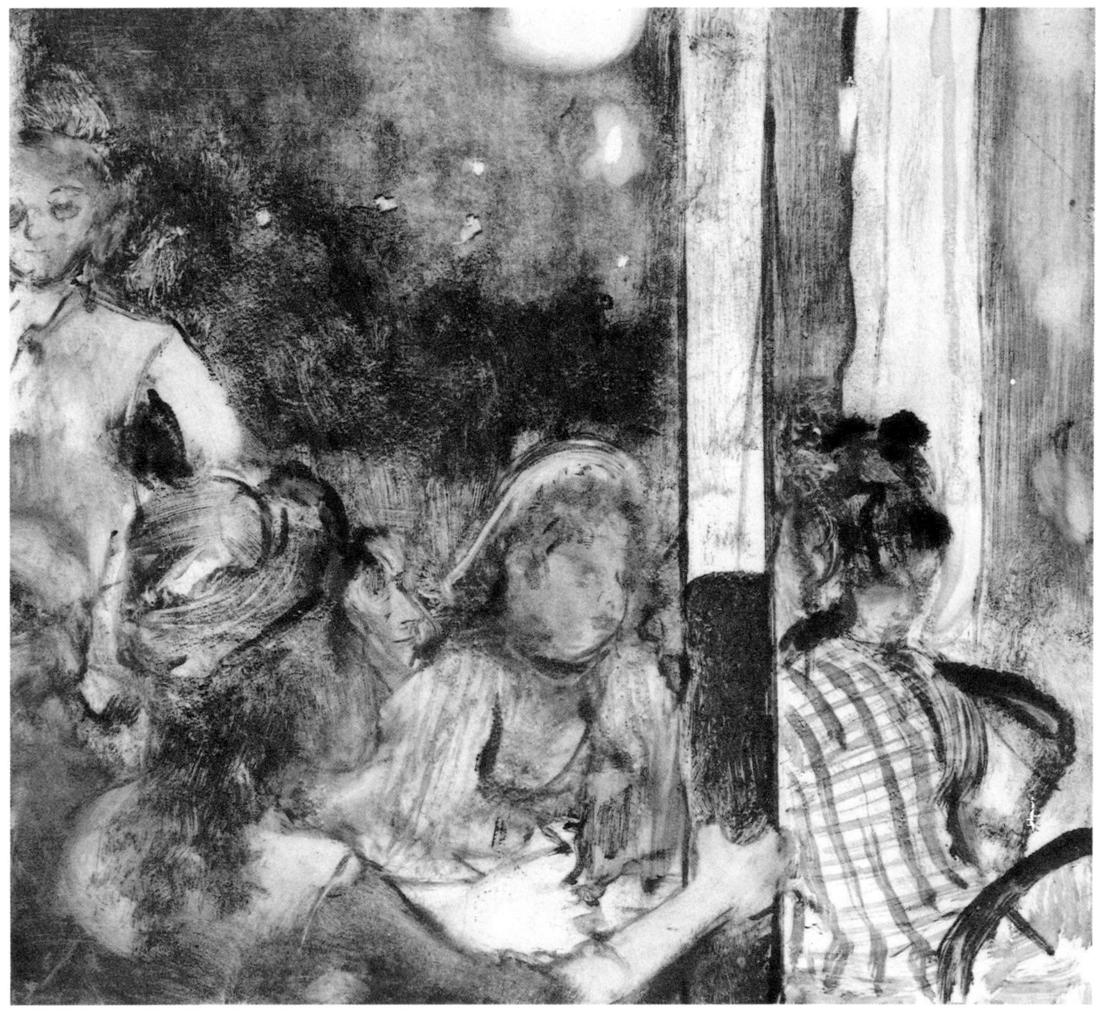

67. Edgar Degas, *Café Scene*, 1876–77, monotype, through a prior bequest of Mr. and Mrs. Martin A. Ryerson, 1990.77.1, Art Institute of Chicago.

connotes the sexual daring of a prostitute's line of work.[155] It brings the subject of sexual commerce into a picture of leisure in an unmistakable and somewhat uncomfortable way. The action of the central figure works as a displaced, risqué, and explicit substitute for the most vulgar form of solicitation (known as *raccrochage*) practiced by the working prostitute (which probably mimicked a form of oral sex). The gesture, then, indirectly summoned up an image of prostitutes' sexual activities. At the same time, Rivière's reading of it as a complaint about business also makes the gesture into a powerful sign of the prostitute's venality. The multiple connotations help fix her character by alluding to specific professional practices. The women in Degas's picture can therefore be read as reactionary and misogynistic figurations. These women are venal and "quasi-bestial" creatures of vice. That Degas's complex and highly sophisticated pictorial machinery serves to *secure* the vulgarity of the street prostitute is a reversal of the progressive values often assigned to modernist ambiguity.

Because the picture straddles and elides the iconographic categories established by other artworks on the subject of boulevard women, we have been able to show that the picture cannot be pinned down to being *either* a picture of prostitutes working to solicit

66. Detail of fig. 64.

customers *or* a depiction of prostitutes taking time off. But my key objective has been to show that the absence of univocal anecdote is *not* the same thing as detachment or open-endedness or vagueness or ambiguity. Indeed, I have made an effort to show that in this case, for all its apparent openness and its avoidance of a single plot, Degas has mustered considerable pictorial resources to establish – by multiple connotation – scurrilous behavioral and moral traits. He has thereby attempted to contain the social and sexual force and threat of such women, but the difficulty of doing so has left traces, and the women in the picture retain their dominion.

This analysis of the picture enables us, on the one hand, to see the central figure in blue as an image produced by bourgeois male disgust and contempt – worthy of Edmond de Goncourt – an observed bit of the sordidness of the common everyday. Yet, on the other hand, she is the keystone of the picture, its triumphant highlight (dismissing male and female spectator alike with her "fuck you" gesture). Even her coloration seems to carry a double meaning – her outfit is an iridescent, luminous blue, but it is also soiled with red as though bloodstained here and there. I do not wish, in the end, to hitch the picture to a monolithic reactionary *or* progressive position. Rather, I hope to highlight two coexisting aspects of its quirky complexities: the picture betrays Degas's effort to dominate and stave off his subject matter, but it is surely not the figuration of a world comfortably controlled by a secure masculine perspective. Like the brothel monotypes, *Women on the Terrace of a Café* plays out at a number of levels a contradictory dialectic of disgust and fascination.[156]

CHAPTER FOUR

Suspicious Professions

Working Women for Sale?

They are seamstresses or milliners according to what's posted. Inside the establishment, the mise en scène *is complete; there are fabrics, patrons, work in progress. In reality, it is a place of debauchery where often, under the pretext of a lucrative business, one takes in young women who quickly allow themselves to become perverted.*

– *C. J. Lecour,* La Prostitution à Paris et à Londres

In the second half of the nineteenth century most French women in the labor force were young single members of the popular classes. Many of those who worked in certain of the classic female professions in Paris, such as the needle trades, were suspected of being prostitutes hiding behind the cover of an honest job. In this chapter I investigate representations of these frequently eroticized young women to find out why painters of the Impressionist circle often chose milliners, for example, as modern motifs when these same female workers were widely believed to be covert prostitutes. A basic knowledge of the legal and social status of women in nineteenth-century France will enable us to conduct an informed discussion of artists' interest in the subject of working women.

French women of all classes had at least one thing in common during this period: as a consequence of marked gender inequalities in the law, they were all considered minors. For example, investigations of paternity were not allowed, but formal inquiries about maternity were permitted. And the penalties for adultery were different for men and women. According to the penal code, a husband's adultery was punishable by a light fine, and only if the act took place within the marital home. For women, however, the offense was punishable no matter where it took place, and the penalty was imprisonment as well as a fine. Indeed, if a man discovered his wife in flagrante delicto with her lover, the husband had the right to kill them both on the spot,[1] a legal circumstance that more than justifies the pitched drama of Jules-Arsène Garnier's *Proof of Adultery* of 1885 (fig. 68).[2]

In spite of the inferior legal status of all women, much separated the middle-class from the lower-class woman. Owing to the power of certain largely middle-class ideas about proper

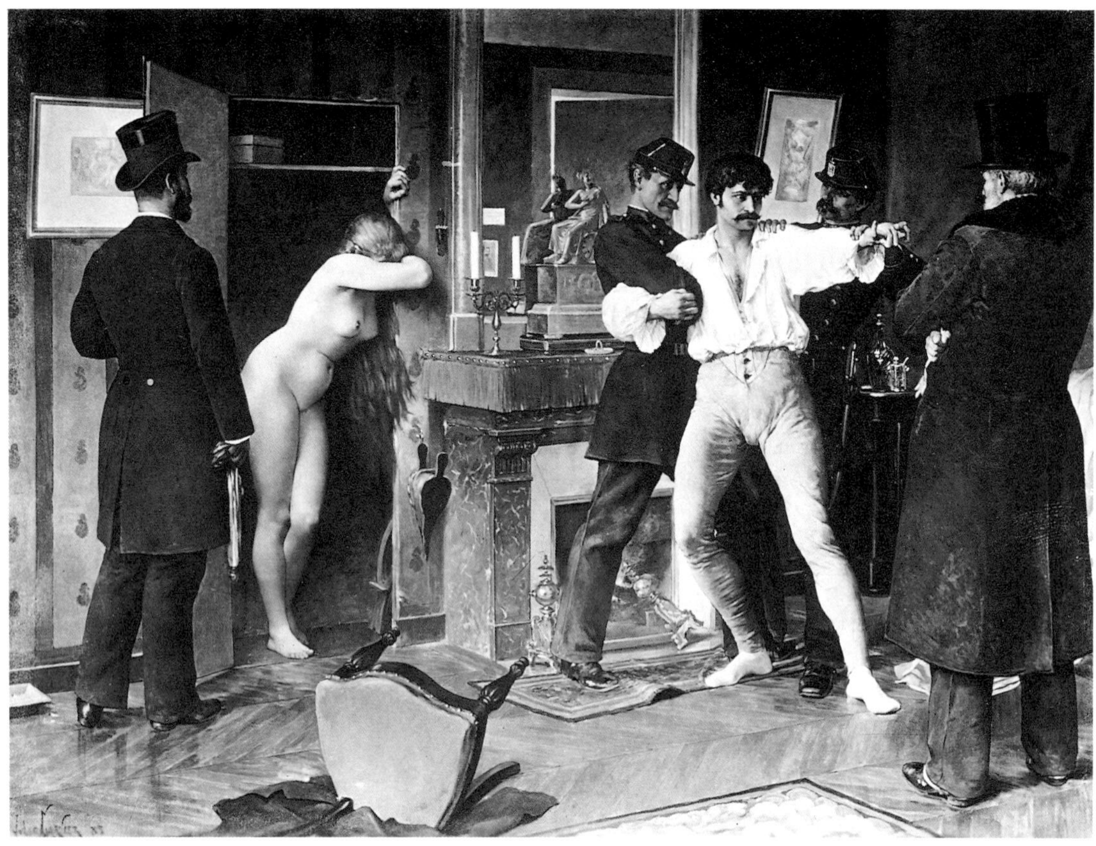

68.
Jules-Arsène Garnier, *Proof of Adultery*, 1885.

female behavior, working women were almost automatically stigmatized in certain circles as socially heterodox if not morally wicked. Bourgeois little girls could pretend – but only pretend – that they would go to work someday in one of the "suspicious" female professions (fig. 69), because paid employment of any sort – let alone work in any of the six jobs pictured – was out-of-bounds for the respectable bourgeoise. Indeed, the middle-class family ideal projected a clear separation between the wife's household responsibilities and the husband's employment. The man was to support the family single-handedly by securing an income outside the home, while the woman was to nurture and organize the family by taking charge of its domestic space and property, children included. Lisa Tickner's gloss on the system of separate spheres is informative: "The 'separate spheres' of men and women were understood as moral (they involved the exercise of different virtues), psychological (men and women had different temperaments) and practical (different activities were appropriate to each)."[3]

In some quarters, of course, women's restrictively defined domestic responsibilities and sexual morality were closely linked. P.-J. Proud'hon's prescription of 1846 was the most merciless. Women had but two alternatives: they were either *ménagères* (housewives) or *courtisanes* (harlots).[4] And the connection between the family ideal and prostitution was cemented in other ways as well. In James McMillan's words, "The doctrine of separate spheres was indistinguishable from the notion of a double standard of morality."[5]

The requirement of uncompromised virtue in the *femme au foyer* linked the issues of domesticity and morality, making prostitutes, recruited from the urban poor, the necessary guard-

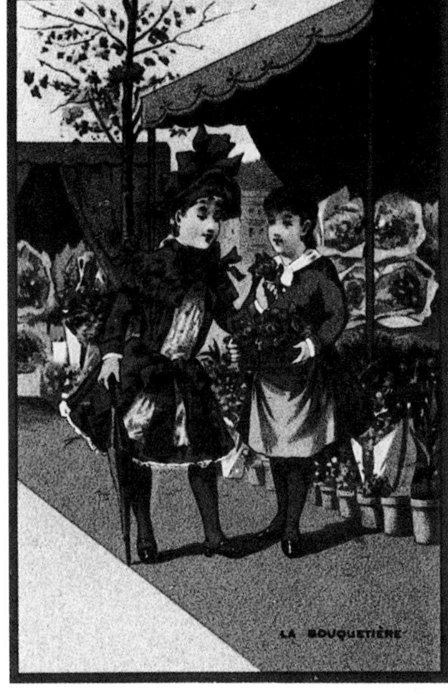

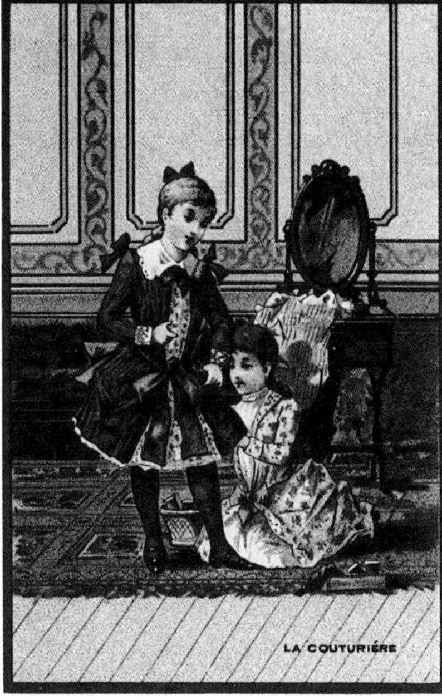

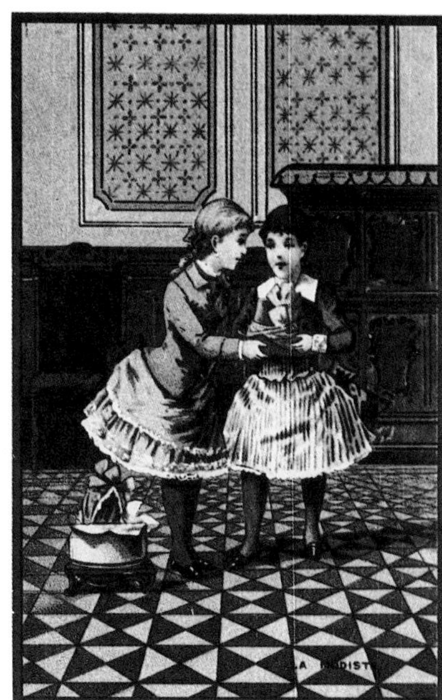

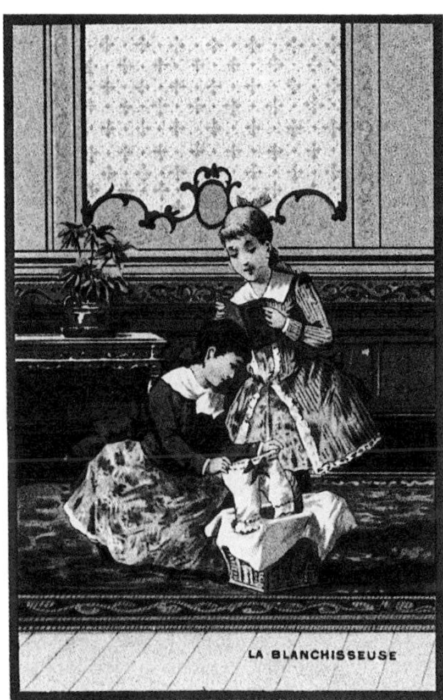

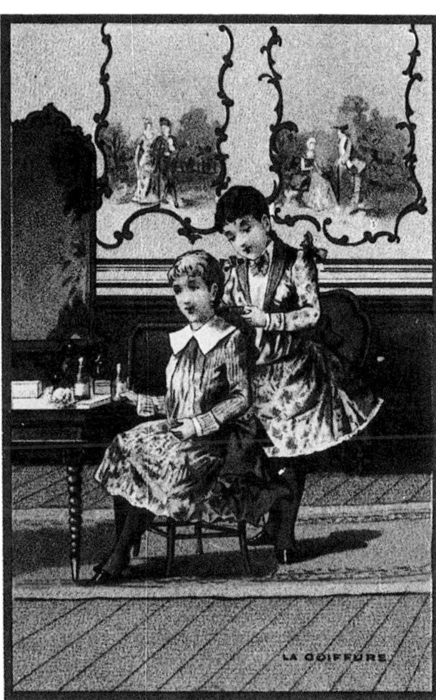

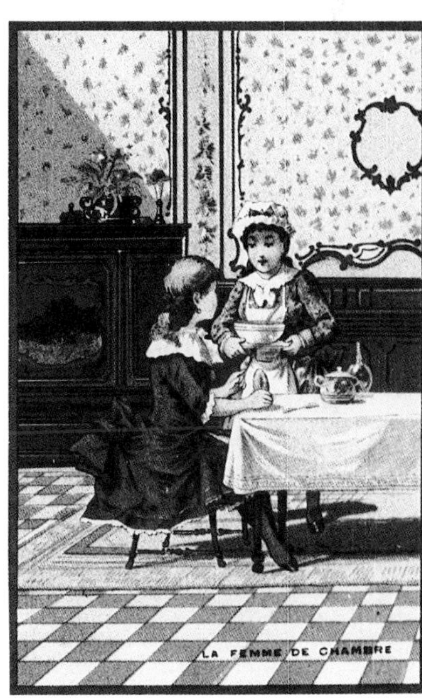

The Flower Girl
The Laundress

The Seamstress
The Hairdresser

The Milliner
The Chambermaid

69. "Little Girls' Jobs," 1890, Cabinet des Estampes, Bibliothèque Nationale, Paris.

ians of the bourgeois woman's virtue. The ideal of the motherly and chaste housewife was hemmed in by the prostitute: if she wavered from the conjugal path, she became one; but by living up to the ideal, she sent her husband into the prostitute's bed. As we have already seen, Parisian réglementation provided an institutionalized sanction of the male double standard and thereby established the sexual vulnerability of lower-class women.

In spite of the ideological dominion of the bourgeois family model in French society during the second half of the nineteenth century, many French women were nonetheless in the labor force. In 1866, 25 percent of French women worked outside the home; by 1896, the proportion had risen to 33 percent.[6] (By 1896, 52 percent of single women were in the work force, and 38 percent of married women also worked outside the home.)[7]

But the phrase "women working outside the home" was oxymoronic as far as the guardians of bourgeois morality and conformity were concerned. They saw outside employment for women as an abandonment of their family responsibilities and ties. Typical is this man's view of poverty-stricken young prostitutes: "It is a sad spectacle watching such young girls abandon the paternal home."[8] On the contrary, being employed outside the home usually did not mean that the woman was rebelling against the period ideal of domesticity; the commitment of working-class women, both mothers and daughters, to the welfare of their families frequently required them to go to work.

In the nineteenth century the majority of French women working outside the agricultural domain were employed in three traditional areas: textiles, the garment industry, and domestic service. The latter two were the most important categories for the female labor force of Paris, especially for single young women. Louise Tilly and Joan Scott have shown that one sign of the authority of domestic ideology was that married working-class women regarded themselves more as housewives and mothers than as workers. This pattern of female self-definition is also partially explained by the nature of women's work in the period: it was almost always sporadic and underpaid, because the traditional areas of women's employment were not stable and women's wage-earning capacity was defined as a reserve resource vis-à-vis the family economy.[9]

Daughters who were sent out of the house to supplement the family income often encountered severe financial problems in their new lives, especially if they were far from home. The idea may have been that they would eventually return to the family they were assisting, but the reality was that they were on their own, and the "sad conclusion will be, that in every line of work, the woman worker's salary falls below what is indispensable for the maintenance of bare subsistance."[10] The low pay and unstable conditions of the garment industry and domestic service, which were the trades of most poor women in Paris, caused many to turn to prostitution. The three principal means of overcoming a life-threatening shortfall of money were prostitution, cohabitation with a man, and suicide.[11] Dr. Octave Commenge's record of the plea of a typical clandestine prostitute following arrest affirms this state of affairs: "Since my work was not sufficient to cover my expenses, I was forced to earn my living some other way."[12]

Milliners, for example – the subject of pictures by Degas, Eva Gonzalès, Manet, and Renoir, which I shall discuss below – earned as low a salary as other minimally skilled female workers: between 2 and 4 francs per day.[13] On the basis of average food costs of the period, even the most thrifty of these women was left with only about 40 centimes a day to pay for everything other than food. It appears that a woman who earned 3.75 francs per day would have found herself at least 200 francs short at the end of the year.[14]

The most reliable employment histories for Parisian prostitutes were compiled by Parent-Duchâtelet in the 1830s, but only for registered prostitutes. His findings reinforce what historians have discovered about the general contours of French women's work in the same years. In Parent-Duchâtelet's sample of 3,120 filles inscrites who declared previous professions at the

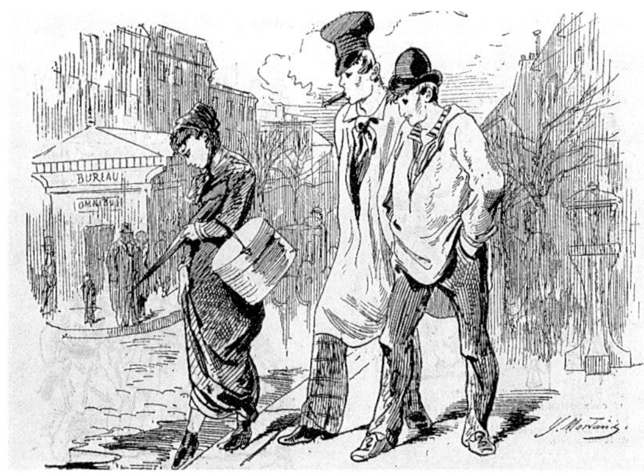

– *So, Lamolle, she's a cute little one, that one.*
– *And they say she's going to slave away all day to earn twenty-five cents. What a shame.*
– *And it's so quickly drunk up.*

70. Victor Morland, "Coupeau, Lantier, Mes-Bottes and Co.," *Le Monde Comique*, 1879–80.

time of their registration, half were makers of luxury clothing accessories, and about two-thirds did not come from Paris.[15] Another study of Paris-based registered prostitutes conducted in 1889 showed the persistence of the pattern: 75 percent of that sample were not born in Paris.[16] Alain Corbin's research has shown that in the 1870s and 1880s, most registered prostitutes came from artisanal trades. Paraphrasing Corbin, the antechambers of the brothel were domestic service, *débits de boissons* (drink shops), laundries, and *ateliers de couture* (sewing studios) – not the factory.[17]

Underpaid female labor was the principal cause of clandestine prostitution as well. A catalog of the professions that fed these ranks would closely resemble a record of the previous jobs held by registered prostitutes. Between 1877 and 1887 in Paris, for example, needlework (a category that encompasses millinery work) was second only to domestic service in furnishing clandestine prostitutes.[18]

Popular images of *modistes* (milliners) on the public thoroughfare presented two contrasting identities: either they were very poor, or they gladly sold themselves. Pictures that foreground poverty avoid converting the unfortunate worker into a prostitute, while the images that telegraph the latter message invariably foreclose any connection between poverty and prostitution by presenting unfailingly sexy milliners. By severing any connection between the two conditions, the cartoons that sexualize the milliner transform prostitution into being "her fault." This is accomplished by converting economic cause into the venal proclivity of the female sexual deviant.

Victor Morland's cartoon of 1879–80, entitled "Coupeau, Lantier, Mes-Bottes and Co." (fig. 70), attempts by direct reference to Zola's *L'Assommoir* to portray the milliner's poverty. He shows a wistful and withdrawn young woman stepping off the sidewalk, heading resolutely off to work nevertheless, her telltale hatbox on her arm. Two men in workers' smocks watch her and lament how little she earns. Perhaps her step aimed toward the gutter is meant to suggest the meanness of her wages and the difficulty of her work, and perhaps, very indirectly, her inevitable immorality. Because Morland's principal target in this picture is male dipsomania, the young woman receives a relatively straightforward and sympathetic treatment.

Morland's "Scenes of Parisian Life" of 1879–80 (fig. 49) makes an altogether different point about a better-dressed young milliner (identifiable as such because she carries hat boxes) who encounters two bourgeois on the street. The younger man tries to make a pass in the clichéd language of sidewalk flirtation: "Miss! miss! listen to a heart who wants only to cherish you!" Her wisecracking but practical response is to inquire about his wallet. His crestfallen rejoinder: "Rats! There are charges." In the former image (fig. 70), which emphasizes the poverty of the milliner, no eroticization takes place, while in the latter, her receptivity to paid sexual adventure is made to appear venal rather than financially necessary. In such popular representations of the milliner, then, the two identities – poor woman and prostitute – are separated.

Milliners were not the only female workers in the garment trades who were shown garnering sexual attention when lugging their work through the city.[19] Pascal-Adolphe-Jean Dagnan-Bouveret's *A Rest by the Seine* of 1880 (fig. 71), for example, presents a laundress on a public thoroughfare in such terms: a pretty young woman rests briefly from carrying two large bundles of laundry, and this innocent pause "naturally" inspires the leering attention of the two swells strolling at the right. As in most pictures that sexualize a chance encounter between a working woman and men-about-town her attractiveness coupled with her profession appear to justify and naturalize the men's impertinence. Indeed, the social and economic gulf between the woman and the men enables this kind of modern-life painting of an apparent commonplace: the most powerful persons (the men) are the active (walking) subjects, while the least powerful person (the working woman) is the passive (seated) object of their gaze. Her appeal certainly depends here upon her being pretty, but it is fundamentally rooted in her gender and her economic inferiority indicated by her dress and bundles of laundry.

An anonymous ink-wash drawing of an *atelier des modistes*, or millinery shop (fig. 72), datable to the late 1870s on the basis of the slim contour of the customer's two-piece day dress, would seem to reinforce C. J. Lecour's declaration, presented at the beginning of this chapter, that millinery shops were places of debauchery. The full range of millinery work is shown in this drawing. At left, three seated women build or ornament hats, while at right a fashionable customer tries on one of the hats, aided by the *marchande à la toilette*, or shopkeeper. A formally dressed, foppish gentleman (complete with monocle) stands silhouetted in the open doorway, peering in with a proprietary air to take in this all-female scene. That milliners were "fair game" for the libidinous *flâneur* – were perhaps in business to meet such a man's sexual requirements – was a widely shared conceit, kept in circulation by many social observers, ranging from naturalist writers to administrators of the service des moeurs. Of course the texts had different functions and audiences, but most agreed that milliners were open to paid sex, and most commentators only begrudgingly acknowledged that this form of prostitution was necessitated by the inadequate wages of the profession.

"Une Modiste," a story published in a journal of naturalist writings in 1880, was a particularly chatty version of the cliché of the alluring milliner. The narrator is the confidant of a young milliner, and, without any ado, the text presumes that the young woman will elicit offers from men on the street because she is carrying a hatbox and that the proprietress of the millinery shop is a procuress. Here are the relevant sections of the story: "All the men turned to look; the hat box gave them assurance. . . . Here is what the proprietress, a woman of forty, told her after having examined her for several seconds: 'My child, you please me physically very much and your look suits me. . . . To avoid hiding anything from you, you will learn that the young women I have here are supported. To tell you the truth, I would like it if you were in the same situation. . . [ellipsis in original] Now, I have the custom of receiving several of my friends in the evening, gentlemen of the world.' "[20]

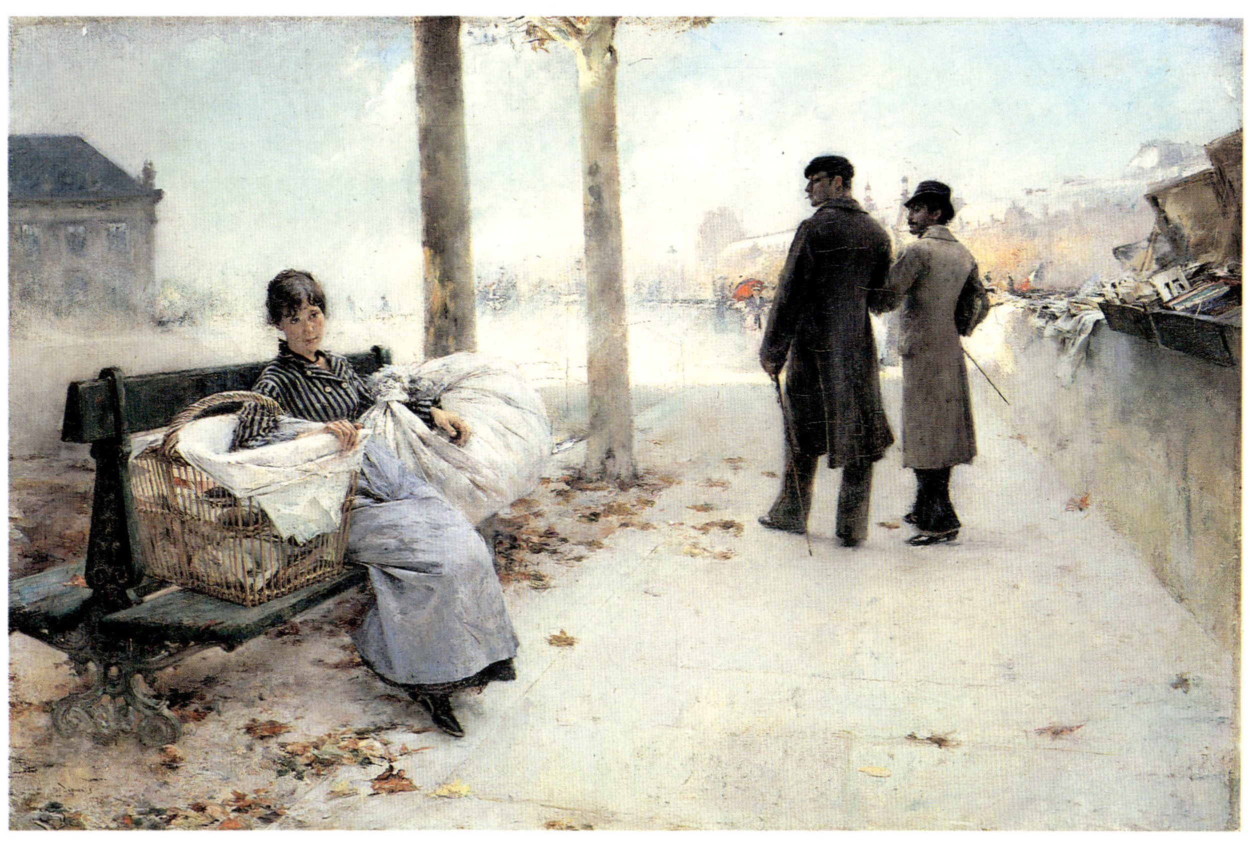

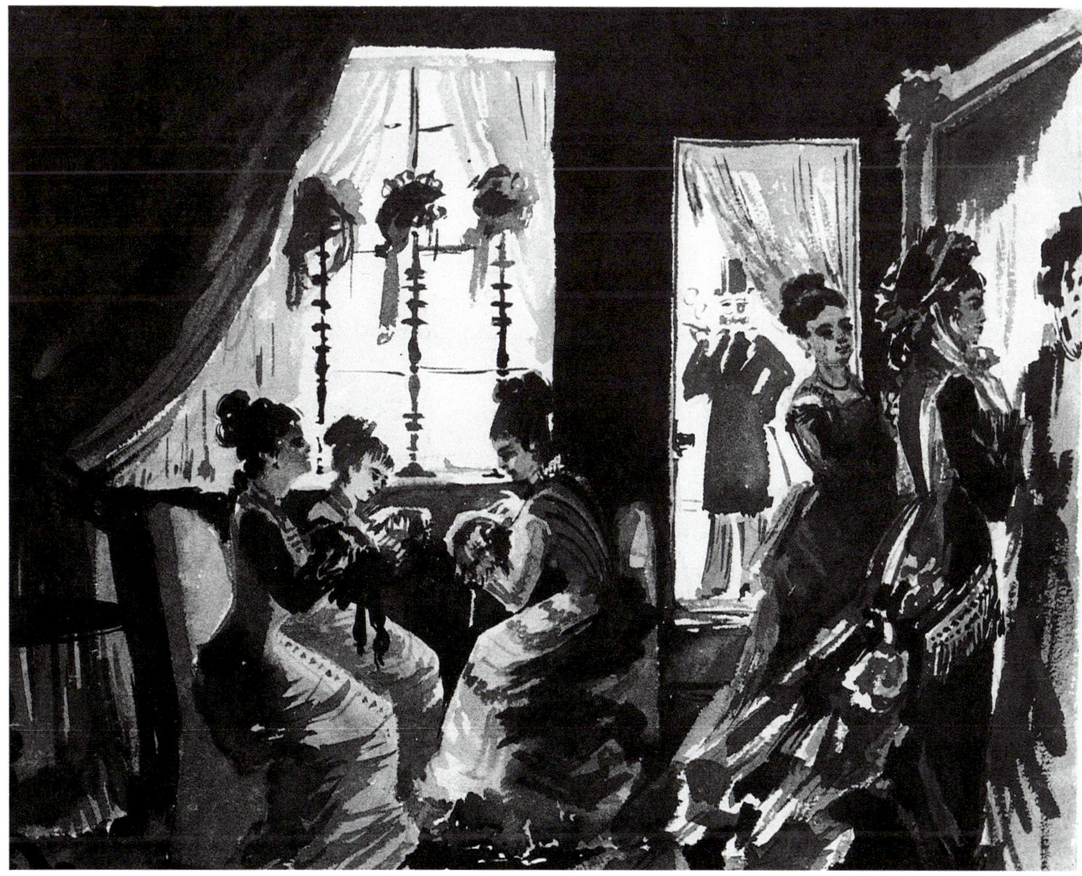

71. Pascal-Adolphe-Jean Dagnan-Bouveret, *A Rest by the Seine*, 1880.

72. *Millinery Shop*, n.d., wash drawing, Cabinet des Estampes, Bibliothèque Nationale, Paris.

We are aware of the prominence of milliners in regulationist accounts of clandestine prostitution, as stated in the epigraph. Lecour prefaced these remarks with a firm avowal: "In this category of procurement ['commerce à la toilette'] the most able cover up their maneuvers under the apparent exercise of a profession in which one actually employs workers."[21] Lecour and others identify the millinery shop of the late 1870s and 1880s as a prototypical *magasin-prétexte*, a shop operating as a front for prostitution. According to most accounts that characterize millinery shops as deceptive forms of enterprise, where hats and sex are merchandised in tandem, the young milliner at the bottom of the pay scale is understood to be a victim who is perverted by the procuress.

Dr. L. Martineau, a medical doctor who specialized in the study and treatment of clandestine prostitutes, observed in 1885 that shop girls employed by many small Parisian specialty stores worked only and quite unmistakably as prostitutes:

> One must follow this prostitution into the less accessible places, where only the knowledgeable public goes, informed by discreet invitations or by the recognizable character of the place. I wish to speak of houses of perfume, gloves, collars, ties, photographs, prints, even book stores, that open onto the great districts of Paris. There one finds a special display of goods for sale which is quite restrained. Between the articles on display inside appear eyes full of promises, and for fear that the *flâneur* will pause before the goods for sale, a wink, a very meaningful gesture, informs him very quickly with what and with whom he might do business.[22]

"Near the Boulevard," a cartoon from an 1879–80 issue of an illustrated paper (fig. 73), falls into line with such assumptions about the "real" labors performed by shop girls: the young employee of a glove shop is said to clean the wallets as well as the gloves of the boulevardiers who frequent the shop.

In most discussions of clandestine prostitution that operated out of the small specialty shop, the role of the proprietress as *entremetteuse* or *proxénète* (procuress or pimp) is stressed. It is consistently differentiated from the role played by her male counterpart, the *souteneur*. Lecour makes a succinct distinction: "The women exploit the debuts; the men come along later."[23] The procuress was apparently considered the recruiter of vulnerable young women, while the pimp was believed to exploit a successful commercial venture.

According to Louis Reuss, a regulationist doctor, the veteran shopkeeper and the younger woman were frequently brought together by the beginner's inability to afford decent clothing.[24] Once again economic hardship shades into a passion for attractive clothing, and that is said to lead in turn to indecorous behavior. It was thought that once a hapless renter was dependent upon such a woman for the necessities and niceties of dress, she was decisively on the hook: "Saying merchant of toiletries is much the same as saying procuress: The insolvent debtor has only to lend an ear to her creditor, who knows how to set up the occasion to free her of debts by procuring clients for her either at her own home or in a *maison de passe*."[25]

Reuss also suggests that some marchandes à la toilette who shepherded young women through the initial stages of clandestine prostitution would use the profits to capitalize a shop, which would be another link between the retail trade in luxury goods and clothing and the procurement of prostitutes: "Those who have amassed a certain quantity of capital open shops to sell gloves, perfume, champagne, curiosities, electroplated ware (*ruolz*), clothing, etc.; others

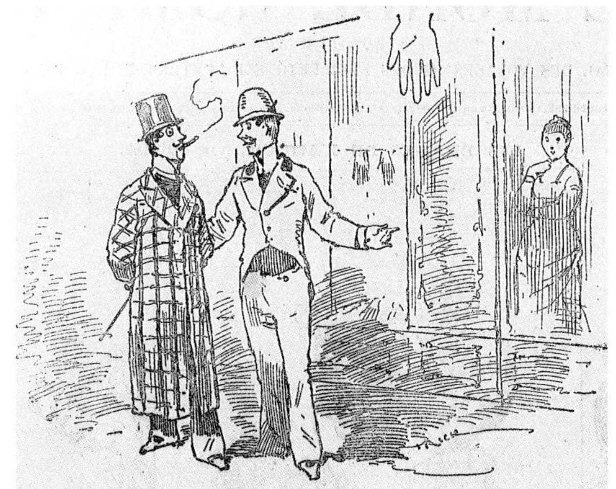

73.
"Near the Boulevard," *Le Monde Comique*, 1879–80.

– *If you need a glove maker, here's mine, whom I can recommend.*
– *And does she do glove cleaning?*
– *And how! she even cleans out wallets!*

become, in appearance at least, laundresses, linen maids, designers, florists, journal saleswomen. The police survey all these fraudulent shops. The police try in vain to close them down; they reappear elsewhere; they are all equipped with a room at the back of the shop which serves as a rendezvous spot."[26]

Artists of the Impressionist avant-garde painted modistes over roughly a ten-year period: the subject was taken up once in pastel and watercolor by Gonzalès circa 1877, painted in oil once by Renoir between 1876 and 1878 and once by Manet in 1881, and depicted repeatedly in oil and pastel by Degas between 1882 and 1885. The reserve and storytelling indefiniteness of the pictures (as well as their compositions and bright palettes) underpin their family resemblance. Their deadpan quality sets them apart from other more interpretively definite and often sexualizing images of milliners in circulation at the same time, some of which we have already discussed (figs. 49 and 72, for example).

Renoir's only treatment of this subject, *At the Milliner* (fig. 74), is a small painting (only 12 3/4" × 9 5/8") that has a complex color scheme, soft focus, and painterly handling that also appear in better-known works by Renoir painted at about the same time, such as the *Bal du Moulin de la Galette* or *Balançoire*, both painted in 1876, now in the Musée d'Orsay.[27] In view of Renoir's pronounced interest in the theme of chance flirtations between men and women, the principal idiosyncracy of his representation of a millinery shop is his conception of it as an exclusively female enclave – not as a place for men to admire sexy milliners. But neither does he show it as a place for women to buy and sell hats.

The face of the central figure, a seated woman, is more clearly rendered than anything else in the painting. The less distinct faces are composed of separate parallel strokes of thick paint. The legibility of the face of the woman at the left edge of the picture is barely secured by the use of black linear eyes and brows, but the extreme blur of the head of the standing figure at the right is unrelieved. And her blurriness makes the subject of the painting especially difficult to sort out. The standing figure's head is summary almost to the point of its obliteration. The crown of her head is defined by overlapping and distinct curved segments of brown. The much looser and greyer strokes covering the plane of her face must describe a veil that attaches to the

74. Pierre-Auguste Renoir, *At the Milliner*, ca. 1876–78, oil on canvas, bequest of Annie Swan Coburn, Fogg Art Museum, Harvard University, Cambridge, Mass.

soft brown, perhaps feathered cloche, but the veil is obscured by several spots of paint in the figure's facial area: two grey-black ovals suggest the shadows of eyesockets, but several short red strokes in the middle of the veil seem to float in front of it, overlapping the auburn hair of the seated figure, and the red strokes do not add up to part of a face seen through transparent material.

In its structure, its loose textures, and the interaction of rich color (for example, the red and purple in the central zone of black), this image of the interaction among three women in a millinery shop is vintage Renoir: an oblique glimpse of a Parisian subject featuring a pretty young woman. It exemplifies an aesthetic of a random and inconsequential glance, but within its structured nonchalance, there is an undertone of strain.

Because two of the figures – the two subsidiary women at either side – wear hats, we assume that they are customers, because an employee in a millinery shop would be hatless. The central figure *is* hatless but occupies the position of a customer; she is seated at a table, surrounded by the others. The illegibility of the woman's face at right makes the position of that leaning figure relative to the seated woman difficult to read precisely. Because of the setting, we read the bending, veiled figure's relationship to the seated woman as part of a commercial transaction, but of what kind?

The seated woman leans slightly forward in a red chair, resting her clasped hands on a table. She looks straight ahead, although placidly, and appears, judging from the position of her head and tightness about her mouth, to be thinking something over. Because Renoir has placed the figure behind her in such a contiguous position – the heads are adjacent, a white, pawlike, gloved hand cups a shoulder – the central figure can be read either as reacting to the implorer behind her or contemplating something or someone in front of them, beyond the picture frame. The third figure, the woman at left, is the outsider. She looks over at them; they look elsewhere. The lines of sight meet at a right or slightly acute angle. Renoir has given the observer (the figure at left) a facial expression that is quite different from that of the central figure: the extreme angle of the observer's black brows hints at tension or strain in her observation of the other two women.

The softness of the forms in this small picture initially draws attention away from the slight but noticeable intensity of the figures' interaction. Renoir produced other pictures in the 1870s that focused upon an observed woman (*The Theater Box* of 1874, for example, in the Courtauld Collection), but the milliner painting in the Fogg Museum seems different because the central figure is contemplating a proposal, the difficulty or challenge of which is set in play by the veiled figure's demeanor and proximity. The secondary motif of the concerned observer strengthens the suggestion of tension in the relationship between the other two.

The small painting portrays informal socializing in the shop rather than merchandising, everyday banality rather than commercial activity. It seems, however, that the tension Renoir built into his otherwise convincingly nonchalant observation suggests his ease with a definition of the millinery shop as a place of female scheming and collusion, where the groundwork might have been laid for sexual dealings, where young women might have been convinced by a proprietress or shop girl to become part of a commerce in sex, which may have been headquartered in the shop.

In this picture, Renoir generally avoids any direct connotations of prostitution and consequently minimizes any eroticization of the hat business. These characteristics of Renoir's paint-

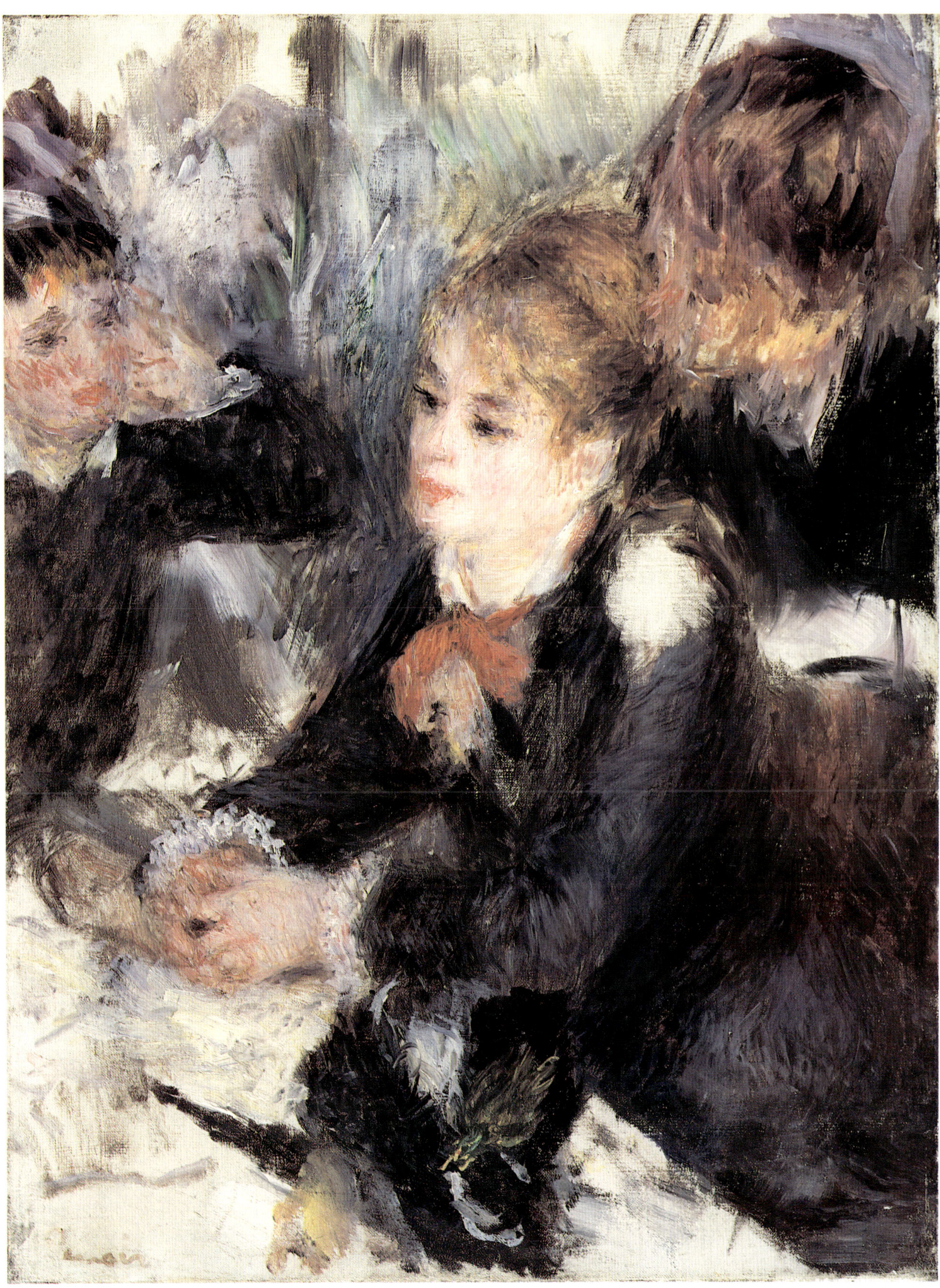

75.
James Tissot, *The Young Lady of the Shop*, 1883–85, oil on canvas, Art Gallery of Ontario, Toronto.

ing of a *magasin de modes* are thrown into sharp relief when compared to another representation of such a shop, *The Young Lady of the Shop* (fig. 75), one of the paintings from James Tissot's series, *The Women of Paris*,[28] painted between 1883 and 1885.

Tissot's series had two showings shortly after its completion: in 1885 at the Galerie Sedelmeyer in Paris and in 1886 at the Arthur Tooth Gallery in London.[29] The London catalog entry for *The Young Lady of the Shop* read: "It is on the boulevard; a scene full of life and movement is passing out of doors and our young lady with her engaging smile is holding open the door till her customer takes the pile of purchases from her hand and passes to the carriage. She knows her business and has learned the first lesson of all, that her duty is to be polite, winning and pleasant. Whether she means what she says, or much of what her looks express, is not the question; enough if she has a smile and an appropriate answer for everybody."[30]

This cheerful and confident description of the work overlooked the secondary narrative at the left side of the painting, which inflects the picture's construction of shop girls and their work. A middle-aged boulevardier peers into the shop window. We have returned to the milieu of the wash drawing of the atelier des modistes (fig. 72) done in the late 1870s. The store clerk coping with a box on a shelf is the focus of his altogether intent gaze; he seems to show little interest in the elaborate display of goods in the vitrine. The shop girl, seen from the back, appears to entice him by returning his look of inspection. There is even a tertiary story that repeats the theme of male-initiated flirtation near the shop. In the distance, behind the right shoulder of the main salesgirl, a young woman walks alone on the sidewalk, eyes downcast; she appears to be saluted by the gentleman in the U-shaped pocket of space between the salesgirl's silhouette and the near edge of the open door.

The painting is an adaptation of the cutoff, causally glimpsed modern-life picture invented and elaborated by Degas, Renoir, Manet, Morisot, and Caillebotte. The work by Renoir, just discussed, is a constructed simulacrum of a casual glance at three women in a shop, in which the substance and meaning of their interaction are not specified. Tissot, however, uses certain of the pictorial conventions of the "glimpse picture" (for example, the stop-action position of the cutoff woman at the left, the perfectly bisected footman and floating horses' heads in the middle distance at right, and the large-scale and diagonal placement of the foreground furniture), but he does so to tell rather specific stories.

Tissot's painting is crowded with crisply painted details of furniture, trimmings, costume, and architecture. At the same time, however, its look of documentary truth is firmly rooted in the male-entrenched view of the female-staffed Parisian haberdashery as a place to ogle the pretty employees and – part and parcel of Tissot's view – to have the women respond. This seems clearly spelled out in the secondary scenario at the left side of the painting. The London catalog text assumed that the shop girl facing out of the picture opens the door for a departing customer, and does so very cordially. Her cordiality may also suggest that a shop girl's simulation of personal warmth toward the buyer was an expected part of her business conduct.

This image of a Parisian specialty store contrasts sharply with Renoir's. Certain of the differences between the two can be explained by the artists' disparate conceptions of fact-based picture making and modernity. Tissot's painting is an uninterrupted assembly of trompe l'oeil renderings of specific physical data. Along with the compositional devices already mentioned, this guarantees an appearance of documentary verisimilitude. The painstaking item-by-item, surface-by-surface inventory of the various inanimate props is the painted equivalent of a

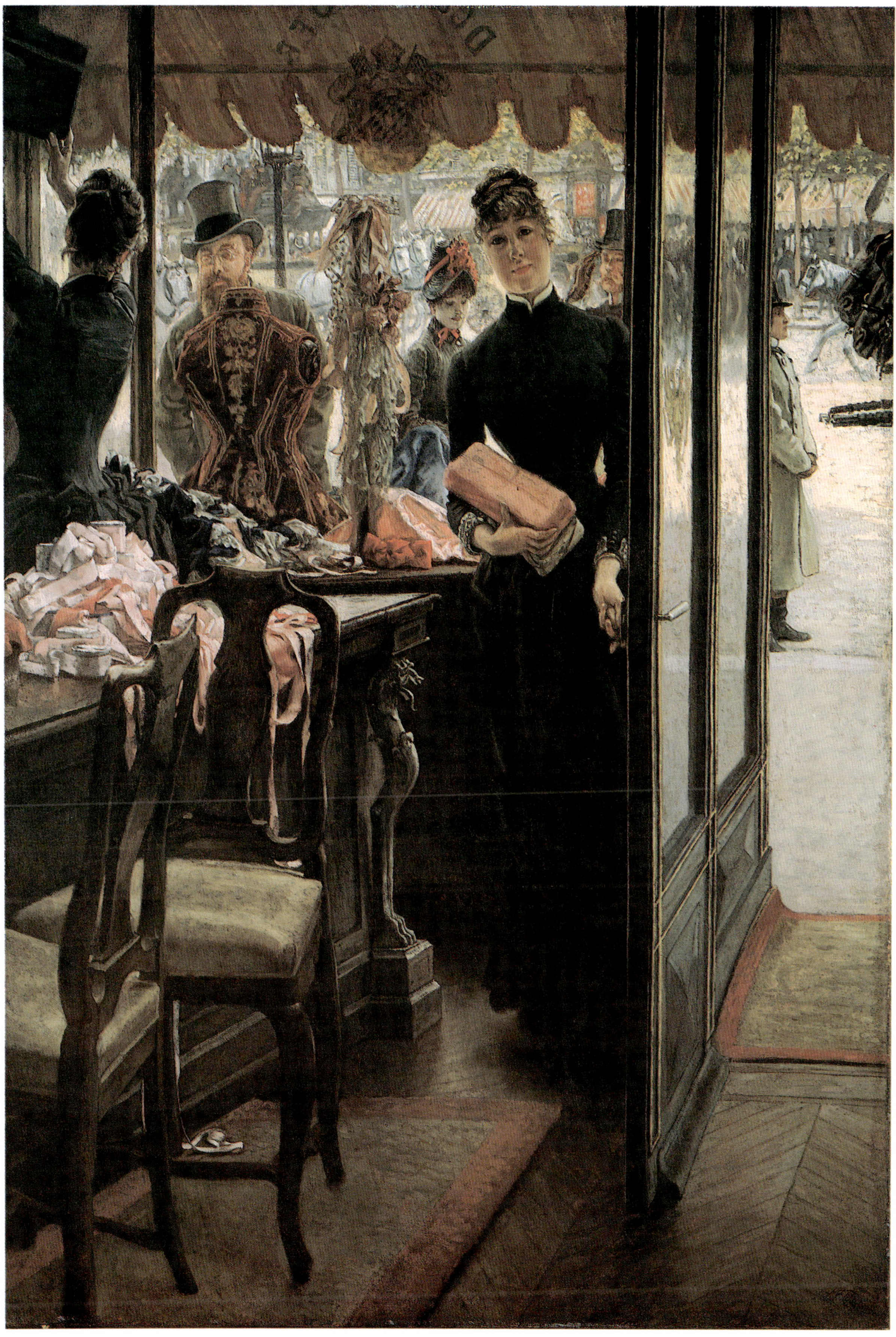

highly artificial way of looking – or imaging that one could look – at the world. The painting appears to be the result of a minute inspection of an obediently frozen motif. This kind of scrutiny is (or would be) highly specialized, because it is foreign to everyday perceptions of one's surroundings and therefore conceivable and practicable only within a representational procedure – in this case, as an aspect of documentary picture making.

Because the conceptual conceit that underlies a picture like Tissot's is the belief in the possibility of accurately recording a particular moment, the inclusion of human figures is automatically subject to certain constraints and destined to follow a preordained pattern. To produce a thoroughly detailed image of a moment that appears plucked from life in media res, the people must be shown in the middle of identifiable, relatively unambiguous action, so that a pose, a face, or a gesture can be as persuasive as a mound of spools of ribbon or an embroidered velvet waistcoast. To give equal weight to all parts of the illusion of *The Young Lady of the Shop*, without allowing it to lapse into a mere still life, Tissot uses a clearly articulated story – that of eroticized commerce in the Parisian shop.

Renoir's *At the Millinery Shop* also pictures a specific contemporary motif that period commentators provided with a sexualized meaning, but the narrative of Renoir's painting is ambiguous and inconclusive, and the conventional identifying signs of a magasin-prétexte have been all but siphoned away. This combination of fluidity and imprecision is markedly different from Tissot's vivid, precise, and frozen image. Renoir constructed inconsequentiality, ambiguity, and the appearance of a gently vibrating motion in things at rest, while Tissot did the opposite.

It seems that Renoir was attracted to and eventually chose the motif of the millinery shop because he found social qualities in it that met his criteria for a suitably interesting subject: the appeal of female sexuality in an ambiguous, secret, and somewhat conspiratorial form, set within a public but intimate marketplace for women's clothing. Renoir obviously found this combination of features appealingly modern – as did Tissot. This strong appeal probably accounts for Renoir's choice of the subject, but the way he painted it reveals his rejection of Tissot's style of grabbing hold of and organizing the motif into something lucid, clear, and unequivocal. Renoir's wispy paint strokes and vibrant color interactions show him to have faced the subject – or his idea of the subject – intent on the primacy of painting, concentrating on the abstract artistic issues of translating the interaction of light and color into oil paint, of enriching black with grey, violet, and crimson, of building a composition to contain the things seen, but without forcing them into a pat and falsely legible hierarchy. It seems that Renoir's attraction to the popular masculine eroticization of the hat shop helped to shape his picture. That the dubious reputation of the millinery shop endowed it with a sexually tantalizing aura of ambiguity and contingency made such a place an appealing subject for a modern painting, and those qualities were carried over into the formal means of the picture. One can see Renoir converting social ambiguity into formal ambiguity. Tissot's more definite interpretation of the motif corresponds, in turn, to his more precise way of depicting it.

Manet's version of the subject, *At the Milliner* (fig. 76), painted in 1881, contains a solitary woman in profile examining a hat. Her pale shoulders are suggestively bared, but she wears a look that is both prim and determined: her lips are pursed and her eyes squint slightly in focused thought. It would be difficult to identify this woman as a customer or the shop's proprietress without recourse to the original title, *The Milliner*, which identifies the woman un-

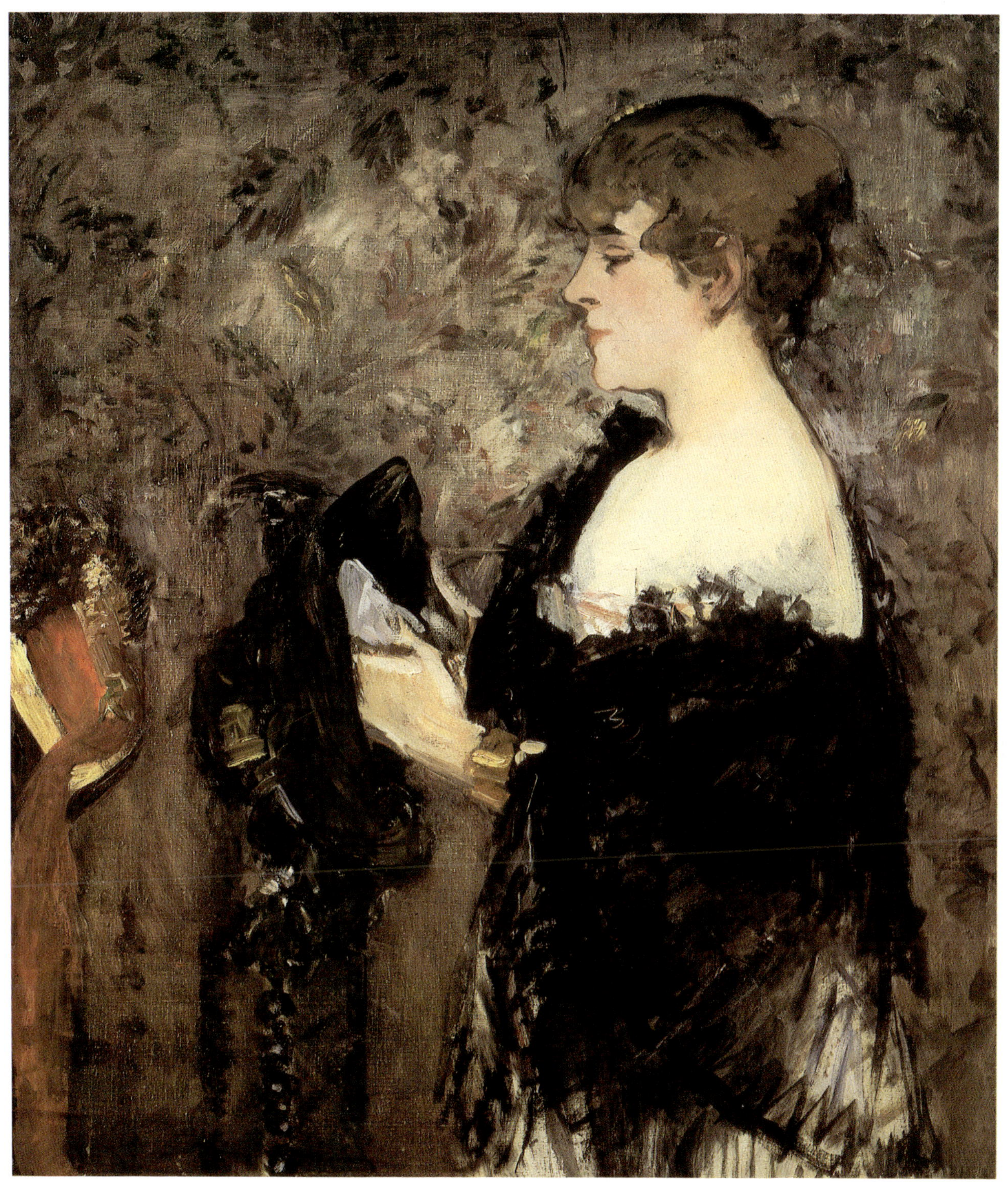

76.
Edouard Manet, *At the Milliner*, 1881, oil on canvas,
California Palace of the Legion of Honor, San Francisco.

equivocally.[31] Her imperious manner, her soigné style of dress, and her action (she appears to adjust the stuffing in a hat on display) fix her identity as the keeper of the shop.[32]

Manet's decision to use a mature, bare-shouldered woman as the sole occupant of the shop may well have been rooted in a familiarity and fascination with the reputation of the manager or owner for organizing millinery shop employees into a clandestine prostitution operation. Although Manet and Renoir were very different kinds of painters, they shared an interest in the subject of the eroticized, contemporary working woman, while, at the same time, leaving aside the telltale signs of her legendary moral corruption.

Beginning in the early 1880s, probably in 1882, Degas did at least sixteen pastels and paintings of milliners.[33] Degas's often-quoted artistic credo and Gustave Coquiot's disparagements of the artist's modiste pictures are apt prefaces to a close study of two of these images. In Degas's words: "No art is less spontaneous than mine. What I do is the result of reflection and of study of the great masters; of inspiration, spontaneity, temperament, I know nothing. One must re-do the same subject ten times, one hundred times. Nothing in art should resemble an accident, even movement."[34] According to Coquiot's 1924 study of Degas's milliner images:

> [In a millinery shop] between 5 and 7, at a shot, everyone on the bridge, the commotion of trying things on, of recriminations, enthusiasms, cries, swoons, rages, jealousies, deceptions. . . . Degas does not go beyond the short anecdote: His paintings and drawings of milliners are not savoury successes. . . . That he cannot give us, Degas, the character of this group of females, so be it! . . . but, in truth, he could have surpassed the photographic document, this painter called artist of "modern truth." . . . Degas has never considered what could really be at the center of feminine thinking![35]

According to Coquiot, Degas recorded the appearance of the women accurately enough, but he did not reveal the meaning of the milliner, because, using Coquiot's terms, the "courte anecdote" and the "document photographique" were inadequate indications of the "vérité" of the subject. By and large, Coquiot's complaints are legitimate: the milliner pictures do lack drama and do not allow an easy interpretation. But, as Degas's remarks remind us, if drama and interpretation are missing, their absence is not due to a lack of probity in method. Those qualities were not part of Degas's interest in the subject or his purpose in presenting it.

One of the pictures, an oil on canvas of 1882–85, entitled *At the Milliner* (fig. 77), contains two women who are readily identifiable as customer and milliner. As usual in Degas's treatment of this particular combination of women, the customer trying on a hat predominates and the milliner plays a subordinate role. Also as usual, his picturing of the transaction is based upon firmly drawn distinctions of class, showing a rigidly maintained social hierarchy. But in this picture Degas's presentation of customer and milliner is odd: the milliner holds a hat for a faceless customer, who dons another and inspects her featureless self in the mirror.

The generally broad handling of the work mitigates the peculiarity of the blank phantom of a face reflected in the mirror as a white, featureless oval laid down in parallel striations of white, as is the balance of the reflection. The blankness of the reflected face is matched by the customer's mittenlike, undifferentiated, orangy, gloved hands. As a result of the schematic features given to the customer, the specificity of the bare pink hands of the milliner reaching in with a hat from the right edge comes as a surprise. Her fingers are separately drawn, and they bend, separate, and arch to the maximum, like claws. They appear exaggerated in the context of this

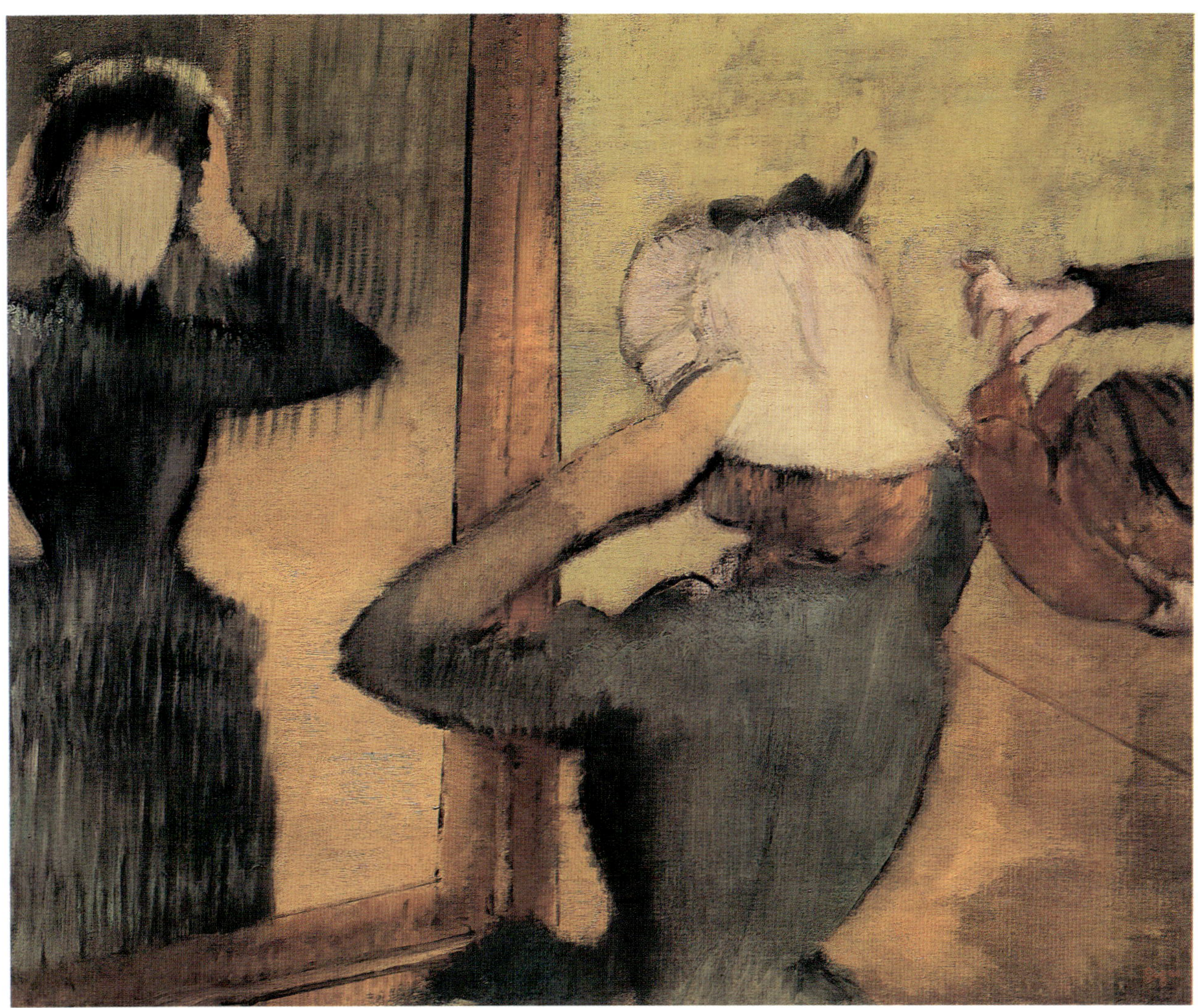

77. Edgar Degas, *At the Milliner*, 1882–85, collection of Mr. and Mrs. Paul Mellon, Upperville, Va.

otherwise sketchily painted work, even somewhat sinister in their overarticulation. The composed and decorous though blank customer forms an eerie contrast to the fussy claws of the shop girl.

The Millinery Shop, a pastel of 1882 by Degas (fig. 78), eliminates entirely the interaction between buyer and seller. Degas marshals his suave compositional skills in a presentation of hats and, in this case, two milliners. We see that both figures are partially covered by the colorful, high-value, warm-hued straw hats and by the work table, and one woman is furthermore cut by the right edge of the picture. This familiar pattern of overlap and fragmentation works to persuade us of the documentary accuracy of the artist's observation. The two milliners in the workroom are not shown as equals, and the differences between them are suggested and underscored by the many contrasts in the picture: the difference between the flowered and ribboned straw hat and the plain one; the difference in position and shape of the plain hat (a round shape seen from above) and the decorated hat (an irregular shape seen from the side); the difference between a woman working and a woman watching; the difference between a young woman (at left) and an older one; the difference between a hat supported by a stand with a slender, turned spiral base and a hat whose black ribbon covers any support and seems almost to float; the

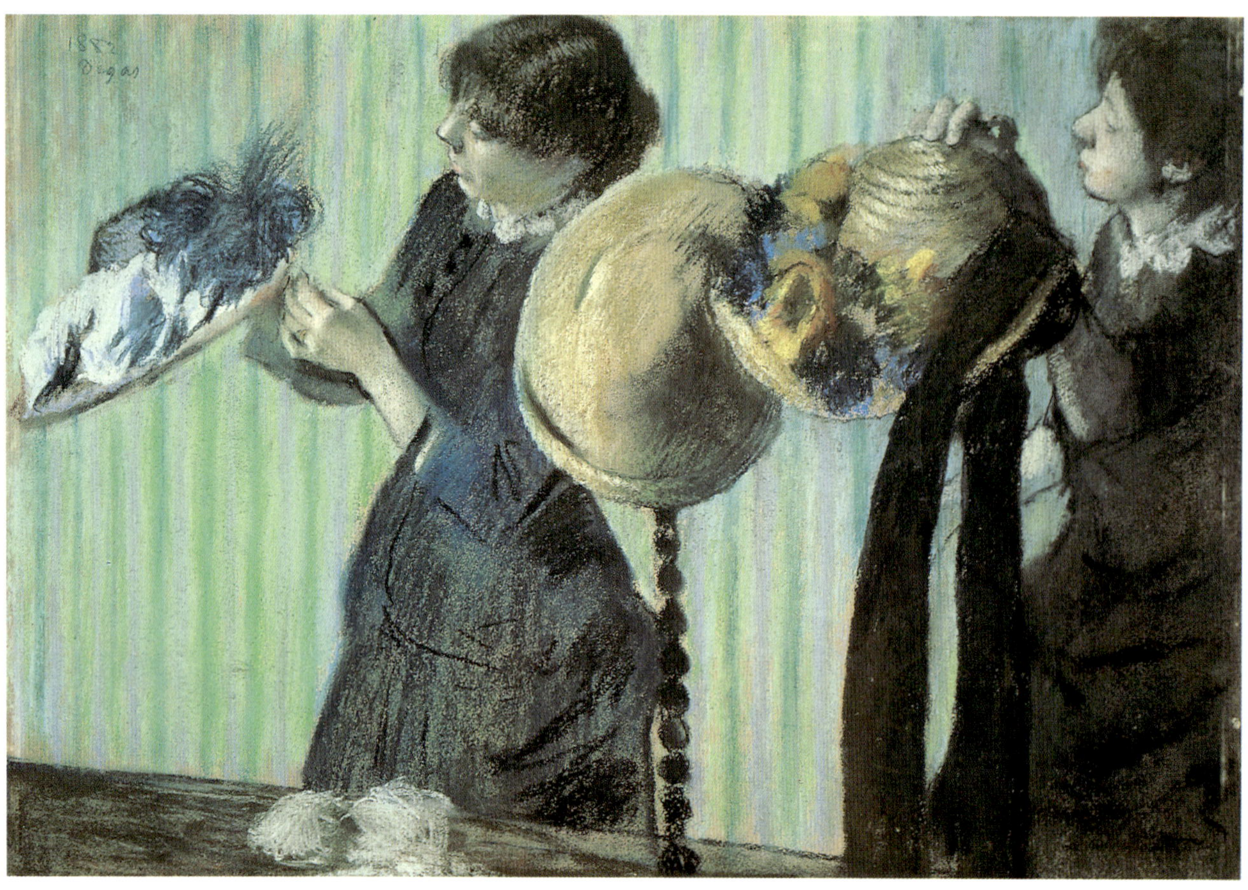

78. Edgar Degas, *The Millinery Shop*, 1882, pastel, Nelson-Atkins Museum of Art, Kansas City, Mo.

ironic contrast between a hat that may appear supportless but that nonetheless supports the large hand resting on it.

The seams do not show in this assembly of contrasts, nor is the professional ranking of the two women fixed by the visual counterpoints particularly obtrusive. The pretty young woman appears to work effortlessly, gently, and unselfconsciously, while the other woman's demeanor, face, and gesture produce the almost opposite effect: that of the surveyor whose serious face suggests the proprietary interest of the workplace supervisor. Her extraordinarily intense left hand, awkwardly perched upon and clutching the edge of the decorated straw hat, reinforces this narrative subtext. Her heavy face and slightly clumsy hand contrast sharply with the lightness and relative delicacy of the younger woman's face and hand.

In both pictures, there is an ambiguous play of relationships – the tension in both cases turning on the odd, forcible realization of a disembodied floating hand. The atmosphere in the pictures is not fully defined by the to-and-fro of work or selling. It seems possible that the tensions in the pictures are Degas's way of acknowledging the legend of the millinery shop as a magasin-prétexte. The tensions may therefore inscribe the artist's undoubted familiarity with the other reputed activities of such a shop – though, to restate my disclaimer, Degas's pictures do not by any means unequivocally define the milliner as a prostitute.

The milliner pictures by Renoir and Manet, and the two by Degas, only barely hint at an erotic subtext, if there is so much as an erotic overtone in any of these pictures. Claiming that the artists were uninterested in the myth of the modiste would not explain their pictures, and arguing that they were ignorant of the lore of the milliner-prostitute is simply implausible. For some late nineteenth-century Parisians, the millinery shop seems to have always denoted elusive, commercialized sex, and it is a matter of importance for us that painters of the Impressionist circle were drawn to the subject of milliners when the profession was so firmly enveloped by an erotic legend.

Introducing *The Milliner*, Eva Gonzalès's pastel and watercolor of circa 1877 (fig. 79), complicates our discussion, but in a productive way. Just like her friend and teacher Manet, she was connected to the Impressionists but exhibited her scenes of everyday life in the Salon only. Like the images of milliners by her male colleagues, her pastel milliner has nothing whatever to say on the subject of prostitution. But that she, too, was interested in portraying a laborer in one of the "suspicious" professions in the late 1870s affirms the strong connection between avant-garde definitions of modernity and the subject matter of sexualized, commodified, anonymous working women – a theme drawn from the exclusive territory of the flâneur.

I am claiming two things as a consequence. First, that this association was operative even though the pictures in question do not overtly sexualize the milliner and her commerce. And second, I am arguing that such an equation not only could be but *was* used by a woman artist. The case of Gonzalès making a modern-life picture on a subject so invested with sexual meanings for men (albeit a picture that stresses the independence, dignity, and calm of the practice of decorating hats) is a clear example of a woman speaking what Elaine Showalter has persuasively called a "'double-voice discourse,' embodying both the social, literary, and artistic heritages of the dominant group and [her] own muted or inflected position within it."[36]

The milliner's work and reputation made a subject for art that brought several interests of the avant-garde into contact and therefore provided appealing representational prospects for the artists' modern-life enterprise. Because "she" and her milieu had a precise physical appearance and set of protocols and her workplace was visually busy and attractive, "she" was eminently paintable in the language of the glimpse. Her reputation made her into a more or less ideal example of the commodified, modern lower-class woman, and thus an ideal trope of modernity for the cruising and painting Parisian observer. A woman who made and sold objects of adornment for a living was also reputed to be for sale herself: supposed to sell hats to women, she allegedly sold herself to men. She was endowed by her myth with a precarious, unstable, and possibly venal sexuality that, according to the legend, equipped her with an unstable purchase on her own subjectivity. This, it seems, was the combination that may account for the painters' attraction to her as a motif and for their elliptical way of depicting her compared to other more definite (and probably exaggerated) contemporary representations. For the avant-garde to have fixed "her" as a sexual libertine would have been to pin down her distinctively ambiguous identity and apparently to lessen her appeal for artists in the process. Yet by keeping their pictures of milliners ambiguous, these painters do not refuse the myth of the modiste. On the contrary, they helped to constitute and shore up the belief that working-class female sexuality was unstable.

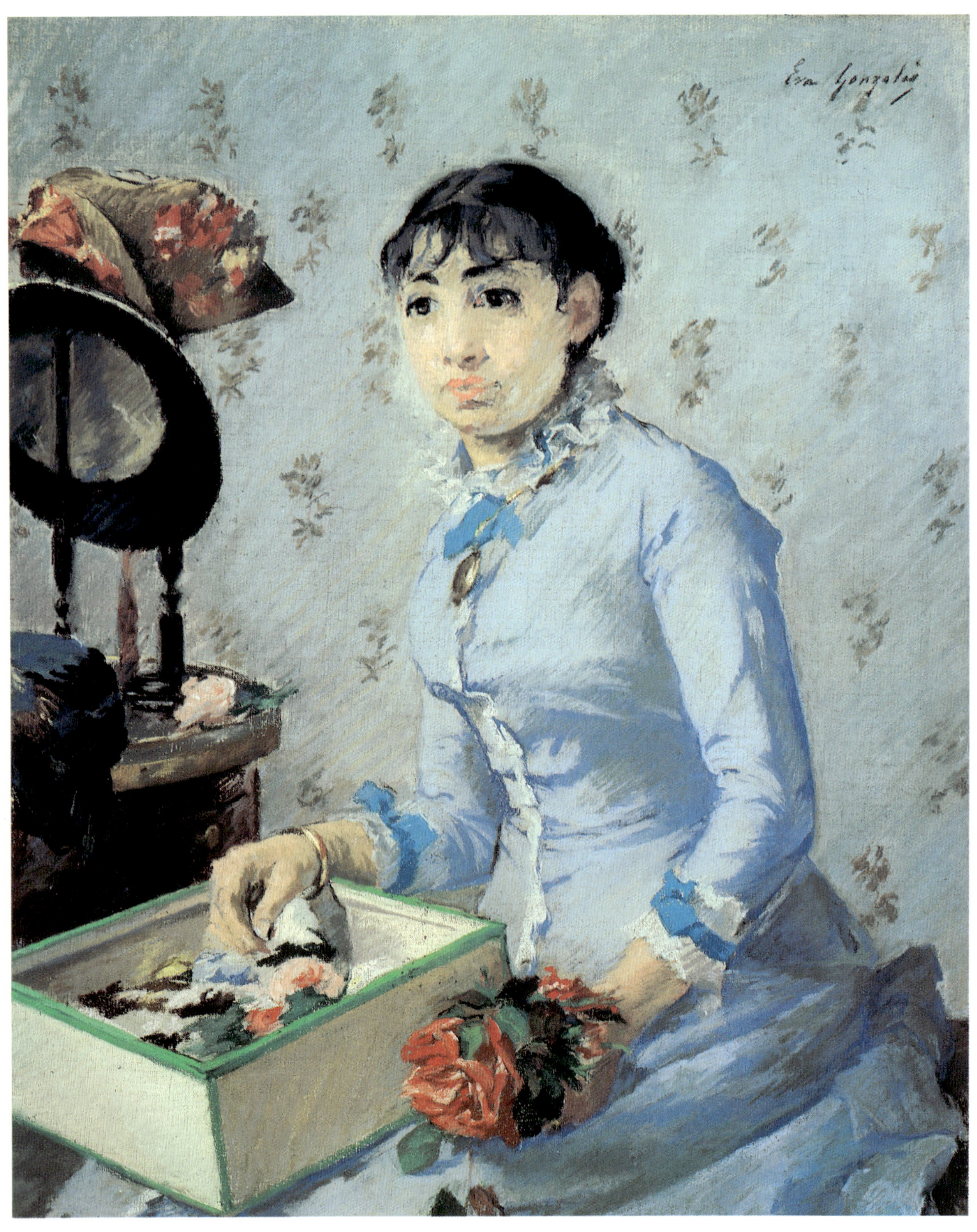

79.
Eva Gonzalès,
The Milliner, ca. 1877, gouache and pastel on canvas,
Lewis Larned Coburn Fund, Art Institute of Chicago.

Mutual Desire in the New Nightspots

Emile Zola addressing Edmond de Goncourt. *"Oh yes, I assure you, he [Alphonse Daudet] likes having his women topsy-turvy."*
Georges Charpentier. *"That's why when he takes me along with him to the brasserie on the rue Medicis, I hear him say, as he encircles the waist of one of the beer-servers, I hear him saying to them: 'Comme je t'enc . . .'"*
Goncourt. *"Gentlemen, you're saying that Daudet's a sex maniac, with a screw loose in the head?"*
Zola. *"Basically, married women just don't have common sense . . . If his wife permitted him the favors accorded him by those girls at the rue Medicis brasserie, theirs would be the happiest home on earth . . . and the rake would turn into a lap dog."*
– *Edmond de Goncourt,* Journal of the Goncourts

The kind of brasserie under discussion by Daudet's literary friends was a distinctive type of Parisian drinking establishment. The principal novelty of these relatively new beer halls was their untraditional use of women as "garçons," or waiters. A female garçon is featured, for example, in an 1878 cartoon entitled "Paris during the Exposition" (fig. 80). Brasseries à femmes, as they were called, first appeared in Paris in the late 1860s, as attractions for visitors to an earlier Exposition Universelle, that of 1867. The new brasseries succeeded in a big way, and such bars continued to open and prosper well into the 1870s and 1880s.

Because the female employees of the new-style brasseries played highly visible commercial roles in a milieu that mingled entertainment and drinking, they acquired a reputation as tramps. For, as we have already learned, independent, attractive, unmarried working women were often peremptorily judged to be libertines, but particular allegations clung to the servers working in brasseries à femmes owing to the way the bars were run. Owners of the new brasseries were merchandising sex in tandem with alcohol in highly organized fronts for clandestine prostitution. The arrangement was supposedly this: the server's primary job was to encourage, in whatever way, the maximum consumption of alcohol. To facilitate brisk sales, the woman would serve the customer his drink, sit down at his side, flirt with him, urge him to drink more and to buy drinks for her, and perhaps entice him to sleep with her – a profit for the house in each case.

Unlike the somewhat ambiguous forms of clandestine prostitution that we have already discussed, there was greater certainty that the brasserie à femmes was an organized outlet of unregulated prostitution, especially in the 1880s. In 1888, for example, Gustave Macé wrote: "The madam of a *tolérance*, in order to escape an overly repressive police hierarchy, transforms her house into a *brasserie à femmes*, a cabaret, or a *garni*."[37] The proliferation of this form of entertainment was an integral part of the decline of official prostitution. The rise of the brasserie à femmes is therefore part of the story of shifting sexual demand and supply in the early

80.
"Paris during the Exposition," *Le Monde Comique*, 1878–79.

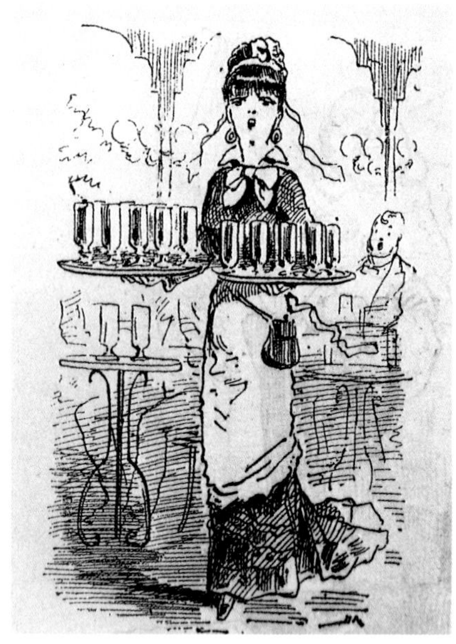

The garçon of a brasserie in the Latin Quarter.

years of the Third Republic in Paris.[38] Alain Corbin considers the advance of the brasserie à femmes to have exemplified the most fundamental change in French prostitution during the last third of the nineteenth century – to wit, "the development of venal outlets that cannot be called clandestine on the part of girls and women who are not courtesans of the highest rank, but escape the regulationist system almost entirely."[39]

Another token of the new sexual order was the combination of true commerce – these new outlets were full-blown business enterprises – with a new prostitutional style based upon the simulation of "real feelings." According to Corbin, "Finally, and perhaps especially for this is what defines them, all these new outlets of prostitution imply that *the prostitute gives her customer the impression that she is letting him seduce her*, and that she is no longer a simple animal deprived of the liberty to refuse him."[40] Several later nineteenth-century commentators adumbrated Corbin's observations about the imitation of sexual feeling in the new beer halls. In his discussion of the simulated flirtations of the *serveuse*, Dr. L. Martineau wrote in 1885: "Sometimes she acts in ways to appear particularly young and overtaken by the madness of being in love which really puts the naive guy on the wrong scent and makes him think he's being seduced, when in fact everything's been calculated."[41] An anonymous source of the same date corroborated this view: "There is the appearance of a conquest and consequently of love in this emphemeral union. They smile, they talk, they like each other. This illusion of independent choice has ruined the prestige of the lowest pleasure-spots."[42]

Starting in 1878, countless visual images of brasseries à femmes were produced. Between 1878 and 1879 Manet did three paintings of waitresses and customers in just such a place (figs. 81, 82, and 83). Further to my observations on these establishments, I shall argue that the atmosphere of contrived mutual desire was central to the historical moder-

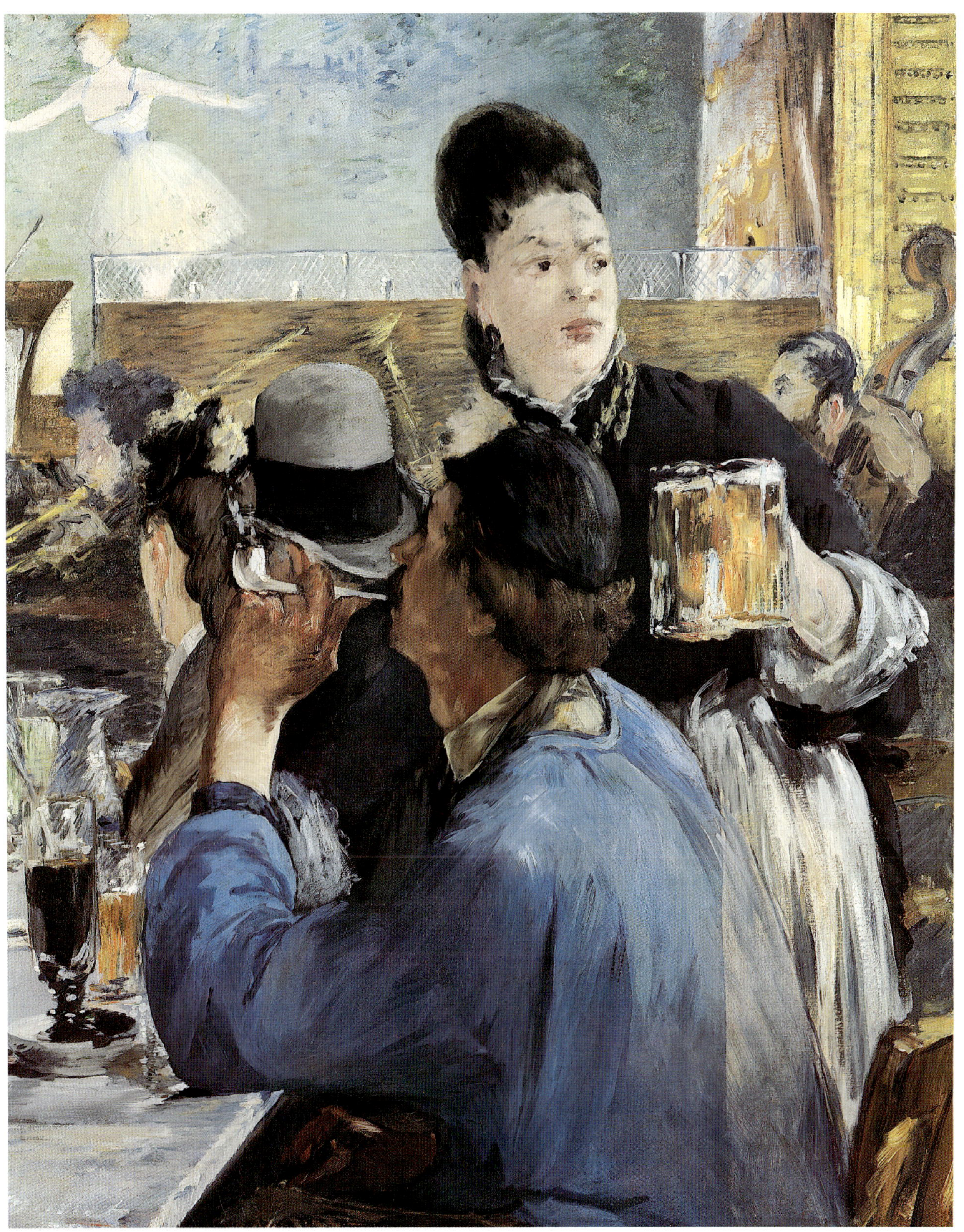

81.
Edouard Manet, *The Waitress*, 1878–79, oil on canvas, National Gallery, London.

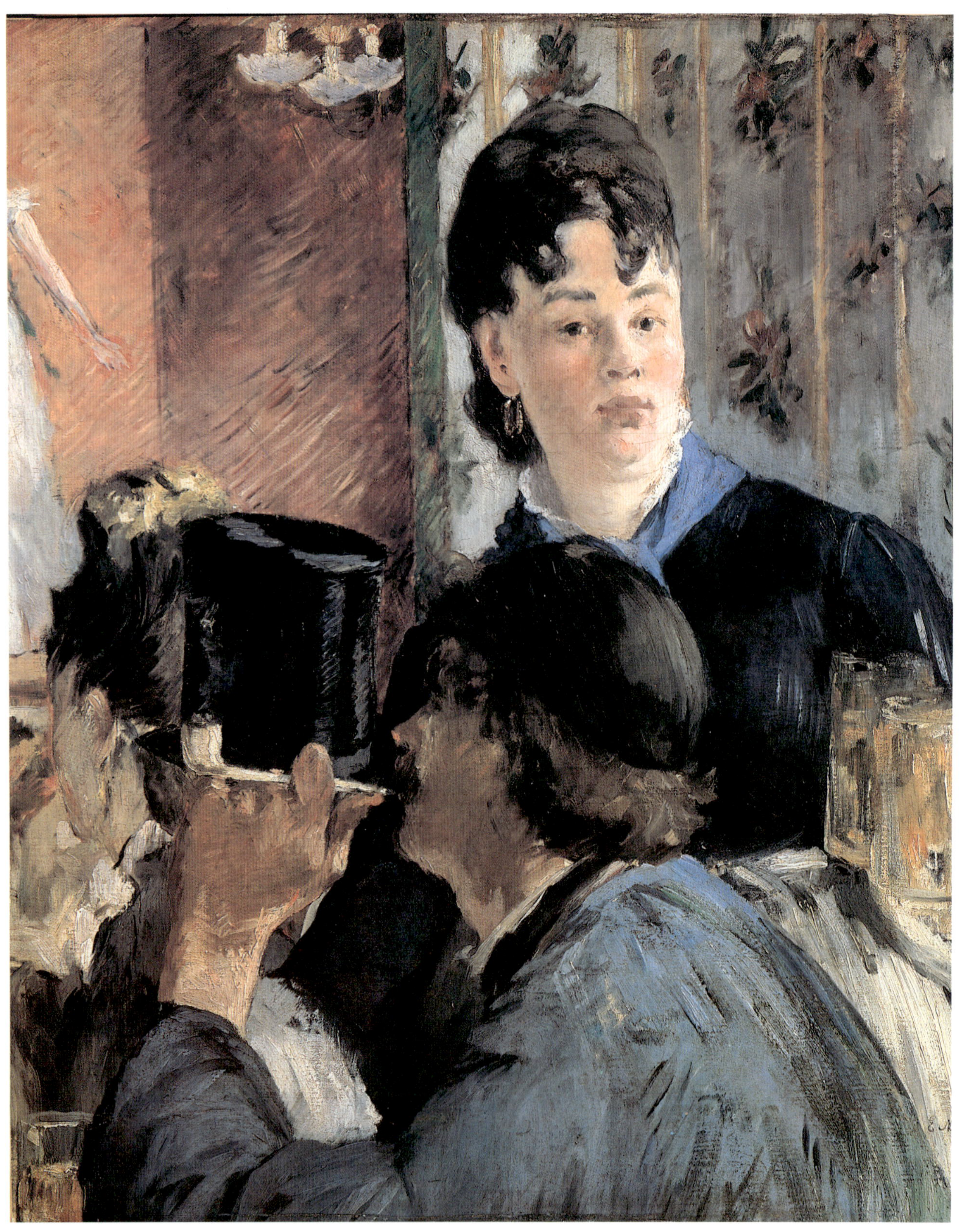

82.
Edouard Manet, *The Waitress*, 1878–79, oil on canvas,
Musee d'Orsay, Paris.

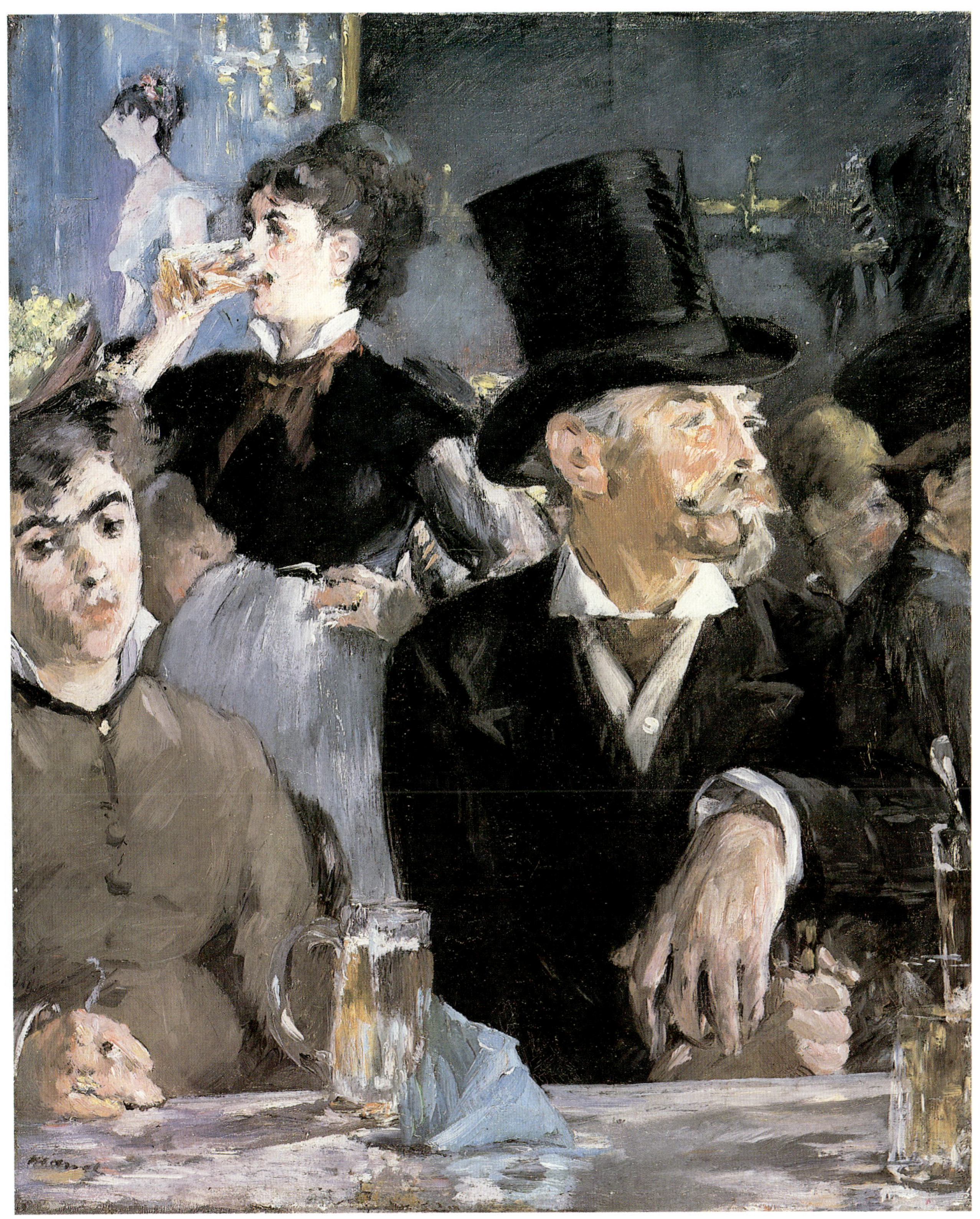

83.
Edouard Manet, *Café-Concert*, 1878, oil on canvas,
Walters Art Gallery, Baltimore.

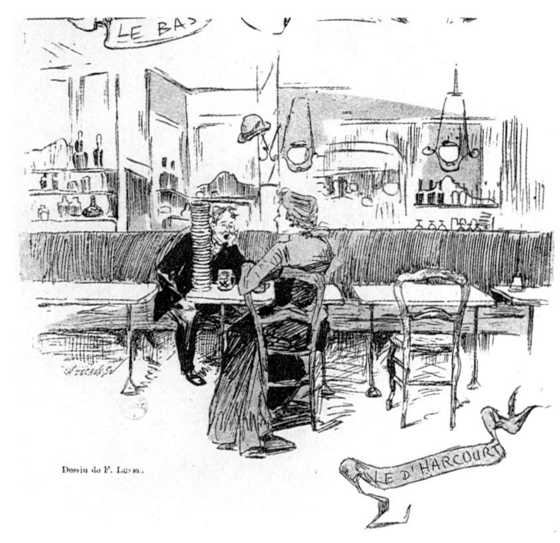

84. Ferdinand Lunel, *Brasserie le Bas-Rhin et le D'Harcourt*, ca. 1888, Cabinet des Estampes, Bibliothèque Nationale, Paris.

Brasseries served by women (fifth arrondissement) – Le Bas-Rhin and le D'Harcourt.

nity of this subject for an avant-garde artist like Manet. Indeed, I shall use our investigation of Manet's paintings of this highly charged subject to reach some conclusions about the meaning of Impressionist ambiguity.

Many popular images of female-staffed brasseries made in the 1880s emphasize intemperate drinking, and most of them show a seated server enticing a man to carouse. Artists often included a stack of saucers (following the French tradition of a saucer standing for one drink served) as the most efficient way of indicating that a customer had had much to drink. In Ferdinand Lunel's drawing of the interior of the brasserie Le Bas-Rhin and le D'Harcourt done in the late 1880s (fig. 84), the tower of saucers shows that the man had exceeded two dozen drinks. The crockery on the table of the principal bon vivant in Jean Béraud's *Brasserie* of 1883 (fig. 85) tells us that he is on his seventh round. The most prominent tippler in Fernand Fau's illustration for A. Carel's book of 1884, *Les Brasseries à femmes à Paris*, has also surpassed the six-drink mark (fig. 86), while another of Fau's illustrations for Carel's text (fig. 87) emphasizes the indecorous physical proximity of waitress and drinker.

The gentleman-student berated by his father in Robida's "New Paris" of 1884 (fig. 88) is clearly shown to have been frequenting brasseries because of his romantic interest in one of the waitresses. Robida therefore avoids the topic of drink by focusing on a persuasively romantic server instead.

Looking back from the vantage point of 1906, Dr. Félix Regnault, a historian of prostitution, stressed the relative decorum of the brasserie waitress's solicitation of a customer: "These establishments resemble ordinary cafés where you sit down to have a beer; soliciting is not brutal. The waitress simply comes over and sits down at the customer's table without being invited, serves herself, encourages the customer to spend money, strikes up a lewd conversation, and finally offers her services. . . . She uses a neighboring hotel to turn the trick. Actually, very few brasseries have rooms on the premises for the client."[45] Martineau also described a relative politeness in the typical brasserie seduction, especially when compared to the rough assaults that took place in the bars known as *débits de vin:* "Soliciting there is less coarse. Sometimes it has a

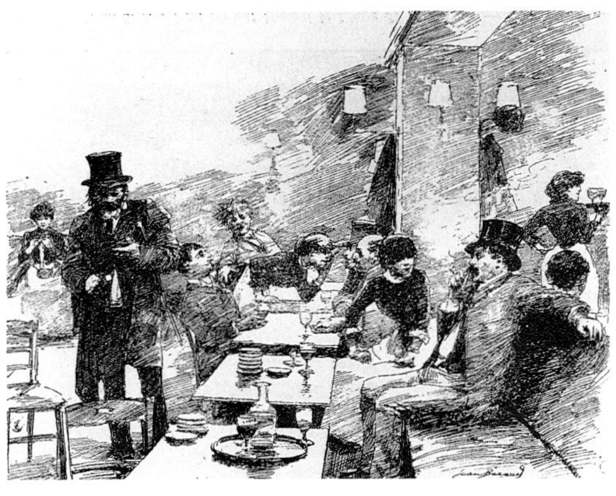

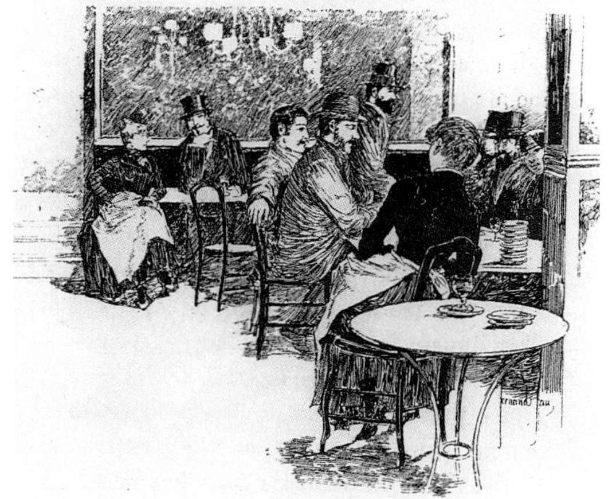

85. (l.) Jean Béraud, *A Brasserie*, from *Salon catalogue illustré*, 1883.

86. (r.) Ferdinand Fau, illustration for A. Carel, *Les Brasseries à femmes de Paris*, Paris, 1884.

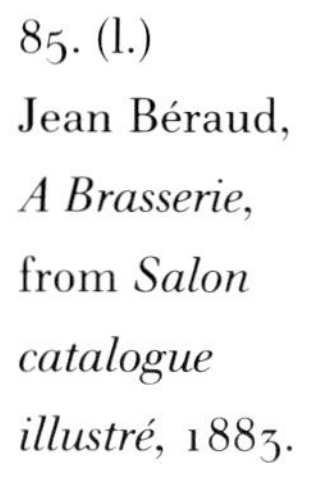

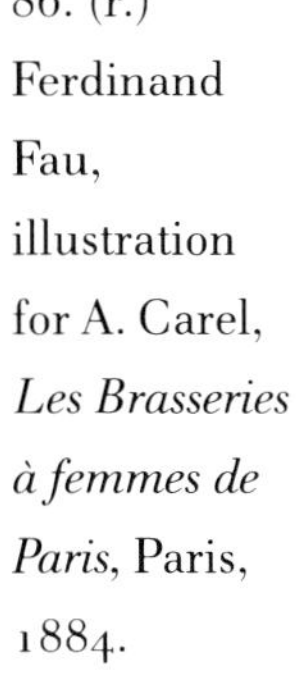

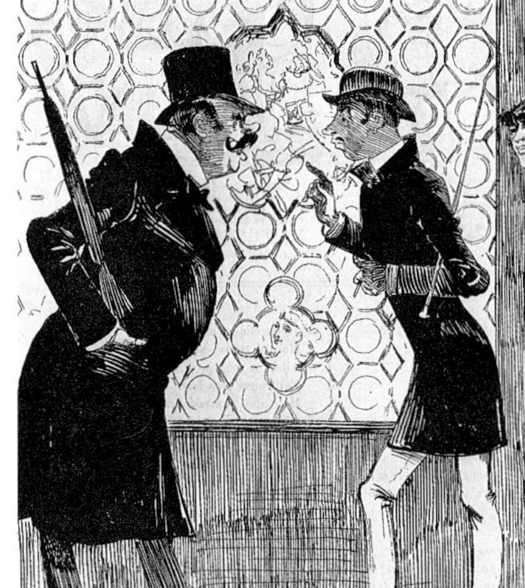

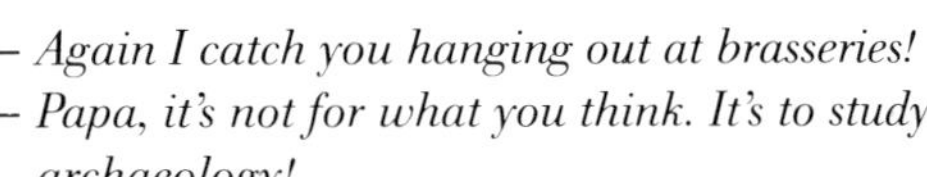

– *Again I catch you hanging out at brasseries!*
– *Papa, it's not for what you think. It's to study archaeology!*

87. (l.) Ferdinand Fau, illustration for A. Carel, *Les Brasseries à femmes de Paris*, Paris, 1884.

88. (r.) Albert Robida, "New Paris," *Le Monde Comique*, 1884.

roundabout quality, even though the introduction of the matter at hand is direct, the woman characteristically comes over to sit down, without being asked, at the drinker's table and strikes up a conversation which always ends with a proposition in secret words of the most easily-understood sort."[44]

According to some later nineteenth-century observers, however, the relatively subtle merchandising of both drink and sex in the 1870s (to which Regnault and Martineau, as well as Zola, apparently refer) was replaced by a more raucous style in the 1880s. Referring to the 1870s with an air of nostalgia, Reuss wrote in 1889: "Everything transpires decently, and if one evening a client takes one of the serving women off to sleep with her, no-one pays any attention."[45] Reuss found the operation of the brasserie of the late 1880s to be quite a different matter: "Those *brasseries à femmes* are virtual *maisons de passe* and houses of prostitution. They even look like them with their opaque windows, their loosely dressed and enticing girls sticking their heads out the partially-opened door, and the boisterous customers that they attract."[46] There is the strong possibility of course that memories of a warmer, more polite kind of solicitation might just be the usual nostalgia for a bygone and therefore more authentic era. The vulgarity of the 1880s may therefore have been exaggerated for effect. However, the fact that popular artists did not even turn their attention to the subject until the occasion of the 1878 Universal Exposition strongly suggests that the female-staffed brasserie acquired a higher public profile (and notoriety?) with the passage of time.

A barrage of reaction in the press greeted the 1881 crackdown on the brasseries attempted by the new police prefect, Jean Camescasse. Charles Flor blamed the police themselves for the appalling state of affairs in the first place. In *Le National,* he wrote: "A police regulation is needed to prevent certain café owners from transforming their establishments into virtual houses of prostitution, replacing the garçons working there with tarts of the lowest rank, for whom the inside of a cabaret is like a convenient and reliable piece of sidewalk, less tiring and protected by agents of the *police des moeurs* who are sometimes truly indiscreet."[47] Flor's detailed depiction of typical solicitation activity in such an establishment reaffirms the view that prostitution in the brasseries became brazen and rowdy after about 1880: "Whoever has gone inside one of these motley establishments, could not help pitying these bare-breasted filles, with raucous voices, dishevelled hair, whose color is either too red or too pale, acting like scum; these miserable creatures generally work themselves to death; they perform a job that even the most robust can't do for long."[48]

According to press reports that appeared in and around 1881, preserved by the prefecture de police, the serveuse's tendency to goad even very young customers to drink excessively was the focus of complaints, and the practice of encouraging intemperance in very young drinkers was the ostensible reason for Camescasse's campaign against the *brasseries.*[49] A parallel complaint was also voiced: a woman who worked in such a place inevitably became an alcoholic herself. We have already learned, thanks to Susanna Barrows's work, that the social meaning of public drunkenness among the lower-classes in general, but especially among women, was a political issue in post-Commune France.[50] The following gloss on the problem of drink in the brasserie à femmes claims that when it came to heavy drinking, the average brasserie waitress was in a league with the indefatigable carousers of Zola's *L'Assommoir:* "The filles pursue an extenuating job that carries the obligation to absorb a quantity of liquids that would make even Bec-Salé, Bibi-la-Grillade and Mes-Bottes recoil."[51]

In spite of complaints and attempts at regulation, the institution of the brasserie à femmes expanded and prospered in Paris from the moment of its conception in 1867.[52] In 1872, there were 40 female-staffed brasseries, employing 125 women. By 1879, the number had increased to 130, employing 582 women, and in 1888, there were 200 such establishments, served by 1,000 women.[53] The rapid growth in the 1880s was undoubtedly helped along by a law of July 17, 1880, which granted increased liberty to the operators of débits de boissons.[54]

According to the findings of Commenge's detailed study of the origins of clandestine prostitutes in the late nineteenth century, the serveuses in the brasseries à femmes tended to be well prepared for the venal work expected of them: "It is usually not girls from the provinces who furnish the personnel for these places; most often women go to work in these establishments after having already gotten their training in other milieux; they have very complete knowledge

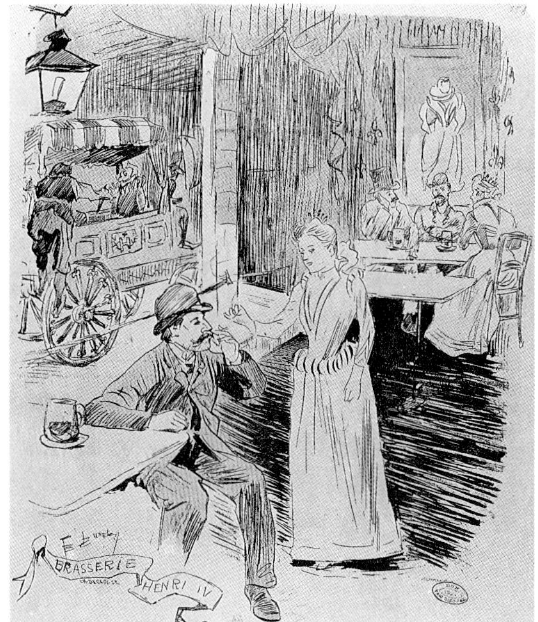

89.
Ferdinand Lunel, *The Henry IV Brasserie,* ca. 1880, Cabinet des Estampes, Bibliothèque Nationale, Paris.

Brasseries served by women – La Brasserie Henri IV.

on these matters and they know for a fact that certain brasseries are nothing but clandestine houses of prostitution, so they are not stunned to learn that the principal service is not serving beer or lighting cigarettes!"[55] There were strong financial reasons for the experienced prostitute to value regular employment in one of the new-style beer halls. The waitress in a brasserie à femmes earned good wages and was likely to make much more than a woman struggling to get by in one of the "suspicious" professions. Even after a number of required work costs were subtracted, the brasserie waitress earned between five and twenty francs a day,[56] or between three and half to thirteen times the daily wage of a milliner or laundress. Compared with other categories of prostitute, it appears that the fille de brasserie maintained a markedly stable employment. The apparently minimal turnover of personnel in these jobs was probably attributable to the relatively good wages and the manageable working hours – generally between mid-afternoon and 2 A.M. It was a very reasonable job for a relatively unskilled woman, if she was willing to fulfill its diverse requirements.

The way in which the server earned her wages varied some from one place to the next. Food was usually provided by the owner, who was, apparently, a man (and hence the occasional use of the expression *proxénétisme masculin* – masculine pimping – in accounts of this phenomenon).[57] The waitress was free to keep the service fees she collected, out of which she paid a daily *droit de servir* (a right-to-work assessment), which was between fifty centimes and three francs.[58] There were other miscellaneous small fees charged by the *patron* (owner), such as the payments based on the profitability of the server's assigned tables and a tax that was proportionate to the number of *passes éffectuées* (tricks turned).[59] She was also generally responsible for paying for her own uniform and for the matches she furnished to customers.[60] Lunel's drawing of the Brasserie Henri IV done around 1880 (fig. 89), for example, makes a point of the thematic outfits worn there and of one costumed waitress who uses her own match to light the customer's smoke.

The drinkers in brasseries a femmes were typically male (as is the case in all the popular pictures illustrated here), but the class, age, and profession of the customers varied with the location of the beer hall in the city.[61] In spite of the gender difference between employees and customers in these brasseries – female workers and male drinkers – the women could not necessarily monopolize the men. The servers faced competition on the job from other women working as prostitutes, because street prostitutes often sought refuge in eating and drinking establishments. Macé reminds us, for example: "On the boulevards that stretch between the Bastille and the Madeleine, there are a hundred cafés-brasseries, half of which serve as refuges for street-walkers. The layout of these establishments do not always permit the women to prostitute themselves [on the premises], nevertheless some of them have basements and furnished rooms." Macé claims that there was in fact a nocturnal attack by prostitutes on brasseries staffed by male servers: "In the morning and afternoon there, you encounter writers, artists, employees of the stock exchange and from commerce; but, once evening falls, they are replaced by crooks, pimps, pickpockets, agents of suspicious business enterprises. Registered and unregistered prostitutes openly demand drinks from customers and solicit until closing time at 2 A.M."[62]

In any case, artists never represented other prostitutes in a brasserie à femmes. Indeed, women who are not waitresses do not appear in this imagery. The only exceptions are the female customers and entertainers that Manet included in his unusual paintings of the subject: *The Waitress* of 1879 (National Gallery, London, fig. 81), *The Waitress* of 1879 (Musée d'Orsay, Paris, fig. 82), and *Café-Concert* of 1878 (Walters Art Gallery, Baltimore, fig. 83).[63] That each of the three works has been known by several titles is not surprising, because none of them permits a clear and easy interpretation, and each has a complex and indirect relationship to its apparent referent, the Parisian beer hall or club staffed by women. Manet's pictures do not use what became a standard iconography for the popular brasserie picture. In the majority of the pictures we have examined – those reproduced in figures 84, 85, 86, 87, and 89 – a brasserie serveuse is shown at work, sitting down at a table with a tippling customer, whereas the waitresses in Manet's images are shown standing in their places of work, delivering (or drinking from) steins of beer.

Two of Manet's brasserie paintings were shown in his solo show of 1880 at *La Vie Moderne* gallery (along with the two *Nana* surrogates we discussed in chapter 3). In the exhibition catalog the London picture was entitled *Café-Concert*, and the Baltimore picture was called *Corner of a Café-Concert.*[64] An india ink and gouache drawing (fig. 90) done after the 1878 Baltimore painting was published in the May 8, 1880, issue of *La Vie Moderne* magazine. The drawing follows the painting called *Corner of a Café-Concert* quite closely but was run in the magazine under the title *The Waitress*. The London picture, known as *Café-Concert* in the 1880 exhibition, was exhibited soon after with the same title, both in the exhibition of Manet's work in Lyon in 1883 and in the posthumous show of his work held at the Ecole des Beaux-Arts in 1884.[65] It appears, however, that *The Waitress* was the title preferred by Manet for both the Paris and London pictures.[66] There is also evidence to suggest that the painter called at least one of the three pictures *L'Assommoir* or *Reichshoffen.*[67]

Manet did preliminary studies for the three works at an establishment called the Reichshoffen, on the boulevard de Rochechouart, which was a café-concert or brasserie or brasserie-concert.[68] I shall argue, however, that it is unlikely that the finished pictures deserve to be

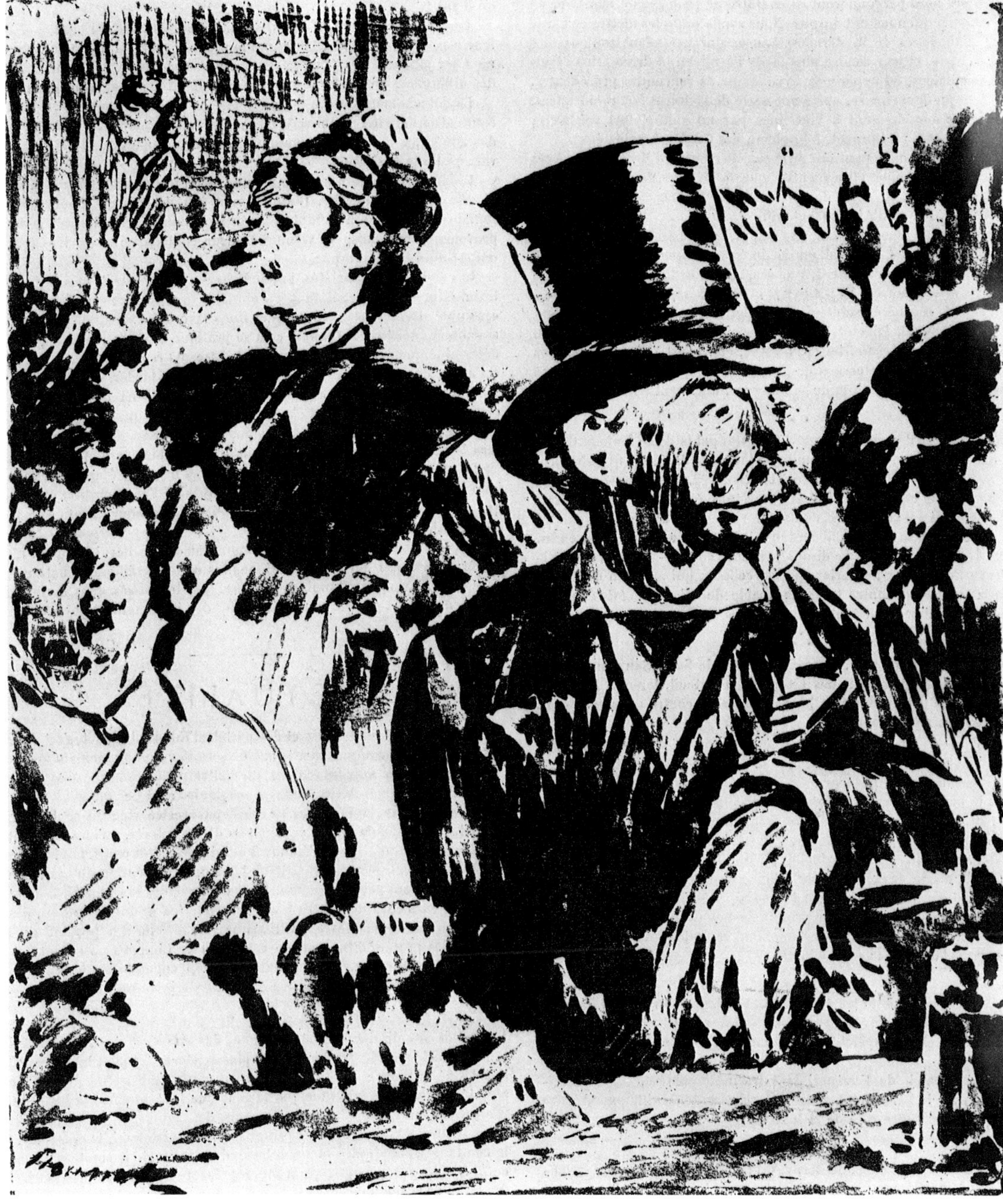

90. Edouard Manet, *The Waitress*, 1878–80, india ink and gouache drawing, reproduced in *La Vie Moderne*, May 8, 1880.

analyzed as pictures of that particular place, or of any other specific club or café. The range of titles alone by which these works have been known over the past century is a sure indication of the composite nature of their studio construction. Unfortunately, very little period commentary on these pictures has come to light, probably because none was shown in a Salon and none achieved the notoriety in Paris that would have attracted journalists as *Nana* had in 1877, for example.[69]

When the London picture (fig. 81) was exhibited in Lyons in 1883 as *Café-Concert*, Adolphe Tabarant, an early twentieth-century scholar, reported (schematically) that the painting was "extremely badly received by the Lyons press."[70] He quotes one example of what he judged to be a poor reaction from Lyons: "Monsieur Manet has sent us a strange canvas from

Paris, carrying the title Café-Concert. M. Manet is a naturalist, that is obvious; a naturalist with bad taste, that is obvious too. His worker is a successful record of a brutalized, sodden type, and his fille de brasserie has a dissolute air. As to his painting, though it has a certain tonal truth, we believe that that is not enough to constitute a tableau."[71] This reviewer built directly upon the primordial "bad taste" of the subject matter and did not let the title of *Café-Concert* stand in the way of pointedly calling the waitress a "fille de brasserie," an epithet with explicit overtones of prostitution.

A generally favorable review of the 1880 show at *La Vie Moderne* gallery (which, recall, included both the London and Baltimore pictures) appeared in *Le Temps*, but the reviewer found Manet's subjects unsavory and Zolaesque: "His subjects [are] taken from the dubious milieux of Parisian bohemia, *skatings*, cafés-concerts and brasseries." The critic found certain paintings "well observed and rigorously rendered," including "*Corner of a Café-Concert* [fig. 83] with its type so cruelly observed of an old fop on the prowl amidst the dregs of society; another *Café-Concert* [fig. 81], larger in size, showing a seated worker smoking his pipe, painted with a singularly male handling."[72] The review placed a premium upon what was taken to be the evidence of Manet's powers of social observation and description. The critic seemed most struck by the documentary aspects of the picture that have been more casually treated by twentieth-century modernist accounts of Manet's art.[73] But too much significance can easily be heaped on the phrase *les bas-fonds* as the predictable epithet for the setting of the picture. It does efficiently tie a certain kind of flâneur to this sort of drinking spot,[74] but it might also and only have been an automatic response to the beer-drinking waitress in view of the invectives hurled at brasseries on the basis of the alleged drunkenness of their employees.

The critic for *L'Artiste*, Josephin Péladan, found the posthumous exhibition of 1884 at the Ecole des Beaux-Arts (in which the London picture [fig. 81] was exhibited as *Café-Concert*) outrageous[75] – even though at that late date Manet's art had been through a twenty-year-long process of neutralization and embrace by the Paris art establishment.[76] Péladan judged Manet to be "without ideal, without conception, without emotion, without poetry, without draftmanship, incapable of a composed *tableau*" and labeled him "only a painter and a painter of pieces at that." Péladan especially disliked the *Café-Concert.*[77]

This modest selection of reactions from the early 1880s to two of Manet's works should open our eyes to the perceived specificity of their subject and its associations. In fact, the notoriety of the brasserie à femmes during this period weighed heavily on the critics, because certain of their terms were more likely descriptions of, or reactions to, an actual brasserie than to Manet's pictures of it. Manet features the "guilty party" (the waitress) in each picture but does little or nothing, as we shall see, to round out her conventional significance – the indecency on the mind of the critics. The terms of Manet's simultaneous confrontation with and avoidance of the trademarks of the brasserie à femmes suggest that these paintings exemplify that peculiar avant-garde enterprise of the late 1870s and early 1880s: constructing an imagery of modernity out of the eroticized, commodified working-class woman in a context of a Parisian public entertainment (or commerce related to clothing and adornment).

Café-Concert or *Corner of a Café-Concert* (the Baltimore painting, fig. 83) is small – only 18 5/8″ × 15 3/8″ – and is synthesized from diverse "facts." It is more crowded with data and is more compositionally complex than any of Manet's other paintings of modern life from the late 1870s. It contains six clearly delineated figures, three of which play the major roles: the two foreground customers seated at the marble table and the waitress behind and between them.

The off-center, slightly incomplete triangle that encompasses the three main figures is the painting's strongest compositional shape and contains a carefully orchestrated assembly of formal contrasts. There is an off-center triangle within the triangle formed by the three heads, but the large size and blackness of the top hat pulls the weight of the triangle in toward the center of the picture. The implied connection between the figures set up by their triangular relationship is undercut, however, by the diversity of the three heads. Each head is positioned differently in space, looks in a different direction, and wears a different kind of facial expression. It is clear that we are to read the physical proximity of the three as the purely accidental if necessary closeness of strangers in a public place. The haphazardness of their encounter is also suggested by the woman customer's blue *pâtisserie* package on the counter next to her beer, indicating that she has just stopped in for a drink on the way home from shopping.[78]

Other devices help to secure further an appearance of the diversity of the materials that the artist observed, as seen, for example, in the handling of the singer. Beyond and to the left of the waitress, an entertainer sings openmouthed on a stage. One is drawn to this area of the painting even though the figure is quite small, because the luminosity and middle value of this light blue area stand out from the dominant black-white scheme of most of the rest of the picture. The placement of the singer suggests that the three foreground figures are ignoring the entertainment, as well as one another. The two partially cut-off figures at the right edge (a working-class couple), then, have also turned their backs to the stage. The background singer indicates that this roomful of socially diverse, unconnected people is, in fact, extraordinarily dispersed, because they are not even facing let alone listening to the stage entertainment. This reading of the architecture of the space, however, places the waitress, who is oblivious to the customers and absorbed in her beer, in a vulnerable position between the stage and the audience.

Manet's handling of the extreme background is another disorienting note in a painting that already contains a number of dislocations. The pale blue background rectangle has a clearly indicated vertical border at its right edge, overlapped by the head of the waitress. This gold border is a mirror frame. The vertical hat rack hanging across the back wall supports the identification of a mirror.[79] Unless that blue area is read as the surface of a mirror, there is an extreme discontinuity in scale between the tiny singer and the brass rack, neatly underplayed, however, by the waitress overlapping the join. The paint handling in this part of the canvas also distinguishes the blue area from its surroundings. The greyed surface surrounding the singer's head and the scumbled, whitish vertical line just inches from the left edge of the picture appear to have been put there to serve as the painted equivalent of light intensified by its reflection in a mirror.

In the related india ink and gouache drawing (fig. 90), Manet considerably simplified the treatment of the back wall. The hat rack is reduced to scant black marks at the far right, and only faint shadows indicate its continuation across the wall and the second hook, which is visible in the painting. But the handling of the far left zone containing the singer reaffirms the role of the wall as a reflective surface. The mirror frame is preserved in the drawing as two straight grey parallel bands directly above the crown of the waitress' head, and the mirror surface itself has been carefully differentiated from the balance of the drawing. Wispy middle-value striations define both the figure and the space that surrounds her. The relative sketchiness and faintness of this area could be atmospheric perspective – a plausible reading, until one looks carefully at the streaks of opaque white gouache there. There are bright highlights on the figure, but the irregularly placed splotches around her especially suggest the glimmer and dazzle of a mirrored surface. Analogous to the treatment of the "mirror area" in the painting, the treatment of this area in the drawing is unlike that of any other part of it.

At first reading, the identification of that partially overlapped blue field as a mirror works to deflate the problem of audience inattention by explaining it away. The majority of the customers, who appeared to be ignoring the small singer in the corner, could now be understood to be looking directly at her, because she and her candelabrum are reflected in that mirror, which is roughly opposite the stage, or at least on the other side of the room. According to this positivist reading of the picture, all the people in the hall, save the most important women (the cigarette-smoking customer at the table and the beer-drinking waitress), are or could be watching the stage. This is surely the architectural structure of the painting's illusion on the most general level, but it is not articulated with anything approaching the exactness and precision that would be required to convey the resolution of an illusionistic conundrum in the puzzle-solving manner of the mirror in, say, Diego Velázquez's *Christ in the House of Mary and Martha* of circa 1618 (now in Dublin).

Looking carefully at Manet's painting, one sees that it does contain a mirror, but its illusionism is not optically precise enough to change fundamentally the look and arrangement of this otherwise rather flattened-out picture. So that even with the mirror identified, the picture remains a network of spatial and social *dis*connections and *dis*unities. The painting's appearance of disunity is also attributable to the ways in which Manet deemphasizes its illusionism by emphasizing its surface.

The introverted, dreamy-eyed, smoking woman in the near left foreground is based upon (if not borrowed from) Degas's besotted Ellen Andrée in his *At the Café* of 1876, better known as *Absinthe* (in the Musée d'Orsay). Manet magnified the gulf between his two adjacent drinkers by substituting a stylish fop for Degas's bedraggled Marcellin Desboutin. Unlike Degas, who places his two figures well back in space and over to one side (their occupation of the fringes of society is reinforced by their placement at the margins of the picture), Manet places his disassociated pair in the center of the foreground of his picture. Their proximity and inertia give them the function of a screen or repoussoir beyond the edges of which we encounter a jigsaw puzzle of smaller-scale data. The smaller, middle-ground server is animated – hand on hip, beer held up to her mouth – and forms a contrast to the inactivity of the large foreground pair. But the fusion of forms at their edges blunts and softens somewhat the vividness of the narrative contrast between the figures. Strokes of brown paint in the female drinker's chair back run over into the white of the server's apron. The greyish taupe area at the back of the woman customer's head – the netting used to secure this kind of hat – appears at the same time to be part of the forward plane of the serving woman's bent right arm. The handling of the negative zone of atmosphere between the behind them (which is roughly in the shape of a lamb chop and hard to read; there may be a face there) also knits their forms together, because its crisp edges – the black line at the edge of the waitress's white apron and the other woman's rigid white collar – convert it into a flat, positive shape that is as strong a part of the overall design as the forms that surround it. The stark white collar point of the gentleman customer is also an emphasized patch of paint – it *is* his collar, to be sure, but it is also an unmodelled shape that sits brightly and flatly on the canvas.

A by-product of this kind of highly aestheticized, deadpan modern-life painting is that the viewer could never be sure that a serveuse like the one to which the painting may refer was (or was expected to be) a prostitute. There were other contemporaneous depictions of brasserie servers in which the women are not shown flirting or enticing men to drink, but their relative straightforwardness does not approach the inexpressiveness of Manet's picture. In *The Waitress* of circa 1875–80 (fig. 91), Henri Somm's brightly colored figure stands ready to perform waitressing duties, and she is exceptionally pretty, shapely, cheerful, and extroverted. The woman in Marcellin Desboutin's print *Fille de brasserie*, an 1886 book frontispiece (fig. 92), is shown in terms of her relationship to her admiring companion, who appears to be an interested customer. She is obviously found appealing by the man who encircles her waist with his arm. Manet's server is unlike these others because she is absorbed in her own refreshment and is not the object of any visible male attention.

Nor would the centrally placed waitresses in the London and Paris versions (figs. 81 and 82) be conclusively identifiable as prostitutes solely on the basis of Manet's paintings of them. These two pictures are similar in many ways: they are about the same size, are similarly composed and populated, and focus on the figure of the waitress. Apart from the changed focus of the server's eyes, the Paris painting is actually a cropped and simplified version of the London picture. As in the Baltimore picture, Manet emphasized the social diversity of the customers: men from either end of the social spectrum sit side by side, and in each the worker is alone and the bourgeois men have equivalently dressed women with them. The waitresses deposit a glass stein of beer on the table, while holding two more for delivery, and are not shown looking at the customers included in the paintings. Perhaps the actions and facial expressions of the serveuses were intended to carry a meaning – a self-contained, slightly bored search for the next customer? – but are too deadpan and equivocal to be definite or clear. They are open to multiple readings.

Of the three paintings, the London picture was exhibited most widely, and as we know, the most extensive reactions to it survive. In 1880 its subject was found Zolaesque because of being taken from the "dubious milieux of bohemia," and in 1883 the review from Lyons called Manet a naturalist of bad taste because of the painting's subjects: the sodden worker and dissolute waitress.[80] The critics' terms do not seem to fit the London picture or the other two closely related works. But because the critics assure us that the brasserie à femmes of the period *was* Manet's point of reference, we are free to face up to the artist's obvious neutralization of the subject and to discuss the meaning of that tactic.

From what we have pieced together about the brasserie with female servers in the late 1870s, it appears that the waitress of sexualized legend worked under conditions that forced her to assume various disguises. She would have been obliged to dissemble her possible sexual venality in the presence of the police, and she would have been obliged to act emotionally involved in her flirtations with customers, all the while energetically serving drinks. It could be argued that her obligatory daily involvement in the commodification of self was even more extreme than that of the brothel or street-walking prostitute insofar as her flirtatious come-ons were to foster the sale of beer and, eventually, the merchandising of her own body. In her legend one could see sexuality transformed into a functioning and efficient part of the commodity economy, and to think about her job was to think about how far the commodity had entered the whole texture of modern social relations. The eroticized coding of the business of the brasserie

91.
Henri Somm [François-Clément Sommier], *The Waitress*, ca. 1875–80, pencil, watercolor, and gouache on buff paper, private collection, England.

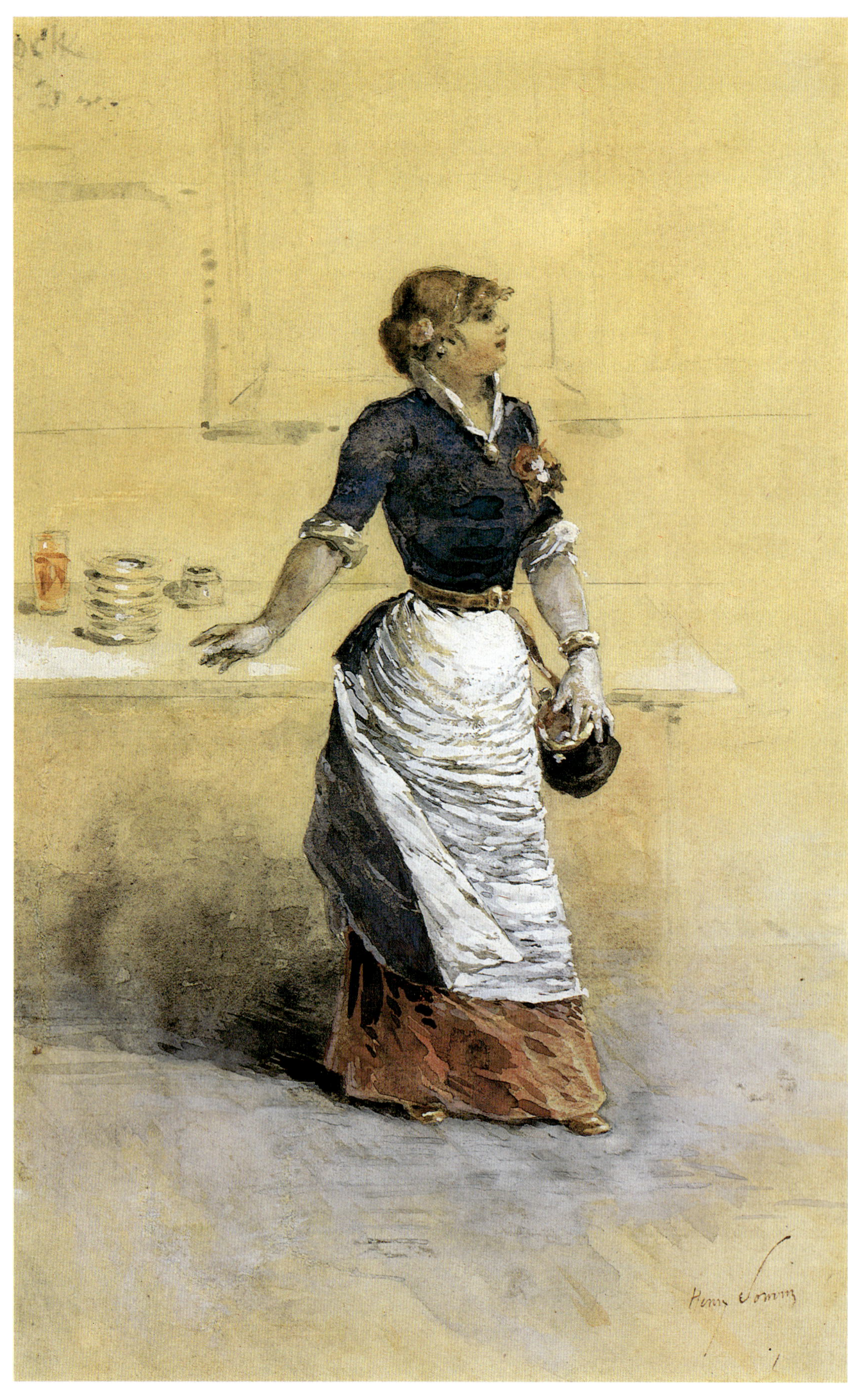

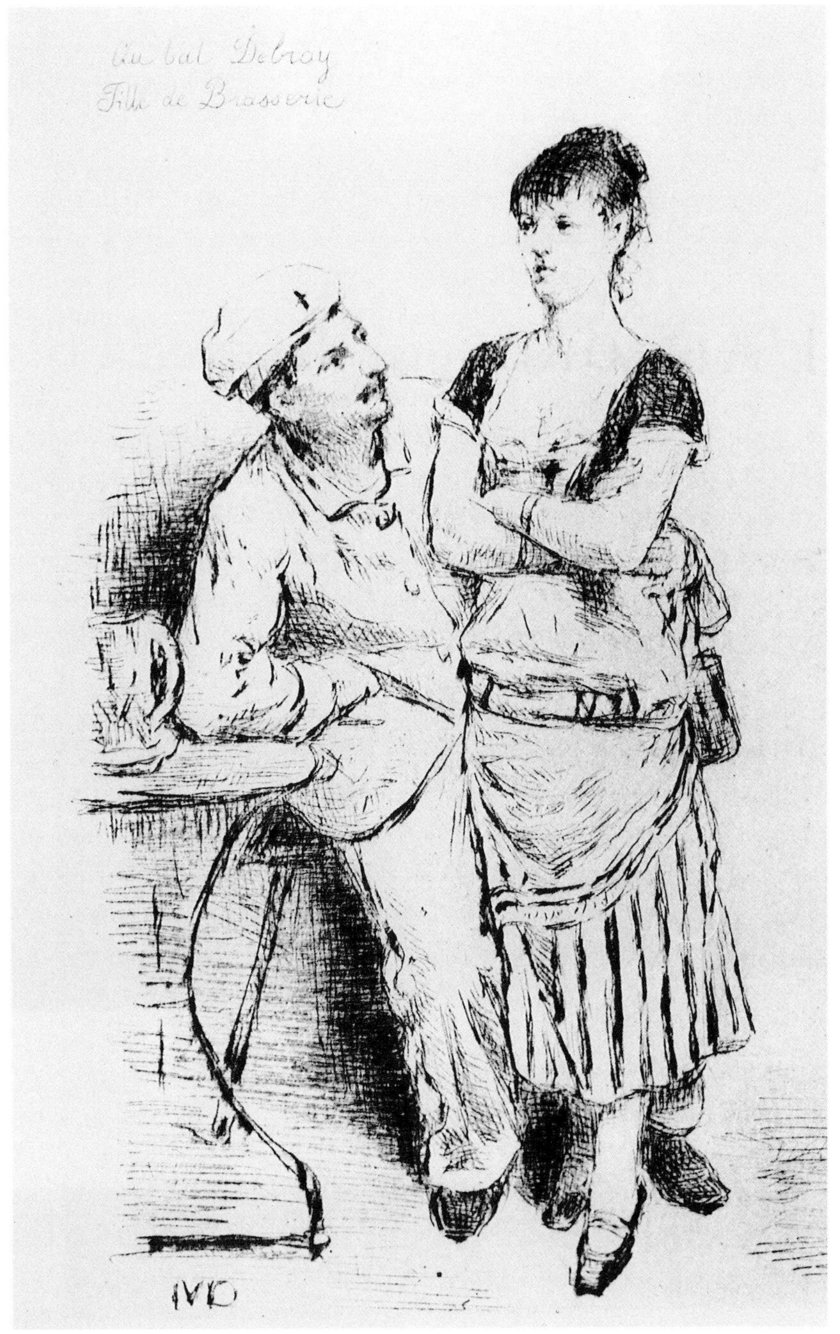

92.
Marcellin Desboutin, *At the Ball Debray – Fille de brasserie*, frontispiece for John Grand-Carteret, *Raphael et Gambrinus, ou l'art dans la Brasserie*, Paris, 1886.

à femmes was a blatant example of the matter-of-fact, modern marketing of the body, because not only was the body of the waitress used to promote the sale of alcohol, but the advertising for it had to simulate "real feelings."

Of all the forms of clandestine prostitution that we have discussed, the brasserie waitress's job must have been the most psychologically demanding because so much acting was required. And she could not risk detachment from the people around her, because remaining aloof could slow sales. But in Manet's representations of Parisian nightlife that center upon the server, he does not show her to be making contact with any of the people in the picture.

In the Baltimore example, she keeps her distance by drinking a beer in an off moment; in the Paris and London pictures, she serves beer but looks elsewhere and so is *between* social transactions. To have shown her at any other stage of her work would have required giving her some kind of warm and welcoming face: somewhere perhaps between familiarity for the police and the professional face of the flirtatious, love-struck "seductress" for the customers. Either of these "faces" would have connected the image to one of the play-acting dimensions of her work. Neither of these options, it seems, would have fit Manet's working definition of a modern representation, which required a dimension of uncertainty to qualify.

As was the case with the milliner pictures discussed in the preceding section, Manet was attracted to an unequivocally commodified and eroticized working-woman subject, although he foreclosed its trademark connotations. He accomplished this by emphasizing and restoring the qualities of moral and narrative contingency to this category of female labor, by representing the fille de brasserie between transactions, amid extremely busy, competing, even distracting surroundings with which she is shown to have no connection, leaving how she would act face-to-face with a man open to speculation.[81] In the Baltimore picture, for example, the alcoholic waitress marks this nightclub as a specific kind of brasserie, but the figure does not forcibly connote participation in the merchandizing of sex. Manet depends on the legibility of the subject to evoke a certain atmosphere while he moves obliquely against it.

That Manet's brasserie waitress paintings do not overtly commodify the women might appear to some viewers as a socially progressive and open-minded way to portray a motif that was so heavily laden with connotations of sexual immorality by the culture at the time. Calling deadpan ambiguity "progressive," however, turns out be an anachronistic, late twentieth-century way of evaluating the sexual politics of the pictures at hand. Manet's pictures (especially the London and Paris versions, figs. 81 and 82) carry out and exemplify an extremely complex form of fence sitting.

Electing to paint a female-staffed brasserie (or brasserie-concert) provides this particular form of entertainment of the late 1870s – a place where beer-serving women were for sale and acted as if they were in love with their buyers! – with membership in the men's club of modern subjects, as was the case with the café and milliner images we have already discussed. As Lisa Tickner puts it, "Genres are not exactly sexed but offer different opportunities for the inscriptions and investments of gender."[82]

That these paradigmatic, elaborately contrived random-glimpse pictures have built into them the destabilizing note of uncertainty regarding the waitresses' emotional, subjective, and sexual investment in their work *might* make us think that Manet has metaphorically come to the rescue of scapegoated and exploited female workers. But it is precisely his ambiguous way of painting them that makes their sexual morality an issue, because it is left as a constantly

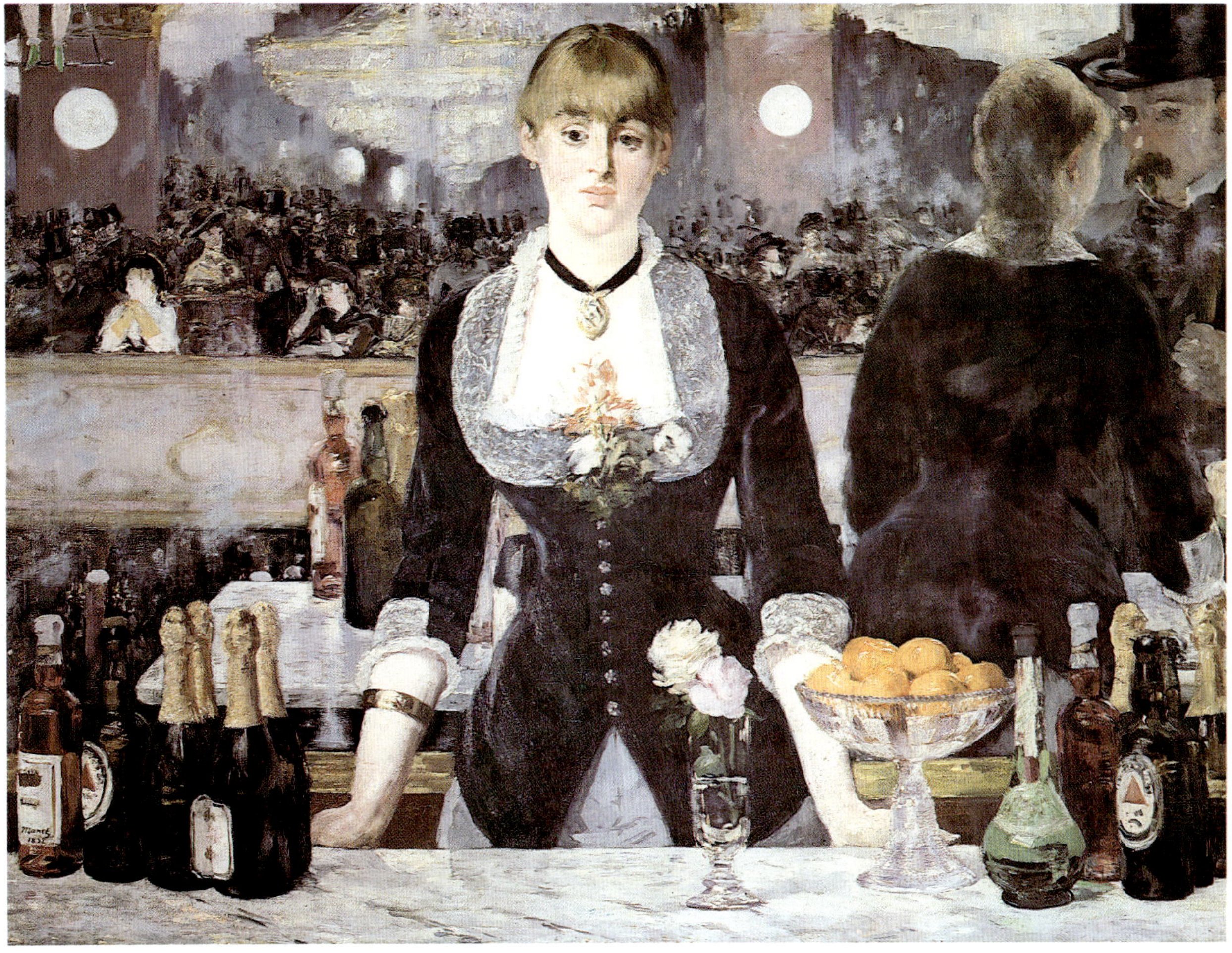

93. Edouard Manet, *A Bar at the Folies-Bergère,* 1882, oil on canvas, Courtauld Institute Galleries, London.

nagging, open question. More than a century after these fact-based canvases were completed, their descriptive specificity continues to encourage social art historians to interrogate the servers' morality. Ambiguity used to represent women working in the "suspicious professions" perpetually calls into question the morality of the women's sexuality. A deadpan treatment of such a subject will always raise the question "Is she or isn't she?"

Manet's last major painting, *A Bar at the Folies-Bergère* of 1881–82 (fig. 93), exhibited in the Salon of 1882, is a widely admired icon of modernist uncertainty.[83] The configuration of its point of equivocation exemplifies, however, the gendered character of ambiguous Impressionist representations of covert prostitution.

That the picture actively addresses the possible double profession of the barmaid – serving and prostitution – was clear to observers in 1882.[84] Critics were, of course, drawing upon their personal knowledge of social life at the Folies-Bergère nightclub, but their assumption that Manet's painting posed explicit questions about the server's morality was encouraged and sustained by the famous conundrum of the double woman.[85] The frontal barmaid stands upright and appears cool, detached, and aloof, whereas the reflected woman leans forward slightly and acts subservient to the adjacent, looming male customer. The plot of the commercial transaction at the bar is eroticized by being provided with two possible outcomes. In one, "she does"; in the other, "she doesn't."

Robert Herbert's commentary targets the sexual overtones of the two key hard-to-read parts of the picture: the woman's face and the reflected barmaid and customer at far right: "In his painting, the whole world of the Folies-Bergère is reduced to this young woman and to our thoughts as we confront her. . . . His disembodied image [of the customer in top hat reflected in the mirror] seems to stand for a male client's hidden thoughts when facing such an attractive woman."[86]

Herbert zeroes in with precision upon the characteristics of *A Bar at the Folies-Bergère* that reveal what a typical avant-garde picture it actually was. The emphasis upon the expressionless young working woman at the center and the client's "hidden thoughts" are the key elements of its programmatic, almost manifestolike rehearsal of an essential article of avant-garde faith. If what the barmaid might be selling is herself, then this double-bodied woman is a veritable summa of modernity. In Manet's *Bar* we encounter a crystallization of what painters of the Impressionist circle found to be modern in modern life, and of the normative protocols of gendered spectatorship, insofar as the answer to the quintessentially modern question – will she or won't she? – is only of interest to a libidinous, heterosexual male interlocutor.

With respect to a narrativization of the woman, the apparatus strains; but the transformation of the woman into spectacle is easy.
– *Mary Ann Doane*, The Desire to Desire

Artists took up "the prostitute" as a standard emblem of modernity in the 1870s and early 1880s when Parisian regulationists saw their project threatened by the increasing number and audacity of clandestine prostitutes. But we have discovered along the way that this was not a straightforward case of mimesis; it was not a story of artists simply describing what was happening around them. The works we have examined demonstrate that although the theme of lower-class urban female prostitution appealed to a wide variety of bourgeois artists, the subject of covert prostitution was especially appropriate to the avant-garde project of detached yet "factual" art making. The lives and legends of the alleged insoumises, women working in various low-paying jobs, helped these painters ideologically to bridge the gap between the two seemingly antithetical qualities of modernity central to the Impressionists: the indeterminacy and fleeting quality of experience and the cold commodification of social relations.

Artists did use directly denotative and narrative pictorial idioms when they acknowledged the uncontrollable and unambiguous sexual and social power of certain kinds of venal women, such as the hyperfashionable courtesan. This was true in the case of Cézanne's early *Olympias*, Duez's *Splendor*, Manet's *Nana*, and Gervex's *Rolla*, as well as many boulevard cartoons. Degas's brothel prints straddle the fence pictorially and philosophically. Those monotypes testify to the complexity of the artist's fascination and disgust with the somatic culture of the pensionnaires of a Parisian brothel. We observed, however, that the avant-garde, especially Degas and Manet, met the alleged prominence of clandestine prostitutes in the modern city with a strategy of elusiveness, incompleteness, and offhandedness, with an apparent refusal to corroborate stereotypes or to narrate precise social transactions. At first viewing, this modernist strategy appears to have acknowledged the ambiguities of public identity that had resulted from the increase in and changing character of clandestine prostitution. However, by singling out sites that were commonly associated with covert prostitution – the boulevard café, the millinery shop, the brasserie, the nightclub – or situations that suggested uncertainty, the avant-garde actually reinforced reductive female stereotypes and exacerbated the commodification of public female identity that prostitution epitomized.

The familiar history of modernism emphasizes and admires ambiguity. In the argument I present here I oppose that pattern of admiration. Rather than serving to avoid the inscription of sexual attitudes, modernist indeterminacy has a vivid and pronounced sexual politics, especially when prostitution is thematized. Rather than beclouding moral and sexual issues, illegibility helps to fix the morality and character of the women portrayed. For the artists repeatedly to have proposed that female sexual availability was a matter of doubt and ambiguity when the types of women regularly chosen for representation were already stigmatized by the culture as likely prostitutes was to produce a seemingly privileged perception of modernity that was in fact based in a kind of ideological banality: Was she or wasn't she?

Ambiguity constituted, then, a male sexual politics. Indeterminacy and open-endedness worked for the painters as ways to master and contain certain male anxieties about women who were found ungovernable, especially sexually open, lower-class women. The use of ellipsis in pictures was a means to limit the threat of female sexual force. The privilege that we habitually accord the vagueness of avant-garde imagery is based on its authors' apparent ability to get some distance on the triteness of questioning every woman's sexual morality. The artists achieved a distance from that cliché by altering its forms, but without ever contradicting it directly. The noncommittal appearance of the art that resulted from this strategy helps to explain our culture's long-standing love affair with these canny, masculinist achievements of the Impressionist avant-garde.

Notes

Introduction

EPIGRAPH: (p. xviii) Luce Irigaray, "Women on the Market," in *This Sex Which Is Not One*, Catherine Porter (trans.), Ithaca, 1977, p. 188.

1. I am grateful to Eli Boderman of Colorado College for an invitation to participate in the 1989 Colorado College Symposium: "Intimacy." In my conference paper I worked out the parallels between the discourse on prostitutes and syphilis in the nineteenth century and that uniting homosexuals and prostitutes to the spread of AIDS in late twentieth-century America. In developing my thoughts, I depended upon many of the contributions to Douglas Crimp's important anthology entitled *AIDS: Cultural Analysis, Cultural Activism* in *October* 43 (Winter 1987), especially Sander L. Gilman's "AIDS and Syphilis: The Iconography of Disease," pp. 87–107. See also Gilman, "Seeing the AIDS Patient," in *Disease and Representation: Images of Illness from Madness to AIDS*, Ithaca, 1988, pp. 245–72; and Debi Brock, "Prostitutes Are Scapegoats in the AIDS Panic," *Resources for Feminist Research* 18, no. 2 (June 1989): 13–17.

2. Luce Irigaray, "Women on the Market," p. 171.

Chapter 1: Painting the Traffic in Women

EPIGRAPHS: (p. 9) Denise Riley, *"Am I That Name?" Feminism and the Category of "Women" in History*, Minneapolis, 1988, p. 103; Simone de Beauvoir, *The Second Sex*, H. M. Parshley (trans. and ed.), New York, 1952, p. xvi; (p. 16) Gayatri Chakravorty Spivak, "Displacement and the Discourse of Women," in Mark Krupnick (ed.), *Displacement: Derrida and After*, quoted in Lisa Tickner, "Feminism, Art History, and Sexual Difference," *Genders* 3 (Fall 1988): 113.

1. The most important study of prostitution in nineteenth-century France is Alain Corbin, *Les Filles de noce: Misère sexuelle et prostitution aux dix-neuvième et vingtième siècles*, Paris, 1978. A good general overview of the rise of urban prostitution across Europe is Richard Evans, "Prostitution, State and Society in Imperial Germany," *Past and Present* 70 (1976): 106–29. The title of this chapter comes from Gayle Rubin, who acknowledges taking it from Emma Goldman. See Rubin, "The Traffic in Women: Notes on the 'Political Economy' of Sex," in *Toward an Anthropology of Women*, Rayna R. Reiter (ed.), New York, 1975, pp. 157–210.

2. See Jill Harsin, *Policing Prostitution in Nineteenth-Century Paris*, Princeton, N.J., 1985.

3. Gordon Wright, *France in Modern Times*, 3d ed. New York, 1981, pp. 178–79 and 294–95; and Louise A. Tilly and Joan W. Scott, "Women's Work and the Family in Nineteenth-Century Europe," in *The Family in History*, Charles E. Rosenberg (ed.), Philadelphia, 1975, pp. 146–47.

4. The best recent discussions of Parent-Duchâtelet's work are Alain Corbin's introduction to an abridged edition of the 1836 work, Alexandre Parent-Duchâtelet, *La Prostitution à Paris au dix-neuvième siècle*, Paris, 1981, pp. 9–55; and Charles Bernheimer, "Of Whores and Sewers: Parent-Duchâtelet, Engineer of Abjection," *Raritan* 6, no. 3 (Winter 1987): 72–90. Charles Bernheimer's *Figures of Ill Repute: Representing Prostitution in Nineteenth-Century France*, Cambridge, Mass., 1989, published after the final draft of this book was complete, appeared too late for my consideration and response.

5. T. J. Clark, *The Painting of Modern Life: Paris in the Art of Manet and His Followers*, New York, 1984, chaps. 1 and 2.

6. On *Olympia*, see Clark, *Modern Life*, chap. 2. On the Courbet, see Patricia Mainardi, "Gustave Courbet's Second Scandal: 'Les Demoiselles de Village,'" *Arts* (Jan. 1979): 95–103; and the discussion of J. P. Proudhon's allegorical interpretation of Courbet's 1856 picture (published in 1865) in Linda Nochlin, "Courbet's Real Allegory: Rereading 'The Painter's Studio,'" pt. 2, "Ending with the Beginning: The Centrality of Gender," *Courbet Reconsidered*, Brooklyn Museum of Art, 1988, pp. 34–36.

7. The classic study of Picasso's picture as a brothel is Leo Steinberg's "The Philosophical Brothel," which first appeared in *Art News* 71, nos. 5 and 6 (Sept. and Oct. 1972). A revised version has appeared in *October* 44 (Spring 1988): 3–74. Also see *Les Demoiselles d'Avignon*, Paris, Musée Picasso, 1987, 2 vols.; and Michael Leja, "'Le Vieux Marcheur' and 'Les Deux Risques': Picasso, Prostitution, Venereal Disease and Maternity, 1899–1907," *Art History* 8, no. 1 (Mar. 1985): 66–87. Emile Bernard's name should be added to that of Toulouse-Lautrec as a major contributor to the fin-de-siècle imagery of prostitution. See Phillip Dennis Cate and Bogomila Welsh-Ovcharov, *Emile Bernard: Bordellos and Prostitutes in Turn-of-the-Century French Art*, New Brunswick, N.J., 1988.

8. Evans, "Prostitution, State, and Society," pp. 106–08; Tilly and Scott, "Women's Work," pp. 145–78.

9. Griselda Pollock, "Modernity and the Spaces of Femininity," in *Vision and Difference: Femininity, Femininism and Histories of Art*, London, 1988, p. 54.

10. In suggesting the earlier dates, I am following the most up-to-date Degas scholarship: Jean Sutherland Boggs, Douglas W. Druick, Henri Loyrette, Michael Pantazzi, and Gary Tinterow, *Degas*, New York and Ottawa, Metropolitan Museum of Art and National Gallery of Canada, 1988, p. 296.

11. On the matter of Impressionist images and ideologies of modernity, the most important (though divergent) work to date has been done by T. J. Clark, *Modern Life*, and Robert L. Herbert, *Impressionism: Art, Leisure and Parisian Society*, New Haven, 1988. The particulars of my debts to (and quibbles with) each are acknowledged in what follows.

12. Alain Corbin, *Les Filles de noce.*

13. Janet Wolff, "The Invisible Flâneuse: Women and the Literature of Modernity," *Theory, Culture and Society* 2, no. 3 (1985): 37–46; and Pollock, *Vision and Difference*, pp. 50–90.

14. Georg Simmel, "The Metropolis and Mental Life" [1903], in *Georg Simmel: On Individuality and Social Forms*, Donald N. Levine (ed.), Chicago, 1971, pp. 324–39.

15. Georg Simmel, "Prostitution" [1907], in Levine, *Georg Simmel*, pp. 121, 122. Compare Marx's position on prostitution: "Prostitution is only a *particular* expression of the *universal* prostitution of the *worker*" (Karl Marx, "Economic and Philosophical Manuscripts," in *Early Writings*, Lucio Colletti [ed.], London, 1975, p. 350 n. 4). On Simmel's ideas about prostitution and objectification, see Guy Oakes, "The Problem of Women in Simmel's Theory of Culture," in *Georg Simmel: On Women, Sexuality, and Love*, Guy Oakes (ed. and trans.), New Haven, 1984, pp. 3–62.

16. Walter Benjamin, "Paris: The Capital of the Nineteenth Century" [1955], in *Charles Baudelaire: A Lyric Poet in the Era of High Capitalism*, Harry Zohn (trans.), London, 1973, p. 171.

17. Charles Baudelaire, "The Painter of Modern Life – Modernity" [1863], translated excerpt reprinted in *Modern Art and Modernism: A Critical Anthology*, Francis Frascina and Charles Harrison (eds.), New York, 1982, p. 23.

18. Quoted in Benjamin, "Some Motifs in Baudelaire," in *Baudelaire*, p. 151.

19. Teresa de Lauretis, "Desire in Narrative," in her *Alice Doesn't: Feminism, Semiotics, Cinema*, Bloomington, Ind., 1984, pp. 149–50.

20. Daniel J. Boorstin, "The Historian: 'A Wrestler With the Angel,'" *New York Times Book Review*, Sept. 20, 1987, p. 28.

21. "Cette degoûtante vie sexuelle est, après tout, la raison même du groupement des femmes et de leur claustration" (Louis Fiaux, *Les Maisons de tolérance, leur fermeture*, Paris, 1892, p. 134). Throughout this book translations from French into English are mine, unless otherwise noted.

22. Corbin, *Les Filles de noce;* and Harsin, *Policing Prostitution.*

23. "L'inscription sur les régistres de la prostitution réglementée l'a fait disparaître, pour toujours, des statistiques concernant les insoumises"

(Docteur O[ctave] Commenge, *Recherches sur les maladies vénériennes à Paris dans leurs rapports avec la prostitution clandestine et la prostitution réglementaire de 1878 à 1887*, Paris, 1890, p. 34).

24. "Malgré ses protestations, elle est apprehendée, inscrite d'office. Des lors, toutes ses préoccupations seront concentrées sur sa vie sexuelle; elle sera sans cesse hantée du désir d'échapper aux policiers, mais sans cesse traquée par eux. Soumise au contrôle, il lui est impossible de songer à retrouver un emploi honnête. Dorenavant, sa grande appréhension sera l'abominable visite qui l'empêchera de s'élèver tant soit peu audessus du plus ignoble terre à terre; sa présence au dispensaire sonnera chaque semaine le glas funèbre de ses affections pures d'autrefois, de ses aspirations vers l'air respirable, de tout élan possible vers le bien. Prostituée! a dit la police, et prostituée elle restera" (Alfred de Meuron, "Police des moeurs," *Revue de morale sociale*, no. 1 [Mar. 1899], pp. 59–60 [preserved in the Archives de la Préfecture de Police (hereafter APP), Paris, D/B 407]). See J.-K. Huysmans's novelistic use of the relentless police pursuit of an "escaped" soumise in his *Marthe, histoire d'une fille* [1876], Paris; 10/18, 1975, p. 53.

25. "Toute femme inscrite est à la disposition complète de la police des moeurs. Aux yeux de la police, toute femme non enregistrée est une insoumise" (Yves Guyot, *La Prostitution*, Paris, 1882, p. 152).

26. See Jeffrey Weeks, *Sex, Politics and Society: The Regulation of Sexuality since 1800*, London and New York, 1981, chap. 1. On the problem of conceptualizing sexuality in history, see Michel Foucault, *The History of Sexuality, vol. 1, An Introduction*, Robert Hurley (trans.), New York, 1978; Martha Vicinus, "Sexuality and Power: A Review of Current Work in the History of Sexuality," *Feminist Studies* 8, no. 1 (Spring 1982): 133–56; and Robert A. Padgug, "Sexual Matters: On Conceptualizing Sexuality in History," *Radical History Review*, no. 20 (Spring/Summer 1979): 2–23.

27. Peter Cominos, "Late Victorian Sexual Respectability and the Social System," *International Review of Social History* 8 (1963): 18–48, 216–50.

28. Jacques Servais and Jean-Pierre Laurend, *Histoire et dossier de la prostitution*, Paris, 1965, p. 207.

29. Corbin, *Les Filles de noce*, pp. 278ff, and for the development of the terminology used here, see Louis Chevalier's classic study, *Classes laborieuses et classes dangéreuses à Paris, pendant la première moitié du dix-neuvième siècle*, Paris, 1958.

30. "Le régime de la police des moeurs constitue donc pour l'homme une véritable compagnie d'assurances contre les risques résultant de son inconduite. Elle le décharge des responsabilités qui lui incombent de la manière la plus formelle" (Meuron, "Police des Moeurs," p. 57).

31. Weeks, *Sex, Politics and Society*, p. 2.

32. "Le monde de la prostitution, établissements et personnel, se transforme d'une manière notable. Le nombre de maisons de tolérance diminue: il ira toujours en décroissant. Au point de vue de la spéculation, ces maisons n'offrent plus guère d'avantages, et elles disparaîtraient si elles n'avaient leur clientèle de voyageurs, de soldats et de journaliers. Ce serait une grave erreur de croire qu'il y a lieu pour la morale publique de se réjouir de ce fait, car il ne tient qu'à un simple changement de forme. Aujourd'hui, on cherche l'*aventure* au grand péril de sa santé, et, dans bien des cas, de sa tranquilité à venir. Question de vanité et de luxe sur un terrain malsain" (C. J. Lecour, *De l'état actuel de la prostitution parisienne*, Paris, 1874, pp. 18–19).

33. "La tolérance pour la galanterie vénale et scandaleuse est entrée dans nos moeurs" (C. J. Lecour, *La Prostitution à Paris et à Londres*, 2d ed., Paris, 1872, p. 2).

34. "Depuis un certain nombre d'années les chances de prosperité des maisons de tolérance ont singulièrement baissé. La prostitution clandestine de jour en jour plus envahissante et plus audacieuse fait à ces maisons une concurrence formidable et leur enlève la meilleure partie de leur clientèle" (Dr. Louis Reuss, *La Prostitution au point de vue de l'hygiène et de l'administration en France et à l'étranger*, Paris, 1889, p. 160).

35. "L'impression d'invasion par l'insoumise traduit bien évidemment la terreur qu'inspire toute idée de libéralisation sexuelle au sein de la bourgeoisie. La demarcation est moins nette que jamais entre adultère, liberté de moeurs, débauche, vice et prostitution" (Corbin, *Les Filles de noces*, p. 43).

36. Peter Brooks, "The Mark of the Beast: Prostitution, Serialization and Narration," chap. 6 of his *Reading for the Plot: Design and Intention in Narrative*, New York, 1984, pp. 143–70.

37. "Les gardes municipaux de service jouissent par devoir du spectacle de la cascade échevelée et

des saturnales que les réglements de police s'éfforcent en vain de contenir dans la décence" (Flévy d'Urville, *Les Ordures de Paris*, Paris, 1874, p. 21).

38. "La femme n'attend plus qu'on l'admire, elle s'exhibe" (ibid., p. 12).

39. "Messieurs, une des pratiques de racolage les plus ordinaires des prostituées consiste à s'installer avec des toilettes ou des allures affichantes, parmi des consummateurs, à la devanture des cafés" (letter from Léon Renault, 1874, Paris, APP, D/B, 407).

40. "L'adultère, c'est vraiment contagieux comme les crises d'hystérie"; and "Ces pauvres femmes du monde arrivent quelquefois à être traitées comme les putains qu'elles sont" (*Journal des Goncourts* [Aug. 19 and 30, 1878], Paris: Flammarion, 1956, vol. 2, pp. 1,249, 1,254).

41. "Dans la bourgeoisie, la jeune fille est gardée pure jusqu'au mariage; seulement, après le mariage, l'effet du milieu gâté et de l'éducation mauvaise se produit et la jette aux bras d'un amant: ce n'est plus la prostitution, c'est l'adultère, il n'y a que le mot de change. Car, il faut bien insister, l'adultère est la plaie de la bourgeoisie, comme la prostitution est celle du peuple" (Emile Zola, "L'Adultère dans la bourgeoisie," *Le Figaro*, Feb. 28, 1881, p. 1).

42. "La prostitution clandestine est bien plus dangéreuse que la prostitution tolérée; elle est bien autrement grave sous le rapport des moeurs et de son influence pernicieuse" (Reuss, *La Prostitution*, p. 163).

43. "Les rassemblements que forment les filles sont une source continuelle de plaintes et de récriminations. . . . Les femmes honnêtes ne peuvent plus s'arrêter aux étalages sans risquer d'être insultées ou d'être en butte aux propositions d'un passant; elles ne veulent pas entrer dans un magasin quand il faut fendre, pour y arriver, un groupe pressé" (ibid., p. 270).

44. "Insultes, propositions: atteintes à l'honneur de la femme honnête dans son intégrité physique pouvant atteindre la conscience qu'elle a d'elle-même. Il n'est plus question ici de l'influence pernicieuse des mauvaises visions sur la moralité féminine mais de la confusion femme honnête/prostituée qu'il convient de combattre"; "La femme honnête doit être l'antithèse de la fille, elle doit avoir rejeté loin d'elle tout désir et plaisirs sexuels" (Martine Callu, "Approche critique du phénomène prostitutionnel parisien de la seconde moitié du dix-neuvième siècle par le biais d'un ensemble d'images: oeuvres de C. Guys, F. Rops, G. Moreau," Mémoire de maîtrise, Université F. Rabelais, Tours, 1977, pp. 91, 96).

45. In Simone de Beauvoir's canny formulation the situation has been and remains this: "In truth woman has not been socially emancipated through man's need – sexual desire and the desire for offspring – which makes the male dependent for satisfaction upon the female" (Beauvoir, *The Second Sex*, p. xx).

46. In Lionello Venturi, *Cézanne: Son art, son oeuvre*, Paris, 1936, the three works are identified as follows: *Une Moderne Olympia*, 1870, no. 106; *Une Moderne Olympia*, 1872–73, no. 225; and *Olympia*, 1875–77, no. 882. In his *Cézanne*, Geneva, 1978, Venturi revised the date of the third work to 1872–74. In dating it ca. 1877, I am following John Rewald, *Paul Cézanne: The Watercolors*, Boston, 1983, no. 135. And in dating the earliest of the three works ca. 1869–70, I am following Lawrence Gowing et al., *Cézanne: The Early Years, 1859–1872*, edited by Mary Anne Stevens, London, Royal Academy of Arts, catalog 40, 1988, pp. 150–51.

47. Meyer Schapiro, "The Apples of Cézanne: An Essay on the Meaning of Still-Life," in *Modern Art: Nineteenth and Twentieth Centuries: Selected Papers*, New York, 1978, pp. 9–10.

48. Venturi, *Cézanne* (1936), vol. 1, p. 115.

49. "D'idéalisation en idéalisation, ils aboutiront à ce degré de romantisme sans frein, où la nature n'est plus qu'un prétexte à rêveries, et où l'imagination devient impuissante à formuler autre chose que des fantaisies personnelles subjectives, sans écho dans la raison générale, parce qu'elles sont sans contrôle et sans vérification possible dans la réalité" (Jules Castagnary, "L'Exposition du boulevard des Capucines, les impressionnistes," *Le Siècle*, Apr. 29, 1874; reprinted in *Centenaire de l'impressionnisme*, 2d ed., Paris, Editions des musées nationaux, 1974, pp. 235, 265).

50. "On se demande s'il n'y a pas là ou une mystification inconvénante pour le public, ou le résultat d'une aliénation mentale qu'on ne pourrait alors que déplorer" (Emile Cardon, "L'Exposition des révoltés" *La Presse*, Apr. 29, 1874; reprinted in *Centenaire de l'impressionnisme*, p. 263).

51. "Le public de dimanche a jugé à propos de ricaner en face de la fantastique figure qui

se présente dans un ciel opiacé, à un fumeur d'opium. Cette apparition d'un peu de chair rose et nue que pousse devant lui, dans le nuageux empyrée, une espèce de démon, où s'incube, comme une vision voluptueuse, ce coin de paradis artificiel, a suffoqué les plus braves, il faut le dire, et M. Cézanne n'apparaît plus que comme une espèce de fou, agité en peignant du *delirium tremens.* L'on a refusé de voir, dans cette création inspirée de Baudelaire, un rêve, une impression causée par les vapeurs orientales et qu'il fallait rendre sous la bizarre ébauche de l'imagination. L'incohérence n'est-elle pas la nature, le caractère particulier du sommeil laudatif? Pourquoi chercher une plaisanterie indécente, un motif de scandale dans L'Olympia? Ce n'est en réalité qu'une des formes extravagantes du haschisch empruntée à l'essaim des songes drôlatiques qui doivent encore se cacher dans de l'hôtel Pimodan" (Marc de Montifaud [Marie-Amélie Chartroule de Montifaud], "Exposition du boulevard des Capucines," *L'Artiste,* May 1, 1874; reprinted in *Centenaire de l'impressionnisme,* pp. 235, 267).

52. Corbin, *Les Filles de noce,* p. 249; and see my discussion in chap. 4, "Mutual Desire in the New Nightspots."

53. Two of Cézanne's earlier watercolors also use a black cat in a context of sexual love. In both of them, the cat joins a naked reclining woman and man who are waited on by a servant bearing food. In Rewald's catalog of the watercolors, *Cézanne's Watercolors,* they are identified as: no. 34, *Le Punch au rhum,* 1866–67, and no. 35, *L'Après-midi à Naples,* 1870–72.

54. There are two of these, one oil on canvas (the work reproduced here) and one watercolor. The oil on canvas version of *L'Eternel féminin,* Venturi (*Cézanne,* 1936), no. 247, is dated 1875–77. The watercolor version, also titled *L'Eternel féminin,* is Rewald, *Cézanne Watercolors,* no. 57, dated 1877. It is Venturi (1936), no. 895, dated 1875–77; Venturi (*Cézanne,* 1978), revised the date to ca. 1877. Simone de Beauvoir (*The Second Sex,* p. 168) reminds us that Cézanne's title is taken from the last lines of Goethe's *Faust:* "The Eternal Feminine/Beckons us upward."

55. "Quand elle sort du bain, la servante [zelée?]/sur son rafraîchi versera les parfums./ Et, les seins palpitants, la tête renversée,/elle vit sans souci des regards importuns." According to Rewald (*Cézanne Watercolors,* p. 118), "[Adrien] Chappuis has deciphered the lines written in ink beneath the watercolor and subsequently blotted out by the artist with a brush (the last word of the first line being cut off)." In Venturi (1936) it is no. 884, dated 1875–77; in Venturi (1978) the author revised the date to 1872–74. I am following the most up-to-date scholarship – Rewald, *Cézanne Watercolors,* no. 137 – in dating it ca. 1880. (This poem sounds about as bad as the one by Zacharie Astruc that Manet appended to his *Olympia* in the Salon of 1865.)

56. Although modernist artists have been granted de facto immunity from such (contaminating) ideas in the normative literature on nineteenth-century French art, some scholars have attempted to point out that, on the plane of ideology, vanguard artists have not been any more progressive about female sexuality than their (ostensibly) less inventive male contemporaries. See, for example, Nochlin, "Courbet's Real Allegory," pp. 31–41, 224–26. In literary studies, see Susan Rubin Suleiman, "Pornography, Transgression, and the Avant-Garde: Bataille's *Story of the Eye,*" in *The Poetics of Gender,* Nancy K. Miller (ed.), New York, 1986, pp. 117–36. And I put Henri Gervex's *Rolla* into contact with Edgar Degas's brothel monotypes in my "*Avant-Garde* and *Pompier* Images of Nineteenth-Century French Prostitution: The Matter of Modernism, Modernity and Social Ideology," in *Modernism and Modernity: The Vancouver Conference Papers,* Benjamin H. D. Buchloh, Serge Guilbaut, and David Solkin (eds.), Halifax, 1983, pp. 43–64.

Chapter 2: In the Brothel

1. The key catalogs of the monotypes are Eugenia Parry Janis, *Degas Monotypes: Essay, Catalogue and Checklist,* Greenwich, Conn., 1968; Jean Adhémar and Françoise Cachin, *Degas: The Complete Etchings, Lithographs and Monotypes,* New York, 1975; *Degas Monotypes,* Arts Council of Great Britain, 1975; and Jean Sutherland Boggs, Douglas W. Druick, Henri Loyrette, Michael Pantazzi, and Gary Tinterow, *Degas,* New York, 1988, pp. 296–302.

Janis (p. xix) provides this essential information: "Degas depicted prostitutes in brothel settings only in monotype. It is the only subject in Degas's work which is limited to one medium." Degas himself seems never to have used the word monotype, preferring "dessins faits à l'encre grasse et imprimés." Unlike his pastels and oils of the same date, which he referred to contemptuously as his "articles," prints were his "serious experiments," and monotypes dominated his prints. According to *Degas* (Arts Council, p. 8), between 1874 and 1884, and again in 1890–92, Degas made perhaps 250 monotypes of which over 400 impressions are documented. Over a longer period of time he made only 66 etchings and lithographs. Boggs et al. (p. 296) argue that "although they are generally dated c. 1879–80, the monotypes appear to belong to an earlier period, c. 1876–77, and it is possible that Degas exhibited some of them in April 1877." It is important to remember that the brothel monotypes are very small, 4 3/4″ × 6 1/4″ or sometimes 6 1/4″ × 8 1/2″.

2. Clement Greenberg, "On the Role of Nature in Modernist Painting" [1949], *Art and Culture*, Boston, 1961, p. 171.

3. Under the (roughly) Greenbergian rubric belong the important early readings of Janis, *Monotypes*, Adhémar and Cachin, *Degas*, and Linda Nochlin, *Realism*, Baltimore, 1971, pp. 204–06. A brilliant synthesis of modernist and deconstructionist viewpoints concerning Degas's dismantling of convention is Carol M. Armstrong, "Edgar Degas and the Representation of the Female Body," in *The Female Body in Western Culture: Contemporary Perspectives*, Susan Rubin Suleiman (ed.), Cambridge, Mass., 1986, pp. 223–42.

4. Charles Bernheimer, "Degas's Brothels: Voyeurism and Ideology," *Representations* 20 (Fall 1987): 172.

5. Alain Corbin, *Les Filles de noce: Misère sexuelle et prostitution aux dix-neuvième et vingtième siècles*, Paris, 1978, chap. 2.

6. Ibid., p. 88.

7. Gustave Macé, *La Police parisienne: Le Gibier de Saint Lazare*, Paris, 1888, p. 264.

8. Ibid., pp. 262–64.

9. "Ces mercenaires de la prostitution officielle, malgré l'absence de désirs physiques, sont en contact perpétuel avec les hommes, et n'ayant que la joie des autres pour vivre, elles se soumettent à un travail absolument mécanique" (ibid., p. 260).

10. "Contrairement aux établissements similaires plus chics où les femmes ne sont vêtues que d'un peignoir ou d'une chémise, les pensionnaires des maisons économiques sont plus habillées" (Mr. Jean, *Les Bas-fonds du crime et de la prostitution*, Paris, n.d. [ca. 1900], p. 59). This distinction was also made by Macé, *La Police*, pp. 260–61: "Les pensionnaires, habillés de diverses couleurs, ont la poitrine et les bras nus. Sur le maillot se noue le petit jupon court s'arrêtant à la naissance des jambes. Rebut du centre de Paris et presque toutes se livrant à l'intempérance, ces femmes, agées de 30 à 40 ans, guettent l'arrivée des clients composés d'ouvriers et de rôdeurs. Si, par hasard, deux ou trois personnes ayant une mise convénable, se présentent, les filles, subitement décontenancées, n'abordent les nouveaux venus qu'après y avoir été invitées par la maîtresse de l'établissement" (The brothel dwellers, dressed in diverse colors, have bare chests and arms. Over their tights is tied a short petticoat that stops just at the top of the legs. These women, between thirty and forty years of age, riffraff from the center of Paris and almost all of them indulging in intemperance, are on the lookout for the customers, all workers and vagrants. If, by chance, two or three decently dressed people present themselves, the filles, suddenly embarrassed, don't approach the new arrivals until being invited to do so by the mistress of the house).

11. The salons were probably on the first floor rather than on the rez-de-chaussée. See Macé, *La Police*, p. 262.

12. The middle-ranked house was permitted to keep a domestic at the door, and under certain circumstances one of the pensionnaires was allowed to circulate on the street in front of the house. See "Maîtresses de Maison, Obligations Générales," 1879, and "Prostitution, Maisons de Tolérance," n.d., in APP, D/B 407; and Dr. Louis Reuss, *La Prostitution au point de vue de l'hygiène et de l'administration en France et à l'étranger*, Paris, 1889, pp. 118ff.

13. Theodore Reff, *The Notebooks of Edgar Degas: A Catalogue of the Thirty-eight Notebooks in the Bibliothèque Nationale and Other Collections*, New York, 1985, vol. 1, pp. 129–30; and Reff, "The Artist and the Writer," in *Degas: The Artist's Mind*, New York, 1976, pp. 172–73.

14. For a discussion of Goncourt's novel, see my Ph.D. dissertation, Susan Hollis Clayson, "Representations of Prostitution in Early Third Republic France," University of California at Los Angeles, 1984, pp. 145–54; and Reff, *Degas: Artist's Mind*, p. 173.

15. "Plus tapageuse, plus braillard continuait l'orgie, en dépit de la somnolence des femmes" (Edmond de Goncourt, *La Fille Elisa* [1877], Paris, 1906, p. 119). See my "Representations of Prostitution," p. 147.

16. Forain's print was intended as an illustration for one of J. K. Huysmans's *Croquis parisiens.* In Marcel Guérin, *J. L. Forain, Aquafortiste*, Paris, 1912, vol. 1, no. 21, the print is entitled *Maison close (planche refusée).*

17. The entry on *Repose* in Boggs et al., *Degas*, considers the woman at the right to be adjusting a stocking.

18. Peter Brooks, "The Sign of the Beast: Prostitution, Serialization, and Narrative," chap. 6 of his *Reading for the Plot: Design and Intention in Narrative*, New York, 1984, p. 155.

19. The abolitionists argued for an end to the licensing and regulating of prostitution, not for the abolition of prostitution per se. The great spokesperson of the pan-European movement was the Englishwoman Josephine Butler. The most important abolitionist in France was Yves Guyot. Norma Broude has recently made the mistake of separating the feminist antiregulationists from their many abolitionist colleagues. See her problematic "Edgar Degas and French Feminism, ca. 1880: 'The Young Spartans,' the Brothel Monotypes, and the Bathers Revisited," *The Art Bulletin* 70, no. 4 (Dec. 1988): 640–59.

20. Four related bather monotypes were dedicated to Degas's friends Philippe Burty, the Viscount Lepic, Henri Michel-Lévy, and P. Rosanna. On the probable limited viewership of the prints, see Richard R. Brettell and Suzanne Folds McCullagh, *Degas in The Art Institute of Chicago*, Chicago, 1984, p. 143. Though I am aware of the problems posed by recognizing, as we all must do, that the circuits of spectatorship are gendered, I have not raised the issue in my discussion of Degas's prints because I have not yet completely sorted out my position. I have not decided yet just how to build into my account the existential, interpretive, and political consequences of acknowledging the difficulty I experience in shuttling between the "imagined" viewer position of a late nineteenth-century bourgeois Frenchman and the "actual" position of a late twentieth-century feminist woman. I used to accept the classic argument of Laura Mulvey that the woman who "enjoyed" or at least understood a paradigmatically male art form (the European nude in the visual arts) was perforce acting masochistically or was at best an uncomfortable transvestite. (See Laura Mulvey's reply to her own article of 1975: Mulvey, "Afterthoughts on 'Visual Pleasure and Narrative Cinema' Inspired by *Duel in the Sun*," *Framework*, nos. 15, 16, 17 [1981]: 12–15.) I am, however, unsatisfied with a psychoanalytic construction of my sexual identity that assumes, for example, that my experience of Degas's monotypes would resemble those of all other women more closely than they would, say, the responses of men (*and* women) of my class, ethnicity, education, and politics. (For illuminating discussions of this problem, see Mary Ann Doane, *The Desire to Desire: The Woman's Film of the 1940s*, Bloomington, Ind., 1987, pp. 6ff; Diane Waldman, "Film Theory and the Gendered Spectator: The Female or the Feminist Reader?" *Camera Obscura* 18 [Sept. 1988]: 80–94; Martha Gever, "Just Looking," *The Nation* [Feb. 5, 1990]: 170–74.) Tania Modleski's suggestion that the female spectator of classic Hollywood cinema (or – my substitution – of a modern European image of an unclad woman) is always caught in "double desire," as she puts it, more closely resembles my own experience: "identifying at one and the same time not only with the passive female (object), but with the active (usually male) subject" (Modleski, *The Women Who Knew Too Much: Hitchcock and Feminist Theory*, New York, 1988, p. 2). Or in Lisa Tickner's words: "There is room for a mobile subject capable of moving in fantasy between positions constituted socially as masculine or feminine" (Tickner, "Feminism, Art History, and Sexual Difference," *Genders* 3 [Fall 1988]: 113).

21. "Le miché sérieux fait son entrée. Aucune femme ne doit lui adresser une invitation verbale particulière; mais toutes lui envoient des regards brûlants, se dandinent, prennent des positions excitantes, sourient, et même agitent la langue, pour faire comprendre clairement qu'elles ont mis à la disposition du client mille raffinements de volupté" (Léo Taxil, *La Prostitution contemporaine: Etude d'une question sociale*, Paris, 1884, quoted in *Le Crapouillot*, special issue: "Petite histoire des maisons closes," n. s., no. 42 [Spring 1977]: 51).

Corbin (*Les Filles de noce*, p. 90) provided this vivid synthetic description: "Au salon de la grande tolérance, haut lieu des plaisirs aristocratiques et bourgeois, règnent le silence et la discrétion. Alors que dans les maisons de bas-étage le bruit, le mouvement, les chants et les danses, alcool, le déshabille suggestif et, plus encore, l'excitation manuelle contribuent à exacerber les sens, dans la maison de luxe, ce sont la nudité presque intégrale, la plastique, les poses suggestives, la sollicitation par le regard ou le geste à distance et le luxe ambiant qui concourent, dans une atmosphere feutrée, à susciter le désir." (In the salon of the grande tolérance, the highest quarter of aristocratic and bourgeois pleasures, silence and discretion reign supreme. While in the low-level houses noise, movement, singing and dancing, alcohol, suggestive states of undress and, still more, manual excitation all contribute to the stirring up of the senses, in the deluxe house, there is almost total nudity, well-formed bodies [*la plastique*] on display, suggestive poses, solicitation by a glance or a gesture at a distance and the surrounding luxury which contributes, in a padded atmosphere, to the arousal of desire.)

Macé (*La Police*, pp. 265–66) gave the following version of this process: "Choisies avec le plus grand soin, les belles filles abondent dans les hautes maisons de plaisir, et le soir, habilement maquillées, elles paraissent fraîches, bien que leur manière de vivre soit accidentée, fatigante et fatale à leur beauté. Depuis huit heures du soir jusqu'à quatre heures du matin, elles sont obligées de se tenir à la disposition des clients et de boire le champagne outre mésure. La plupart ont leurs habitués, et gagnent énormément d'argent, si on en juge d'après le carnet de celles qui tiennent leur comptabilité au jour le jour. . . . Les toilettes de *salon* confectionnées dans les tolérances changent à chaque trimestre: les filles portent soit des vêtements uniformes, soit des corsages et maillots de différentes couleurs, ou ne sont couvertes que d'un léger voile de gaze permettant d'exhiber leurs charmes" (Chosen with the greatest care, beautiful filles abound in houses of pleasure of the highest rank, and in the evening, artfully made up, they appear fresh, even though their chequered way of life is fatiguing and fatal to their beauty. From eight o'clock in the evening until four o'clock in the morning, they are obliged to put themselves at the disposition of the customers and to drink quantities of champagne beyond measure. Most of them have their regular customers, and gain enormous amounts of money, if one can judge from the notebook kept by the women who keep track of their accounts from day to day. . . . The toilettes produced for wear in the salon change every trimester: the filles wear identical outfits, or tights and bodices of different colors, or they cover themselves with just a light veil of gauze permitting the exhibition of their charms).

22. "Le scintillement des glaces ouvragées, la profusion des dorures, l'éclat les lumières . . ." (Macé, *La Police*, pp. 262–63).

23. T. J. Clark, *The Painting of Modern Life: Paris in the Art of Manet and His Followers*, New York, 1985, p. 131.

24. "Ce qui est prodigieux dans cette oeuvre, c'est la puissance de réalité qui s'en dégage; ces filles sont des filles de maison et pas d'autres filles, et de leurs postures, leur irritante odeur, leur faisandé de peau, sous les flammes du gaz qui éclaire cette aquarelle lavée de gouache, avec une précision de vérité vraiment étrange, sont, pour la première fois sans doute, aussi fermément, aussi carrément rendus, leur caractère, leur humanité béstiale ou puérile ne l'est pas moins. Toute la philosophie de l'amour tarifé est dans cette scène où, après être volontairement entré, poussé par un désir bête, le monsieur réfléchit et, devenu plus froid, finit par demeurer insensible aux offres" (J.-K. Huysmans, "L'Exposition des indépendants en 1880," reprinted in *L'Art moderne/Certains*, Paris, 1975, pp. 120–21).

25. On Huysmans's notorious venting of similar ideas explicitly in reaction to Degas's works, see Charles Bernheimer, "Degas's Brothels," pp. 161–63; and Martha Ward's discussion of Huysmans's 1886 criticism of some of the bather pastels: Ward, "1886, The Eighth Exhibition: The Rhetoric of Independence and Innovation," in *The New Painting: Impressionism, 1874–1886*, Charles S. Moffett (ed.), 1986, Fine Arts Museums of San Francisco, pp. 421–42.

26. Alexandre Parent-Duchâtelet, *De la prostitution dans la ville de Paris*, Paris, 1936, vol. 1, chap. 3, "Considérations physiologiques sur les prostitutées," pp. 193–282.

27. "Les défauts particuliers aux prostituées," Parent-Duchâtelet, vol. 1, pp. 138–42; and Reuss, *La Prostitution*, pp. 66–69.

28. "Les bonnes qualités de prostituées," Parent-Duchâtelet, *De la prostitution*, vol. 1, pp. 143–51; Corbin, *Les Filles de noce*, pp. 21–22; and Reuss, *La Prostitution*, pp. 55–61, 126–27.

29. "Etranges filles que ces pensionnaires. Jolies, laides, bêtes, spirituelles, toutes ont leur minute de folie et de désespoir; elles passent simultanément du rire aux larmes, des ménaces aux caresses. Si on écoute leurs confidences, elles imputent à la fatalité la cause de leur premier abandon, et pour mieux exciter la pitié des clients, elle renouvellent cette éternelle et vieille histoire de filles séduites. Aucune n'était née pour ce genre de vie et c'est par besoin qu'elles exercent ce repugnant travail. La corruption morale est rarement complète, car dans leur chambre particulière, nue, délabrée, se trouvent des objets de piété, des fleurs dessechées, souvenirs du pays, et des livres honnêtement écrits. . . . La plupart de ces filles sont superstitieuses à l'excès" (Macé, *La Police*, pp. 258–59).

30. The other two monotypes on this subject are Janis, *Degas Monotypes*, checklist nos. 88 and 90. Fig. 22 is Janis no. 89.

31. See my "Representations of Prostitution," pp. 139–54.

32. Of an imagery of graphic heterosexual physical contact, few monotypes survive. The one unequivocal and fully legible representation of sexual activity survives only as a once-broken, now-mended zinc plate (Janis, *Degas Monotypes*, no. 108). In it two prostitutes attend to a corpulent, mustachioed man; all three are naked. The prone woman appears to perform fellatio on him, while the other woman stands aside but touches the leg of her colleague. In a similar but less legible image known as *Sur le lit* (once owned by John Richardson, now in the Musée Picasso; apparently considered too daring to be shown along with Picasso's other Degas monotypes in *Donation Picasso*, Paris, 1978; Janis, *Degas Monotypes*, no. 109), a naked woman sits upright between the legs of a supine naked man. His outstretched right leg rests on her splayed left thigh; his left leg folds behind her buttocks. Because of the angle of their bodies, the genital areas are not visible, but her hands appear in position for a manipulation of his genitals. She looks away from him, to her left. Her position does not seem to suggest the imminence of coitus, but rather her convenient access to either manual or oral manipulation of him. The images are not very clear, and we will never know what other monotypes were destroyed before the studio sale in 1918. Anything we might say must be provisional, but judging from the fragmentary pictorial evidence to have survived, the traditionally "intimate" form of sexual intercourse (partners reclining face-to-face) is not included in the repertory of his prostitutes. There are also two legibly lesbian monotypes (Janis, nos. 117 [fig. 29] and 118).

33. Other monotypes in this format include Janis, *Degas Monotypes*, checklist nos. 92, 95, 97, and 104.

34. Bernheimer, "Degas's Brothels," p. 165.

35. Janis, *Degas Monotypes*, p. xx.

36. John Richardson, "The Catch in the Late Picasso," *New York Review of Books*, July 19, 1984, p. 26.

37. Lisa Tickner, *The Spectacle of Women: Imagery of the Suffrage Campaign, 1907–1914*, Chicago, 1988, pp. 172, 173.

38. Douglas Druick, "La Petite Danseuse et les criminels: Degas moraliste?" in *Degas inédit*, Actes du Colloque Degas, Paris: Musée d'Orsay (Apr. 18–21, 1988), pp. 224–50. A splendid overview of nineteenth-century physiognomic theory can be found in Neil McWilliam, "Making Faces," *Art History* 7, no. 1 (Mar. 1984): 115–19.

39. Linda Nochlin, "Degas on the Dreyfus Affair: A Portrait of the Artist as an Anti-Semite," in *The Dreyfus Affair: Art, Truth, and Justice*, Norman L. Kleeblatt (ed.), Berkeley, 1988, pp. 103, 111.

40. Anthea Callen, "The Flesh Made Word: Voyeurism and Sexual Guilt in Degas' Brothel Monotypes," paper presented at the annual meeting of the Association of Art Historians, London, Apr. 9, 1989. Nochlin ("Dreyfus Affair," p. 105) proposes that Degas's representation of his Jewish friend Ludovic Halévy in the artist's illustrations for Halévy's *La Famille Cardinal* came close to resembling "coarse Semitic-featured 'protectors' who appeared leering down the *décolletages* of ballet-girls in caricature of the time." Nochlin surmises that this resemblance *may* help to explain Halévy's rejection of Degas's illustrations. Insofar as the *Famille Cardinal* pictures were made ca. 1878 – at roughly the same time or slightly later than the brothel monotypes – Nochlin's construal serves to support Callen's discovery of negative Semitic faces in the brothel monotypes.

41. Alan Sekula, "The Body and the Archive," *October* 39 (Winter 1986): 3–64.

42. T. E. Perkins quoted in Tickner, *Spectacle of Women*, p. 172.

43. For example, Roy McMullen (*Degas: His*

Life, Times, and Work, London, 1985, p. 238) writes: "A renunciation of statistically normal love was perhaps a necessary condition for the creation of this brilliant universe of looking." Richard Thomson (*Degas: The Nudes*, London, 1988, p. 101) discusses the rumor that Degas was an inadequate lover, which Thomson thinks might explain Degas's lack of attachment to any women: "It might also promote the related idea that he frequented brothels, as a convenient outlet for a fragile sexuality without risk of humiliation, and that the creation of images showing both the place and the means to satisfy such an appetite was perhaps some kind of substitute for the performance."

44. "X . . . [Degas] vit comme un petit notaire et n'aime pas les femmes, sachant que s'il les aimait et les b . . . [baisait] beaucoup, cérébralement malade, il deviendrait inepte en peinture. La peinture de X . . . est virile et impersonnelle justement parce qu'il a accepté de n'être personnellement qu'un petit notaire ayant un horreur de faire la noce. Il regarde des animaux humains plus forts que lui, b . . . et b . . . , et il les peint bien, justement parce qu'il n'a pas tant que ça le prétention de b . . ." (Vincent van Gogh, "Lettre 9," *Lettres de Vincent van Gogh à Emile Bernard*, Paris: Ambroise Vollard, 1911, p. 102, ellipses in original). I thank Carol Zemel for telling me about this letter. The English translation is taken from "Letter to Bernard B14," Arles, August 1888, *The Complete Letters of Vincent van Gogh*, vol. 3, Greenwich, Conn., 1958, p. 509.

45. John Richardson, "The Late Picasso," pp. 21–28; William S. Rubin and Milton Esterow, "Visits with Picasso at Mougins," *Art News* 72, no. 6 (Summer 1973): 42–43; *Pablo Picasso: Das Spätwek, Themen 1964–1972*, Christian Geelhaar (ed.), Basel Kunstmuseum, 1971, pp. 44–52; Gert Schiff, *Picasso, The Last Years, 1963–1973*, New York, 1983, pp. 59–61; Pierre Cabanne, "Degas chez Picasso," *Connaissance des Arts* 262 (Dec. 1973): 146–51; Christian Geelhaar, "Ausstellung Picasso," *Pantheon* 36 (July/Aug./Sept. 1978): 288–89.

46. Schiff, *Picasso*, p. 59; Cabanne, "Degas chez Picasso," p. 147; Rubin and Esterow, "Visits with Picasso," p. 42.

47. Quoted in Schiff, *Picasso*, p. 61.

48. I am paraphrasing Bernheimer, "Degas's Brothels," p. 170.

49. Richardson, "The Late Picasso," p. 25.

50. Sander Gilman, "The Hottentot and the Prostitute: Toward an Iconography of Female Sexuality," chap. 3 of his *Difference and Pathology: Stereotypes of Sexuality, Race and Madness*, Ithaca, 1985. Sigmund Freud's discussion of the "Wolf Man's" neurotic preference for women's posteriors appears in "From the History of an Infantile Neurosis" [1918] in Freud, *Three Case Histories*, New York, 1963, pp. 227ff.

51. Gilman, "The Hottentot," p. 90.

52. Richard Sennett, *The Fall of Public Man: On the Social Psychology of Capitalism*, New York, 1976.

53. Carol Armstrong and I disagree on this issue (Carol M. Armstrong, "Duranty, Degas and the Realism of the Third Republic," paper presented to the 1987 meeting of Nineteenth-Century French Studies, Northwestern University). Armstrong writes (p. 19): "The brothel monotypes . . . represent the most dramatic and thoroughgoing conversion of the physiognomic text of the body into a private spectacle of corporeal sensation and gestural effect."

Chapter 3: Testing the Limits

EPIGRAPHS: (p. 89) Thorstein Veblen, *A Theory of the Leisure Class: An Economic Study of Institutions* [1899], New York, 1931, pp. 181–82, emphasis added; (p. 93) *Paris after Dark: Night Guide for Gentlemen*, 13th ed., Paris, n.d. (ca. 1870), p. 19; (p. 94) Georges Grison, *Paris horrible et Paris original*, Paris, 1882, pp. 296–97, emphasis in original: "Car ce n'est plus la nuit, le soir, *d'allumage de gaz à onze heures* que les *hétaïres* opèrent. C'est toute la journée. Ce n'est pas dans les quartiers extérieures qu'elles cherchent leur butin, c'est au centre le plus vivant de Paris. Passez donc de midi à minuit sur le trottoir de gauche du faubourg Montmartre, – vous voyez que je précise, – vous rencontrerez vingt, trente, quarante filles, âgées de quinze à dix-huit ans – il y en a de douze! – en cheveux, *décolletées*, provocantes, éhontées, vous frôlant du coude ou de l'épaule, vous barrant le passage en vous disant à haute voix des mots à faire rougir un carabinier. D'où sortent-elles? A leur allure il est facile de le voir; elles marchent traînant les pieds, genées par les bottines à hauts talons dont elles n'ont pas l'habitude, embarrassées par les corsets qu'elles ne portent que depuis peu. C'est le rebut des *bals de barrière* qui, alleché par l'impunité, a fait sa descente dans Paris."

1. Thorstein Veblen, *The Theory of the Leisure Class: An Economic Study of Institutions* [1899], New York, 1931, p. 167.

2. Richard Sennett, *The Fall of Public Man: On the Social Psychology of Capitalism*, New York, 1977, p. 164; and Lisa Tickner, *The Spectacle of Women: Imagery of the Suffrage Campaign, 1907–1914*, Chicago, 1988, p. 169.

3. Alexandre Parent-Duchâtelet, *De la prostitution dans la ville de Paris*, Paris, 1836, vol. 1, pp. 362–63. The policy cited by Parent-Duchâtelet applied, of course, to the 1830s, but the same general code remained in force at least until the late 1880s. This summary for instance was written in 1888: "Les filles soumises ne doivent pas racoler sur la voie publique en taille, en cheveux ou dans les toilettes de nature à se faire remarquer. . . . Des tenues par trop affichantes motivent l'arrestation" – Registered prostitutes may not solicit in public without a coat, without a hat, or in any clothing that will attract attention. . . . Outfits that are too flashy will occasion arrests (Gustave Macé, *La Police parisienne: Le Gibier de Saint-Lazare*. Paris, 1888, pp. 290–91). I believe that Alain Corbin commits his only factual error on the issue of proscribed hatlessness. In his *Filles de noce*, he wrote (p. 129): "Elles [les filles en carte] doivent éviter les toilettes comme les allures provocantes et ne peuvent circuler qu' 'en cheveux'" (Registered prostitutes must avoid provocative toilettes and ways of walking and can only circulate "in their hair," or hatless). In her review of *Filles de noce*, Michelle Perrot, eminent French historian, repeated the error when she wrote: "On leur interdisait le racolage et le port du chapeau, signe de bourgeoise" – Forbidden to them are solicitation and the wearing of a hat, sign of a bourgeois woman (Perrot, "Les Filles de noce," *L'Histoire*, no. 9 [Feb. 1979]: 83). Corbin repeated this mistake in a recent essay: "In public spaces, the prostitute will not wear a hat; she must circulate bare-headed" (Corbin, "Commercial Sexuality in Nineteenth-Century France: A System of Images and Regulations," *Representations* 14 [Spring 1986]: 217).

4. See John Berger, *Ways of Seeing*, London, 1972, pp. 45–64; and Anne Hollander, *Seeing Through Clothes*, New York, 1978.

5. Sennett, *Public Man*, pp. 166–67.

6. Michael B. Miller, *The Bon Marché: Bourgeois Culture and the Department Store, 1869–1920*, Princeton, 1981.

7. Sennett, *Public Man*, pp. 141–49; Elizabeth Wilson, *Adorned in Dreams: Fashion and Modernity*, London, 1985, pp. 144–52; and Russell Lewis, "Everything under One Roof: World's Fairs and Department Stores in Paris and Chicago," *Chicago History* 12, no. 3 (Fall 1983): 28–47.

8. Elaine S. Abelson, "Urban Women and the Emergence of Shopping" and "The World of the Store," *When Ladies Go A-Thieving: Middle-Class Shoplifters in the Victorian Department Store*, New York, 1989, pp. 13–62. On the continuation of this trend into the twentieth century, especially in the U.S., see Mary Ann Doane, *The Desire to Desire: The Woman's Film of the 1940s*, Bloomington, Ind., 1987, p. 27.

9. Georg Simmel, "Fashion" [1904], in *On Individuality and Social Forms*, Donald N. Levine (ed.), Chicago, 1971, pp. 309, 310. Theodore Zeldin's shrewd observation (*France, 1848–1945*, vol. 1, *Ambition, Love and Politics*, Oxford, 1973, p. 234) also applies: "The simultaneous idealisation and repression of women . . . was one of the ways by which French society developed its peculiar characteristics. Repression was compensated for and mitigated by giving women considerable power in strictly limited fields."

10. Sheila Rowbotham, *Women, Resistance and Revolution*, New York, 1972, p. 39.

11. Wilson, *Adorned in Dreams*, p. 29.

12. "Quel poète oserait, dans la peinture de plaisir causé par l'apparition d'une beauté, séparer la femme de son costume? Quel est l'homme qui, dans la rue, au théâtre, au bois, n'a pas joui, de la manière la plus désintéressée, d'une toilette savamment composée, et n'en a pas emporté une image inséparable de la beauté de celle a qui elle appartenait, faisant ainsi des deux, de la femme et de la robe, une totalité indivisible?" (Charles Baudelaire, "Le Peintre de la vie moderne," [1863], *Curiosités esthétiques, l'art romantique, et autres oeuvres critiques*, Paris: Editions Garnier Frères, 1962, p. 489).

13. Simone de Beauvoir, *The Second Sex* [1949], H. M. Parshley (trans. and ed.), New York, 1952, p. 148.

14. Wilson, *Adorned in Dreams*, p. 29.

15. Ibid., p. 32.

16. Beauvoir, *Second Sex*, p. 533.

17. "Le désir de se procurer des jouissances ou de beaux vêtements, surtout à Paris . . ." (F. F. A. Béraud, *Les Filles publiques de Paris et la police qui les régit*, Brussels, 1839, p. 89).

18. "[Les] raisons sont tout simplement les trois quarts des péchés capitaux: la coquetterie, la paresse, la gourmandise – et le reste" (Alfred Delvau, "La Prostitution," *Paris Guide par les principaux écrivains et artistes de la France*, Paris, 1867, p. 1,882).

19. "Alors, trottant dans la boue, éclaboussée par les voitures, aveuglée par le résplendissement des étalages, elle avait des envies qui la tortillaient à l'éstomac, ainsi que des frigales, des envies d'être bien mise, de manger dans les restaurants, d'aller au spectacle, d'avoir une chambre à elle avec de beaux meubles. Elle s'arrêtait toute pâle de désir, elle sentait monter du pavé du Paris une chaleur le long de ses cuisses, un appetit féroce de mordre aux jouissances dont elle était bousculée, dans la grande cohue des trottoirs" (Emile Zola, *L'Assommoir* [1877], Paris: Garnier-Flammarion, 1969, pp. 376–77).

20. "Grâce aux journaux mondains qui s'occupent des toilettes, des attelages, des amants, des raoûts et de l'installation des filles, aux pièces de théâtre et aux romans dont beaucoup ont soutenu, avec un incontestable talent, la rehabilitation de la courtisane, il s'est fait dans les moeurs une évolution singulière; à la curiosité évidemment malsaine, qui poussait les honnêtes femmes, au debut de cette évolution, vers les courtisanes, mais qui ne les empêchait pas de garder leur distance, a succedé peu à peu un autre sentiment. Jalouses des filles qui leur enlevaient, de haute lutte, leurs maris, leurs frères ou leurs fiancés, elles se sont mises à les imiter, à les copier. Les salons se sont transformés; la *cocodette* y a fait son apparition, aux applaudissements des jeunes gens blasés et des vieillards ramollis qui retrouvaient en elle le sans gêne, le langage, et jusqu'au parfum de la *cocotte* à la mode" (Dr. Louis Reuss, *La Prostitution au point de vue de l'hygiène et de l'administration en France et à l'étranger*, Paris, 1889, p. 166).

21. "*La Dame aux Camélias* . . . [ellipsis Vanier's] ne pourrait plus être écrite aujourd'hui. . . . On se prêta des patrons de robes entre courtisanes et femmes du monde . . . [ellipsis Vanier's] Non seulement on eût les mêmes toilettes, on eût le même langage" (Dumas, quoted in Henriette Vanier, *La Mode et ses metiers: Frivolités et luttes des classes, 1830–1870*, Paris, 1960, p. 203).

22. "Si vous aviez, ô matrones, la même jeunesse que les filles, et si vous jeunes demoiselles, aviez la même élégance; si vous, dignes bourgeois, pouviez obtenir leurs faveurs sans vous ruiner outre mésure, et si vous, pâles jeunes gens, osiez aussi avoir le courage de votre opinion, personne ne hurlerait contre les filles!" (D. Servet, "Paradoxe: Les Filles," *Revue Moderne et Naturaliste* [1878–79]: 82).

23. Beauvoir, *Second Sex*, p. 539.

24. Phillipe Perrot, *Les Dessus et les dessous de la bourgeoisie: Une histoire du vêtement au dixneuvième siècle*, Paris, 1981, p. 63.

25. Ibid., p. 227.

26. Ibid., pp. 330–31 n. 2.

27. See Charles Blanc du Collet, "Contribution à l'histoire du rétablissement du divorce en France en 1884, étude faite d'après les travaux préparatoires de la loi Naquet," thesis, Université de Paris, Faculté de Droit, 1939; and Alexandre Laya, *Causes célèbres du mariage ou les infortunes conjugales*, Paris, 1883.

28. Quoted in Miller, *Bon Marché*, p. 167 n. 2.

29. "La création de ces grands bazars a fait naître dans l'ordre moral comme dans l'ordre pathologique de nouvelles passions . . . [ellipsis in original]. A coup sûr, il y a là un mode nouveau de névrose!" (Ignotus, "Les Grands Bazars," *Le Figaro*, Mar. 23, 1881, p. 1). See also Perrot *Dessus et dessous*, pp. 120–21; and Octave Uzanne, *Parisiennes de ce temps en leurs divers milieux, états et conditions. Etudes pour servir* . . . , Paris, 1910, pp. 345–46. On female kleptomania, see Rachel Bowlby, *Just Looking: Consumer Culture in Dreiser, Gissing and Zola*, New York, 1985; Abelson, *When Ladies Go A-Thieving;* and Miller, *Bon Marché.*

30. Quoted in Miller, *Bon Marché*, p. 177.

31. "Les femmes que je vois, ont le costume du jour. Le corset fait saillir les hanches. La robe sans plis à la taille, dessine les formes, comme une robe mouillée. La pointe des seines apparaît sous l'étoffe, comme sous le marbre de certaines statues florentines. De temps en temps, la femme cherche dans sa poche la bourse miniscule. On s'étonne qu'un être qui dépense tant ait une bourse si petite!" (Ignotus, "Les Grands Bazars," p. 1).

32. "La femme de race relativement élevée – que les saines passions maternelles ou conjugales

ont preservée de cette névrose particulière – ne va chercher dans les grands bazars qu'une économie très précieuse pour son ménage" (ibid.).

33. Simmel, "Fashion," p. 311.

34. *Equivoques: Peintures françaises du dix-neuvième siècle*, Paris, Musée des Arts Décoratifs, 1973, n.p. (see entry on Duez, *Splendor*).

35. As much as a thirty-year difference, according to Paul Mantz, "Le Salon," *Le Temps*, June 10, 1874, p. 2.

36. Even though *Misère* hung at the left, according to Louis Gonse, "Salon de 1874," *La Gazette des Beaux-Arts*, 2d ser., vol. 10 (July–Dec. 1874): 42.

37. The "before and after" narrative format was a strong English tradition (familiar from the work of William Hogarth, for example) and was often used in earlier nineteenth-century prints as well (in the work of Gustave Doré and Gavarni [Guillaume Sulpice Chevallier], for example).

38. Emile Zola, "Lettre de Paris," *Le Sémaphore de Marseille*, May 4, 1874; reprinted in *Zola: Mon salon, Manet, écrits sur l'art*, Paris: Garnier Flammarion, 1970, p. 207.

39. See the discussion of then-current fashion in the analysis of Gervex's *Rolla* later in this chapter.

40. On the social and moral semiology of dogs, see Richard Thomson, "'Les Quat' Pattes': The Image of the Dog in Late Nineteenth-Century French Art," *Art History* 5, no. 3 (Sept. 1982): 323–37.

41. See chap. 3, "The Invasion of the Boulevard."

42. "C'est très bien, à lui, de faire ressortir par son talent la rigueur, le poignant de ces deux contrastes. La vue de la hideuse chiffonnière arrêtera-t-elle, par la peur de finir de même celles qui seraient tentées de commencer comme elle? j'en doute" (L. Janmot, "Salon de 1874: Quelques considérations générales," excerpt from *Contemporain*, June 1–July 1, 1874, p. 38). Emile Zola's brief descriptive remarks ("Lettre de Paris," p. 207) also acknowledge an ethical message in the diptych: "Une fille à cheveux rouges, superbe de crânerie, et une vieille chiffonnière, la hotte au dos; le titre *Splendeur et Misère* suffit à faire comprendre l'antithèse" (A fille with red hair, superb in her daring, and an old ragpicker, basket on her back; the title *Splendor and Misery* suffices to make the antithesis understood).

43. "C'est un diptyque fort moral ou, du moins, fort mélangé de littérature. . . . [On one side] superbe et jeune, les cheveux teints en jaune, la joue enfarinée de veloutine, insolente, radieuse, elle va, faisant craquer sur l'asphalte du boulevard le petit talon de sa bottine victorieuse. . . . Voici, tout à côté, la même petite dame vue trente ans après, ratatinée, sordide, en haillons, laissant deviner à toutes ses déchirures la misère et le vice, et tenant à la main comme un symbole ironique des folies passées une vieille paire de souliers de satin rose" (Paul Mantz "Le Salon," p. 2). Mantz goes on to offer an interpretation of the moral of the story, which is, he judges, presented in "les proportions du grand poème": "Quant à la moralité du conte. Il n'y a pas à la discuter. Nous sommes ici à l'Ambigu: le public exige que le vice soit puni. J'entends dire autour de moi que ces galantes cigales ne finissent pas toujours aussi misérables et aussi dépourvues que M. Duez veut nous le faire croire. Cette enquête n'a pas été essayée, et combien elle serait difficile? Ceux qui s'occupent de la biographie de ces dames ne s'intéressent peut être qu'à leur première manière" (As for the morality of the story. There is not a basis for discussion. We are faced with Ambiguity: the public demands that vice be punished. Around me I hear people saying that these gallant grasshoppers do not always end up as miserable and as destitute as Mr. Duez would like us to think. This inquiry has not been attempted, and just how difficult would it be? Those who occupy themselves with the biography of these women are probably only interested in their initial phase).

Louis Gonse, of the *Gazette des Beaux-Arts*, disavowed any interest in the moral content of the paintings but went on at some length nevertheless about Duez's use of a Gavarni-era cliché – that clothing tells all. Status and morality were immanent in dress, hence Gonse's resuscitation of the passé term *lorette* for the occasion (p. 42): "N'insistons pas sur le côté littéraire, moral et philosophique, c'est-à-dire prétentieux et antipictural, du sujet lui-même, qui vise un peu trop au souvenir de Gavarni, et ne considérons que la valeur pittoresque de la peinture. . . . Il a vu avant tout dans l'opposition de ces deux figures un motif de décoration. . . . C'est un diptyque, un panneau à deux compartiments qui encadre les deux termes d'une comparaison: l'*alpha* et l'*oméga*, le commencement et la fin, le haut et le bas de la courtisane. A droite, c'est la lorette jeune, indolente, insouciante et tapageuse, une reine de la tribu des chignons rouges qui croit à l'éternité de ces vingt-deux printemps; à gauche, en regard, c'est la lorette vieillie, ratatinée et sordide qui promène sa misère en haillons et cherche pâture dans l'inconnu sinistre de la fange et du ruisseau: – 'Les poètes de mon temps m'ont couronnée des roses . . . [ellipsis in original] et ce matin je n'ai pas eu ma goutte! et pas de tabac pour mon pauvre nez!' – Il était facile de glisser dans la cynisme de la satire. Le sujet étant admis, il faut reconnaître que M. Duez est resté élégant et bien élevé" (Let us not insist upon the literary, moral and philosophical aspect, that is to say the pretentious and antipictorial side, of the subject itself, that alludes a bit too closely to a memory of Gavarni, and let us consider only the pictorial quality of the painting. . . . Before anything else, he saw in the opposition between the two figures a decorative motif. . . . It is a diptych, a panel of two compartments that frames the two terms of the comparison: the *alpha* and the *omega*, the beginning and the finish, the high and low points of the courtesan. At right, it is the young *lorette*, indolent, insouciant and showy, a queen of the tribe of red chignons who believes in the eternity of her twenty-second springtime; at left, by comparison, it is the old lorette, shrivelled and sordid who promenades her misery in tatters and seeks refuge in the sinister unknown of the mire and the gutter: – "The poets of my day crowned me with roses . . . and this morning I haven't had my drink! and no tobacco for my poor nose!" – It was easy to slip into the cynicism of satire. Having admitted the subject, we must recognize that Mr. Duez remained elegant and correct).

44. "Elle doit se dorer pour être adorée" (Baudelaire, "Le Peintre," p. 492).

45. See my discussion of this concept in chap. 4, "Working Women for Sale?"

46. Eunice Lipton was the first to study this in her "Manet: A Radicalized Female Imagery," *Artforum* (Mar. 1975): 48–53.

47. Emily Apter has written persuasively about the presence of "visual feasting" in Manet's *Nana*. According to Apter, "The picture perfectly captures the built-in stereoscopy of the cabinet: a scene of secret beholding is itself 'caught in the act of looking' because of the projection of an imaginary spectator, who, though anonymous and intangible, is no less fully present." And, in her judgment, the structures of viewing in the picture constitute a "voyeuristic *mise en abyme*, composed of viewer-gazing-at-viewer-gazing-at-object-of-desire" (Emily Apter, "Cabinet Secrets: Fetishism, Prostitution, and the Fin de Siècle Interior," *Assemblage: A Critical Journal of Architecture and Design Culture* 9 [June 1989]: 10).

48. Sander Gilman, *Difference and Pathology: Stereotypes of Sexuality, Race and Madness*, Ithaca, N.Y., 1985, p. 102. And Gilman noticed that Manet gave Nana a "Darwin's ear."

49. For the record, Françoise Cachin agrees (*Manet, 1832–1883*, Paris: Editions de la Réunion des musées nationaux, 1983, p. 393), while Anne Coffin Hanson (*Manet and the Modern Tradition*, New Haven, 1977, p. 66) disagrees.

50. "Das Mädchen Nana ist gleichsam eine moderne Allegorie der Kauflichkeit. Der Mann ist eine Allegorie des betrogenen Käufers" (Gotthard Jedlicka, *Edouard Manet*, Zurich, 1941, p. 191; quoted in Werner Hofmann, *Nana: Mythos und Wirklichkeit*, Köln, 1973, p. 46).

51. See my remarks on Simmel's ideas about prostitution in chap. 1. Georg Simmel, "Prostitution" [1907], in *On Individuality and Social Forms*, Donald N. Levine (ed.), Chicago, 1971, pp. 121–26.

52. See Hofmann's discussion of this in *Nana*, p. 46–47.

53. Beauvoir, *Second Sex*, p. 536.

54. Hofmann, *Nana*, p. 66; Robert Herbert, *Impressionism: Art, Leisure and Parisian Society*, New Haven, 1988, p. 113. Herbert has also suggested (p. 113) that the possible identifiability of Manet's model, the actress Henriette Hauser, then the mistress of the Prince of Orange, may have helped to impute a note of immodesty to the picture.

55. Hofmann, *Nana*, pp. 21, 22; and George Holden, in his introduction to *Nana*, Middlesex, Penguin, 1972, p. 14.

56. Cachin (*Manet*, p. 393) argues that Zola was clearly responsible for providing the title for the painting before its submission to the Salon. For additional materials regarding the connection between the two Nanas, see my "Representations of Prostitution in Early Third Republic France," Ph.D. diss., University of California at Los Angeles, 1984, pp. 280–81.

57. See Cachin, *Manet*, pp. 392–93; and Hofmann, *Nana*, pp. 21–23, for detailed discussions of this question.

58. By the end of 1868, Zola had settled on the

idea of building a novel around the character of a courtesan from the lower classes. (This matter is discussed by Roger Ripoll in his introduction to *Nana*, Paris; Garnier-Flammarion, 1968, pp. 9–10.) Paul Alexis did the same in his novella *La Fin de Lucie Pellegrin*, written ca. 1874. Certain newspapers and illustrated journals became obsessed with pointing out the inaccuracies of Zola's "factual" novels. See, for example, "Quelques Erreurs de Nana," *La Vie Parisienne*, Feb. 28, 1880, p. 125.

59. "Appetit du luxe et des jouissances faciles . . ." (Ripoll, introduction to *Nana*, p. 9). These are Zola's words, used in his preliminary Rougon-Marquart series outline, prepared for the publisher Lacroix in 1869.

60. Beatrice Farwell, *Manet and the Nude: A Study in Iconography in the Second Empire*, New York, 1981, p. 332 n. 16.

61. "Cocotte parisienne n'a rien de véritablement fatal"; "sans connotation amère ou tragique . . ." (Cachin, *Manet*, p. 394).

62. "Le caractère béstial de la femme sexuée est également rendu tangible par le mélange de malpropreté, d'étroitesse étouffante, de chaleur suffocante et nauséabonde qui marque tous les lieux de l'intimité féminine dans *Nana*" (Chantal Bertrand-Jennings, *L'Eros et la femme chez Zola*, Paris, 1977, p. 93).

63. "Pris d'un malaise, d'une répugnance mêlée de peur . . ." (Zola, *Nana*, Paris: Garnier-Flammarion, 1968, p. 148); "l'étouffement de l'air, épaissi, surchauffée, où traînait une odeur forte . . ." (p. 149); "hâtant sa marche, fuyant presque, en emportant à fleur de peau le frisson de cette trouée ardente sur un monde qu'il ignorait . . ." (p. 150); "sentiment de vertige . . ." and "craignant de défaillir dans cette odeur, decuplée sous le plafond bas, il s'assit" (p. 151).

64. "Tranquillement, pour aller à la toilette, elle passa en pantalon au milieu de ces messieurs" (ibid., p. 152); "elle voulut se montrer sensible au compliment du vieillard, elle s'agita en balançant les hanches" (p. 155); "Lui que n'avait jamais vu la comtesse Muffat mettre ses jarretières, il assistait aux détails intimes d'une toilette de femme . . . au milieu de cette odeur si forte et si douce. . . . Mais il se promettait d'être fort. Il saurait se défendre" (p. 156).

65. "Alors, Muffat, la tête en feu, voulut rentrer à pied. Tout combat avait cessé en lui. Un flot de vie nouvelle noyait ses idées et ses croyances de quarante années. Pendant qu'il longeait les boulevards, le roulement des dernières voitures l'assourdissait du nom de Nana, les becs de gaz faisaient danser devant ses yeux des nudités, les bras souples, les épaules blanches de Nana; et il sentait qu'elle le possedait, il aurait tout renié, tout vendu, pour l'avoir une heure, le soir même. C'était sa jeunesse qui s'eveillait enfin, une puberté goulue d'adolescent, brûlant tout à coup dans sa froideur de catholique et dans sa dignité d'homme mur" (ibid., p. 170).

66. "Des viveurs prennent à leur solde des courtisanes, non pour le plaisir qu'ils trouvent avec elles, mais par un sentiment de ridicule vanité" ("Courtisane," *Le Grand Dictionnaire universel du dix-neuvième siècle*, vol. 5; quoted in Perrot, *Dessus et dessous*, p. 330 n. 2).

67. On Renoir's ambitions as a book illustrator, see John Rewald, "Auguste Renoir and His Brother," *Gazette des Beaux-Arts* (Mar. 1945): 171–88; and Charles Léger, "Renoir Illustrateur," *L'Art Vivant* 9 (1938): pp. 8, 9.

68. Zola inscribed this passage from the novel on the wash drawing by Renoir that preceded the ink drawing referred to here. (Information provided by Martha Tedeschi, Department of Prints and Drawings, Art Institute of Chicago.)

69. "Le petit corsage et la tunique de soie bleue collant sur le corps, relevés derrière les reins en un pouf énorme, ce qui déssinait les cuisses d'une façon hardie, par ces temps de jupes ballonnées" (Zola, *Nana*, pp. 327–28); "ce n'était pas pressé de travailler au succès d'une sale fille qui les écrasait toutes, avec ses quatre chevaux blancs, ses postillons, son air d'avaler tout le monde" (p. 336).

70. "Il n'y avait . . . plus qu'une foule, qu'un vacarme, autour de son landau" (ibid., p. 340); "Comme l'entrée de l'enceinte du pésage était absolument interdite aux filles, Nana faisait des remarques pleines d'aigreur sur toutes ces femmes comme il faut, qu'elle trouvait fagotées, avec de drôles de tête" (p. 337).

71. David Kunzle, "The Corset as Erotic Alchemy: From Rococo Galanterie to Montaut's Physiologies," in *Woman as Sex Object: Studies in Erotic Art, 1730–1970*, Thomas B. Hess and Linda Nochlin (eds.), New York, 1972, p. 164 n. 54. Although in a letter (1983), David Kunzle told me that Nana's corset in Manet's painting is "too short to be a true cuirasse." On the quite definite up-to-dateness of other items of clothing in the painting, especially the decorated stockings, see J.-K. Huysmans, "Le Nana de Manet," *L'Artiste*

de Bruxelles, May 13, 1877, pp. 148–49; and Perrot, *Dessus et dessous*, p. 282, who observes that only pale-colored plain stockings were worn by respectable women.

In the following Goncourt journal entry of Dec. 4, 1878 (*Journal des Goncourts*, Paris, 1956, vol. 2, p. 1,274), a man makes known his sexual excitement with his wife by offering an erotic gift of special stockings: "Il doit y avoir pas mal de libertinage dans les honnêtes ménages bourgeois. Aujourd'hui, une de ces bourgeoises que je vois chez Burty montrait à sa femme une série de cartons remplis de bas excitants. . . . Donc, il arrive de certains jours où l'on voit tout à coup son grave et prudhommesque mari, qui est juge au Tribunal de Commerce, se précipiter soudain dehors, comme s'il avait la plus grave affaire, et rapporter au bout d'une heure une paire de bas de la dernière cocotterie, demandant à sa femme de l'essayer immédiatement" (There must be a fair amount of libertinism in bourgeois marriages. Today, one of the bourgeois women whom I see at Burty's was showing her maid a series of boxes filled with exciting stockings. . . . So it happens that on certain days one sees her somber and conventional husband, who is a Court of Commerce judge, suddenly running outside, as though he had the most serious item of business to attend to, bringing home in an hour's time a pair of stockings of the most complete coquettry, demanding of his wife that she try them on immediately).

72. D. A. Miller, "The Novel and the Police," *Glyph* 8 (1981): 139ff.

73. For all its *un*typicality vis-à-vis the avant-garde record on this theme, Manet's avoidance of certain conventions in *Nana* – emphasizing appearance over action (although there is somewhat more "action" here than is usual in Impressionist figure paintings) – is a point of similarity with most other pictures on the subject of prostitution turned out in the 1870s and early 1880s by him and other members of the Impressionist circle.

74. The former was exhibited as *La Toilette*, catalog no. 16; it is no. 22 in vol. 2 of Denis Rouart and Daniel Wildenstein, *Manet: Catalogue raisonné*, Lausanne, 1975. The latter was catalog no. 8; it is no. 264 in vol. 2 of Rouart and Wildenstein. For a complete list of works included in *La Vie Moderne* exhibition, see *La Vie Moderne*, Apr. 10, 1880, p. 239.

75. The references to Nana were no doubt also encouraged by the recent appearance of Zola's *Nana* in feuilleton in *Le Voltaire*, starting in October 1879.

76. Hofmann (*Nana*) reports tantalizingly but without follow-through that the police had to be called. I have not undertaken an analysis of the critical reaction to *Nana* in 1877 that comes close to the scale or extent of my study of the reaction to Gervex's *Rolla* in 1878 (see below). This is *not* because I fancy one picture or event over the other, but because art critical writing about *Nana* was regrettably very limited. Indeed, the sparseness of 1877 writings on *Nana* encouraged me to move on to a discussion of closely related displays in Manet's 1880 exhibition at *La Vie Moderne*.

77. "Le Monde Parisien," *Le Soleil*, May 3, 1877, p. 3.

78. "Plus que nue, en chemise, elle étale, la fille,/Ses appas et sa chair qui tente. La voilà./Elle a mis son corset de satin et s'habille/Calme, près d'un monsieur, pour la voir venu là" ("Nana," *Le Tintamarre*, May 13, 1877, p. 2).

79. "Elle est cent fois infame cette grue" (ibid.).

80. Huysmans, "Nana," p. 148. This was three years prior to his writing on Forain, quoted and discussed in chap. 2.

81. "Le luxe des dessous entrevus . . ." (ibid., p. 148). He especially admired the stockings (p. 149): "Observation profond: les bas que des personnes peu habituées sans doute aux déshabilles emphatiques des filles, trouvent invraisemblables et durement rendus, sont absolument vrais; ce sont ces bas à la trame serrée, ces bas qui luisent sourdement et se fabriquent, je crois, à Londres" (Profound observation: the stockings that people undoubtedly unaccustomed to the affected *déshabille* of prostitutes find unrealistic and harshly rendered, are absolutely true; these are tightly woven stockings, which have a dull shine and are manufactured, I believe, in London); "L'aristocracie du vice se reconnaît au linge."

82. "La soie, c'est la marque de fabrique des courtisanes qui se louent cher. . . . Nana est donc arrivée, dans le tableau du peintre, au sommet envié par ses semblables et, intelligente et corrompue comme elle est, elle a compris que l'élégance des bas et des mules . . . était, à coup sûr, l'un des adjuvants les plus précieux que les filles de joie aient inventés pour culbuter les hommes" (ibid., p. 149).

83. Cachin, *Manet*, p. 392.

84. Paul Alexis, "Manet," *Revue Moderne et Naturaliste* (1880): 293.

85. "Chacun est de sa race, de son temps et de son milieu; les femmes du monde sont de vraies femmes du monde, les filles de vraies filles, les voyous de vrais voyous, et Nana est vraiment Nana!" (Gustave Goetschy, "Edouard Manet," *La Vie Moderne*, Apr. 17, 1880, p. 250).

86. For example, Goetschy was undoubtedly referring to this work when he wrote, "les filles [sont] de vraies filles" (ibid.).

87. "Il ne faut pas oublier . . . une des oeuvres qui attirent le plus le public par le risqué du sujet: c'est une femme en déshabille qui attache ses jarretières, et dont la position penchée fait voir ce qu'en poésie on appelérait 'les trésors opulents du corsage.' Ceci est du pur naturalisme, quelque chose comme une page de *Nana*" (Paul Sébillot, quoted by Trois Etoiles, "Les Petits Salons à côté du Grand Salon," *L'Artiste* [July 1880]: 32).

88. David Kunzle, *Fashion and Fetishism: A Social History of the Corset, Tight-Lacing and Other Forms of Body-Sculpture in the West*, Totowa, N.J., 1982, p. 180.

89. "Que vient faire ici cette horrible femme qui, tournée sans pudeur vers le public, tire son bas bleu au-dessus duquel se drapent des linges sordides et que surmonte un corset retenant avec peine une gorge affreuse, dont les plis tortueux et repugnants debordent éffrontement du côté du spectateur? Pourquoi?" (Bertall [Charles Albert Arnoux], quoted by Trois Etoiles, "Les Petits Salon," pp. 30–31).

90. "En ce genre séduisant il y a là des morceaux de choix. Je ne parle pas de la *Toilette* de cette grosse fille penchée et tirant un bas de soie blanc" ("Chronique," *Le Temps*, Apr. 10, 1880, p. 2).

91. In his *History of Impressionism* (4th ed., New York, 1973, p. 403) John Rewald mistakenly identified this cartoon as a delayed attack on *Nana*. Edmond de Goncourt reported that the radically compressed chest of a Russian noblewoman (to the degree that her nipples showed above her corset) provoked the most base sexual passions in his friend Gustave Flaubert (reported in the journal entry of Mar. 8, 1877).

92. "L'une, *la Toilette*, representant une femme décolletée, avançant sur la sortie de sa poitraille, un sommet de chignon et un bout de pif, tandis qu'elle attache une jarretière sur un bas bleu, fleure à plein nez la prostituée qui nous est chère. Envelopper ses personnages de la senteur du mode auquel ils appartiennent, telle a été l'une des plus constantes préoccupations de M. Manet" (J.-K. Huysmans, "Le Salon officiel en 1880, IV," in *L'Art moderne/Certains*, Paris, 10/18, 1975, p. 164).

93. From about the time of his public debut in 1873 until at least the end of the 1870s, Henri Gervex (1852–1929) managed to juggle a successful academic career with a social life among artists on the institutional fringes of the early Third Republic. This balancing act never imperiled his academic respectability, nor did it dampen the enthusiasm of his vanguard friends for his company, at least not until the early 1880s. The *Rolla* scandal of 1878 in no way interrupted his eventual meteoric rise. As early as 1879, he was able to move out of Montmartre to the rue de Rome in the fashionable Europe quarter. In 1882, he was made a chevalier of the Legion of Honor.

A Parisian by birth, he began to study painting at the age of fifteen with Pierre Brisset, continuing as a student of Alexandre Cabanel and Eugène Fromentin at the Ecole des Beaux-Arts. He debuted in the Salon in 1873 at the age of twenty-one. The following list of his Salon exhibits through 1878 verifies two important aspects of his career: his early success and his calculated switch in 1876 from mythological or religious to modern-life subjects:

1873, *Baigneuse endormie*, purchased by the State for 2,000 F.

1874, *Satyre jouant avec une bacchante*, second-class medal, purchased by the State for 3,500 F (collection of the Musée de Luxembourg).

1875, *Diane et Endymion*, purchased by the State for 1,500 F.
Job
Portrait de Mlle. T. de Réfuge

1876, *Autopsie à l'Hôtel-Dieu*, honorable mention, purchased by the State for 3,000 F.
Dans les bois

1877, *La Communion à l'Eglise de la Trinité*, purchased by the State for 4,000 F.
Portrait de mon ami Brispot

1878, *Portrait de Mme. G . . .*
Portrait de M. E. Paz

(See the Gervex dossier, Archives Nationales, Paris, F21 4311.)

His friends in the 1870s included not only Degas, Monet, Guy de Maupassant, and Renoir – Gervex is one of the dancers in the middle ground of Renoir's *Moulin de la Galette* of 1876 – but also Alfred Stevens, Princess Mathilde Bonaparte, and Ernest Meissonnier. There is no evidence that Gervex was ever invited to show with the Independents (the Impressionists), even in 1874 and 1876, when their invitation list was very broad – though in their 1879 *Salons*, Castagnary, Huysmans, and Zola discussed Gervex in the same breath with Renoir, Degas, and Manet. But by the early 1880s, Gervex was considered to be the "enemy" by most members of the Impressionist-naturalist circle. On June 13, 1883, Camille Pissarro, for example, wrote to his son Lucien: "Il ne faut pas juger l'art anglais comme ici on juge l'art français sur Bastien-Lepage et Gervex" (One must not judge English art the way French art is judged, based on Bastien-Lepage and Gervex). And the obsequious, successful pompier Fagerolles, of Zola's 1886 *L'Oeuvre*, was based on Gervex. He remained in favor with Degas, however. (Gervex appears in Degas's 1885 pastel *Six Friends at Dieppe*.)

According to Gervex's memoirs, Edmond Turquet was responsible for the removal of *Rolla* in 1878: "Cependant à peine ma toile était-elle accrochée dans une des salles, que le surintendant des Beaux-Arts, Turquet, donnait l'ordre brutal de l'enlever sous prétexte d'immoralité, et cela avec le complicité tacite du jury du Salon. Seul, parmi ses membres, Hébert avait fait entendre une voix de protestation!" – Meanwhile my canvas had only just been hung in one of the exhibition rooms when Turquet, the superintendent of Beaux-Arts, gave the brutal order to remove it on the pretext of immorality, and this was done with the tacit complicity of the Salon jury. Alone, among its members, Hébert let be heard a dissenting voice! (Henri Gervex, *Souvenirs*, collected by Jules Bertaut, Paris, 1924, p. 34). It seems Gervex's memory may have been faulty, because Turquet was still a deputy in the Chambre des Députés in the spring of 1878, and Phillipe de Chennevières was still the Directeur des Beaux-Arts. Turquet did not become an official of the Ministère des Beaux-Arts until 1879, when he was named to the position of Sous-secrétaire d'Etat in the Ministère de l'Instruction Publique et des Beaux-Arts (according to the 1879 *Salon Livret*). Dossier F21 566 in the Archives Nationales, however, makes some sense of Gervex's naming Turquet. A manuscript entitled "Salon de 1878, Procès-verbal de l'élection du Jury d'admission et de récompenses" gives the names of all the jury members and votes received in their election. There were fifteen jurors for the painting section, as well as three supplementary jurors, the runners-up in votes to the first fifteen. Then five jurors designated by the administration are listed, followed by: "Mr. E. Turquet, deputy, supplementary juror designated by the administration." Another nineteenth-century source explains that "*Rolla* fût refusé par le jury sur les instances de M. Turquet, alors membre de la Commission artistique des Beaux-Arts" – Because of the entreaties of Mr. Turquet, then a member of the Artistic Commission of the Fine Arts, *Rolla* was refused by the jury (J. Uzanne, "Henry Gervex," *Figures contemporaines* tirées de l'Album Mariani, Paris, 11 vols., 1896–1908, vol. 6, n.p.). The Archives Nationales dossier titled "Salons annuels, 1873–1882" (F21 535) contained nothing for 1878.

94. Musset's poem was first published in the *Revue des Deux Mondes* on August 15, 1833, and appeared in his *Poésies complètes* of 1840. In a letter of 1983, Albert Boime suggested to me that Gervex's selection of Musset's "Rolla" as the basis of his 1878 modern-life picture was probably an attempt to bolster his modernity by the use of a "traditional, intellectually safe source." Boime also believes that interest in prostitution during the early Third Republic may be connected to the days of the July Monarchy in other ways as well, especially in view of the prominent themes of the orgy, the courtesan, and moral degradation in the work of Thomas Couture and other artists active between 1830 and 1848. On this and the importance of Musset to artists of the July Monarchy, see Albert Boime, *Thomas Couture and the Eclectic Vision*, New Haven, 1980, pp. 84, 86, 124–25, 148, 152, 162, 168–75, 368–70, and p. 622 n. 35.

95. "Le plus grand débauché"; "où le libertinage est à meilleur marché, de la plus vieille en vice et de la plus féconde." I have used the text of "Rolla" in Alfred de Musset, *Premiers Poésies. Poesies nouvelles* (edited and annotated by Patrick Berthier), Paris: Editions Gallimard, 1976,. pp. 203–27.

96. "Ce qui l'a dégradée, hélas! c'est la misère/Et non l'amour de l'or"; "Vos amours sont

dorés, vivants et poétiques; . . . vous n'êtes pas publiques"; "les rideaux honteux de ce hideux repaire," "dans un bouge," "les murs de cette chambre obscure et délabrée."

97. Rolla considère d'un oeil mélancolique
La belle Marion dormant sur son grand lit;
Je ne sais quoi d'horrible et presque diabolique
Le faisait jusqu'aux os frissonner malgré lui.
Marion coûtait chèr. – Pour lui payer sa nuit,
Il avait dépensé sa dernière pistole.
Ses amis le savaient. Lui-même, en arrivant,
Il s'était pris la main et donné sa parole
Que personne, au grand jour, ne le verrait vivant.
. . . .
Quand Rolla sur les toîts vit le soleil paraître,
Il alla s'appuyer au bord de la fenêtre.
. . . .
Rolla se détourna pour regarder Marie.
Elle se trouvait lasse, et s'était rendormie.
Ainsi tous deux fuyaient les cruautés du sort,
L'enfant dans le sommeil, et l'homme dans la mort!

The three sections quoted here come from cantos 3 and 5 of the poem (Musset, pp. 213 n. 105, 220, 221). The first quoted section appeared in "Chronique," *Le Temps*, Apr. 21, 1878, p. 2. The latter two were quoted in Le Sphinx, "Echos de Paris, hier, aujourd'hui, demain," *L'Evénement*, Apr. 21, 1878, p. 1. The photograph of *Rolla* by Goupil et cie. (Cabinet des Estampes, Bibliothèque Nationale, Paris, negative C30307) reproduced the second and third verses, too. Many warm thanks to Michal Ginsburg and Gerry Mead for translating "Rolla."

98. At the end of the poem, there is an episode of "redemption." At the very last moment, Rolla, who had never loved, is touched by the purity of Marion's offer to sell her jewelry to save him from financial ruin. He takes poison and dies anyway, but not before bestowing a chaste kiss upon her necklace and experiencing love. In Musset's words: "Dans ce chaste baiser son âme était partie,/Et, pendant un moment, tous deux avaient aimé" (In that chaste kiss his soul had parted,/ And, for a moment, both had loved). The moment of redemption does not figure in Gervex's painting, because Marion is asleep.

99. "De pesants chariots commencaient à rouler"; "un groupe délaissé de chanteurs ambulants murmuraient sur la place une ancienne romance."

100. Le Sphinx, "Echoes," p. 1.

101. A preliminary oil study for the male figure, showing a distinctly premodern urban prospect out the window, survived until recently. It was in the collection of M. Henry Basset of Paris and Montauban, but in 1984 the small oil was stolen from his Montauban residence, the Château de Cabarieu. I discuss it in my "Representations of Prostitution," pp. 16–19; it is reproduced badly there as plate 2. After 1878 – the exact date is unknown – Gervex made a medium-scale (33 3/4″ × 42 3/4″), almost identical replica of the Bordeaux *Rolla* (the replica is in the collection of Pyms Gallery, London). See KMcC's discussion of the two *Rollas* in *Rural and Urban Images: An Exhibition of British and French Paintings, 1870–1920*, London, Pyms Gallery, Oct. 24–Nov. 30, 1984, pp. 26–28. Pyms Gallery bought the replica from Sotheby's, London, on June 19, 1984, no. 79. My sincere thanks to Mme. Françoise Claverie Garcia of the Musée des Beaux-Arts in Bordeaux for this information.

102. "Est-ce sur de la neige, ou sur une statue/ Que cette lampe d'or, dans l'ombre suspendue,/ Fait onduler l'azur de ce rideau tremblant?/ Non. la neige est plus pâle, et le marbre est moins blanc./C'est un enfant qui dort." A stanza quoted in *Le Temps* (Apr. 21, 1878), it appears in canto 3 of the poem (Musset, *Premiers Poésies*, p. 209).

103. Some careless critics mistakenly described Rolla as looking at Marion, consistent with the Musset text. "Il se détourna pour regarder Marion dormant dans son grand lit" (He turned aside to look at Marion sleeping in her big bed), wrote Roger Ballu ("Le Salon de 1878: Peintres et Sculpteurs," excerpt from the *Gazette des Beaux-Arts*, July and Aug. 1878, p. 41). "Rolla, rêveur, jetant sur elle un regard de commisération et de pitié . . ." (Rolla, dreamer, casting a look of commiseration and pity . . .), wrote Emile Cardon ("Les Beaux-Arts – L'Ecole française en 1878, 9," *Le Soleil*, June 16, 1878, p. 3). The anonymous notice published in *Le Temps* (Apr. 21, 1878) quoted the relevant Musset text without correc-

tion. Paul Sébillot's was the least correct of all: "Rolla regarde vaguement dans la rue avec l'air fatal des héros romantiques" – Rolla looks off vaguely onto the street with the fatal air of romantic heroes ("Chronique des arts," *Le Bien Public*, May 1, 1878, p. 3).

104. This list includes all the mentions of Gervex's art that I found in the Parisian press from the spring and summer of 1878. In parentheses following each item, I characterize the length, coverage, and general opinion of the article, if any. All subsequent references to reviews of Gervex's art in 1878 refer to this list. Some of the early mentions of *Rolla* appeared in society columns, because the removal from the Salon was a social as well as an artistic event. But, for obvious reasons, *Rolla* did not figure very often in the usual 1878 Salon reviews.

Of the nineteen mentions of Gervex's art that I gathered from the 1878 press, one item discussed the portraits only. Of the remaining eighteen, five were neutral about *Rolla*, six were positive, and seven were negative. ("Positive" means against the removal of *Rolla* from the Salon and enthusiastic in some measure about the painting; "negative" therefore means in favor of the exclusion of *Rolla* from the Salon and unfavorable about the picture.) Overall, then, the opinion on *Rolla* appears to have been evenly divided. Counting only the lengthy and serious accounts of *Rolla*, however (and eliminating reprints of an identical text), the tally is five positive and three negative. In the press, at least, *Rolla* had more thoughtful supporters than detractors. In the serious positive column, I am placing Balsamo, Emile Cardon, Jacques Liber, Paul Sébillot (May 1), and Le Sphinx (Apr. 20). The serious negative opinions were those of Anonymous in *Le Temps*, Roger Ballu, and Alexandre Weill.

Anon., "Chronique," *Le Temps*, Apr. 21, p. 2 (lengthy discussion of *Rolla;* negative).

Anon., "Echos," *Le Courrier du Soir*, Apr. 23, p. 4 (five paragraphs on *Rolla*, leading up to Weill's letter; negative).

Anon., "Le Monde parisien," *Le Soleil*, Apr. 15, p. 3 (brief announcement; neutral).

Anon., "Nouvelles," *La Chronique des Arts et de la Curiosité* (supplement to the *Gazette des Beaux-Arts*), Apr. 27, p. 130 (brief announcement; negative).

Anon., "Prime à nos lecteurs," *Paris-Plaisir* 1, no. 6 (Apr. 21): 1; 1, no. 7 (Apr. 28): 1 (advertisements for photos of *Rolla* and brief announcement; neutral).

Roger Ballu, "Le Salon de 1878 – Peintres et sculpteurs," excerpt from the *Gazette des Beaux-Arts*, July–Aug., pp. 41–42 (lengthy discussion of *Rolla;* negative).

Balsamo, "Echos de Paris," *Le Petit Parisien*, Apr. 16, p. 2 (five paragraphs on *Rolla;* positive).

Emile Cardon, "Les Beaux-Arts–L'Ecole française en 1878. IX," *Le Soleil*, June 16, p. 3 (lengthy discussion of *Rolla;* positive).

Desgenais, "Au Jour le jour," *Le Bien Public*, Apr. 12, p. 3 (brief announcement; neutral).

L'inconnu, "Le Salon de 1878 V: Les portraits," *L'Univers Illustré*, June 22, p. 391 (one line on the portraits; negative).

Louis Leroy, "Le Salon pour rire III. Les Tableaux à l'Ecole," *Le Charivari*, June 4, p. 2 (facetious remarks on *Rolla* and one portrait; neutral).

Jacques Liber, "Beaux-Arts: Le Cas d'Henri Gervex," *Paris-Plaisir* 1, no. 5 (Apr. 14): 4 (lengthy discussion of *Rolla;* positive).

Paul Sébillot, "Chronique des arts," *Le Bien Public*, Apr. 4, p. 3, (brief mention of *Rolla* before its removal; positive).

Paul Sébillot, "Chronique des arts," *Le Bien Public*, May 1, p. 3 (lengthy discussion of *Rolla;* positive).

Spavento, "Echos de partout," *L'Estafette*, Apr. 14, p. 3 (brief announcement; neutral).

Le Sphinx, "Echos de Paris–hier, aujourd'hui, demain," *L'Evénement*, Apr. 20, p. 1 (lengthy discussion of *Rolla;* positive).

Le Sphinx, "Echos de Paris–hier, aujourd'hui, demain. Un mea culpa," *L'Evénement*, Apr. 23, p. 1 (retraction and publication of Weill's letter; negative).

Pierre Veron, "Chronique parisienne. Le Salon de 1878," *Journal Amusant*, July 6, p. 3 (brief comment on *Rolla* and portraits; negative on *Rolla;* positive on portraits).

Alexandre Weill, "Letter to Edmond Magnier, publisher of *l'Evénement*," published in Le Sphinx (Apr. 23) and Anon., *Le Courrier du soir* (lengthy discussion of *Rolla;* negative).

105. "A sortir des sentiers battus et du poncif académique . . ." (Liber, "Beaux-Arts"). In any discussion of journalistic reaction to a work of art,

the question naturally arises as to whether there are connections between the political and aesthetic ideologies of a newspaper. The conditions under which journalists were operating in 1878 tended to blur the clearer relations of earlier years between ideas about art and ideas about politics. The Parisian press had been subject to the caprices of government censorship from the time of the provisional declaration of the Republic in 1870. This state of affairs continued – with periodic ups and downs – until the passage of the liberal, relaxed press law in July 1881. Because government censorship throughout the 1870s focused relentlessly on the press of the extreme left, there was no trenchantly critical paper on that side during the decade, with the exception of *La Lanterne*, the only successful radical paper of the period (which did not review Gervex's picture). The years of President McMahon's *septennat*, 1873–1879, were hard ones for the press, but government restrictions on the press generally lessened beginning in 1876 (in spite of the crackdown on the press during the 1877 elections). Owing to Republican successes in the elections of 1876 and 1877, the crisis of May 16, 1877, and the press amnesty of February 1878, the press operated with relative freedom in the spring of 1878. Of overarching importance, however, is this: as the press of the Third Republic became less and less subject to censorship, it generally became less and less political. (See Robert Justin Goldstein, *Political Censorship of the Arts and the Press in Nineteenth-Century Europe*, Houndmills, Eng., 1989, which appeared just as these notes were being completed.)

Paris-Plaisir, Liber's paper, was made up of social tidbits, theater and fashion news, sports, "chroniques de la semaine," and "variétés" and featured Huysmans's "Croquis Parisiens." The paper published only seven issues, appearing seven Sundays in a row during March and April of 1878. It offered ten-franc photographs of *Rolla* under the heading "Prime à nos lecteurs" in the issues of April 21 and 28.

L'Evénement, which published both Le Sphinx's defense of *Rolla* and Weill's denunciation of it, was a republican paper of medium size: in 1880 its circulation was 14,085, making it twenty-fifth among the sixty Parisian dailies and eighteenth among exclusively republican papers. (To provide some context for these circulation figures, *Le Petit Journal*, the giant of its day, sold 583,820 copies daily, and the second largest paper, *La Petite République*, sold 196,372.) The publishers of *L'Evénement* had ambitions to make it into "*le Figaro* de gauche," a mass circulation republican paper (*Figaro* was the conservative daily with the largest circulation, 104,924). Because of the discordant opinions of Gervex's work published in the same paper, it is hard to see any hard and fast connections between the paper's cultural and political reporting. The second publisher of Weill's letter, *Le Courrier du soir*, was also a republican paper, but a very small one. It originated in February 1878, and by 1880 it had the lowest circulation of any of the Parisian dailies.

Le Petit Parisien, publisher of Balsamo's positive review, was a popular republican paper (selling for only one *sou*) that became slowly more radical beginning in 1878. Its circulation of 39,419 in 1880 placed it eleventh among the daily papers. *Le Soleil*, which published Emile Cardon's positive evaluation, was a powerful newspaper: "le premier grand journal politique à un sou," it espoused a conservative center-right position in politics (essentially monarchist in orientation, it nevertheless preached a "ralliement à la République") and maintained a large circulation (45,190, which made it ninth of the sixty dailies in 1880).

Le Temps, which published an anonymous condemnation of *Rolla*, was a conservative republican paper, strongly opposed to radicals allied with Léon Gambetta. With a circulation of 22,764 in 1880, it was twelfth of the thirty-four republican dailies. The *Gazette des Beaux-Arts*, another source of condemnation of *Rolla*, lacked an explicit political viewpoint because it reported only on art, although it was known for its hidebound conservatism in cultural matters.

Le Bien Public, home to Paul Sébillot's defense of *Rolla*, was a generally conservative paper; since 1874, it had been a Protestant, anticlerical republican paper. It became *Le Voltaire* in July 1878 (a daily circulation of 10,451 established its rank of thirty-first in 1880). *Le Bien Public* and then *Le Voltaire* had a long-standing relationship with Zola, which reminds us again of the difficulty of directly correlating political and aesthetic ideas in the press in these years. Zola published feuilletons of *L'Assommoir*, *Nana*, and *Une page d'amour* in these papers and had also written theater and literary criticism for *Le Bien Public* from 1876 to 1878. (He broke with *Le Voltaire* late in 1880.)

My principal sources of information on the press in the 1870s are: Jacques Lethève, *Impressionnistes et symbolistes devant la presse*, Paris, 1959; Jacques Lethève, *La Caricature et la presse sous la troisième République*, Paris, 1961; Claude Bellanger et al., *Histoire générale de la presse française*, vol. 3: *1871–1940*, Paris, 1969; Phillipe Jones, *La Presse satirique illustrée entre 1860 et 1890*, Paris, 1956; René de Livois, *Histoire de la presse française*, vol. 1: *Des origines à 1881*, Lausanne, 1965; Raymond Manévy, *La Presse de la troisième République*, Paris, 1955.

106. Indeed, an attack on the administration's hypocrisy takes up most of Liber's review. He writes: "Quelle est donc, au bout du compte, cette censure qui s'effarouche si facilement. C'est la censure qui autorise toutes les petites oeuvres polissonnes, saletés érotiques ou scandales se retroussant aux devantures des librairies, suivant le mot des Goncourts. . . . C'est elle qui, sous prétexte d'antiquités, laisse acheter pour nos musées nationaux, des *Lédas* aux poses lesbiennes se pâmant sous les caresses de volatiles en rût. Il y a là un scandale public intolérable et nous espérons que justice sera faite" – What is this censorship, after all, that gets embarrassed so easily. It is the same censorship that authorizes all the smutty little works, erotic rubbish, or scandals pulling up their skirts in the windows of bookstores, as the Goncourts would put it. . . . It is the same censorship that, using the pretext of antiquity, lets our national museums buy *Ledas* in lesbian poses swooning under the caresses of birds in heat. This is an intolerable public scandal and we hope that justice will be done (Liber, "Beaux-Arts").

107. "Avez-vous vu le tableau de Rolla? C'est d'une laideur idéale. Rolla a l'air d'un brosseur militaire qui s'apprête à donner une friction à une créature anémique aux mamelles retrécies en citrons, aux jambes de fuseau déchiquetées encore par le drap blanc – plutôt linceul que drap – et aux traits de sainteté rentrée et purie. Il n'y a rien d'immoral dans ce tableau, excepté peut-être le parti pris de vouloir faire passer l'artiste comme une victime de l'administration. L'administration a bien fait de le refuser ou de ne pas l'admettre. L'artiste fera mieux une autre fois" (Weill, "Letter to Edmond Magnier").

108. See my discussion of the nude in chap. 2.

109. "Nous croyons que l'administration a fait preuve . . . d'une susceptibilité éxagerée, d'une pudibonderie farouche. La jeune fille est nue, certainement. Mais si on va s'amuser à proscrire les études academiques du Salon, il y a tous les ans les nudités plus nues les unes que les autres" (Balsamo, "Echoes de Paris").

110. "Pour ma part, la différence profonde qui existe entre les deux tableaux, c'est que le Bouffon est vêtu d'un superbe costume de velours rouge tel qu'en portaient les fous de François 1er, tandis que le Rolla de M. Gervex est en bras de chémise, et porte un pantalon de chez Renard ou Dussautoy" (Cardon, "Les Beaux-Arts").

111. "Ici, ce sont les accéssoires qui ont tout gâté. Le nu est assez beau en lui-même pour se passer d'un ragoût qui le rend tout à coup indécent: près du lit, s'entasse un tas de jupons empesés que coiffe ironiquement un chapeau noir haute forme, la canne n'est pas loin. Voilà l'anecdote qui fait tache, l'amorce au rire malsain. Ce malheureux chapeau, une jarretière égarée dans les jupes: on dirait les artifices de vaudeville au beau milieu d'un drame" (anon., *Le Temps*).

112. "Le matin d'une orgie d'amour . . ."; "Je voudrais pouvoir admirer sans réserve ce corps d'un ton si fin, d'une coloration si fraîche au milieu des blancheurs de sa couche: mais, hélas! ces blancheurs représentent un lit défait et foulé, des draps tombants: tout l'appareil hideux de la débauche. Les détails sont peints avec une franchise de touche et une vérité de couleur d'un mérite incontestable, mais savez-vous quels sont des détails? c'est une jarretière de soie rose, un jupon empesé, tombé dans le désordre par terre; c'est un chapeau d'homme insolent et brutal, qui s'étale sur la robe précipitamment jetée et roulée dans ce fauteuil! Oh! être jeune, avoir l'honneur d'être artiste, sentir le talent en soi, et faire une pareille oeuvre! Se servir de l'art sacré pour surexciter les instincts lubriques, cela est une profanation: je le dis du fond du coeur" (Ballu, "Le Salon de 1878").

113. "Sur un lit qu'on aperçoit à peine sous les draps blancs et brodés et les riches oreillers, Marion dort toute nue, une jambe pendante hors du lit, l'autre à moitié repliée: les jupons, les robes et tous les accéssoires de la toilette moderne couvrent de leur désordre pittoresque les fauteuils capitonnés; le collier et les bijoux qui jouent un rôle dans le poème sont posés sur un table de nuit richement orné, et qui disparaît presque sous le fouillis qui la couvre et l'entoure, et parmi ces

blancheurs et ces objets clairs un chapeau à haute forme met sa note noire" (Sébillot, "Chronique des Arts," May 1).

114. "Conçue dans un sentiment moderne"; "absolument dans la donnée du poème qui lui a servi de thème." "Mais la modernité appliquée à certains sujets n'a point encore triomphé des préjugés de l'école: c'est la modernité qui a fait exclure le tableau du Salon"; "Je sais bien qu'il y a dans un coin un chapeau noir: c'est, paraît-il, ce chapeau noir qui est le vrai coupable, c'est lui qui rend scabreux un tableau qui sans cela ne l'eût pas été. . . . On est habitué à la nudité des héros et des héroines de l'antiquité: le nu moderne choque, non pas notre pudeur, mais nos préjugés d'école et d'éducation, et un tableau devient dangéreux pour les moeurs suivant la noblesse des accéssoires" (Sébillot, "Chronique des Arts," May 1).

115. "M. Gervex, quoique tout jeune, est hors concours; par conséquent, le jury n'a pas eu à l'admettre ou à le refuser. C'est donc la pudeur administrative seule qui s'est scandalisée. Oui, cette même administration qui admet avec tant d'enthousiasme les lupanars de M. Gérôme, n'entend pas que Rolla se permette de vivre en plein Paris, qu'il s'habille chez le bon faiseur, que sa chemise fripée, brisée par l'orgie, sorte de chez le fournisseur en vogue. Non! non! Oh! nos censeurs sont à cheval sur la morale . . . [ellipsis in original] ou plutôt sur les morales, car ils en ont deux. . . . Mettez la jeune Marie sur un divan moelleux et coiffez Rolla d'un turban . . . [ellipsis in original] vous ferez l'admiration de ces messieurs; on vous placera à la cimaise, et sans danger la fille conduira sa mère devant votre 'compétition.' Mais une jeune fille sur un lit parisien *moderne* (quoique du plus pur style Louis XVI), avec un homme en manches et chemise, et, sur un fauteuil, un chapeau noir haut de forme, dernière mode, un parapluie (*bone Deus*!), un corset (horreur!), et sur le tapis, une jupe! . . . [ellipsis in original] Vite, jeune homme, remportez-nous ça!" (Le Sphinx, "Echos de Paris," Apr. 20).

116. Degas also coached Gervex on his first major modern-life effort in 1876. Seeing the *Autopsie à l'Hôtel-Dieu* in the studio, Degas is reported by Vollard to have suggested, "Mais ce carabin qui prend des notes quand le professeur parle, où as-tu vu cela? Il roule une cigarette" – But this medical student who takes notes when the professor speaks, where has he seen that? He is rolling a cigarette (Ambroise Vollard, *Degas*, Paris, 1924, p. 43). According to Fénéon's interview with Gervex, Degas's words were: "Alors vous savez que les carabins ne s'émeuvent pas pour un corps ouvert. Faites donc tout simplement rouler à votre bonhomme une cigarette" – In a case like that you know that medical students are not the least moved by a cut-open corpse. So show that fellow of yours rolling a cigarette (Félix Fénéon, *Oeuvres plus que complètes* [textes réunies et présentés par Joan U. Halperin], vol. 1: *Chroniques d'art*, Geneva, 1970, p. 377). In either case, Gervex took the advice.

117. "Il faut qu'on comprenne que 'ta' femme n'est pas un modèle. Où est la robe qu'elle a quittée? Mets donc un corset par terre!" (Vollard, *Degas*, p. 44).

118. "C'est à son instigation que j'installe au premier plan ce jupon si róidement empesé, ce corset, tout ce linge" (Fénéon, *Oeuvres*, p. 378).

119. "Tu vois . . . on a compris que c'est une femme qui se déshabille" (Vollard, *Degas*, p. 44).

120. "On aurait passé, à la rigueur, sur ce nu que n'éclairait pas un jour de l'atelier, sur ce conflit de la clarté de la lampe et la clarté de l'aube naissante, mais cette dépouille féminine donnaît, paraît-il, à l'oeuvre un trop irritant piment de modernité" (Fénéon, *Oeuvres*, p. 378).

121. "Quelques détails qui paraissaient très audacieux à l'époque, comme l'écroulement du linge féminin près du lit, son amoncellement près de la chair nue de la femme . . ." (Gervex, *Souvenirs*, p. 33).

122. The nude was, of course, not new to Gervex in 1878: he had learned the genre as a student and had shown uncontroversial nudes in the Salons of 1873, 1874, and 1875.

123. Anne Hollander, *Seeing Through Clothes*, New York, 1978, p. 213; and David Kunzle, "The Corset as Erotic Alchemy: From Rococo Galanterie to Montaut's Physiologies," in *Woman as Sex Object: Studies in Erotic Art, 1730–1970*, Thomas B. Hess and Linda Nochlin (eds.), New York, 1972, p. 121. See also Kunzle, *Fashion and Fetishism: A Social History of the Corset, Tight-Lacing and Other Forms of Body-Sculpture in the West*, Totowa, N.J., 1982. I wish to thank David Kunzle for generously sharing his knowledge of corsetry with me.

124. Blanche Payne, *History of Costume from the Ancient Egyptians to the Twentieth Cen-*

tury, New York, 1965; Nancy Bradfield, *Costume in Detail, Women's Dress, 1730–1930*, Boston, 1968; Kunzle, "The Corset as Erotic Alchemy," pp. 134–39; Norah Waugh, *Corsets and Crinolines*, London, 1954; and Theodore Zeldin, *France, 1848–1945*, vol. 2: *Intellect, Taste and Anxiety*, Oxford, 1977, p. 437.

125. Kunzle, "The Corset as Erotic Alchemy," p. 164.

126. Ibid., pp. 120–27.

127. "Genées par les bottines à hauts talons dont elles n'ont pas l'habitude, embarassées par les corsets qu'elles ne portent que depuis peu . . ." (Georges Grison, *Paris horrible et Paris original*, Paris, 1882, pp. 296–97).

128. An alternative reading of the corset is possible, but it will be found controversial if not infuriating to certain feminist analysts of the tyrannies of the nude. I have put this analysis in a note rather than in the text because I am not so sure of its validity myself. In other words, I believe I have changed my mind since 1987, when I wrote the following.

A woman who wore a showy red corset may have donned the item of her own accord, in order to please herself. And the pleasure in question is sexual. Although David Kunzle has called attention to "a kind of female sexual assertion" in corset-wearing, an advertisement for the possession of an active, publicly displayed sexuality (David Kunzle, *Fashion and Fetishism*, p. xviii), I refer here to a form of masturbation, to the inner-directed and autoerotic, to a salutary form of female *jouissance*. A minority strain of present-day feminist thought addresses this issue: "High heels and corsets provide intense kinaesthetic stimulation for women, appealing to the sense of touch but extending more than skin deep. These frivolous accessories are not just visual stimuli for men; they are also tactile stimuli for women" (Beatrice Faust, *Women, Sex, and Pornography: A Controversial and Unique Study*, New York, 1980, p. 53. I learned of this extraordinary book thanks to Elizabeth Wilson, *Adorned in Dreams*). In Gervex's *Rolla*, the discarded corset had already overdetermined Marion's illicit sexuality, but that a tight corset might have given erotic pleasure to its wearer would certainly have been an unspeakable and infuriating consideration, especially since this standpoint claims a power of resistance for the tight-laced prostitute.

My demoting this minority report from text to note is an explicit by-product of my disagreement with certain strains of feminist admiration for the videos of Madonna produced in the late 1980s. I find myself increasingly uncomfortable with interpretations of her work that argue that Madonna-in-black-merry-widow has achieved a salutary, critical political distance from the woman-objectifying, pornographic tropes that she often relies upon in her performances. See, for example, Ramona Curry, "Madonna from Marilyn to Marlene – Pastiche and/or Parody?" *Journal of Film and Video* 42, no. 2 (Summer 1990): 15–30. Because I think Madonna is rehearsing those worrisome conventions rather than parodying them, I have found myself rethinking my own earlier thoughts about Marion and her corset, too.

129. "Ce jupon si roidement empesé . . ." (Fénéon, *Oeuvres*, p. 378).

130. See my "Representations of Prostitution," pp. 90–94.

131. Another example of this type of text is that of E. de la Bédollière, "Les Boulevards de la Porte Saint-Martin à la Madeleine," in *Paris Guide par les principaux écrivains et artistes de la France*, vol. 2, Paris, 1867, p. 1,296: "A 6 h., grand remue-ménage! le faubourg déscend! Les habitantes des quartiers Bréda et Notre Dame de Lorette s'avancent à la conquête des Boulevards. C'est une légion que signalent de loin le cliquetis du jais, l'odeur du musc, le frissonnement de la soie. . . . Cette troupe féminine s'égaie, comme disaient les chouans, et prend des positions stratégiques, depuis le passage Jouffroy jusqu'à la rue de la Chaussée-d'Antin. Jamais ni d'un côté, ni de l'autre, elle ne va plus loin" (At 6 o'clock, great hullabaloo! the outskirts of town descend! The inhabitants of the Bréda and Notre Dame de Lorette neighborhoods advance to conquer the boulevards. It is a legion that signals from afar the jingle of jet, the odor of musk, the flutter of silk. . . . This feminine troop makes merry, as the Chouans [the Breton royalists] would say, and takes up strategic positions, from the Jouffroy passage all the way to the rue de la Chaussée-d'Antin. They never go beyond this territory at either end).

132. Gustave Macé (*La Police parisienne: Un joli monde*, Paris, 1888, p. 329) spotlights the notoriety of the same section of boulevard in very specific terms. For an evening eyeful of vice and debauchery, he recommends the corner of the rue du

Faubourg-Montmartre to observe "[ce] qui fait actuellement l'honneur de nos boulevards" (what constitutes these days the honor of our boulevards). In groups of three, four, or five, the filles constitute "un marché à prix variés, accompagné de paroles . . . [ellipsis in original] toujours invariables" (a marketplace with varied prices, accompanied by words . . . that are always the same). The following, he suggests, was typical: "Regardez la hardiesse de celles-ci, assez grandes, têtes nues, coiffées à la chien; elles gesticulent, tournent sur elles-mêmes. . . . Et ces jeunes filles, habituées des passages, courent après les hommes avec plus d'audace que des vieilles créatures de la rue des Filles-Dieu, et cependant l'ainée ne paraît pas avoir quinze ans" (Look at the audacity of these girls, rather big, bareheaded, with wild hair; they make gestures and twirl around. . . . And these young girls, habitués of the passages, run after men with more audacity than the ancient creatures of the rue des Filles-Dieu, and meanwhile the oldest does not appear to be even fifteen years old).

Pairing the lowest forms of prostitution with this particular quarter of the city is the basis of Guy de Maupassant's story "L'Odysée d'une Fille," first published in *Gil Blas* in 1883 (the following quotes are taken from *Le Rosier de Madame Husson*, Paris: Editions Gallimard–Collection Folio, 1976, p. 211). The story recounts the life of an unfortunate, orphaned country girl who becomes a street walker in Paris out of dire necessity. In the opening paragraph, the narrator explains his view of the nocturnal insoumise: "J'ai touché ce fond noir de la misère humaine: j'ai compris l'impossibilité de la vie honnête pour quelques-uns" (I experienced the darkest nadir of human misery; I understood the impossibility of an honest life for some people). Here is Maupassant's description of a group of such filles looking for customers after midnight on a rainy rue Drouot: "Les filles, la jupe relevée, montrant leurs jambes, laissant entrevoir un bas blanc à la lueur terne de la lumière nocturne, attendaient dans l'ombre des portes, appelaient, ou bien passaient, pressées, hardies, vous jetant à l'oreille deux mots obscurs et stupides. Elles suivaient l'homme quelques secondes, se serrant contre lui, lui soufflant au visage leur haleine putride; puis, voyant inutiles leurs exhortations, elles le quittaient d'un mouvement brusque et mécontent, et se remettaient à marcher en frétillant des hanches" (The filles, skirt pulled up, showing their legs, revealing a glimpse of white stocking in the dim glimmering of the nocturnal light, were waiting in the shadow of doorways, calling, or even passing by, urgent, audacious, tossing two obscure and stupid words into your ear. They were following a man for several seconds, pressing against him, blowing their putrid breath into his face; then, seeing that their exhortations are useless, they left him with a brusque and displeased movement, and resumed their walking while wriggling their hips).

An 1889 guide to the immoral women of the city ventured an obscure commentary on the preferences of customers in this neighborhood (*L'Indicateur des grues de Paris: Nouveau Guide des étrangers pour l'Exposition 1889*, Paris, p. 5): "Faubourg Montmartre', la *Moderne* / Par ses habitués pervers, / Rappell' de Mossieu Jul's Verne, / *Vingt mille lieues sous les mers*" (The Montmartre neighborhood, the Modern style / Thanks to its perverse habitués, / Recalls Mister Jules Verne, / *Twenty Thousand Leagues under the Sea*).

133. "La ville des nourritures ouvertes . . ." (Corbin, *Les Filles de noce*, pp. 301ff).

134. "Il s'y forma une série de rues, dont la partie septentrionale, sur la rive droite de la Seine surpasse aujourd'hui toutes les rues de l'univers, tant par la richesse de son architecture que par le luxe de ses magasins et la décoration splendide de ses cafés" (K. Baedeker, *Paris, Ses environs et les principaux itinéraires des pays limitrophes à Paris*, 3d ed., Paris, 1874, p. 69).

135. "Le moment le plus convenable pour cette promenade est la matinée, de 9 h. à midi, lorsque la foule n'est pas encore trop compacte. Plus tard, entre 2 et 6 h., et le soir de 8 à 11 h., il y a une telle foule, surtout de la Madeleine au boulevard de Sébastopol, qu'il ne peut plus être question d'examiner à son aise les édifices, les magasins, etc. Néanmoins on répétera cette promenade le soir, où des centaines de milliers de becs de gaz transforment la nuit en jour, et où l'on peut voir aussi l'intérieur de tous ces beaux magasins, grâce au brillant système d'éclairage qu'ils ont pour la plupart adopté" (ibid., p. 70). Some tourist guides to the boulevard differentiated between the various sections of boulevard. Most concurred that the boulevard des Italiens was the toniest, including the *Guide de l'étranger dans Paris et ses environs*,

Paris: Grand-Hôtel, 1874, p. 30.

136. See Roland Barthes, "The Blue Guide" [1950s], in *Mythologies*, Annette Lavers (trans.), New York, 1972, pp. 74–77, for the classic analysis of the dehistoricizing procedures of the guidebook.

137. See T. J. Clark's discussion of the meretricious quality of Monet's picture in *The Painting of Modern Life: Paris in the Art of Manet and His Followers*, New York, 1984, pp. 70–72.

138. *L'Assommoir* was first published in 1877 by Renoir's patron, the publisher Georges Charpentier. The first illustrated edition (with sixty illustrations) was issued the following year by the Parisian publishers Marpon and Flammarion. The Prints and Drawings Department of the Art Institute of Chicago recently acquired a copy of this edition (no. 67 out of an edition of 130).

139. "'Monsieur, écoutez donc' . . . L'homme la régarda de côté et s'en alla en sifflant plus fort" ("Sir, please listen" . . . The man gave her a side glance and went on, whistling even louder).

140. Susanna Barrows, "After the Commune: Alcoholism, Temperance, and Literature in the Early Third Republic," in *Consciousness and Class Experience in Nineteenth-Century Europe*, John M. Merriman (ed.), New York, 1979, pp. 205–18.

141. Susanna Barrows, *Distorting Mirrors: Visions of the Crowd in Late Nineteenth-Century France*, New Haven, 1981, p. 61.

142. Theresa Ann Gronberg uses the phrase "urban slut" to describe the woman in Manet's *La Prune* ("Femmes de Brasserie," *Art History* 7, no. 3 [Sept. 1984]: 335). Theodore Reff is also very sure (overdefinite, I think) about the moral semiology of depictions of female smoking and drinking. He calls Manet's sitter a "well-dressed prostitute" and a "wistful prostitute" (*Manet and Modern Paris*, Washington, D.C.: National Gallery of Art, 1982, p. 76).

143. Jean Sutherland Boggs et al., *Degas*, New York: Metropolitan Museum of Art, 1988, entry no. 173, pp. 288–89.

144. I acknowledge Robert Herbert's assistance in "reading" this picture: *Impressionism: Art, Leisure and Parisian Society*, New Haven, 1988, p. 71.

145. In P. A. Lemoisne, *Degas et son oeuvre*, Paris, 1946, vol. 2, no. 419, the work is subtitled "Un café, Blvd. Montmartre." Gronberg ("Femmes de Brasserie") has identified the kind of café depicted by Degas as a *boîte à femmes*.

146. "M. Degas, comment parler bien de cet artiste essentiellement parisien, dont chaque oeuvre contient autant de talent littéraire et philosophique que d'art linéaire et de science de coloration? . . . Puis voici des femmes à la porte d'un café, le soir. Il y en a une qui fait claquer son ongle contre sa dent, en disant: 'pas seulement ça,' qui est tout un poème. Une autre étale sur la table sa grande main gantée. Dans la fond, le boulevard dont le grouillement diminue peu à peu. C'est encore une page d'histoire bien extraordinaire" (Georges Rivière, "L'Exposition des impressionnistes," *L'Impressionniste*, no. 1 [Apr. 6, 1877]; reprinted in Lionello Venturi, *Les Archives de l'Impressionnisme*, Paris, 1939, vol. 2, p. 313).

147. Carol Armstrong, "Duranty, Degas, and the Realism of the Third Republic," paper presented at the annual meeting of the Nineteenth-Century French Studies, Evanston, Ill., 1987.

148. "M. Degas semble avoir jeté un défi aux philistins, c'est-à-dire aux classiques. *Les Femmes devant un café, le soir* sont d'un réalisme effrayant. Ces créatures fardées, flétries, suant le vice, qui se rancontent avec cynisme leurs faits et gestes du jour, vous les avez vues, vous les connaissez et vous les retrouverez tout à l'heure sur le boulevard" (Alexandre Pothey, "Beaux-Arts," *Le Petit Parisien*, Apr. 7, 1877; reprinted in Venturi, *Les Archives*, pp. 303–04). I have used the English translation in Clark, *Painting of Modern Life*, p. 101.

149. "M. Degas ne manque ni de fantaisie, ni d'esprit, ni d'obsérvation dans ses aquarelles. Il a ramassé devant les tables d'éstaminet, dans les cafés-concerts, dans le corps de ballet, des types d'une vérité cynique et quasi-béstiale, portant tous les vices de la civilisation écrits en grosses lettres sur leur triple couche de plâtre. Mais son esprit a la main lourde et l'expression crue" (Bernadille, *Le Français*, Apr. 13, 1877; quoted in Clark, *Painting of Modern Life*, pp. 101, 291 n. 78). I have used Clark's translation.

150. "Les études dans les cafés du boulevard ne sont pas moins finies ni moins curieuses, bien que cruelles passablement. Il est permis de critiquer une certaine accentuation des détails. Mais l'ensemble constitue une page incomparable du livre anecdotique contemporain" (Jacques, *L'Homme Libre*, Apr. 12, 1877, quoted in Clark, *Painting of Modern Life*, 291 n. 80).

151. Regulationist rules required that prostitutes

at work on the street wear a hat. Edmond de Goncourt's version of one such showy hat was this: "un chapeau de velours noir avec un bouquet de géraniums ponceau" – a black velvet hat with a poppy-red bouquet of geraniums (*La Fille Elisa* [1877] Paris: Charpentier, 1906, p. 94).

152. Interestingly, the most well-informed present-day commentators on the same picture, writing in 1988 and early 1989, joined the 1877 critics in seeing this quintessentially modernist work as social description. But they ran into snags and contradictions in their attempts to tie the pastel-enhanced monotype to an exact plot. See Robert Herbert, *Impressionism*, pp. 44–46; Kathleen Adler, "Nineteenth-Century Studies," *Art in America* 77, no. 1 (Jan. 1989): 27; and Boggs et al., *Degas*, p. 289. I discuss and compare these interpretations of the narrative in Degas's picture in my forthcoming article, "The Sexual Politics of Impressionist Illegibility: A Case Study," *Dealing with Degas*, Richard Kendall and Griselda Pollock (eds.), London, 1991.

153. Richard Thomson brought this to my attention in his *Degas, The Nudes*, London, 1988, p. 106. To my knowledge, these are the only uses (let alone repetition) of this gesture in Degas's art. In view of the redating of the brothel monotypes to 1876–77 by the Degas Exhibition Committee (Boggs et al., *Degas*), Degas may have worked on *Femmes devant un café* and *L'Attente* around the same time.

154. It probably looked very *mannish* too at the time, as both Patricia Simons and Lisa Tickner have credibly and generously suggested. I thank Gloria Groom for pointing out to me that Balzac had his character Vautrin use the same gesture as one of categorical dismissal in *Le Père Goriot:* "Qu'est-ce qu'un homme pour moi? Ça! fit-il en faisant claquer l'ongle de son pouce sous une de ses dents" – What's a man in my book? That! he uttered, clicking the nail of his thumb under one of his teeth (Honoré de Balzac, *Le Père Goriot*, New York: Scribner's, 1928, p. 173).

155. Although in an earlier article (Clayson, "Prostitution and the Art of Later Nineteenth-Century France: On Some Differences Between the Work of Degas and Duez," *Arts* 60, no. 4 [Dec. 1985]: 40–45) I described *Women on a Café Terrace* similarly and highlighted its evasiveness, the conclusions I reached there are quite different from those that appear here. In that essay, I argued that the general absence of precise anecdote in that picture foreclosed on the sexual connotations of its subject.

156. I thank Alex Potts sincerely for his thoughtful commentary on an earlier version of a portion of this chapter. His suggestions shaped my concluding remarks.

Chapter 4: Suspicious Professions

EPIGRAPHS: (p. 113) "Par l'enseigne, elles sont couturières ou modistes. Dans la maison, la mise en scène est complète; il y a des étoffes, des patrons, des travaux en train. En réalité, c'est un lieu de débauche où souvent, sous prétexte d'un travail lucratif, on entraîne des jeunes filles qui ne tardent pas à se laisser pervertir" (C. J. Lecour, *La Prostitution à Paris et à Londres, 1789–1877*, 3d ed., Paris, 1877, p. 198); (p. 133) "Mais si, je vous l'assure, il a le goût de prendre les femmes à l'envers." – "C'est donc pour cela, que lorsqu'il m'émmène avec lui à la brasserie de la rue Medicis, je l'entends, quand il entoure la taille d'une de ces femmes qui servent des bocks, je l'entends leur dire: 'Comme je t'enc . . . [ellipsis in original].' " (I left "comme je t'enc . . ." alone because it is a shortening of "comme je t'encule," the meaning of which is not really conveyed by "I intend to sodomize you.") – "Messieurs, Daudet serait un érotomane, un cerveau où il y a une case malade?" – "Au fond, les femmes légitimes n'ont pas le sens commun . . . [ellipsis in original] Si sa femme lui permettait ce que lui accordent les bonnes de la brasserie de la rue Medicis, ce serait l'intérieur le plus heureux de la terre . . . [ellipsis in original] et le coureur deviendrait un caniche de fidelité" (Edmond de Goncourt, *Journal des Goncourts*, Paris: Flammarion, 1956, vol. 3, pp. 26–27 [June 10, 1879, entry]); many thanks to Michal Ginsburg and Gerry Mead for their expert help in translating this tricky passage; (p. 152) Mary Ann Doane, *The Desire to Desire: The Woman's Film of the 1940s*, Bloomington, Ind., 1987, pp. 5–6.

1. James F. McMillan, *Housewife or Harlot: The Place of Women in French Society, 1870–1940*, New York, 1981, p. 17.

2. Parisians were especially touchy about adulteries after passage of a divorce bill, *la loi Naquet*, in 1884, after which verifiable adultery was grounds for divorce.

3. Lisa Tickner, *The Spectacle of Women: Imagery of the Suffrage Campaign, 1907–1914*, Chicago, 1988, p. 304 n. 18.

4. "Courtisane ou ménagère," from Pierre-Joseph Proud'hon, *Contradictions économiques: La propriété*, vol. 2, Paris, 1846, p. 197.

5. McMillan, *Housewife or Harlot*, p. 16.

6. Louise A. Tilly and Joan W. Scott, "Women's Work and the Family in Nineteenth-Century Europe," in *The Family in History*, Charles E. Rosenberg (ed.), Philadelphia: University of Pennsylvania Press, 1975, p. 146. See also Louise A. Tilly, Joan W. Scott, and Miriam Cohen, "Women's Work and European Fertility Patterns," *Journal of Interdisciplinary History* 6, no. 3 (Winter 1976): 447–76, as well as Tilly and Scott's slightly later book, *Women, Work and Family*, New York, 1978.

7. Tilly and Scott, "Women's Work," p. 149. Among the reasons that France had a large proportion of married women in the nonagricultural labor force was that the French population contained a relatively high proportion of married women (McMillan, *Housewife or Harlot*, p. 40). Married working-class women in France provided about 20 percent of the nonagricultural female labor force (p. 39).

8. "C'est un spéctacle douloureux de voir de si jeunes filles abandonner le domicile paternel" (Dr. O[ctave] Commenge, *Recherches sur les maladies vénériennes à Paris . . . de 1878 à 1887*, Paris, 1890, p. 49).

9. Tilly and Scott, "Women's Work," pp. 152–53, 157, 148.

10. "La conclusion malheureuse sera, qu'en tout genre de travail, il arrive que le salaire de l'ouvrière tombe un peu plus bas que ce qui est indispensable pour lui procurer la subsistance" (Dr. O[ctave] Commenge, *La Prostitution clandestine à Paris*, Paris, 1904, p. 21).

11. Tilly and Scott, "Working Women," p. 170.

12. Commenge, *La Prostitution*, p. 21.

13. On milliners' wages, see Commenge, *La Prostitution*, pp. 20–23; *Paris after Dark: Night Guide for Gentlemen*, 13th ed., Paris, n.d. (ca. 1870), p. 50; and Eunice Lipton's groundbreaking article, "The Laundress in Late Nineteenth-Century French Culture: Imagery, Ideology and Edgar Degas," *Art History* 3, no. 3 (Sept. 1980): 301. See her revision of this material in Lipton, "Images of Laundresses: Social and Sexual Ambivalence," chap. 3 of *Looking into Degas: Uneasy Images of Women and Modern Life*, Berkeley, 1986, pp. 116–50.

14. René Gonnard, *La Femme dans l'industrie*, Paris, 1906; quoted in Lipton, "The Laundress," p. 302.

15. A. J. B. Parent-Duchâtelet, *De la prostitution dans la ville de Paris*, vol. 1, Paris, 1837, pp. 71–75.

16. Dr. Louis Reuss, *La Prostitution au point de vue de l'hygiène et de l'administration en France et à l'étranger*, Paris, 1889, p. 13.

17. Alain Corbin, *Les Filles de noce: Misère sexuelle et prostitution aux dix-neuvième et vingtième siècles*, Paris, 1978, pp. 78–81.

18. Ibid., p. 242.

19. See Lipton's discussion of the laundress, for example ("The Laundress," pp. 295–313).

20. "Tous les hommes se retournaient; le carton à chapeau leur donnait de l'aplomb. . . . Voici ce que la maîtresse, une femme d'une quarantaine d'années, lui avait dit après l'avoir examinée quelques instants: 'Mon enfant, vous me plaisez beaucoup physiquement et votre tenue me convient. . . . Pour ne vous rien cacher, vous saurez que les jeunes filles que j'ai ici sont entretenues. A vous dire vrai, j'aimerais que vous fussiez dans la même situation . . . [ellipsis in original] Maintenant, j'ai l'habitude de recevoir le soir plusieurs de mes amis, des Messieurs du monde'" (Henry Detouche, "Une Modiste," *Revue Moderne et Naturaliste* [1880]: 190). And see the similar though later remarks of Gustave Coquiot, *Degas*, 2d ed., Paris, 1924, p. 130.

21. "Dans cette catégorie du proxénétisme ['commerce à la toilette'], les plus habiles dissimulent leurs manoeuvres sous l'exercice apparent d'une profession où l'on emploie des ouvrières" (Lecour, *La Prostitution*, p. 198).

22. "Il faut suivre cette prostitution dans des milieux moins accessibles, où le public n'entre qu'à bon escient, éclairé qu'il est par les invitations discrètes ou par le caractère bien reconnaissable du lieu. Je veux parler des maisons de parfumerie, gants, cols, cravates, photographies, gravures, ganteries, librairies même, qui s'ouvrent dans les grands quartiers de Paris. On y voit un étalage spécial, assez restreint. Entre les articles en montre apparaissent à l'intérieur des yeux pleins de promesse, et pour peur que le flâneur hésite devant l'étalage, un clignement, un geste très significatif, lui dit bien vite à quoi et à qui il a

affaire" (Dr. L. Martineau, *La Prostitution clandestine*, Paris, 1885, p. 82).

23. "Celles-là exploitent les débuts; ceux-ci viennent ensuite" (Lecour, *La Prostitution*, p. 204).

24. Reuss, *La Prostitution*, p. 181.

25. "Qui dit marchande à la toilette, dit quelque peu proxénète: La débitrice insoluble n'aura qu'à prêter l'oreille aux conseils de sa créancière, qui saura lui ménager l'occasion de se libérer envers elle, en lui procurant des clients, soit chez elle, soit dans une maison de passe" (ibid., p. 182).

26. "Celles qui ont un certain capital devant elles ouvrent des magasins de gants, de parfumerie, de vins de champagne, de curiosités, d'objets en ruolz, de modes, etc.; les autres se font, en apparence du moins, blanchisseuses, lingères, couturières, fleuristes, marchandes de journaux. La police surveille tous ces magasins interlopes. Elle a beau les fermer, ils renaissent ailleurs; tous sont munis d'une arrière-boutique qui sert de lieu de rendezvous" (ibid., pp. 184–85).

27. See Joel Isaacson, *The Crisis of Impressionism, 1878–1882*, Ann Arbor, Mich., 1980, p. 17.

28. David S. Brooke and Henri Zerner, *James Jacques Joseph Tissot, 1836–1902: A Retrospective Exhibition*, Providence, Rhode Island School of Design Museum of Art, 1968, entries 35 and 39.

29. Ibid., entry 35.

30. Ibid., entry 39.

31. Denis Rouart and Daniel Wildenstein, *Edouard Manet: Catalogue raisonné*, Lausanne, 1975, vol. 1, no. 373. Rouart and Wildenstein report that the painting has been retouched, thus problematizing any discussion of the picture's object qualities. According to the authors, *The Milliner*, used in the 1883 inventory of Manet's work, was the original title. The present owner, the California Palace of the Legion of Honor in San Francisco, prefers *At the Milliner*.

32. S. Lane Faison, Jr., identifies the woman as a customer. See his "Edouard Manet (1832–1883), The Milliner," *Bulletin of the California Palace of the Legion of Honor* (Aug. 1957), n.p.

33. Degas did about eighteen pastels and paintings on this subject between ca. 1882 and 1898; ten of them were done prior to 1890. See P. A. Lemoisne, *Degas et son oeuvre*, Paris, 1946–49, vols. 2 and 3, nos. 681, 682, 683, 705, 709, 729, 774, 827, 832, 835, 1,023, 1,110, 1,315, 1,316, 1,317, 1,318, 1,319. On the question of the chronology of the milliner pictures, see Ronald Pickvance, *Degas 1879*, National Galleries of Scotland and the Edinburgh Festival Society, 1979, no. 72, p. 63. For a recent discussion of Degas's depiction of milliners that differs from mine, see Colin B. Bailey's entry on *At the Milliner's*, which Bailey dates to 1881 in *Masterpieces of Impressionism and Post-Impressionism: The Annenberg Collection*, Philadelphia, 1989, pp. 18–21.

A complex period commentary on one of Degas's such pictures is that written by his English crony George Moore, who in 1891 described a milliner's window as depicted by Degas like this: "full of the dim, sweet, sad poetry of female work. For are not those bonnets the signs and symbols of long hours of weariness and dejection? and the woman that gathers them iron-handed fashion has moulded and set her seal upon. See the fat woman trying on the bonnet before the pier-glass, the shopwomen around her. How the lives of those poor women are epitomized and depicted in a gesture! Years of servility and obeisance to customers, all the life of the fashionable woman's shop is there" (George Moore, *Impressions and Opinions*, London, 1891, p. 316; quoted in Theresa Ann Gronberg, "Femmes de Brasserie," *Art History* 7, no. 3 [Sept. 1984]: 331).

34. "Aucun art n'est aussi peu spontané que le mien. Ce que je fais est le résultat de la réflexion et de l'étude des grands maîtres; de l'inspiration, la spontanéité, le tempérament, je ne sais rien. Il faut refaire dix fois, cent fois le même sujet. Rien en art ne doît ressembler à un accident, même le mouvement" (Edgar Degas, quoted in Jacques Lassaigne and Fiorello Minervino, *Tout l'oeuvre peint de Degas*, Paris, 1974, p. 13).

35. "[In a millinery shop] de 5 à 7, c'est le coup de feu, le tout le monde sur le pont, le branle-bas des essayages, des récriminations, des enthousiasmes, des cris, des évanouissements, des colères, des jalousies, des déceptions. . . . Degas . . . ne dépassa point la courte anecdote. Ses peintures et ses dessins de modistes ne sont point de savoureuses réussites. . . . Qu'il ne puisse pas vous donner, Degas, l'aspect d'ensemble de toutes ces femelles, soit! . . . mais, en vérité, il eût pu aller au délà du document photographique, ce peintre dit de la 'vérité moderne.' . . . Il n'a donc jamais considérée, Degas, ce que peut être dans la formation de la pensée féminine!" (Gustave Coquiot, *Degas*, 2d ed., Paris, 1924, pp. 132–34).

36. Lisa Tickner, "Feminism, Art History, and Sexual Difference," *Genders* 3 (Fall 1988): 102. Against Showalter's conception of a doubled voice, Luce Irigaray would argue that the repetition by women of male forms is to be expected, for women can do nothing but copy male systems. Irigaray writes: "*Socially*, they [women] are 'objects' for and among men and furthermore they cannot do anything but mimic a 'language' that they have not produced; *naturally*, they remain amorphous, suffering from drives without any possible representatives or representations" (Irigaray, "Women on the Market," in *This Sex Which Is Not One*, Ithaca, 1977, p. 189, emphasis in original).

37. "La maîtresse de tolérance, pour se soustraire à une hiérarchie policière trop compressive, métamorphose sa maison en brasserie à femmes, cabaret ou garni" (Gustave Macé, *La Police parisienne: Le Gibier de Saint Lazare*, Paris, 1888, p. 289). Macé was not alone in describing direct transformations of brothels into brasseries. In the same vein, an outraged anonymous author reported: "L'institution [of the *brasserie*] . . . a dégénéré. Le salon est devenu un bouge. . . . C'est l'héritage direct des cloîtres numerotés du boulevard extérieur dont le peuple se déshabitue. . . . Une révolution s'était accomplie. La maison aux volets clos avait absorbé la brasserie. Elle avait quitté les persiennes désertes où les réglements de police la parquaient pour la grande voie du plaisir et de l'amour, les Boulevards" – The institution [of the brasserie] . . . has degenerated. The salon has become a brothel. . . . This is the direct heritage of the numbered cloisters of the exterior boulevard that the people have stopped frequenting. . . . A revolution had been accomplished. The house with closed shutters had absorbed the brasserie. It [the brothel] had left the deserted Venetian blinds in which police regulations had confined it for the high road of pleasure and love, the Boulevards ("Les Petites Cythères," *La Vie des Boulevards*, n.d. [ca. 1888], pp. 203–06; Paris, APP, D/B, 173–75). See also "Irruption des brasseries: Une révolution française des moeurs?" *Cafés, bistrots et compagnie*, Expositions itinérantes CCI no. 4, Paris, Centre National d'Art et de Culture Georges Pompidou, Centre de Création Industrielle, 1977, p. 50; and Dr. Félix Regnault, *L'Evolution de la prostitution*, Paris, 1906, p. 159.

38. As well as a shift in politics, according to Theresa Ann Gronberg. See her "Femmes de Brasserie," p. 344 n. 36, and compare her general characterization of the rise of this distinctive form of Parisian entertainment, pp. 336–37.

39. "Le développement de conduites vénales, que l'on ne peut plus qualifier de clandestines, de la part de filles et de femmes qui, sans être des courtisanes de haut rang, échappent presque totalement au système réglementariste . . ." (Corbin, *Les Filles de noce*, p. 249).

40. "Enfin, et peut-être surtout car c'est ce qui les définit, toutes ces nouvelles conduites prostitutionelles impliquent que *la fille donne à son client l'impression qu'elle s'est laissé séduire* et qu'elle n'est plus un simple animal privé de la liberté de se refuser" (ibid., p. 249, emphasis in original).

41. "Parfois elle s'y pare de quelque apparence de jeunesse et de folie amoureuse qui donne le change au naif et lui fait volontiers croire à un entraînement, là où il n'y a qu'un calcul" (Martineau, *La Prostitution clandestine*, p. 78).

42. "Il y a apparence de conquête et partant d'amour dans ce rapprochement éphémère. On se sourit, on se parle, on se convient. Cette indépendance pour le choix a ruiné la prestige des basses Cythères" ("Les Petites Cythères," p. 204).

43. "Ces établissements ressemblent aux cafés ordinaires où on s'attable pour prendre un bock; le racolage n'y est pas brutal. La serveuse vient simplement s'asseoir, sans en être priée, à la table du consommateur, se fait servir, pousse à la dépense, engage une conversation égrillarde, et finalement fait ses offres de service. . . . Elle se rend dans un hôtel voisin pour se faire sa passe. En effet bien peu de brasseries ont des chambres installées pour recevoir le client" (Regnault, *Prostitution*, pp. 115–16).

44. "Le racolage y est moins grossier. Il revêt parfois une forme detournée, bien que l'entrée en matière soit bien directe, la femme venant habituellement s'asseoir, sans en être priée, à la table du consommateur et engageant un entretien qui se termine toujours par quelque proposition à mots couverts des plus faciles à comprendre" (Martineau, *La Prostitution clandestine*, pp. 78–80).

45. "Tout s'y passait décemment, et si un client émmenait le soir une des filles de salle pour un coucher, personne ne s'en aperçevait" (Reuss, *La Prostitution*, p. 195).

46. "Ces brasseries à femmes sont donc de véritables maisons de passe et de prostitution. Elles en ont l'apparence avec leurs vitraux opaques, leurs

Bibliography

Items that are parts of published works or archive dossiers, though individually cited in notes, are not repeated here.

ARCHIVAL SOURCES

Archives de la Préfecture de Police (APP), Paris: ser. D/B, nos. 173–175, 407, 408.

Archives Nationales, Paris: ser. F21, nos. 297, 300, 306, 524, 535, 538, 558, 566, 4,311.

Musée des Beaux-Arts, Bordeaux: Henri Gervex dossier.

Service d'Etude et de Documentation, Musée du Louvre, Paris: Henri Gervex dossier.

PUBLISHED SOURCES

Abelson, Elaine S. *When Ladies Go A-Thieving: Middle-Class Shoplifters in the Victorian Department Store.* New York, 1989.

Adhémar, Jean, and Françoise Cachin. *Degas: Graveurs et Monotypes.* Paris, 1973.

———. *Degas: The Complete Etchings, Lithographs and Monotypes.* New York, 1975.

Alexis, Paul. "Manet." *Revue Moderne et Naturaliste* (1880): 293.

Alis, Harry. "La Décadence artistique." *Revue Moderne et Naturaliste* (1878–79): 289–92.

———. "La Vénus des boulevards." *Revue Moderne et Naturaliste* (1878–79): 203.

Anderson, J. A. "Critique d'art." *Revue Moderne et Naturaliste* (1878–79): 18–19.

Apter, Emily. "Cabinet Secrets: Fetishism, Prostitution, and the Fin de Siècle Interior." *Assemblage: A Critical Journal of Architecture and Design Culture* 9 (June 1989): 6–19.

Ariès, Philippe. "Le Dix-neuvième Siècle et la révolution des moeurs familiales." In *Renouveau des idées sur la famille,* edited by Robert Prigent. Paris, 1954, pp. 111–18.

Armstrong, Carol M. "Duranty, Degas and the Realism of the Third Republic." Paper presented at the annual meeting of Nineteenth-Century French Studies, Evanston, Ill., October 1987.

Aron, Jean-Paul, ed. *Misérable et glorieuse, la femme au dix-neuvième siècle.* Paris, 1980.

Artinian, Artine. *Maupassant Criticism in France, 1880–1940.* 1941, Reprint. New York, 1969.

Aubert, Jacques. *L'Etat et sa police en France, 1789–1914.* Geneva, 1979.

Baedeker, K[arl]. *Paris: Ses environs et les principaux itinéraires des pays limitrophes à Paris.* 3d ed. Paris, 1874.

Ballu, Roger. "Le Salon de 1878: Peintres et sculpteurs." *La Gazette des Beaux-Arts* (July and August 1878): 41–42.

Balsamo. "Echos de Paris." *Le Petit Parisien,* April 16, 1878, p. 2.

Bareau, Juliet Wilson. *The Hidden Face of Manet.* London, 1986.

Barrows, Susanna. *Distorting Mirrors: Visions of the Crowd in Late Nineteenth-Century France.* New Haven, 1981.

Barthes, Roland. "Nana: La Mangeuse d'hommes." Paris: Théâtre National de l'Opéra, n.d. (1976).

———. *Mythologies.* Translated by Annette Lavers. New York, 1972.

Baudelaire, Charles. *Curiosités esthétiques, l'art romantique et autres oeuvres critiques.* Paris: Editions Garnier Frères, 1962.

Beauvoir, Simone de. *The Second Sex* [1949]. Translated and edited by H. M. Parshley. New York, 1952.

Béllanger, Claude, Jacques Godechot, Pierre

Guiral, and Fernand Terrou. *Histoire générale de la presse française.* Vol. 3, *1871 à 1940.* Paris, 1969.

Benjamin, Harry, and R. E. L. Masters. *Prostitution and Morality.* New York, 1964.

Benjamin, Walter. *Charles Baudelaire: A Lyric Poet in the Era of High Capitalism.* Translated by Quintin Hoare. London: New Left, 1973.

Béraud, F. F. A. *Les Filles publiques de Paris et la police qui les régit.* Brussels, 1839.

Berger, John. *Ways of Seeing.* London, 1972.

Bernheimer, Charles. "Prostitution and Narrative: Balzac's *Splendeurs et misères des courtisanes.*" *L'Esprit Créateur* 25, no. 2 (Summer 1985): 22–31.

———. "Degas's Brothels: Voyeurism and Ideology." *Representations* 20 (Fall 1987): 158–86.

———. "Of Whores and Sewers: Parent-Duchâtelet, Engineer of Abjection." *Raritan* 6, no. 3 (Winter 1987): 72–90.

Bertrand-Jennings, Chantal. *L'Eros et la femme chez Zola.* Paris, 1977.

Bloch, Louis, and Sagari. *Paris qui danse.* Paris, 1888.

Boime, Albert. *Thomas Couture and the Eclectic Vision.* New Haven, 1980.

Boiron, N. M. *La Prostitution dans l'histoire, devant le droit, devant l'opinion.* Nancy, 1926.

Bomford, David. "Manet's *The Waitress:* An Investigation into Its Origins and Development." *National Gallery Technical Bulletin* 7 (1983): 3–19.

Boorstin, Daniel J. "The Historian: 'A Wrestler With the Angel.'" *New York Times Book Review,* September 20, 1987, pp. 1, 28–29.

Boucher, François. *Twenty Thousand Years of Fashion: The History of Costume and Personal Adornment.* New York, 1967.

Bowker, Lee H. *Women, Crime and the Criminal Justice System.* Lexington, Mass., 1978.

Bowlby, Rachel. *Just Looking: Consumer Culture in Dreiser, Gissing and Zola.* New York, 1985.

Bradfield, Nancy. *Costume in Detail: Women's Dress, 1730–1930.* Boston, 1968.

Braun-Ronsdorf, Margarete. *The Wheel of Fashion: Costume since the French Revolution, 1789–1929.* London, 1964.

Brettell, Richard R., and Suzanne Folds McCullagh. *Degas in The Art Institute of Chicago.* Chicago, 1984.

Brooke, David S., and Henri Zerner. *James Jacques Joseph Tissot, 1836–1902: A Retrospective Exhibition.* Providence: Rhode Island School of Design Museum of Art, 1968.

Brooks, Peter. *Reading for the Plot: Design and Intention in Narrative.* New York, 1984.

Broude, Norma. "Degas's 'Misogyny.'" *Art Bulletin* 59, no. 1 (March 1977): 95–107.

———. "Edgar Degas and French Feminisms, ca. 1880: 'The Young Spartans,' the Brothel Monotypes, and the Bathers Revisited." *Art Bulletin* 70, no. 4 (December 1988): 640–59.

Browse, Lillian. *Forain the Painter, 1852–1891.* London, 1978.

Buchloh, Benjamin H. D., Serge Guilbaut, and David Solkin, eds. *Modernism and Modernity: The Vancouver Conference Papers.* Halifax, Press of Nova Scotia College of Art and Design, 1983.

Bullough, Vern, and Bonnie Bullough. *Prostitution: An Illustrated Social History.* New York, 1978.

Buskirk, Martha. "Degas's Brothel Monotypes and the Limits of History." Paper presented to the annual meeting of Nineteenth-Century French Studies, Evanston, Ill., October 1987.

Cabanne, Pierre. "Degas chez Picasso." *Connaissance des Arts* 262 (December 1973): 146–51.

Cafés, bistrots et compagnie. Paris: Centre de Création Industrielle, Centre National d'Art et de Culture Georges Pompidou (Expositions itinérantes C.C.I. no. 4), 1977.

Callen, Anthea. "The Flesh Made Word: Voyeurism and Sexual Guilt in Degas's Brothel Monotypes." Paper presented at the annual meeting of the Association of Art Historians, London, April 1989.

Callu, Martine. "Approche critique du phénomène prostitutionnel parisien de la seconde moitié du dix-neuvième siècle par le biais d'un ensemble d'images: Oeuvres de C. Guys, F. Rops, G. Moreau." Mémoire de maîtrise, Université F. Rabelais, Tours, 1977.

Cardon, Emile. "Le Salon." *Le Soleil,* May 30, 1878, p. 3.

———. "Les Beaux-Arts: L'Ecole française en 1878, 9." *Le Soleil,* June 16, 1878, p. 3.

Carel, Alfred. *Les Brasseries à femmes de Paris.* Paris, 1884.

Castagnary, Jules Antoine. *Salons.* Vol. 1, *1857–1870;* vol. 2, *1872–1879.* Paris, 1892.

Cate, Phillip Dennis, and Bogomila Welsh-Ovcharov. *Emile Bernard: Bordellos and Prostitutes in Turn-of-the-Century French Art.* New Brunswick, N.J., 1988.

Centenaire de l'impressionnisme. Paris: Editions des Musées Nationaux, 1974.

Cézanne: The Early Years, 1859–1872. London: Royal Academy of Arts, 1988.

Chevalier, Louis. *Classes laborieuses et classes dangéreuses à Paris, pendant la première moitié du dix-neuvième siècle.* Paris, 1958.

———. *Montmartre du plaisir et du crime.* Paris, 1980.

"Chronique." *Le Temps,* April 21, 1878, p. 2.

"Chronique." *Le Temps,* April 10, 1880, p. 2.

Clark, T. J. *The Painting of Modern Life: Paris in the Art of Manet and His Followers.* New York, 1984.

Clayson, [Susan] Hollis. "Representations of Prostitution in Early Third Republic France." Ph.D. diss., University of California at Los Angeles, 1984.

———. "Prostitution and the Art of Later Nineteenth-Century France: On Some Differences Between the Work of Degas and Duez." *Arts* 60, no. 4 (December 1985): 40–45.

Collet, Charles Blanc du. "Contribution à l'histoire du rétablissement du divorce en France en 1884: Etude faite d'après les travaux préparatoires de la loi Naquet." Thesis, Université de Paris, Faculté de Droit, 1939.

Cominos, Peter. "Late Victorian Sexual Respectability and the Social System." *International Review of Social History* 8 (1963): 18–48, 216–50.

Commenge, Dr. O[ctave]. *Recherches sur les maladies vénériennes à Paris dans leurs rapports avec la prostitution clandestine et la prostitution réglémentaire de 1878 à 1887.* Paris, 1890.

———. *La Prostitution clandestine à Paris.* Paris, 1904.

Coquiot, Gustave. *Degas.* 2d ed. Paris, 1924.

Corbin, Alain. *Les Filles de noce: Misère sexuelle et prostitution aux dix-neuvième et vingtième siècles.* Paris, 1978.

———. "Commercial Sexuality in Nineteenth-Century France: A System of Images and Regulations," *Representations* 14 (Spring 1986): 209–19.

"Curiosités anecdotiques: Les boulevards." *Le Bulletin Français,* April 26, 1878, p. 453.

Davies, Martin, and Cecil Gould. *National Gallery Catalogues: French School; Early Nineteenth Century, Impressionists, Post-Impressionists, etc.* London: National Gallery, 1970.

Degas. New York and Ottawa: Metropolitan Museum of Art and National Gallery of Canada, 1988.

Degas inédit: Actes du colloque Degas. Paris: Musée d'Orsay and Ecole du Louvre, 1988.

Degas Monotypes. London: Arts Council of Great Britain, 1975.

Delvau, Alfred. *Plaisirs de Paris.* Paris, 1867.

Desgenais. "Au jour le jour." *Le Bien Public,* April 12, 1878, p. 3.

Desgranges, Ovide. "De la Madeleine à la Bastille." *Le Petit Journal Pour Rire* 128 (1878): 2.

Detouche, Henry. "Croquis moderne, le grue." *Revue Moderne et Naturaliste* (1880): 77.

———. "Une Modiste." *Revue Moderne et Naturaliste* (1880): 189–92.

Doane, Mary Ann. *The Desire to Desire: The Woman's Film of the 1940s.* Bloomington, Ind., 1987.

Donation Picasso: La Collection personnelle de Picasso. Paris: Ministère de la culture et de la communication, Editions de la Réunion des musées nationaux, 1978.

Duchet, Claude, ed. *Mythes et représentation de la femme au dix-neuvième siècle.* Paris, 1976.

Dumesnil, René. "Essai de Classement." In *Oeuvres complètes de Guy de Maupassant.* Vol. 15, *Chroniques, études, correspondance.* Paris, 1938.

"Echos." *Le Courrier du Soir,* April 23, 1878, p. 4.

Equivoques, peintures françaises du dix-neuvième siècle. Paris: Musée des arts décoratifs, 1973.

Euloge, Georges-André. *Histoire de la police et de la gendarmerie des origines à 1940.* Paris, 1985.

Evans, Richard. "Prostitution, State and Society in Imperial Germany." *Past and Present* 70 (1976): 106–129.

Explication des ouvrages de peinture, sculpture, architecture, gravure, et lithographie des artistes vivants, exposés au palais des Champs-Elysées. Paris: Imprimerie Nationale, 1872–80.

"A l'exposition de peinture: Modes et confections pour l'année 1877." *La Vie Parisienne,* May 12, 1877, pp. 258–59.

Faison, S. Lane, Jr. "Edouard Manet (1832–1883), The Milliner," *Bulletin of the California*

Palace of the Legion of Honor (August 1957): n.p.

Farwell, Beatrice. *The Cult of Images: Baudelaire and the Nineteenth-Century Media Explosion.* Santa Barbara, 1977.

———. *Manet and the Nude: A Study in Iconography in the Second Empire.* New York, 1981.

Faunce, Sarah, and Linda Nochlin, eds. *Courbet Reconsidered.* Brooklyn: Museum of Art, 1988.

Faust, Beatrice. *Women, Sex, and Pornography: A Controversial and Unique Study.* New York, 1980.

Feuillet, Octave. *Histoire d'une parisienne.* Paris, 1881.

Fiaux, Louis. *Les Maisons de tolérance, leur fermeture.* Paris, 1892.

Finnegan, Francis. *Poverty and Prostitution.* Cambridge, Eng., 1979.

Flexner, Abraham. *Prostitution in Europe.* 1914. Reprint. Montclair, N.J., 1969.

Forster, Robert, and Orest Ranum, eds. *Deviants and the Abandoned in French Society.* Translated by Elborg Forster and Patricia M. Ranum. *Selections from the Annales,* vol. 4. Baltimore, 1978.

Foucault, Michel. *The History of Sexuality.* Vol. 1, *An Introduction.* Translated by Robert Hurley. New York, 1978.

French Salon Paintings in Southern Collections. Atlanta: High Museum of Art, 1982.

Frisby, David. *Fragments of Modernity: Theories of Modernity in the Work of Simmel, Kracauer and Benjamin.* Cambridge, Eng., 1985.

Geelhaar, Christian, ed. *Pablo Picasso: Das Spätwerk, Themen 1964–1972.* Basel: Kunstmuseum, 1971.

———. "Ausstellung Picasso." *Pantheon* 36 (July/Aug./Sept. 1978): 288–89.

Gervex, Henri. *Souvenirs.* Edited by Jules Bertaut. Paris, 1924.

Gibson, Mary. "The State and Prostitution: Prohibition, Regulation, or Decriminalization." In *History and Crime,* edited by James A. Inciardi. Beverly Hills, 1980, pp. 193–207.

Gilman, Sander L. *Difference and Pathology: Stereotypes of Sexuality, Race and Madness.* Ithaca, 1985.

Goetschy, Gustave. "Edouard Manet." *La Vie Moderne,* April 17, 1880, pp. 247, 250.

———. "Ateliers et vitrines: Ernest Duez." *La Vie Moderne,* July 16, 1881, pp. 461–62.

Gogh, Vincent van. *Lettres de Vincent van Gogh à Emile Bernard.* Paris: Ambroise Vollard, 1911.

———. *The Complete Letters of Vincent van Gogh.* Vol. 3. Greenwich, Conn., 1958.

Goncourt, Edmond de. *La Fille Elisa* [1877]. Paris: Charpentier, 1906.

Goncourt, Edmond de, and Jules de Goncourt. *Journal des Goncourts.* Vols. 2 and 3. Paris: Flammarion, 1956.

Gonse, Louis. "Salon de 1874." *La Gazette des Beaux-Arts,* 2d ser., no. 10 (July-December 1874): 42–44.

Grand-Carteret, John. *Raphael et Gambrinus, ou l'art dans la brasserie.* Paris, 1886.

Grant, Richard B. *The Goncourt Brothers.* New York, 1972.

Greenberg, Clement. *Art and Culture.* Boston, 1961.

Grison, Georges. *Paris horrible et Paris original.* Paris, 1882.

Gronberg, Theresa Ann. "Femmes de brasserie." *Art History* 7, no. 3 (September 1984): 329–44.

Guérin, Marcel. *J. L. Forain, Aquafortiste.* Vol. 1. Paris, 1912.

Guide de l'étranger dans Paris et ses environs. Paris: Grand-Hôtel, 1874.

Guyot, Yves. *La Prostitution.* Paris, 1882.

Hadjiha, Ali. "Le Problème du mariage dans la drame naturaliste en Europe: Henrik Ibsen, Gerhard Hauptmann, G. B. Shaw et les auteurs naturalistes français." Thesis, Université des Sciences Humaines, Strasbourg, 1974.

Halperin, Joan U., ed. *Félix Fénéon: Oeuvres plus que complètes.* Vol. 1, *Chroniques d'art.* Geneva, 1970.

Hanson, Anne Coffin. *Edouard Manet, 1832–1883.* Philadelphia: Museum of Art, 1966.

———. *Manet and the Modern Tradition.* New Haven, 1977.

Harsin, Jill. *Policing Prostitution in Nineteenth-Century Paris.* Princeton, N.J., 1985.

Herbert, Robert L. *Impressionism: Art, Leisure and Parisian Society.* New Haven, 1988.

Hervilly, Ernest d'. *Mesdames les parisiennes.* Paris, 1875.

Hess, Thomas B., and Linda Nochlin. *Woman as Sex Object: Studies in Erotic Art, 1730–1970.* New York, 1972.

Hines, Norman E. *Medical History of Contraception.* 1936. Reprint. New York, 1970.

Hofmann, Werner. *Nana: Mythos und*

Wirklichkeit. Köln, 1973.

Hollander, Anne. *Seeing Through Clothes.* New York, 1978.

Huysmans, J[oris]-K[arl]. "La Nana de Manet." *L'Artiste de Bruxelles,* May 13, 1877, pp. 148–49.

———. *L'Art moderne/Certains.* Paris: 10/18, 1975.

Ignotus. "Les Grands Bazars." *Le Figaro,* March 23, 1881, p. 1.

———. "La Sûreté et les moeurs." *Le Figaro,* April 13, 1881, p. 1.

Impressionist and Post-Impressionist Masterpieces: The Courtauld Collection. New Haven, 1987.

Un impressionniste. "Nana." *Le Tintamarre,* May 13, 1877, p. 2.

L'Indicateur des grues de Paris. Nouveau guide des étrangers pour l'Exposition 1889. Paris: Imprimerie polyglotte, n.d. (ca. 1889).

Irigaray, Luce. *This Sex Which Is Not One.* Translated by Catherine Porter. Ithaca, 1977.

Isaacson, Joel. *The Crisis of Impressionism, 1878–1882.* Ann Arbor: University of Michigan Museum, 1980.

Janis, Eugenia Parry. *Degas Monotypes: Essay, Catalogue and Checklist.* Greenwich, Conn., 1968.

Janmot, L. "Salon de 1874: Quelques considérations générales." *Le Contemporain,* June 1 and July 1, 1874, p. 38.

Jardine, Alice A. *Gynesis: Configurations of Woman and Modernity.* Ithaca, 1985.

Jean. *Les Bas-fonds du crime et de la prostitution.* Paris, n.d. (ca. 1900).

Jones, Philippe. *La Presse satirique illustrée entre 1860 et 1890.* Paris, 1956.

Kleeblatt, Norman L., ed. *The Dreyfus Affair: Art, Truth, and Justice.* Berkeley, 1988.

Kunzle, David. *Fashion and Fetishism: A Social History of the Corset, Tight-Lacing and Other Forms of Body-Sculpture in the West.* Totowa, N.J., 1982.

Lafargue, Paul. "Les Femmes nues du Salon." *Le Citoyen,* May 23, 1882, pp. 1–2.

Lambert, Nicholas. *Les Amours et galanteries des grandes dames, des actrices et des cocottes célèbres de Paris.* Paris, 1871.

Lassaigne, Jacques, and Fiorello Minervino. *Tout l'oeuvre peint de Degas.* Paris: Flammarion, 1974.

Lauretis, Teresa de. *Alice Doesn't: Feminism, Semiotics, Cinema.* Bloomington, Ind., 1984.

Laya, Alexandre. *Causes célèbres du mariage, ou les infortunes conjugales.* Paris, 1883.

Lecour, C. J. *La Prostitution à Paris et à Londres, 1789–1877.* 2d and 3d eds. Paris, 1872, 1877.

———. *De l'état actuel de la prostitution parisienne.* Paris, 1874.

Leja, Michael. "'Le Vieux Marcheur' and 'Les Deux Risques': Picasso, Prostitution, Venereal Disease and Maternity, 1899–1907," *Art History* 8, no. 1 (March 1985): 66–87.

Lemoisne, P. A. *Degas et son oeuvre.* 4 vols. Paris, 1946–49.

Leroy, Louis. "Le Salon Pour Rire," Pt. 3, "Les Tableaux à l'école." *Le Charivari,* June 4, 1878, p. 2.

Lethève, Jacques. *Impressionnistes et symbolistes devant la presse.* Paris, 1959.

———. *La Caricature et la presse sous la troisième République.* Paris, 1961.

Lewis, Russell. "Everything Under One Roof: World's Fairs and Department Stores in Paris and Chicago." *Chicago History* 12, no. 3 (Fall 1983): 28–47.

Liber, Jacques. "Beaux-Arts: Le Cas d'Henri Gervex." *Paris-Plaisir* 1, no. 5 (April 14, 1878): 4.

Lipton, Eunice. "Manet: A Radicalized Female Imagery." *Artforum* (March 1975): 48–53.

———. *Looking into Degas: Uneasy Images of Women and Modern Life.* Berkeley, 1986.

Livois, René de. *Histoire de la presse française.* Vol. 1, *Des origines à 1881.* Lausanne, 1965.

Livret illustré du musée du Luxembourg. Paris, 1884.

McBride, Teresa. "A Woman's World: Department Stores and the Evolution of Women's Employment, 1870–1920." *French Historical Studies* 10, no. 4 (Fall 1978): 664–83.

McC, K. *Rural and Urban Images: An Exhibition of British and French Paintings, 1870–1920.* London: Pyms Gallery, 1984.

Macé, Gustave. *La Police parisienne: Le Gibier de Saint Lazare.* Paris, 1888.

———. *La Police parisienne: Un joli monde.* Paris, 1888.

McMillan, James F. *Housewife or Harlot: The Place of Women in French Society, 1870–1940.* New York, 1981.

McMullen, Roy. *Degas: His Life, Times, and Work.* London, 1985.

McWilliam, Neil. "Making Faces." *Art History* 7, no. 1 (March 1984): 115–19.

Mainardi, Patricia. "Gustave Courbet's Second Scandal: 'Les Demoiselles de Village,'" *Arts* (January 1979): 95–103.

Mancini, Jean-Gabriel. *Prostitution et proxénétisme*. Que sais-je? no. 999. Paris: Presses Universitaires de France, 1972.

Manet, 1832–1883. Paris: Editions de la Réunion des musées nationaux, 1983.

Manévy, Raymond. *La Presse de la troisième République*. Paris, 1955.

Mantz, Paul. "Le Salon." *Le Temps*, June 10, 1874, p. 2.

Marcus, Steven. *The Other Victorians: A Study of Sexuality and Pornography in Mid-Nineteenth Century England*. New York, 1964.

Martineau, Dr. L. *La Prostitution clandestine*. Paris, 1885.

Maupassant, Guy de. *Le Rosier de Madame Husson*. Introduced by Pierre Cogny. Paris: Garnier-Flammarion, 1976.

Mayeur, Jean-Marie. *Les Débuts de la troisième République: 1871–1898*. Paris, 1973.

Medina, Elizabeth. "Gervex's *Rolla*, Manet's *Nana* and *Olympia:* The Depiction of Underwear in the Nineteenth Century as Images of Female Resistance." Northwestern University, 1986. Typescript.

Merriman, John M., ed. *Consciousness and Class Experience in Nineteenth-Century Europe*. New York, 1979.

Mignard, Annie. "Propos élémentaires sur la Prostitution." *Les Temps Modernes* 31 (March 1976): 1526–47.

Miller, D. A. "The Novel and the Police." *Glyph* 8 (1981): 127–47.

Miller, Michael B. *The Bon Marché: Bourgeois Culture and the Department Store, 1869–1920*. Princeton, N.J., 1981.

Modleski, Tania. *The Women Who Knew Too Much: Hitchcock and Feminist Theory*. New York, 1988.

"Le Monde parisien." *Le Soleil*, May 3, 1877, p. 3.

"Le Monde parisien." *Le Soleil*, April 15, 1878, p. 3.

Mosse, George L. *Nationalism and Sexuality: Respectability and Abnormal Sexuality in Modern Europe*. New York, 1985.

Le Musée du Luxembourg en 1974. Paris: Editions des Musées Nationaux, 1974.

Musset, Alfred de. *Premières Poésies, poésies nouvelles*. Paris: Editions Gallimard, 1976.

Nadar [Tournachon, Félix]. "A une courtisane." *Revue Moderne et Naturaliste* (1878–79): 408–09.

Nead, Lynda. *Myths of Sexuality: Representations of Women in Victorian Britain*. Oxford, 1988.

Nield, Keith, ed. *Prostitution in the Victorian Age: Debates on the Issue from Nineteenth Century Critical Journals*. Westmead, Eng., 1973.

Nochlin, Linda. *Realism*. Baltimore, 1971.

"Nouvelles." *La Chronique des Arts et de la Curiosité*, April 17, 1878, p. 130.

Padgug, Robert A. "Sexual Matters: On Conceptualizing Sexuality in History." *Radical History Review* 20 (Spring/Summer 1979): 2–23.

Parent-Duchâtelet, A. J. B. *De la prostitution dans la ville de Paris*. 2 vols. Paris, 1837.

———. *La Prostitution à Paris au dix-neuvième siècle*. Introduction by Alain Corbin. Paris, 1981.

Paris after Dark: Night Guide for Gentlemen. 13 ed. Paris, n.d. (ca. 1870).

Paris: Guide par les principaux écrivains et artistes de la France. Vol. 2. Paris, 1867.

Payne, Blanche. *History of Costume from the Ancient Egyptians to the Twentieth Century*. New York, 1965.

Pearson, Michael. *The Age of Consent: Victorian Prostitution and Its Enemies*. Newton Abbot, Eng., 1972.

Péladan, Josephin. "Le Procédé de Manet d'après l'Exposition de l'Ecole des Beaux-Arts." *L'Artiste*, February 1884, pp. 101–17.

Perrot, Philippe. *Les Dessus et les dessous de la bourgeoisie: Une histoire du vêtement au dix-neuvième siècle*. Paris, 1981.

Perry, Mary Elizabeth. "'Lost Women' in Early Modern Seville: The Politics of Prostitution." *Feminist Studies* 4 (February 1978): 195–215.

"Petite Histoire des maisons closes." *Le Crapouillot* (special issue), n.s. 42 (Spring 1977).

Pickvance, Ronald. *Degas, 1879*. Edinburgh: National Galleries of Scotland and Edinburgh Festival Society, 1979.

Pollock, Griselda. *Vision and Difference: Femininity, Feminism and Histories of Art*. London, 1988.

Pontmartin, Alexandre de. "Promenade au Salon de 1878." *Le Correspondant* 3 (1878): 807.

Radzinowicz, Leon. "Certain Political Aspects of the Police of France." In *A History of English Criminal Law and Its Administration from 1750*. Vol. 3. London, 1957, pp. 539–74.

Reff, Theodore. *The Notebooks of Edgar Degas: A Catalogue of the Thirty-Eight Notebooks in the Bibliothèque Nationale and Other Collections.* New York, 1985.

———. *Manet and Modern Paris.* Washington, D.C.: National Gallery of Art, 1982.

———. *Degas: The Artist's Mind.* New York, 1976.

Réglement. Paris: Préfecture de Police, Service des Moeurs, October 1878.

Regnault, Dr. Félix. *L'Evolution de la prostitution.* Paris, 1906.

Reuss, Dr. Louis. *La Prostitution au point de vue de l'hygiène et de l'administration en France et à l'étranger.* Paris, 1889.

Rewald, John. *Paul Cézanne: The Watercolors.* Boston, 1983.

Ricatte, Robert. *La Génèse de "La Fille Elisa."* Paris, 1960.

Richardson, Joanna. *The Courtesans.* Cleveland, 1967.

Richardson, John. "The Catch in the Late Picasso," *New York Review of Books*, July 19, 1984, pp. 21–28.

Riley, Denise. *"Am I That Name?" Feminism and the Category of "Women" in History.* Minneapolis, Minn., 1988.

Romi. *Maisons closes.* 2 vols. Geneva, 1979.

Rosenberg, Charles E., ed. *The Family in History.* Philadelphia, 1975.

Rouart, Denis, and Daniel Wildenstein. *Edouard Manet: Catalogue raisonné.* 2 vols. Lausanne, 1975.

Rowbotham, Sheila. *Women, Resistance and Revolution.* New York, 1972.

Rubin, Gayle. "The Traffic in Women: Notes on the 'Political Economy' of Sex." In *Toward an Anthropology of Women*, edited by Rayna R. Reiter. New York, 1975, pp. 157–210.

Rubin, William S., and Milton Esterow. "Visits with Picasso at Mougins." *Art News* 72, no. 6 (Summer 1973): 42–43.

Schapiro, Meyer. "The Nature of Abstract Art." *Marxist Quarterly* 1, no. 1 (1937): 77–98.

———. *Modern Art, Nineteenth and Twentieth Centuries: Selected Papers.* New York, 1978.

Schiff, Gert. *Picasso: The Last Years, 1963–1973.* New York, 1983.

Sébillot, Paul. "Chronique des arts." *Le Bien Public*, April 4, 1878, p. 3.

———. "Chronique des arts." *Le Bien Public*, May 1, 1878, p. 3.

Sekula, Alan. "The Body and the Archive." *October* 39 (Winter 1986): 3–64.

Sennett, Richard. *The Fall of Public Man: On the Social Psychology of Capitalism.* New York, 1977.

Servais, Jacques, and Jean-Pierre Laurend. *Histoire et dossier de la prostitution.* Paris, 1965.

Servet, D. "Paradoxe: Les Filles." *Revue Moderne et Naturaliste* (1878–79): 81–84.

Seymour-Smith, Martin. *Fallen Women: A Sceptical Inquiry into the Treatment of Prostitutes, Their Clients and Their Pimps in Literature.* London, 1969.

Simmel, Georg. *On Individuality and Social Forms: Selected Writings*, edited by Donald N. Levine. Chicago, 1971.

———. *On Women, Sexuality, and Love.* Translated and introduced by Guy Oakes. New Haven, 1984.

Spavento. "Echos de partout." *L'Estafette*, April 14, 1878, p. 3.

Le Sphinx. "Echos de Paris, hier, aujourd'hui, demain." *L'Evénement*, April 20, 1878, p. 1.

———. "Echos de Paris, hier, aujourd'hui, demain. Un mea culpa." *L'Evénement*, April 23, 1878, p. 1.

Steinberg, Leo. "The Philosophical Brothel." *October* 44 (Spring 1988): 3–74.

Suleiman, Susan Rubin, ed. *The Female Body in Western Culture: Contemporary Perspectives.* Cambridge, Mass., 1986.

Sullerot, Evelyne. *Women, Society and Change.* London, 1981.

Sutcliffe, Anthony. *The Autumn of Central Paris: The Defeat of Town Planning, 1850–1970.* London, 1970.

Tabarant, A[dolphe]. *Manet, histoire catalographique.* Paris, 1931.

———. *Manet et ses oeuvres.* Paris, 1947.

Thomson, Richard. "'Les Quat' Pattes': The Image of the Dog in Late Nineteenth-Century French Art." *Art History* 5, no. 3 (September 1982): 323–37.

———. *Degas: The Nudes.* London, 1988.

Tickner, Lisa. "Feminism, Art History, and Sexual Difference." *Genders* 3 (Fall 1988): 92–128.

———. *The Spectacle of Women: Imagery of the*

Suffrage Campaign, 1907–1914. Chicago, 1988.

Tilly, Louise A., and Joan W. Scott. *Women, Work and Family.* New York, 1978.

Tilly, Louise A., Joan W. Scott, and Miriam Cohen. "Women's Work and European Fertility Patterns." *Journal of Interdisciplinary History* 6, no. 3 (Winter 1976): 447–76.

Trois Etoiles. "Les Petits Salons à côté du Grand Salon." *L'Artiste* (July 1880): 30–33.

Trudgill, Eric. "Prostitution and Paterfamilias." In *The Victorian City: Images and Realities,* edited by H. J. Dyos and Michael Wolff. Vol. 2. London, 1973, pp. 693–705.

Urville, Flévy d'. *Les Ordures de Paris.* Paris, 1874.

Uzanne, J. *Figures contemporaines tirées de l'album Mariani.* 11 vols. Paris, 1896–1908.

Uzanne, Octave. *Parisiennes de ce temps en leurs divers milieux, états et conditions. . . .* Paris, 1910.

Vanier, Henriette. *La Mode et ses métiers: Frivolités et luttes des classes, 1830–1870.* Paris, 1960.

Veblen, Thorstein. *The Theory of the Leisure Class: An Economic Study of Institutions* [1899]. New York, 1931.

Venturi, Lionello. *Cézanne: Son art, son oeuvre.* 2 vols. Paris, 1936.

———. *Les Archives de l'Impressionnisme.* Vol. 2. Paris, 1939.

Veron, Pierre. "Chronique parisienne: Le Salon de 1877." *Le Journal Amusant,* no. 1,081 (May 19, 1877): 7.

———. "Chronique parisienne: Le Salon de 1878." *Le Journal Amusant,* no. 1,140 (July 6, 1878): 3.

———. *Les Mangeuses d'homme.* Paris, 1878.

Vicinus, Martha. "Sexuality and Power: A Review of Current Work in the History of Sexuality," *Feminist Studies* 8, no. 1 (Spring 1982): 133–56.

"La Vie à Paris." *Le Courrier du Soir,* April 26, 1878, p. 4.

La Vie Moderne, April 10, 1880.

Un Vieux Petit Employé. *La Préfecture de police: Procès de "La Lanterne."* Paris, 1879.

Vollard, Ambroise. *Degas.* Paris, 1924.

Walkowitz, Judith. *Prostitution and Victorian Society: Women, Class, and the State.* Cambridge, Eng., 1980.

Waugh, Norah. *Corsets and Crinolines.* London, 1954.

Weeks, Jeffrey. *Sex, Politics and Society: The Regulation of Sexuality since 1800.* London, 1981.

Weill, Alexandre. "Letter to Edmond Magnier, publisher of *L'Evénement.*" *L'Evénement,* April 23, 1878, p. 1; and *Le Courrier du Soir,* April 23, 1818, p. 4.

Weston, Elisabeth Anne. "Prostitution in Paris in the Later Nineteenth Century: A Study of Political and Social Ideology." Ph.D. diss., State University of New York, Buffalo, 1979.

Wilson, Elizabeth. *Adorned in Dreams: Fashion and Modernity.* London, 1985.

Wilson, Michael. *Manet at Work.* London: National Gallery, 1983.

Wolff, Janet. "The Invisible Flâneuse: Women and the Literature of Modernity." *Theory, Culture and Society* 2, no. 3 (1985): 37–46.

Wright, Gordon. *France in Modern Times.* 3d ed. New York, 1981.

Zeldin, Theodore. *France 1848–1945.* Vol. 1, *Ambition, Love and Politics;* vol. 2, *Intellect, Taste and Anxiety.* Oxford, 1973–77.

Zola, Emile. *L'Assommoir* [1877]. Paris: Garnier-Flammarion, 1969.

———. *Nana* [1879–80]. Paris: Garnier-Flammarion, 1968.

———. "L'Adultère dans la bourgeoisie." *Le Figaro,* February 28, 1881, p. 1.

———. *Zola: Mon salon, Manet, écrits sur l'art.* Paris: Garnier-Flammarion, 1970.

———. *Le Bon Combat: De Courbet aux Impressionnistes.* Edited by Gaetan Picon and Jean-Paul Bouillon. Paris, 1974.

Index

Abolitionism, 11, 12, 35, 161n19. *See also* Regulationism
"Actualities," 13, *14*
Adultery, 14, 113, 181n2. *See also* Marriage
Alexis, Paul, 5, 78
Ambiguity and confusion, 6, 19, 20–21, 23, 46–47, 99, 107, 111, 121, 126, 131, 145–46, 147, 187nn83–85. *See also* Avant-garde art; Glimpse pictures; Narrative; Stereotypes
Ancourt, Edward: "Au boulevard" ("On the Boulevard"), *101;* "Sur le boulevard" ("On the Boulevard"), 96, *98*
Anti-Semitism, 48, 163n40
Apparel. *See* Clothing; Fashion
Atelier des modistes (Millinery Shop), 118, *119*, 121
Augier, Emile, 2
Avant-garde art: prostitution as a characteristic theme, 1–3, 5–9, 16, 26, 27, 33, 69, 113, 116, 121, 126, 128, 130–31, 134, 138, 144, 152–53, 170n73; and narrative, 3, 6, 33, 107, 126; male perspective, 6, 7, 20, 112, 152, 159n56; glimpse pictures, 6, 26, 27, 33, 35, 107, 122, 124, 131, 150; documentary accuracy, 27, 35, 124, 126, 128, 152; ambiguity, 35, 99, 111–12, 124, 138, 144, 147, 150–53, 187n83; and nudes, 85–87. *See also* Modern life

Baedeker, Karl, 94–95, 96
Ballu, Roger, 86–87
Balsamo, 85
Balzac, Honoré de, 2, 33, 67, 181n154
Barrière, Théodore, 2
Baudelaire, Charles, 2, 7–9, 19, 58, 69, 75
Beauvoir, Simone de, 9, 58–60, 63, 158n45
Bédollière, E. de la, 178n131
Benjamin, Walter, 7–9
Béraud, Jean, *Brasserie*, 138, *139*
Bernadille, 106
Bernard, Emile, 49
Bertall (Charles Albert Arnoux), 78, *79*
Blanchard, Edouard Théophile, *Le Bouffon (The Buffoon)*, 85, *86*
Bodies, of prostitutes: distinguishing characteristics, 20, 42–44, 47–48, 50, 55, 69, 106; in Degas, 28, 36, 39, 40, 43–44, 47–48, 50–51, 55, 108, 164n55; in Forain, 41; in Manet, 69–70; and corsets, 89. *See also* Faces; Nudes and nudity; Sexuality
Boldini, Giovanni, *Conversation au café (Café Conversation)*, 103, *105*
Bonaparte, Mathilde, 88
Boulanger Affair, 12
Boulevards, 28, 65, 82, 92–96, 103, 120, 124, 142, 178–79nn131–32, 179n135, 184n37
Bourgeoisie, bourgeois, middle class: sexual morality, 11–12, 14; sexual ideals, 19; shopping, 63–64; family model, 114–16. *See also* Class; Commodification; Working class
Brasseries à femmes: in art, 5–6, 142–47, 150–52, 186n71, 187n81; clandestine prostitution, 6, 133–34, 138–42, 147, 150, 184n37, 185n49, 185n59. *See also* Cafés
"Bréda Street," 90, *91*
Brothels: regulation of, 10, 12; numbers of, 12, 13, 28; deluxe, 19, 28–29, 35–36, 161–62n21; prostitutional styles in, 28–29, 35–36, 40, 161–62n21; *maisons populaires*, 28–29, 134, 162n21; prostitutes' dress in, 29, 35, 36, 92, 160n10, 162n21; layout of, 29, 36, 160n12; social interactions in, 29–30, 33, 35–36, 46–47; brasseries as, 139–41. *See also* Prostitution
Buland, J. E., *Deux ans à la ville [retour aprés] (The Return after Two Years in the City)*, 96, *98*
Buttocks, 50–51, 55

Cabanel, Alexandre, 82
Cafés, 94, 96, 99, 101, 103, 107, 138, 143. *See also Brasseries à femmes*
Caillebotte, Gustave, 103

Camescasse, Jean, 140
Capitalism, 8. *See also* Bourgeoisie; Commodification
Cardon, Emile, 19, 85
Caricatures, 6, 96. *See also* Popular art; individual artists
Castagnary, Jules, 17, 19
"Ces dames et l'Exposition" ("These Women and the Exposition"), *92*
Cézanne, Paul: sexual feelings, 16–17, 19, 23, 26, 159n53; contemporary criticism, 17, 19
—works: *L'éternal féminin (The Eternal Feminine)*, 23, *24; Une Moderne Olympia (A Modern Olympia) (1869–70)*, 5, 16, *17*, 20–21, 23, 152; *Une Moderne Olympia (A Modern Olympia) (1872–73)*, 5, 16, 17, *18*, 19, 21, 41, 152; *Olympia (1877)*, 5, 21, 22, 23, 152; *La Toilette de la courtisane (The Courtesan's Toilette)*, 23, *25*, 26
Charpentier, Georges, 133
Clandestine prostitution: increase in, 2, 7, 12–13, 19, 35; courtesans, 2, 19; millinery shops, 6, 113, 120–21, 126, 128, 130; *brasseries à femmes*, 6, 133–34, 138–42, 147, 150, 184n37, 185n49, 185n59; and regulationism, 12–13, 14–15, 46, 94, 120–21, 133–34, 140, 185n49; in literature, 118. *See also* Courtesans; Prostitution
Class: of prostitutes' customers, 1, 11–12, 28, 47; boundaries blurred by prostitution, 2, 7, 12, 72; working-class women and prostitution, 6, 14, 15, 75, 90, 91, 92–93, 108, 115, 117–18, 131, 153; distinctions and female sexuality, 13, 15, 128; stereotypes, 48; indicated by clothing, 56, 59, 64, 91–92: and propriety of women's work, 113–14. *See also* Bourgeoisie; Working class
Clients. *See* Customers; Men
Clothing: in brothels, 29, 35, 36, 92, 160n10, 162n21; indicates social class, 56, 59, 64, 91–92; to designate prostitutes, 56, 108, 165n5, 180–81n151; and sexuality, 58–59, 64–65, 72, 91, 167–68n43; of courtesans, 59–60, 62–64, 65, 67, 74–75, 91–92, 167–68n43. *See also* Corsets; Department stores; Fashion; Hats; Underwear
Coindre, Gaston, "Le Ridicule" ("Ridicule"), *59*, 92
Commenge, Octave, 116
Commodification: sexual marketplace, 7, 19, 23; prostitution and, 7–10, 33, 35, 39–40, 41–42, 70, 147, 150; in modern life, 8–9, 35, 131, 144, 150, 152–53; in art, 28, 33, 35, 39–40, 46, 50, 150. *See also* Bourgeoisie
Commune, Paris, 7, 12, 94, 96
Confusion. *See* Ambiguity
Consumption. *See* Commodification; Department stores; Fashion
Contraception, 5
Conventional art. *See* Pompier art; Popular art; Salon art
Coquiot, Gustave, 128
Corsets, 69, 70, 75–76, 78–79, 83, 89–92, 108, 169n71, 171n91, 178n128. *See also* Clothing; Fashion; Underwear
Coté, Hippolyte, "Croquis parisien" ("Paris Sketch"), *99*
Courbet, Gustave, *Les Demoiselles des bords de la Seine [été] (Young Ladies on the Banks of the Seine [Summer])*, 2, *3*, 6
Courtesans: as clandestine prostitutes, 2, 19; clothing of, 59–60, 62–64, 65, 67, 74–75, 91–92, 167–68n43. *See also* Clandestine prostitution; Prostitutes
Couture, Thomas, 2, 172n94
Customers: social class of, 1, 11–12, 28, 47; feelings of, 46–47 (*see also* Desire). *See also* Brothels; Men

Dagnan-Bouveret, Pascal-Adolphe-Jean, *Repos à côté de la Seine (A Rest by the Seine)*, 118, *119*
Daudet, Alphonse, 133
David, Paul, "Boulevardières" ("Boulevard Women"), *101*
Degas, Edgar: date of brothel monotypes, 5, 27, 156n10; elliptical treatment of prostitution in public works, 6; milliner pictures, 6, 116, 121, 128–30, 183n33; brothel monotypes, 27, 30, 33, 35–36, 39–42, 44, 46–51, 55, 152, 159–60n1, 163n32; construction of the body, 28, 36, 39, 40, 43–44, 47–48, 50–51, 55, 108, 164n55; literary influences, 29, 33; his sexuality, 48–50, 163n32, 163–64n43; and Gervex, 87–89, 177n116; and narrative, 103, 106–07, 109, 111–12, 128, 130, 181n152
—works: *Absinthe*, 146; *L'Atelier de la modiste (The Millinery Shop)*, 129–30; *L'Attente (Waiting)*, *51; L'Attente (Waiting)*, 108, *109; L'Attente (Waiting for the Client)*, 36, *37*, 39; *Au Café (Café Scene)*, 108, *111; Au Salon (In the Salon)*, 39, *40; Chez la modiste (At the Milliner)*, 128–29, *129; Le Client (The Customer)*, 20, *38*, 39, 46, 47; *Le Client sérieux (The Serious Customer)*, *34*, 35, 46, 47, 51; *Conversation*, 51, *52; Dans le salon d'une maison close (In a Brothel Salon)*, *51; Deux femmes [scène de maison close] (Two Women [Scene in a Brothel])*, 51, *54; L'Entremetteuse (The Procuress)*, 51, *53; Femme dans un café (Woman in a Café)*, 99, 101;

Femmes devant un café, le soir (Women on the Terrace of a Café in the Evening), 103, *106*, 106–09, *110*, 111–12, 181n152, 181n154; *La Fête de la patronne (The Madam's Name Day)*, 44, *45*; *La Fille Elisa* notebook drawings, 29–30, *30*, 47; *Le Repos (Repose)*, *32*, 33; *Repos sur le lit (Resting on the Bed)*, 46, 47, *47*
Delacroix, Eugène, 16
Demi-monde. *See* Courtesans
Department stores, 58, 63–64. *See also* Fashion
Desboutin, Marcellin, *Fille de Brasserie*, 147, *149*
Desire: male, and sexual needs, 12, 13, 16, 158n45; simulated by prostitutes, 19, 26, 28–29, 35, 36, 41, 134, 147, 150; male, ambivalence of, 71–72; female, deviance of, 90; and spectatorship, 161n20. *See also* Fantasy; Sexuality
Deviance, sexual, 9–10, 11, 13, 15, 19, 33, 48, 55, 71, 72, 90, 92. *See also* Sexuality
Divorce, 63, 181n2. *See also* Marriage
Double standard, 11–12, 13, 15, 114–15
Draner, Jules (Jules Renard), *Au salon (At the Salon)*, 41, *42*
Drinking: by prostitutes, 96, 99, 101, 140, 180n142; public concern about, 96, 140, 185n49; by respectable women, 101, 103; in *brasseries à femmes*, 133, 138, 140, 142, 144, 185n49
Duez, Ernest-Ange, 6; *Splendeur (Splendor)* and *Misère (Misery)*, 65, *66*, 67, 167–68nn42–43
Dumas, Alexandre fils, 2, 36, 62
Duranty, Edmond, 103, 106

Estaminets, 29. *See also* Brothels
Exhibitions: Salon, 2, 3, 65, 70, 75, 79, 83, 85, 88, 92, 96; Impressionist, 17, 48, 103, 172n93; of *Nana* at Giroux, 69, 75, 170n76; Manet's, at *La Vie Moderne*, 75, 78–79, 142, 144, 170n76; of *Rolla* at M. M. Bague, 81
Exposition Universelle *(1878)*, 28, 36, 92, 140

Faces, 23, 47–48, 69, 83, 128, 163n40. *See also* Bodies
Fantasy, 5, 17, 19, 20–21, 23, 26, 41, 91. *See also* Desire
Fashion: vehicle of power for women, 58–59, 74–75; of courtesans, 59–63, 65, 67, 69, 74–75, 92; leads to immorality, 60–61, 63–64, 67, 120; women compete via, 63; and corsets, 89–90, 91–92. *See also* Clothing; Department stores
Fau, Fernand, illustrations for *Les Brasseries à Femmes de Paris*, 138, *139*
Fénéon, Félix, 88
Feydeau, Ernest, 2
Flaubert, Gustave, 2, 14
Flor, Charles, 140
Forain, Jean-Louis, 6; *Le Client (The Customer)*, 40–42, *41*, 47; *Maison close (Brothel)*, 30, *31*

Garnier, Jules-Arsène, *Le Constat d'adultère (Proof of Adultery)*, 113, *114*
Gervex, Henri, 6, 171–72n93
—works: *Autopsie à l'Hôtel-Dieu (Autopsy at the Hospital)*, 177n116; *Groupe à table (Group at Table)*, 103, *105*; *Rolla*, 5, 79, *80*, 81–83, *84*, 85–93, 152, 171–72nn93–94, 173n101, 173–76nn103–06, 177n122, 178n128
Gillot, "Fantaisies parisiennes" ("Parisian Fantasies"), 96, *98*, 109
Giraud, Eugène, *La Salle des pas perdus (The Hall of Missteps)*, *92*
Glimpse pictures, 6, 26, 27, 33, 35, 107, 122, 124, 131, 150. *See also* Ambiguity; Avant-garde art; Narrative; Realism
Goetschy, Gustave, 78
Goncourt brothers, 2, 14; Edmond de, 5, 29, 33, 112, 133, 171n91, 180–81n151
Gonse, Louis, 167–68n43
Gonzalès, Eva, *La Modiste (The Milliner)*, 116, 121, 131, *132*
Grison, Georges, 94
Guyot, Yves, 11
Guys, Constantin, 2

Hadol, Paul, "L'Araignée du soir" ("Evening Spider"), *98*, 99
Haenen, P. de, *Paris qui s'en va—Le Cabaret du Père Lunette (Disappearing Paris—The Cabaret of "Papa Eyeglasses")*, 72, *73*
Halévy, Ludovic, 163n40
Hats, 74, 108, 165n5, 180–81n151. *See also* Clothing
Haussmann, Baron Georges, 2, 15
Huysmans, Joris-Karl, 5, 33, 42, 78, 79, 170n81

Ignotus, 63
Impressionism, group identity, 6, 172n93. *See also* Avant-garde art; Modern life
Impressionist exhibitions, 172n93; *1874*, 17; *1877*, 103; *1881*, 48. *See also* Exhibitions

Jacques, 106–07
Janmot, L., 67
July Monarchy, 1, 2–3, 12, 81, 172n94

Kemplen, Alfred Richard, *L'Assommoir* illustrations, 96, *97*

Labor, women's: demand for, and prostitution, 1, 5; participation in the work force, 113, 115–16, 182n7; wages, 116, 118, 141; in brasseries, 133, 141. *See also* Milliners
Lecour, C. J., 12, 113, 118, 120
Lefèbvre, Jules Joseph; *Femme couchée, étude (Reclining Woman, Study), 36*, 36, 39, 51; *Odalisque*, 51, *54*, 55
Liber, Jacques, 83, 85, 176n106
Literature, prostitution in: significance, 1–2, 5, 6, 7; connections with art, 26, 33, 70–73, 75; artists' illustrations, 29, 73–74; clandestine, 118. *See also* Zola, Emile; and other individual writers
Louis-Philippe, 1
Lower class. *See* Working class
Lunel, Ferdinand: *Brasseries le Bas-Rhin et le D'Harcourt, 138; La Brasserie Henri IV, 141*

Macé, Gustave, 29, 43, 133, 142, 160n10, 162n21, 165n5, 178–79n132
Madams, 39, 44, 118. *See also* Brothels
Magasins-prétextes. *See* Clandestine prostitution; Milliners
Maisons. *See* Brothels
Make-up, 69. *See also* Fashion
Manet, Edouard, 88; treats prostitution elliptically, 6, 144; *La Vie Moderne* exhibition *(1880)*, 75, 78–79, 142, 144, 170n76
—works: *Un bar aux Folies-Bergère (A Bar at the Folies-Bergère)*, 5–6, *151*, 151–52, 187nn 83–85; *Les Bockeuses (Women Drinking Beer)*, 101, *102; Le Café-concert*, 134, *137*, 142, 144–47, 150, 187n81; *Chez la modiste (At the Milliner)*, 116, 121, 126, *127*, 128, 150, 183n31; *Devant la glace (Before the Mirror)*, 75, *76*, 78; *La Femme à la jarretière (The Garter)*, 75, *77*, 78–79; *Nana*, 5, 67, *68*, 69–73, 75–76, 78, 79, 81, 92, 143, 152, 168n47, 168n54, 168n56, 169n71, 170n73, 170n76, 170n81; *Olympia*, 2, *4*, 6, 16; *La Prune (The Plum)*, 99, *100*, 101, 180n142; *La Servante de bocks (The Waitress)*, 142, *143*, 145–46; *La Serveuse de bocks (The Waitress)* [London], 134, *135*, 142, 143–44, 147, 150, 187n81; *La Serveuse de bocks (The Waitress)* [Paris], 134, *136*, 142, 147, 150, 187n81
Mantz, Paul, 67, 167n43
Marriage, 5, 182n7. *See also* Adultery; Divorce
Martineau, L., 120, 134, 138–39
Marx, Karl, 156n15
Maupassant, Guy de, 5, 44, 46, 179n132
Men: define female sexuality, 11, 15–16, 91; needs and desires, 11–12, 14, 16, 19, 46; as spectators, 55, 69, 72–73, 91, 112, 118, 152, 153, 187n84; support women's conspicuous consumption, 63, 70, 73; doctrine of separate spheres, 114. *See also* Customers; Sexuality; Women
Meuron, Alfred de, 11
Milliners, 6, 113, 116–18, 120–22, 124, 126, 128–31, 150, 183n33. *See also* Clandestine prostitution
Modern life: prostitution and, 1–2, 6, 7–9, 33, 35, 111–12, 126, 131, 134, 150, 152, 172n94; commodification, 8–9, 35, 131, 144, 150, 152–53; urban, 8, 9, 94. *See also* Avant-garde art
Monet, Claude, *Boulevard des Capucines*, 95–96
Monotypes. *See* Degas
Montaud, Henri de, 91
Montifaud, Marc de (Marie-Amélie Chartroule de Montifaud), 19
Moore, George, 183n33
Morel-Retz, Louis Pierre Gabriel Bernard. *See* Stop
Morland, Victor: "Ces petites dames" ("These Little Women"), *62;* "Coupeau, Lantier, Mes-Bottes et cie.," *117;* "Scènes de la vie parisienne" ("Scenes of Parisian Life"), 92, *93*, 117–18, 121
"M. Manet édudiant la belle nature" ("Mr. Manet Studying Beautiful Nature"), *79*
Musset, Alfred de, 2, 81–82, 172n94, 173n98, 173–74n103

Napoléon Bonaparte, 1
Napoléon III, 2, 28
Narrative, 2–3, 6, 33, 65, 67, 103, 106–107, 109, 111–12, 124, 126, 152, 167n37, 167nn42–43, 181n152. *See also* Ambiguity; Glimpse pictures
Neo-regulationism. *See* Regulationism
Nudes and nudity, 23; in Salon art, 23, 36, 40, 41, 51, 82–83, 85–86, 88, 90, 91, 176n106, 177n122; Degas, 28, 36, 40; in brothels, 35, 36, 160n10, 162n21. *See also* Bodies; Clothing

"Occupations des fillettes," 114, *115*

Parent-Duchâtelet, A. J. B., 1, 43, 56, 116–17
Paris: prostitute population, 1, 2, 5, 7; migration to, 1, 94, 117; boulevards, 28, 65, 82, 92–96, 103, 120, 124, 142, 178–79nn131–32, 179n135, 184n37; rebuilding of, 28, 82
Paris, arts exhibitions in. *See* Exhibitions; Salon exhibitions
Paris Commune. *See* Commune
"Paris pendant l'Exposition" ("Paris during the Exposition"), 133, *134*

Péladan, Josephin, 144, 186n75
Péry, "Les Cocottes" ("The Tarts"), 60, *62*
Picasso, Pablo, 44, 48–50, 51, 108, 163n32; *Demoiselles d'Avignon*, 5; *Le 16 mars 1971 (March 16, 1971)*, *49*
Pimps, 120, 141
Police, 1, 11, 140. *See also Réglementation;* Regulationism
Pompier art, 5, 6, 64–65. *See also* Salon art; individual artists
Popular art, 5, 138; illustrated press, 3. *See also* Caricatures; individual artists
Pothey, Alexandre, 106
"Prés du boulevard" ("Near the Boulevard"), 120, *121*
Press censorship, 175n105
Prostitutes: number in Paris, 1, 2, 5, 7; stereotypes of temperament, 2, 42, 43, 44, 46; working-class women, 6, 14, 15, 75, 90, 91, 92–93, 108, 115, 117–18, 131, 153; sexual deviance, 9–10, 48, 72, 90, 92; temporary, 10; exhibition of desire by, 19, 26, 28–29, 35, 36, 41, 134, 147, 150; stereotypes of appearance, 20, 42–44, 47–48, 50, 55, 69, 106; faces, 23, 47–48, 69, 83, 128; childlike, 39, 42, 43, 44, 82; venal, 43, 44, 46, 60–61, 67, 81, 111, 118; sentimental, 43, 46; registered, 44, 116, 165n5; *filles en carte*, 56; distinctive clothing, 56, 108, 165n5, 180–81n151; competition between, 63, 65, 67, 142; friendship between, 101, 103, 106–07; earnings, 141. *See also* Brothels; Courtesans; Prostitution; and other individual topics
Prostitution: modern public problem, 1–2, 5, 6–7, 94; and social boundaries, 2, 7, 12, 72; and public morality, 2, 7, 14–15, 61, 67, 71, 72, 92–93; and the commodification of sexuality, 7–10, 33, 35, 39–40, 41–42, 70, 147, 150; a state not a job, 10–11, 42–43, 108, 111; changes in styles of, 12, 19, 28, 35, 40, 133–34; economic causes, 60, 81, 116–18, 120, 141, 179n132. *See also* Brothels; Clandestine prostitution; Customers; Prostitutes; Regulationism
Proud'hon, P. J., 114

Quidam, Jean (Douglas Jerrold), "Un monsieur qui suit les femmes" ("A Man Who Follows Women"), 56, *57*

Raccrochage. See Solicitation
Racolage. See Solicitation
Realism: Degas, 27, 33, 40, 129; as modern goal, 27, 35, 124, 126, 128, 152; Manet, 144. *See also* Avant-garde art; Glimpse pictures
Réglementation (regulation of prostitution): established, 1; debated, 7; function of, 11–12, 14; and clandestine prostitution, 12–13, 46, 94, 120–21, 133–34, 140, 185n49; of prostitute's appearance, 56, 108, 165n5, 180–81n151; decline of official prostitution, 133–34. *See also* Abolitionism; Clandestine prostitution; Regulationism
Regnault, Félix, 138
Regulation of prostitution. *See Réglementation;* Regulationism
Regulationism: categorization of prostitutes, 10–11, 42–43; justifications for, 11–12, 43, 44, 46, 115; neoregulationism, 12–13, 94, 140. *See also* Abolitionism; Clandestine prostitution; *Réglementation*
Renard, Jules. *See* Draner, Jules
Rénault, Léon, 13–14
Renoir, Pierre Auguste, 6; *L'Assommoir* illustrations, 5, 73–75, *74*, 169n68; *Au Café (At the Café)*, 103, *104*; *Chez la modiste (At the Milliner)*, 116, 121–22, *123*, 124, 126
Reuss, Louis, 62, 120–21, 139–40
Rivière, Georges, 103, 106, 108, 111
Robida, Albert, "Paris Nouveau" ("New Paris"), 138, *139*

Salon art: narrative in, 3; exclusion from, 5, 67, 70, 75, 79, 83, 85, 88, 172n93, 176n106; nudes in, 23, 36, 40, 41, 51, 82–83, 85–86, 88, 90, 91, 176n106, 177n122. *See also* Pompier art
Salon exhibitions: *1857*, 2; *1865*, 2; *1874*, 65; *1877*, 67, 70, 75, 92; *1878*, 3, 79, 83, 85, 88; *1881*, 96. *See also* Exhibitions
Sébillot, Paul, 78, 79, 87
Second Empire, 2–3, 6, 11, 12, 59, 74
Second Republic, 2
Servet, D., 62
Sexuality: instability, 6, 7, 13, 131, 152–53; marketplace, 7, 19, 23 (*see also* Commodification); and women's place, 9, 11, 158n45; deviance, 9–10, 11, 13, 15, 19, 33, 48, 55, 71, 72, 90, 92; prostitution as public, 11; increase in, 13; women's responsibility for men's 13–14; artistic containment of, 26; and fashion, 58–59, 64; corsets and, 90–91, 178n128. *See also* Desire; Men; Women
Shopping. *See* Department stores; Fashion
Simmel, Georg, 7–9, 58, 64, 70
Smoking: by women, 96, 180n142; in brasseries, 141
Solicitation: in brothels, 35–36, 41, 162n21; on the boulevards, 94, 96, 179n132; in cafés and brasseries, 101, 111, 138–39, 140, 142;

Solicitation (*continued*)
raccrochage, 111. *See also* Desire, simulated by prostitutes
Somm, Henri (François-Clément Sommier), *La Serveuse de bocks (The Waitress)*, 147, *148*
Spectatorship: male, 55, 69, 72–73, 91, 112, 118, 152, 153, 187n84; female, 161n20; gendered, 161n20; and desire, 168n47
"Sphinx, Le," 87, 89
Stereotypes: prostitutes' temperaments, 2, 42, 43, 44, 46; prostitutes' bodies, 20, 42–44, 47–48, 50, 55, 69, 106; social classes, 48; women, 48; Jews, 48, 163n40. *See also* Ambiguity; Narrative
Stevens, Alfred, 88
Stop (Louis Pierre Gabriel Bernard Morel-Retz), *Les Prêtresses de l'amour vénal (The High Priestesses of Venal Love)*, 60, *61*, 67
Sue, Eugène, 2, 33

Tabarant, Adolphe, 143–44
Taverns. *See Brasseries à femmes;* Cafés
Third Republic, 6–7, 11, 172n94, 175n105
Tissot, James, 6; *La Demoiselle de magasin (The Young Lady of the Shop)*, 124, *125*, 126
Toulouse-Lautrec, Henri de, 3
Travel guides, 93–96, 178–79nn131–32, 179n135
Tricoche, *Paris régénéré (Paris Regenerated)*, 7, 56
Turquet, Edmond, 172n93

Underwear, 69, 73, 75–76, 78, 86, 87–88, 169–70n71, 170n81. *See also* Clothing; Corsets; Fashion

"Une Modiste," 118
Urville, Flévy d', 13

Van Gogh, Vincent, 48, 49
Vély, Anatole, *L'Amour et l'argent (Love and money)*, 3, *4*
Verdi, Giuseppe, 2
Vollard, Ambroise, 44, 87–88, 177n116

Waitresses. *See Brasseries à femmes;* Labor
Weill, Alexandre, 85, 90
Women: difficulties telling "honest" from "loose," 7, 43, 50, 56, 58, 64, 91–92, 150–52; opposition between "honest" and "loose," 11, 13, 15, 43, 63, 114–15; infection of "honest" by "loose," 14–15, 60, 61–63, 67, 74; stereotypes of, 48; consumption and power of, 58–59, 74, 165n9; legal status of, 113; paid work by, 113, 115–16, 182n7; doctrine of separate spheres, 113–15; self-definition, 116, 184n36. *See also* Men; Prostitutes; Sexuality; and other individual topics
Work. *See* Labor
Working class: women as prostitutes, 6, 14, 15, 75, 90, 91, 92–93, 108, 115, 117–18, 131, 153; agitation, 96. *See also* Bourgeoisie; Class
Worth, Charles Frederick, 59

Zola, Emile, 33, 65, 133, 139, 167n42; on sexual morality, 14; on fashion, 63, 64
—works: *L'Assommoir*, 5, 60, 69, 70–71, 73–74, 96, 117, 140, 169n68; *Nana*, 5, 69, 71–73, 74–75, 78, 168n56, 168–69n58; Thérèse Raquin, 2, 14